# ALGORITHMIC THINKING

## 2ND EDITION

## Learn Algorithms to Level up Your Coding Skills

by Daniel Zingaro

**no starch press®**

San Francisco

**ALGORITHMIC THINKING, 2ND EDITION.** Copyright © 2024 by Daniel Zingaro.

Printed in the United States of America

First printing

27 26 25 24 23      1 2 3 4 5

ISBN-13: 978-1-7185-0322-9 (print)
ISBN-13: 978-1-7185-0323-6 (ebook)

Published by No Starch Press®, Inc.
245 8th Street, San Francisco, CA 94103
phone: +1.415.863.9900
www.nostarch.com; info@nostarch.com

Publisher: William Pollock
Managing Editor: Jill Franklin
Production Manager: Sabrina Plomitallo-González
Production Editor: Sydney Cromwell
Developmental Editor: Alex Freed
Cover Illustrator: Rob Gale
Interior Design: Octopod Studios
Technical Reviewers: Naaz Sibia and Larry Yueli Zhang
Copyeditor: George Hale
Proofreader: Elizabeth Littrell

*The Library of Congress has catalogued the first edition as follows:*

Name: Zingaro, Daniel, author.
Title: Algorithmic thinking : a problem-based introduction / by Daniel Zingaro.
Includes bibliographical references and index.
Identifiers: LCCN 2020031510 (print) | LCCN 2020031511 (ebook) | ISBN 9781718500808 (paperback) |
    ISBN 1718500807 (paperback) | ISBN 9781718500815 (ebook)
Subjects: LCSH: Computer algorithms--Problems, exercises, etc. | Computer programming--Problems, exercises, etc.
Classification: LCC QA76.9.A43 Z56 2020  (print) | LCC QA76.9.A43 (ebook) | DDC 005.13--dc23
LC record available at https://lccn.loc.gov/2020031510
LC ebook record available at https://lccn.loc.gov/2020031511

For customer service inquiries, please contact info@nostarch.com. For information on distribution, bulk sales, corporate sales, or translations: sales@nostarch.com. For permission to translate this work: rights@nostarch.com. To report counterfeit copies or piracy: counterfeit@nostarch.com.

[S]

# PRAISE FOR
## *ALGORITHMIC THINKING, 2ND EDITION*

"*Algorithmic Thinking* will empower you—whether you're looking to get a leg up on technical interviews, enter the world of competitive programming, or just want to sharpen your skills."

—JOSH LOSPINOSO, PHD, AUTHOR OF
*C++ CRASH COURSE*

"This book . . . is by far the quickest way to get hands-on experience with algorithms, and is also a great supplement to more theoretical expositions."

—RICHARD PENG, ASSOCIATE PROFESSOR
AT THE UNIVERSITY OF WATERLOO'S
CHERITON SCHOOL OF COMPUTER
SCIENCE

"*Algorithmic Thinking* provides the theoretical background and detailed problem explanations required to stay ahead of our human and robotic competitors."

—DUNCAN SMITH, SENIOR SOFTWARE
ENGINEER AT MICROSOFT

"Not only does *Algorithmic Thinking* guide readers on how to approach tackling problems, but Zingaro also helps them understand why these approaches work."

—SUSHANT SACHDEVA, PHD,
ALGORITHMS PROFESSOR AT
THE UNIVERSITY OF TORONTO

"The step-by-step solution explanations are so detailed, it feels like Zingaro is directly teaching us, his readers. This second edition is a worthy update to an already excellent text."

—DR STEVEN HALIM, SENIOR
LECTURER AT NATIONAL
UNIVERSITY OF SINGAPORE

"*Algorithmic Thinking* discusses many interesting problems from programming contests and presents useful techniques that are not often included in algorithm textbooks."

—ANTTI LAAKSONEN,
UNIVERSITY OF HELSINKI

To Doyali

## About the Author

Dr. Daniel Zingaro is an associate teaching professor of computer science and award-winning teacher at the University of Toronto. His main area of research is computer science education, where he studies how students learn computer science material.

## About the Technical Reviewer

Naaz Sibia is an MSc student of computer science at the University of Toronto with an interest in computer science education research and human computer interaction (HCI). Her research focuses on identifying challenges faced by students in computing and utilizing HCI principles to design interventions that improve their learning experience.

## About the First Edition Technical Reviewer

Larry Yueli Zhang is an assistant professor of computer science in the Department of Electrical Engineering and Computer Science at York University's Lassonde School of Engineering. His teaching and research span a wide range of topics, including introductory programming, algorithms, data structures, operating systems, computer networks, and social network analysis, all underscored by a passion for computing education. Larry holds a PhD in computer science from the University of Toronto.

# BRIEF CONTENTS

# CONTENTS IN DETAIL

## 2
## TREES AND RECURSION          37

## 3
## MEMOIZATION AND DYNAMIC PROGRAMMING          77

# 6
# SHORTEST PATHS IN WEIGHTED GRAPHS     197

# 7
# BINARY SEARCH     231

# 9
# UNION-FIND
**331**

# 10
# RANDOMIZATION
**375**

# FOREWORD

For the novice tennis player, keeping the ball in the court is hard enough (especially from the backhand side). Only after months of practice, once the basic rallying skills have been mastered, does the sport and its addictive nature begin to reveal itself. You add to your repertoire more advanced tools—a slice backhand, a kick serve, a drop volley. You strategize at a higher level of abstraction—serve and volley, chip and charge, hug the baseline. You develop intuition for which tools and strategies will be most effective against different types of opponents—there's no silver-bullet approach that works well against everyone.

Programming is like tennis. For the beginning coder, coaxing the computer to understand what you want it to do—to execute your solution to a problem—is hard enough. Graduate from this white-belt level and the true problem-solving fun begins: How do you come up with the solution in the first place? While there's no silver-bullet approach that solves every computational problem efficiently, there are enduringly useful, advanced tools and strategies: hash tables, search trees, recursion, memoization, dynamic programming, graph search, and more. And to the trained eye, many problems and algorithms offer dead giveaways as to which tools are the right ones. Does your algorithm perform repeated lookups or minimum computations? Speed it up with a hash table or min-heap, respectively! Can you build a solution to your problem from solutions to smaller subproblems? Use recursion! Do the subproblems overlap? Speed up your algorithm with memoization!

Be it tennis or programming, you can't up your game to the next level without two things: practice and a good coach. To this end, I give you

*Algorithmic Thinking: Learn Algorithms to Level up Your Coding Skills* and Daniel Zingaro. This book teaches all the concepts that I've mentioned, but it is no mere laundry list. With Zingaro as a tutor by your side, you'll learn, through practice on challenging competition problems, a repeatable process for figuring out and deftly applying the right algorithmic tools for the job. And you'll learn it all from a book that exudes clarity, humor, and just the right dose of Canadian pride. Happy problem-solving!

Tim Roughgarden
New York, NY
May 2020

# ACKNOWLEDGMENTS

What an idyllic experience it was to work with the folks at No Starch Press. They're all laser-focused on writing books to help readers learn. I've found my people! Liz Chadwick supported my book from the start (and unsupported another one—I'm grateful for that!). It is a gift to have worked with Alex Freed, my developmental editor. She's patient, kind, and always eager to help me improve how I write instead of just fixing my mistakes. I thank all those involved in the production of the second edition of this book, including my copyeditor, George Hale; production editor, Sydney Cromwell; and cover designer, Rob Gale.

I thank the University of Toronto for offering me the time and space to write. I thank Naaz Sibia, my technical reviewer, for her careful review of the manuscript and for finding the time to help me.

I thank Tim Roughgarden for authoring the book's foreword. Tim's books and videos are examples of the kind of clarity that we need to strive for when teaching algorithms.

I thank my colleagues Larry Zhang, Jan Vahrenhold, and Mahika Phutane for their review of draft chapters.

I thank everyone who contributed to the problems that I used in this book and to competitive programming in general. I thank the DMOJ administrators for their support of my work. Special thanks to Tudor Brindus, Radu Pogonariu, and Maxwell Cruickshanks for their help in improving and adding problems.

I thank my parents for handling everything—*everything*. All they asked me to do was learn. I thank Doyali, my partner, for giving some of our time to this book and for modeling the care it takes to write.

Finally, I thank all of you for reading this book and wanting to learn.

# INTRODUCTION

I'm assuming that you've learned to use a programming language such as C, C++, Java, or Python ... and I'm hoping that you're hooked. It's hard to explain to nonprogrammers why solving problems through programming is so rewarding and fun.

I'm also hoping that you're ready to take your programming skill to the next level. I have the privilege of helping you do that.

## What We'll Do

I could start by teaching you some fancy new techniques, telling you why they're useful, and comparing them to other fancy techniques, but I won't. That material would lay inert, holding on for a little, waiting for the opportunity to spring into action—if in fact some opportunity ever did present itself.

Instead, what I do throughout this book is pose problems: hard problems. These are problems that I hope you cannot solve, problems that I hope stymie your current approaches. You're a programmer. You want to solve problems. Now it's time for learning those fancy techniques. This book is all about posing hard problems and then solving them by bridging between what you know and what you need.

You won't see traditional textbook problems here. You won't find an optimal way to multiply a chain of matrices or compute Fibonacci numbers. I promise: you won't solve the Towers of Hanoi puzzle. There are many excellent textbooks out there that do these things, but I suspect that many people are not motivated by those kinds of puzzles.

My approach is to use new problems that you haven't seen before. Each year, thousands of people participate in programming competitions, and these competitions require new problems to measure what participants can come up with on their own rather than who can google the fastest. These problems are fascinating, riffing on the classics while adding twists and context to challenge people to find new solutions. There is a seemingly endless stream of programming and computing knowledge encompassed by these problems. We can learn as much as we like by choosing the right problems.

Let's start with some basics. A *data structure* is a way to organize data so that desirable operations are fast. An *algorithm* is a sequence of steps that solves a problem. Sometimes we can make fast algorithms without using sophisticated data structures; other times, the right data structure can offer a significant speed boost. My goal is not to turn you into a competitive programmer, though I'd take that as a happy side benefit. Rather, my goal is to teach you data structures and algorithms using problems from the competitive programming world—and to have fun while doing so. You can reach me at *daniel.zingaro@gmail.com*. Email me if you have learned. Email me if you have laughed.

## New to the Second Edition

I've thoroughly enjoyed the opportunity to discuss the first edition of this book with readers. Their feedback has led to many of the changes and improvements in this new edition.

I've made small improvements and additions throughout, but here are the major highlights of what's new:

**Chapter 1**   I removed the Compound Words problem, as it can be solved in ways that did not require a hash table. Instead, now we have a problem about passwords on a social networking website. I've also streamlined the code in this chapter to help those without a C/C++ programming background, and I added more information about the efficiency of hash tables.

**Chapter 3**   I added more guidance for how to discover the needed subproblems when solving a problem with dynamic programming.

**Chapter 4**   This chapter is completely new, and it focuses on more advanced uses of memoization and dynamic programming. This was a frequent request of readers, and I'm excited to have been able to add this. You'll learn how to look at dynamic programming problems in reverse (and why you'd want to), how to work with more dimensions in your subproblem arrays, and how to further optimize your dynamic programming code when it's just not fast enough.

**Chapter 5, previously Chapter 4**  I added guidance on how to choose between using dynamic programming and using a graph.

**Chapter 8, previously Chapter 7**  I added further discussion of why we implement heaps as arrays rather than as explicit trees.

**Chapter 10**  This chapter is completely new and teaches you how to use randomization, a topic not often covered in books. Randomization is a technique that can help you design algorithms that are simple and fast. You'll use two types of randomization algorithms to solve problems that would otherwise be very difficult. You'll also learn what to look for in a problem when trying to decide whether to use randomization in the first place.

## Who This Book Is For

This book is for any programmer who wants to learn how to solve tough problems. You'll learn many data structures and algorithms, their benefits, the types of problems they can help you solve, and how to implement them. You'll be a better programmer after this!

Are you taking a course on data structures and algorithms and getting your butt kicked by a wall of theorems and proofs? It doesn't have to be that way. This book can serve as a companion text for you, helping you get to the core of what's going on so that you can write code and solve problems.

Are you looking for an edge in your next coding interview? You need to be able to compare and contrast different approaches for solving a problem, choose the best data structure or algorithm, and explain and implement your solution. You'll practice all of these skills over and over as you read this book. Never fear hash tables, recursion, dynamic programming, trees, graphs, or heaps again!

Are you an independent learner working toward expertise in data structures and algorithms? Piecing together stuff from all over the internet can be tiring and lead to knowledge gaps if the right resources are not found. This book will provide you the solid foundation and consistent presentation that you need to become an expert.

As explored further in the next section, all code in this book is written in the C programming language. However, this isn't a book on learning C. If your prior programming experience is in C or C++, then jump right in. If instead you've programmed in a language such as Java or Python, I suspect that you'll pick up most of what you need by reading, but you may wish to review some C concepts now or on first encounter. In particular, I'll use pointers and dynamic memory allocation, so, no matter what your prior experience, you might like to brush up on those topics. The best C book I can recommend is *C Programming: A Modern Approach*, 2nd edition, by K. N. King. Even if you're okay with C, read it anyway. It's that good and a wonderful companion any time you get tripped up by C stuff.

# Our Programming Language

I've chosen to use C as the programming language for this book, rather than some higher-level language such as C++, Java, or Python. I'll discuss why and also justify a couple of other C-related decisions I've made.

## Why Use C?

The primary reason for using C is that I want to teach you data structures and algorithms from the ground up. When we want a hash table, we'll build it ourselves. There will be no reliance on dictionaries or hashmaps or similar data structures of other languages. When we don't know the maximum length of a string, we'll build an extensible array: we won't let the language handle memory allocation for us. I want you to know exactly what's going on, with no tricks up my sleeve. Using C helps me toward this goal.

Solving programming problems in C, as we do in this book, is a useful primer should you decide to continue with C++. If you become serious about competitive programming, then you'll be happy to know that C++ is the most popular language used by competitive programmers, thanks to its rich standard library and ability to generate code that favors speed.

## Static Keyword

Regular local variables are stored on what's called the *call stack*. On each call of a function, some of the call stack memory is used to store local variables. Then, when the function returns, that memory is freed up for other local variables to use later. The call stack is small, though, and isn't appropriate for some of the massive arrays that we'll meet in this book. Enter the static keyword. When used on a local variable, it changes the storage duration from automatic to static, which means that the variable maintains its value between function calls. As a side effect, these variables are *not* stored in the same memory area along with regular local variables, since then their values would be lost when a function is terminated. Instead, they're stored in their own separate segment of memory, where they don't have to compete with whatever else might be on the call stack.

One thing to watch out for with this static keyword is that such local variables are only initialized once! For a quick example, see Listing 1.

```
int f(void) {
❶ static int x = 5;
  printf("%d\n", x);
  x++;
}

int main(void) {
  f();
  f();
  f();
```

```
    return 0;
}
```

*Listing 1: A local variable with a static keyword*

I've used static on local variable x ❶. Without that, you'd expect 5 to be printed three times. However, since static is there, you should see this output instead:

```
5
6
7
```

## Include Files

To save space, I don't include the #include lines that should be added to the start of C programs. You'll be safe if you include the following:

```
#include <stdio.h>
#include <stdlib.h>
#include <string.h>
#include <time.h>
```

## Freeing Memory

Unlike Java or Python, C requires the programmer to free all memory that is manually allocated. The pattern is to allocate memory using malloc, use that memory, and then free the memory using free.

For two reasons, though, I do not free memory here. First, freeing memory adds clutter, distracting from the primary teaching purpose of the code. Second, these programs are not long-lived: your program will run on a few test cases, and that's it. The operating system reclaims all of the unfreed memory on program termination, so there's nothing to worry about even if you run a program many times. Of course, not freeing memory is quite irresponsible in practice: no one is happy with a program that consumes more and more memory as it runs. If you'd like to practice freeing memory, you can add calls of free to the programs presented in this book.

# Topic Selection

The fields of data structures and algorithms are too large to be corralled by one book (or by this one author!). I used three criteria to help me decide what topics made the cut.

First, I chose topics of broad applicability: each can be used to solve not only the corresponding problems in the book but many other problems as well. In each chapter, I focus on at least two problems. I generally use the first problem to introduce the data structure or algorithm and one of its prototypical uses. The other problems are meant to give a sense of what else the data structure or algorithm can do. For example, in Chapter 6, we study Dijkstra's algorithm. If you google it, you'll see that Dijkstra's algorithm is used to find shortest paths. Indeed, in the first problem of the chapter, we use it for that very purpose. However, in the second problem, we go further, tweaking Dijkstra's algorithm to find not only the shortest path but also the number of shortest paths. I hope that, as you progress through each chapter, you learn more and more about the affordances, constraints, and subtleties of each technique.

Second, I chose topics whose implementation did not overwhelm the surrounding discussion. I wanted the solution to any problem to top out at around 150 lines. That includes reading the input, solving the problem itself, and producing the output. A data structure or algorithm whose implementation took 200 or 300 lines was for practical reasons not suitable.

Third, I chose topics that lend themselves to correctness arguments that I hope are convincing and intuitive. Teaching you specific data structures and algorithms is of course one of my goals, because I am imagining that you're here to learn powerful problem-solving approaches and how to implement them. Meanwhile, I'm also hoping that you're interested in *why* what you're learning works, so I have more quietly pursued another goal: convincing you that the data structure or algorithm is correct. There won't be formal proofs or anything like that. Nonetheless, if I have succeeded in my secret goal, then you'll learn about correctness right along with the data structure or algorithm. Don't be content in merely tracing code and marveling that it magically works every time. There is no magic, and the insights that make code tick are within your grasp, just as is the code itself.

If you'd like to go beyond the chapters of this book, I recommend starting with Appendix B. There, I've included some additional material related to Chapters 1, 3, 5, 8, 9, and 10.

Many readers will benefit by practicing or reading additional material as they progress through the book. The Notes sections at the end of the chapters point to additional resources, some of which contain further examples and sample problems. There are also online resources that offer a curated, categorized list of problems and their solution strategies. The *Methods to Solve* page by Steven Halim and Felix Halim is the most comprehensive that I've found; see *https://cpbook.net/methodstosolve*.

## Programming Judges

Each problem that I have chosen is available on a programming-judge website. Many such websites exist, each of which generally contains hundreds of problems. I've tried to keep the number of judges that we use small but large enough to give me the flexibility to choose the most appropriate problems. For each judge website, you'll need a username and password; it's worth setting up your accounts now so that you don't have to stop to do so while working through the book. Here are the judges that we'll use:

**Codeforces**  *https://codeforces.com*

**DMOJ**  *https://dmoj.ca*

**POJ**  *http://poj.org*

**SPOJ**  *http://spoj.com*

**UVa**  *https://uva.onlinejudge.org*

Each problem description begins by indicating the judge website where the problem can be found and the particular problem code that you should use to access it.

While some problems on the judge websites are written by individual contributors, others are originally from well-known competitions. Here are some of the competitions from which problems in this book originate:

**International Olympiad in Informatics (IOI)**  This is a prestigious annual competition for high school students. Each participating country sends up to four participants, but each participant competes individually. The competition runs over two days, with multiple programming tasks on each day.

**Canadian Computing Competition (CCC) and Canadian Computing Olympiad (CCO)**  These annual competitions for high school students are organized by the University of Waterloo. CCC (aka Stage 1) takes place at individual schools, with the top performers moving on to take the CCO (aka Stage 2) at the University of Waterloo. The top performers in Stage 2 represent Canada at the IOI. When I was a high school student, I participated in the CCC, but I never made it to the CCO—I wasn't even close.

**Croatian Open Competition in Informatics (COCI)**  This online competition is offered many times per year. Performance is used to determine the Croatian IOI team.

**National Olympiad in Informatics in Province (NOIP)**  This is an annual competition for high school students in China, similar in function to the CCC. The top performers are invited to the National Olympiad in Informatics (NOI), China. The top NOI contestants are eligible for further training and possible selection to China's IOI team.

**South African Programming Olympiad (SAPO)**  This competition is offered in three rounds per year. The rounds increase in difficulty, from Round 1 to Round 2 to the Final Round. Performance is used to select students to represent South Africa at the IOI.

**USA Computing Olympiad (USACO)**  This online competition is offered several times per year, the most challenging of which is the US Open competition. In each competition, you'll encounter four levels of problems: bronze (easiest), silver, gold, and platinum (hardest). Performance is used to determine the American IOI team.

**East Central North America (ECNA) Regional Programming Contest**  In this annual competition for university students, the top performers are invited to the annual International Collegiate Programming Contest (ICPC) world finals. Unlike the other competitions here, where students compete individually, ECNA and the world finals competitions are team competitions.

**DWITE** This was an online programming contest designed to help students practice for annual competitions. Unfortunately, DWITE is no longer running, but the old problems—and they are good ones!—are still available.

See Appendix C for the source of each problem in this book.

When you submit code for a problem, the judge compiles your program and runs it on test cases. If your program passes all test cases, and does so within the allotted time, then your code is accepted as correct; judges show AC for accepted solutions. If your program fails one or more test cases, then your program is not accepted; judges show WA (for "Wrong Answer") in these cases. A final popular outcome is for when your program is too slow, in which case judges show TLE ("Time-Limit Exceeded"). Note that TLE does not mean that your code is otherwise correct: if your code times out, the judges do not run any further test cases, so there may be some WA bugs hidden behind the TLE.

At the time of publication, my solution for each problem passes all test cases within the allotted time with the specified judge. Within those base requirements, my aim has been to make the code readable and to choose clarity over speed. This is a book about teaching data structures and algorithms, not squeezing further performance out of a program that otherwise gets the job done.

## Anatomy of a Problem Description

Before solving a problem, we must be precise about what we are being asked to do. This precision is required not only in understanding the task itself but also in the way that we should read input and produce output. For this reason, each problem begins with a problem description of three components:

**The Problem** Here, I provide the context for the problem and what we are being asked to do. It's important to read this material carefully so that you know exactly what problem we're solving. Sometimes, misreading or misinterpreting seemingly small words can lead to incorrect solutions. For example, one of our problems in Chapter 3 asks us to buy "at least" a certain number of apples: if you instead buy "exactly" that many apples, your program will fail some of the test cases.

**Input** The author of the problem provides test cases, all of which must be passed for a submission to be deemed correct. It's our responsibility to read each test case from the input so that we can process it. How do we know how many test cases there are? What is on each line of each test case? If there are numbers, what are their ranges? If there are strings, how long can they be? All of this information is provided here.

**Output** It can be very frustrating to have a program that produces the correct answer but fails test cases because it does not output answers in the correct format. The output portion of a problem description dictates exactly how we should produce output. For example, it will tell us how many lines of output to produce for each test case, what to put on each line, whether blank lines are required between or after test cases, and so on. In addition, I provide the time limit for the problem here: if the program does not output the solution for all test cases within the time limit, then the program does not pass.

I have rewritten the text of each problem from the official description so that I can maintain a consistent presentation throughout. Despite these tweaks, my description will convey the same information as the official description.

For most problems in this book, we'll read input from standard input and write output to standard output. (There are only two problems where standard input and output are not involved; they are in Chapter 7.) This means we should use C functions such as scanf, getchar, printf, and so on and not explicitly open and close files.

## Starter Problem: Food Lines

Let's familiarize ourselves with a sample problem description. I'll provide some commentary in parentheses along the way, directing your attention to the important bits. Once we understand the problem, I can think of nothing better to do than solve it. Unlike the other problems in the book, we'll be able to do so with programming constructs and ideas that I hope you already know. If you can solve the problem on your own or work through my solution with little or no trouble, then I think you're ready for what's to come. If you get seriously stuck, then you may wish to revisit programming fundamentals and/or solve a few other starter problems before continuing.

This is DMOJ problem 1kp18c2p1. (You might like to go now to the DMOJ website and search for this problem so that you're ready to submit our code once we're done.)

### The Problem

There are $n$ lines of people waiting for food. We know the number of people that are already waiting in each line. Then, each of $m$ new people will arrive, and they will join a shortest line (a line with the fewest number of people). Our task is to determine the number of people in each line that each of the $m$ people joins.

(Spend a little time interpreting the above paragraph. There's an example coming next, so if anything is unclear, try to remedy it with the combination of the above paragraph and the example below.)

Here's an example. Suppose that there are three lines of people, with three people in Line 1, two people in Line 2, and five people in Line 3. Then, four new people arrive. (Try to work out what happens for this case before reading the rest of this paragraph.) The first person joins a line with two people, Line 2; now Line 2 has three people. The second person joins a line with three people, Line 1 or Line 2—let's say Line 1; Line 1 now has four people. The third person joins a line with three people, Line 2; Line 2 now has four people. The fourth and final person joins a line with four people, Line 1 or Line 2—let's say Line 1; Line 1 now has five people.

### Input

The input contains one test case. The first line of input contains two positive integers, $n$ and $m$, giving the number of lines of people and number of new people, respectively. $n$ and $m$ are at most 100. The second line of input contains $n$ positive integers, giving the number of people in each line of people before the new people arrive. Each of these integers is at most 100.

Here's the input for the above test case:

---

```
3 4
3 2 5
```

---

(Note how there is exactly one test case here. Therefore, we should expect to read exactly two lines of input.)

### Output

For each of the $m$ new people, output a line containing the number of people in the line that they join.

The correct output for the above test case is:

---

```
2
3
3
4
```

---

The time limit for solving the test case is three seconds. (Given that we have to handle at most 100 new people for each test case, three seconds is a long time. We won't need any fancy data structures or algorithms.)

## Solving the Problem

For problems involving data structures that are difficult to build by hand, I may start by reading the input. Otherwise, I tend to save that code for last. The reason for this is that we can generally test the functions we're writing by calling them with sample values; there is no need to worry about parsing the input until we're ready to solve the whole problem.

The key data that we need to maintain are the number of people in each line. The appropriate storage technique is an array, using one index per line. We'll use a variable named lines for that array.

Each new person that arrives chooses to join a shortest line, so we'll need a helper function to tell us which line that is. That helper function is given in Listing 2.

```
int shortest_line_index(int lines[], int n) {
  int j;
  int shortest = 0;
  for (j = 1; j < n; j++)
    if (lines[j] < lines[shortest])
      shortest = j;
  return shortest;
}
```

*Listing 2: Index of a shortest line*

Now, given a lines array and n and m, we can solve a test case, the code for which is given in Listing 3:

```
void solve(int lines[], int n, int m) {
  int i, shortest;
  for (i = 0; i < m; i++) {
    shortest = shortest_line_index(lines, n);
    printf("%d\n", lines[shortest]);
❶ lines[shortest]++;
  }
}
```

*Listing 3: Solving the problem*

For each iteration of the for loop, we call our helper function to grab the index of the shortest line. We then print the length of that shortest line. This person then joins that line: that's why we must increment the number of people in that line by one ❶.

All that's left is to read the input and call solve; that's done in Listing 4.

```
#define MAX_LINES 100

int main(void) {
  int lines[MAX_LINES];
  int n, m, i;
  scanf("%d%d", &n, &m);
  for (i = 0; i < n; i++)
    scanf("%d", &lines[i]);
  solve(lines, n, m);
  return 0;
}
```

*Listing 4: The main function*

Putting together our shortest_line_index, solve, and main functions and adding the required #include lines at the top gives us a complete solution that we can submit to the judge. When doing so, be sure to choose the correct programming language: for the programs in this book, you want to find GCC, or C99, or C11, or however the judge refers to a compiler for C.

If you want to test your code locally before submitting it to the judge, then you have a few options. Since our programs read from standard input, one thing you can do is run the program and type a test case by hand. That's a reasonable thing to do for small test cases, but it's tedious doing that over and over, especially for large test cases. (You may also need to issue an end-of-file control code after you type the input, such as CTRL-Z on Windows or CTRL-D on other operating systems.) A better option is to store the input in a file and then use *input redirection* from the command prompt to have the program read from that file instead of the keyboard. For example, if you store a test case for the present problem in file *food.txt*, and your compiled program is called *food*, then try:

```
$ food < food.txt
```

This makes it easy to play with many test cases: just change what's in *food.txt* and then run the program with input redirection again.

Congratulations! You've solved your first problem. Moreover, you now know our game plan for each problem in the book, as we'll use the same general structure I have given here. We'll first understand the problem itself and work through some examples. Then we'll start writing code to solve the problem. We won't always get it right the first time, though. Maybe our code will be too slow or fail some specific test cases. That's okay! We'll learn new data structures and algorithms and then strike back at the problem. Eventually, we will solve each one—and after each such experience, we will know more and be better programmers than when we started.

Let's get to it.

## Online Resources

Supplementary resources for this book, including downloadable code and additional exercises, are available at *https://nostarch.com/algorithmic -thinking-2nd-edition*.

## Notes

Food Lines is originally from the 2018 LKP Contest 2, hosted by DMOJ.

# 1

## HASH TABLES

It's amazing how often computer programs need to search for information, whether it's to find a user's profile in a database or to retrieve a customer's orders. No one likes waiting for a slow search to complete.

In this chapter, we'll solve two problems whose solutions hinge on being able to perform efficient searches. The first problem is determining whether or not all snowflakes in a collection are identical. The second is determining how many passwords can be used to log in to someone's account. We want to solve these problems correctly, but we'll see that some correct approaches are simply too slow. We'll be able to achieve enormous performance increases using a data structure known as a hash table, which we'll explore at length.

We'll end the chapter by looking at a third problem: determining how many ways a letter can be deleted from one word to arrive at another. Here we'll see the risks of uncritically using a new data structure—when learning something new, it's tempting to try to use it everywhere!

## Problem 1: Unique Snowflakes

This is DMOJ problem cc007p2.

## The Problem

We're given a collection of snowflakes, and we have to determine whether any of the snowflakes in the collection are identical.

A snowflake is represented by six integers, where each integer gives the length of one of the snowflake's arms. For example, this is a snowflake:

3, 9, 15, 2, 1, 10

Snowflakes can also have repeated integers, such as

8, 4, 8, 9, 2, 8

What does it mean for two snowflakes to be identical? Let's work up to that definition through a few examples.

First, we'll look at these two snowflakes:

1, 2, 3, 4, 5, 6

and

1, 2, 3, 4, 5, 6

These are clearly identical because the integers in one snowflake match the integers in their corresponding positions in the other snowflake.

Here's our second example:

1, 2, 3, 4, 5, 6

and

4, 5, 6, 1, 2, 3

These are also identical. We can see this by starting at the 1 in the second snowflake and moving right. We see the integers 1, 2, and 3 and then, wrapping around to the left, we see 4, 5, and 6. These two pieces together give us the first snowflake.

We can think of each snowflake as a circle as in Figure 1-1.

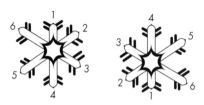

Figure 1-1: Two identical snowflakes

The two snowflakes are identical because we can start at the 1 in the second snowflake and follow it clockwise to get the first snowflake.

Let's try a different kind of example:

1, 2, 3, 4, 5, 6

and

3, 2, 1, 6, 5, 4

From what we've seen so far, we would deduce that these are not identical. If we start with the 1 in the second snowflake and move right (wrapping around to the left when we hit the right end), we get 1, 6, 5, 4, 3, 2. That's not even close to the 1, 2, 3, 4, 5, 6 in the first snowflake.

However, if we begin at the 1 in the second snowflake and move left instead of right, then we do get exactly 1, 2, 3, 4, 5, 6! Moving left from the 1 gives us 1, 2, 3, and wrapping around to the right, we can proceed leftward to collect 4, 5, 6. In Figure 1-2, this corresponds to starting at the 1 in the second snowflake and moving counterclockwise.

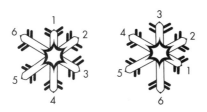

Figure 1-2: Two other identical snowflakes

That's our third way for two snowflakes to be identical: two snowflakes are identical if they match when we move counterclockwise through the numbers.

Putting it all together, we can conclude that two snowflakes are identical if they are the same, if we can make them the same by moving rightward through one of the snowflakes (moving clockwise), or if we can make them the same by moving leftward through one of the snowflakes (moving counterclockwise).

### Input

The first line of input is an integer $n$, the number of snowflakes that we'll be processing. The value $n$ will be between 1 and 100,000. Each of the following $n$ lines represents one snowflake: each line has six integers, where each integer is at least 0 and at most 10,000,000.

### Output

Our output will be a single line of text:

- If there are no identical snowflakes, output exactly No two snowflakes are alike.

- If there are at least two identical snowflakes, output exactly Twin snowflakes found.

The time limit for solving the test cases is one second.

## Simplifying the Problem

One general strategy for solving competitive programming challenges is to first work with a simpler version of the problem. Let's warm up by eliminating some of the complexity from this problem.

Suppose that instead of working with snowflakes made of multiple integers, we're working with single integers. We have a collection of integers, and we want to know whether any are identical. We can test whether two integers are identical with C's == operator. We can test all pairs of integers, and if we find even one pair of identical integers, we'll stop and output

```
Twin integers found.
```

If no identical integers are found, we'll output

```
No two integers are alike.
```

Let's make an identify_identical function with two nested loops to compare pairs of integers, as shown in Listing 1-1.

```
void identify_identical(int values[], int n) {
  int i, j;
  for (i = 0; i < n; i++) {
❶   for (j = i + 1; j < n; j++) {
      if (values[i] == values[j]) {
        printf("Twin integers found.\n");
        return;
      }
    }
  }
  printf("No two integers are alike.\n");
}
```

Listing 1-1: Finding identical integers

We feed the integers to the function through the values array. We also pass in n, the number of integers in the array.

Notice that we start the inner loop at i + 1 and not 0 ❶. If we started at 0, then eventually j would equal i, and we'd compare an element to itself, giving us a false positive result.

Let's test identify_identical using this small main function:

```
int main(void) {
  int a[5] = {1, 2, 3, 1, 5};
  identify_identical(a, 5);
  return 0;
}
```

Run the code and you will see from the output that our function correctly identified a matching pair of 1s. In general, I won't provide much test code in this book, but it's important that you play with and test the code yourself as we go along.

## Solving the Core Problem

Let's take our `identify_identical` function and try to modify it to solve the Snowflake problem. To do so, we need to make two extensions to our code:

1. We have to work with six integers at a time, not one. A two-dimensional array should work nicely here: each row will be a snowflake with six columns (one column per element).

2. As we saw earlier, there are multiple ways for two snowflakes to be identical. Unfortunately, this means we can't just use == to compare snowflakes. We need to take into account our "moving right" and "moving left" criteria (not to mention that == in C doesn't compare contents of arrays anyway!). Correctly comparing snowflakes will be the major update to our algorithm.

To begin, let's write a pair of helper functions: one for checking "moving right" and one for checking "moving left." Each of these helpers takes three parameters: the first snowflake, the second snowflake, and the starting point for the second snowflake.

### Checking to the Right

Here is the function signature for `identical_right`:

```
int identical_right(int snow1[], int snow2[], int start)
```

To determine whether the snowflakes are the same by "moving right," we scan snow1 from index 0 and snow2 from index start. If we find corresponding elements that are not equal, then we return 0 to signify that we haven't found identical snowflakes. If all the corresponding elements do match, then we return 1. Think of 0 as representing false and 1 as representing true.

In Listing 1-2 we make a first attempt at writing this function's code.

```
// bugged!
int identical_right(int snow1[], int snow2[], int start) {
  int offset;
  for (offset = 0; offset < 6; offset++) {
❶ if (snow1[offset] != snow2[start + offset])
      return 0;
  }
  return 1;
}
```

Listing 1-2: Identifying identical snowflakes moving right (bugged!)

As you may notice, this code won't work as we hope. The problem is start + offset ❶. If we have start = 4 and offset = 3, then start + offset = 7.

The trouble is snow2[7], as snow2[5] is the farthest index to which we are allowed to go.

This code doesn't take into account that we must wrap around to the left of snow2. If our code is about to use an erroneous index of 6 or greater, we should reset our index by subtracting six. This will let us continue with index 0 instead of index 6, index 1 instead of index 7, and so on. Let's try again with Listing 1-3.

```
int identical_right(int snow1[], int snow2[], int start) {
  int offset, snow2_index;
  for (offset = 0; offset < 6; offset++) {
    snow2_index = start + offset;
    if (snow2_index >= 6)
      snow2_index = snow2_index - 6;
      if (snow1[offset] != snow2[snow2_index])
      return 0;
  }
  return 1;
}
```

Listing 1-3: Identifying identical snowflakes moving right

This works, but we can still improve it. One change that many programmers would consider making at this point involves using %, the mod operator. The % operator computes remainders, so x % y returns the remainder of integer-dividing x by y. For example, 9 % 3 is 0, because there is no remainder when dividing 9 by 3. 10 % 4 is 2, because 2 is left over when dividing 10 by 4.

We can use mod here to help with the wraparound behavior. Notice that 0 % 6 is 0, 1 % 6 is 1, . . . , 5 % 6 is 5. Each of these numbers is smaller than 6, and so will itself be the remainder when dividing 6. The numbers 0 to 5 correspond to the legal indices of snow2, so it's good that % leaves them alone. For our problematic index 6, 6 % 6 is 0: 6 divides 6 evenly, with no remainder at all, wrapping us around to the start. That's precisely the wraparound behavior we wanted.

Let's update identical_right to use the % operator. Listing 1-4 shows the new function.

```
int identical_right(int snow1[], int snow2[], int start) {
  int offset;
  for (offset = 0; offset < 6; offset++) {
    if (snow1[offset] != snow2[(start + offset) % 6])
      return 0;
  }
  return 1;
}
```

Listing 1-4: Identifying identical snowflakes moving right using mod

Whether you use this "mod trick" is up to you. It saves a line of code and is a common pattern that many programmers will be able to identify. However, it doesn't always easily apply, even in cases that exhibit similar wraparound behavior, such as identical_left. Let's turn to this now.

## Checking to the Left

The function identical_left is very similar to identical_right, except that we need to move left and then wrap around to the right. When traversing right, we had to be wary of erroneously accessing index 6 or greater; this time, we have to be wary of accessing index −1 or less.

Unfortunately, our mod solution won't directly work here. In C, -1 / 6 is 0, leaving a remainder of −1, and so -1 % 6 is −1. We'd need -1 % 6 to be 5.

Let's just do this without using mod. In Listing 1-5, we provide the code for the identical_left function.

```
int identical_left(int snow1[], int snow2[], int start) {
  int offset, snow2_index;
  for (offset = 0; offset < 6; offset++) {
    snow2_index = start - offset;
    if (snow2_index <= -1)
      snow2_index = snow2_index + 6;
    if (snow1[offset] != snow2[snow2_index])
      return 0;
  }
  return 1;
}
```

*Listing 1-5: Identifying identical snowflakes moving left*

Notice the similarity between this function and that of Listing 1-3. All we did was subtract the offset instead of adding it and change the bounds check at 6 to a bounds check at -1.

## Putting It Together

With these two helper functions, identical_right and identical_left, we can finally write a function that tells us whether two snowflakes are identical. Listing 1-6 gives the code for an are_identical function that does this. We simply test moving right and moving left for each of the possible starting points in snow2.

```
int are_identical(int snow1[], int snow2[]) {
  int start;
  for (start = 0; start < 6; start++) {
❶   if (identical_right(snow1, snow2, start))
      return 1;
❷   if (identical_left(snow1, snow2, start))
      return 1;
  }
```

```
    return 0;
}
```

*Listing 1-6: Identifying identical snowflakes*

We test whether snow1 and snow2 are the same by moving right in snow2 ❶.
If they are identical according to that criterion, we return 1 (true). We then
similarly check the moving-left criterion ❷.

It's worth pausing here to test the are_identical function on a few sample
snowflake pairs. Please do that before continuing!

## Solution 1: Pairwise Comparisons

When we need to compare two snowflakes, we just deploy our are_identical
function instead of ==. Comparing two snowflakes is now as easy as comparing two integers.

Let's revise our earlier identify_identical function (Listing 1-1) to work
with snowflakes using the new are_identical function (Listing 1-6). We'll
make pairwise comparisons between snowflakes, printing out one of two
messages depending on whether we find identical snowflakes. The code is
given in Listing 1-7.

```
void identify_identical(int snowflakes[][6], int n) {
  int i, j;
  for (i = 0; i < n; i++) {
    for (j = i + 1; j < n; j++) {
      if (are_identical(snowflakes[i], snowflakes[j])) {
        printf("Twin snowflakes found.\n");
        return;
      }
    }
  }
  printf("No two snowflakes are alike.\n");
}
```

*Listing 1-7: Finding identical snowflakes*

This identify_identical function on snowflakes is almost, symbol for symbol, the same as the identify_identical function on integers in Listing 1-1. All
we've done is swap == for a function that compares snowflakes.

### Reading the Input

We're not quite ready to submit to our judge. We haven't yet written the
code to read the snowflakes from standard input. Revisit the problem description at the start of the chapter. We need to read a line containing integer *n* that tells us how many snowflakes there are and then read each of the
following *n* lines as an individual snowflake.

Listing 1-8 is a main function that processes the input and then calls
identify_identical from Listing 1-7.

```
#define SIZE 100000

int main(void) {
❶ static int snowflakes[SIZE][6];
  int n, i, j;
  scanf("%d", &n);
  for (i = 0; i < n; i++)
    for (j = 0; j < 6; j++)
      scanf("%d", &snowflakes[i][j]);
  identify_identical(snowflakes, n);
  return 0;
}
```

*Listing 1-8: The main function for Solution 1*

Notice that the snowflakes array is a static array ❶. This is because the array is huge; without using such a static array, the amount of space needed would likely outstrip the amount of memory available to the function. We use static to place the array in its own, separate piece of memory, where space is not a concern. Be careful with static, though. Regular local variables are initialized on each call of a function, but static ones retain whatever value they had on the previous function call (see "Static Keyword" on page xxvi).

Also notice that we've allocated an array of 100,000 snowflakes ❶. You might be concerned that this is a waste of memory. What if the input has only a few snowflakes? For competitive programming problems, it's generally okay to hardcode the memory requirements for the largest problem instance: the test cases are likely to stress test your submission on the maximum size anyway!

The rest of the function is straightforward. We read the number of snowflakes using scanf, and we use that number to determine the number of iterations of the outer for loop. For each such iteration, we loop six times in the inner for loop, each time reading one integer. We then call identify_identical to produce the appropriate output.

Putting this main function together with the other functions we have written gives us a complete program that we can submit to the judge. Try it out . . . and you should get a "Time-Limit Exceeded" error. It looks like we have more work to do!

### Diagnosing the Problem

Our first solution was too slow, so we got a "Time-Limit Exceeded" error. Let's understand why.

For our discussion here, we'll assume that there are no identical snowflakes. This is the worst-case scenario for our code, since then it doesn't stop processing early.

The reason that our first solution is slow is because of the two nested for loops in Listing 1-7. Those loops compare each snowflake to every other snowflake, resulting in a huge number of comparisons when the number of snowflakes $n$ is large.

Let's figure out the number of snowflake comparisons our program makes. Since we might compare each pair of snowflakes, we can restate this question as asking for the total number of snowflake pairs. For example, if we have four snowflakes numbered 1, 2, 3, and 4, then our scheme performs six snowflake comparisons: Snowflakes 1 and 2, 1 and 3, 1 and 4, 2 and 3, 2 and 4, and 3 and 4. Each pair is formed by choosing one of the $n$ snowflakes as the first snowflake and then choosing one of the remaining $n - 1$ snowflakes as the second snowflake.

For each of $n$ decisions for the first snowflake, we have $n - 1$ decisions for the second snowflake. This gives a total of $n(n - 1)$ decisions. However, $n(n - 1)$ double-counts the true number of snowflake comparisons that we make—it includes both of the comparisons 1 and 2 and 2 and 1, for example. Our solution compares these only once, so we can divide by 2, giving $n(n - 1)/2$ snowflake comparisons for $n$ snowflakes.

This might not seem so bad, but let's substitute some values of $n$ into $n(n - 1)/2$ and see what happens. Substituting 10 gives $10(9)/2 = 45$. Performing 45 comparisons is a piece of cake for any computer and can be done in milliseconds. How about $n = 100$? That gives 4,950: still no problem. It looks like we're okay for a small $n$, but the problem statement says that we can have up to 100,000 snowflakes. Go ahead and substitute 100,000 for $n$ in $n(n - 1)/2$: this gives 4,999,950,000 snowflake comparisons. If you run a test case with 100,000 snowflakes on a typical laptop, it will take something like three minutes. That's far too slow—we need at most one second, not several minutes! As a conservative rule of thumb for today's computers, think of the number of steps that we can perform per second as about 30 million. Trying to make nearly 5 billion snowflake comparisons in one second is not doable.

If we expand $n(n - 1)/2$, we get $n^2/2 - n/2$. The largest exponent there is 2. Algorithm developers therefore call this an $O(n^2)$ algorithm, or a *quadratic-time algorithm*. $O(n^2)$ is pronounced "big O of $n$ squared," and you can think of it as telling you that the rate at which the amount of work grows is quadratic relative to the problem size. For a brief introduction to big O, see Appendix A.

We need to make such a large number of comparisons because identical snowflakes could show up anywhere in the array. If there were a way to get identical snowflakes close together in the array, we could quickly determine whether a particular snowflake was part of an identical pair. Maybe we can try sorting the array to get the identical snowflakes close together?

## Sorting Snowflakes

C has a library function called qsort that we can use to sort an array. The key requirement is a comparison function: it takes pointers to two elements to sort, and it returns a negative integer if the first element is less than the second, 0 if they are equal, and a positive integer if the first is greater than the second. We can use are_identical to determine whether two snowflakes are equal; if they are, we return 0.

What does it mean, though, for one snowflake to be less than or greater than another? It's tempting to just agree on some arbitrary rule here. We might say, for example, that the snowflake that is "less" is the one whose first differing element is smaller than the corresponding element in the other snowflake. We do that in Listing 1-9.

```
int compare(const void *first, const void *second) {
  int i;
  const int *snowflake1 = first;
  const int *snowflake2 = second;
  if (are_identical(snowflake1, snowflake2))
    return 0;
  for (i = 0; i < 6; i++)
    if (snowflake1[i] < snowflake2[i])
      return -1;
  return 1;
}
```

*Listing 1-9: A comparison function for sorting*

Unfortunately, sorting in this way will not help us solve our problem. You might try writing a program that uses sorting to put identical snowflakes next to each other so that you can find them quickly. But here's a four-snowflake test case that would likely fail on your laptop:

```
4
3 4 5 6 1 2
2 3 4 5 6 7
4 5 6 7 8 9
1 2 3 4 5 6
```

The first and fourth snowflakes are identical—but the message No two snowflakes are alike. may be output. What's going wrong?

Here are two facts that qsort might learn as it executes:

1.  Snowflake 4 is less than Snowflake 2.

2.  Snowflake 2 is less than Snowflake 1.

From this, qsort could conclude that Snowflake 4 is less than Snowflake 1, without ever directly comparing Snowflake 4 and Snowflake 1! Here it's relying on the transitive property of less than. If $a$ is less than $b$, and $b$ is less than $c$, then surely $a$ should be less than $c$. It seems like our definitions of "less" and "greater" matter after all.

Unfortunately, it isn't clear how one would define "less" and "greater" on snowflakes so as to satisfy transitivity. If you're disappointed, perhaps you can take solace in the fact that we'll be able to develop a faster solution without using sorting at all.

In general, collecting similar values with sorting can be a useful data-processing technique. As a bonus, good sorting algorithms run quickly—certainly faster than $O(n^2)$, but we aren't going to be able to use sorting here.

## Solution 2: Doing Less Work

Comparing all pairs of snowflakes and trying to sort the snowflakes proved to be too much work. To work up to our next, and ultimate, solution, let's pursue the idea of trying to avoid comparing snowflakes that are obviously not identical. For example, if we have snowflakes

```
1, 2, 3, 4, 5, 6
```

and

```
82, 100, 3, 1, 2, 999
```

there's no way that these snowflakes can be identical. We shouldn't even waste our time comparing them.

The numbers in the second snowflake are very different from the numbers in the first snowflake. To devise a way to detect that two snowflakes are different without having to directly compare them, we might begin by comparing the snowflake's first elements, because 1 is very different from 82. But now consider these two snowflakes:

```
3, 1, 2, 999, 82, 100
```

and

```
82, 100, 3, 1, 2, 999
```

These two snowflakes *are* identical even though 3 is very different from 82. We need to do more than just look at first elements.

A quick litmus test for determining whether two snowflakes might be identical is to use the *sum* of their elements. When we sum our two example snowflakes, for 1, 2, 3, 4, 5, 6, we get a total of 21, and for 82, 100, 3, 1, 2, 999, we get 1,187. We say that the *code* for the former snowflake is 21 and the code for the latter is 1,187.

Our hope is that we can throw the "21 snowflakes" in one bin and throw the "1,187 snowflakes" in another, and then we never have to compare the 21s to the 1,187s. We can do this binning for each snowflake: add up its elements, get a code of $x$, and then store it along with all of the other snowflakes with code $x$.

Of course, finding two snowflakes with a code of 21 does not guarantee they are identical. For example, both 1, 2, 3, 4, 5, 6 and 16, 1, 1, 1, 1, 1 have a code of 21, and they are surely not identical.

That's okay, because our "sum" rule is designed to weed out snowflakes that are clearly not identical. This allows us to avoid comparing all pairs—the source of the inefficiency in Solution 1—and only compare pairs that have not been filtered out as obviously nonidentical.

In Solution 1, we stored each snowflake consecutively in the array: the first snowflake at index 0, the second at index 1, and so on. Here, our storage strategy is different: sum codes determine snowflakes' locations in the array! That is, for each snowflake, we calculate its code and use that code as the index for where to store the snowflake.

We have to solve two problems:

1.  Given a snowflake, how do we calculate its code?

2.  What do we do when multiple snowflakes have the same code?

Let's deal with calculating the code first.

### Calculating Sum Codes

At first glance, calculating the code seems easy. We could just sum all of the numbers within each snowflake like so:

```
int code(int snowflake[]) {
  return (snowflake[0] + snowflake[1] + snowflake[2]
          + snowflake[3] + snowflake[4] + snowflake[5]);
}
```

This works fine for many snowflakes, such as 1, 2, 3, 4, 5, 6, and 82, 100, 3, 1, 2, 999, but consider a snowflake with huge numbers, such as

```
1000000, 2000000, 3000000, 4000000, 5000000, 6000000
```

The code that we calculate is 21000000. We plan to use that code as the *index* in an array that holds the snowflakes, so to accommodate this, we'd have to declare an array with room for 21 million elements. As we're using at most 100,000 elements (one for each snowflake), this is an outrageous waste of memory.

We're going to stick with an array that has room for 100,000 elements. We'll need to calculate a snowflake's code as before, but then we must force that code to be a number between 0 and 99999 (the minimum and maximum index in our array). One way to do this is to break out the % (mod) operator again. Taking a nonnegative integer mod $x$ yields an integer between 0 and $x - 1$. No matter the sum of a snowflake, if we take it mod 100,000, we'll get a valid index in our array.

This method has one downside: taking the mod like this will force *more* nonidentical snowflakes to end up with the same code. For example, the sums for 1, 1, 1, 1, 1, 1 and 100001, 1, 1, 1, 1, 1 are different—6 and 100006—but once we take them mod 100,000, we get 6 in both cases. This is an acceptable risk to take: we'll just hope that this doesn't happen much; when it does, we'll perform the necessary pairwise comparisons.

We'll calculate the sum code for a snowflake and mod it, as displayed in Listing 1-10.

```
#define SIZE 100000

int code(int snowflake[]) {
    return (snowflake[0] + snowflake[1] + snowflake[2]
            + snowflake[3] + snowflake[4] + snowflake[5]) % SIZE;
}
```

Listing 1-10: Calculating the snowflake code

### Snowflake Collisions

In Solution 1, we used the following fragment to store a snowflake at index i
in the snowflakes array:

```
for (j = 0; j < 6; j++)
    scanf("%d", &snowflakes[i][j]);
```

This worked because exactly one snowflake was stored in each row of
the two-dimensional array.

However, now we have to contend with the 1, 1, 1, 1, 1, 1 and 100001,
1, 1, 1, 1, 1 kind of collision, where, because they'll end up with the same
mod code and that code serves as the snowflakes index in the array, we need
to store multiple snowflakes in the same array element. That is, each array
element will no longer be one snowflake but a collection of zero or more
snowflakes.

One way to store multiple elements at the same array index is to use a
*linked list*, a data structure that links each element to the next. Here, each
element in the snowflakes array will point to the first snowflake in the linked
list; the remainder of the snowflakes can be accessed through next pointers.

We'll use a typical linked list implementation. Each snowflake_node contains both a snowflake and a pointer to the next snowflake. To collect these
two components, we'll use a struct. We'll also make use of typedef, which allows us to later use snowflake_node instead of the full struct snowflake_node:

```
typedef struct snowflake_node {
    int snowflake[6];
    struct snowflake_node *next;
} snowflake_node;
```

This change necessitates updates to two functions, main and identify
_identical, because those functions use our old two-dimensional array.

### The New main Function

You can see the updated main code in Listing 1-11.

```
int main(void) {
❶ static snowflake_node *snowflakes[SIZE] = {NULL};
❷ snowflake_node *snow;
    int n, i, j, snowflake_code;
```

```
    scanf("%d", &n);
    for (i = 0; i < n; i++) {
❸    snow = malloc(sizeof(snowflake_node));
      if (snow == NULL) {
        fprintf(stderr, "malloc error\n");
        exit(1);
      }
      for (j = 0; j < 6; j++)
❹      scanf("%d", &snow->snowflake[j]);
❺    snowflake_code = code(snow->snowflake);
❻    snow->next = snowflakes[snowflake_code];
❼    snowflakes[snowflake_code] = snow;
    }
    identify_identical(snowflakes);
    // deallocate all malloc'd memory, if you want to be good
    return 0;
}
```

*Listing 1-11: The main function for Solution 2*

Let's walk through this code. First, notice that we changed the type of our array from a two-dimensional array of numbers to a one-dimensional array of pointers to snowflake nodes ❶. We also declare snow ❷, which will point to snowflake nodes that we allocate.

We use `malloc` to allocate memory for each `snowflake_node` ❸. Once we have read in and stored the six numbers for a snowflake ❹, we use `snowflake_code` to hold the snowflake's code ❺, calculated using the function we wrote in Listing 1-10.

The last thing to do is to add the snowflake to the `snowflakes` array, which amounts to adding a node to a linked list. We do this by inserting the snowflake at the beginning of the linked list. We first point the inserted node's next pointer to the first node in the list ❻, and then we set the start of the list to point to the inserted node ❼. The order matters here: if we had reversed the order of these two lines, we would lose access to the elements already in the linked list!

Notice that, in terms of correctness, it doesn't matter where in the linked list we add the new node. It could go at the beginning, the end, or somewhere in the middle—it's our choice. So we should do whatever is fastest, and adding to the beginning is fastest because it doesn't require us to traverse the list at all. If we instead chose to add an element to the end of a linked list, we'd have to traverse the entire list. If that list had a million elements, we'd have to follow the next pointers a million times until we got to the end—that would be very slow!

Let's work on a quick example of how this `main` function works. Here's the test case:

```
4
1 2 3 4 5 6
8 3 9 10 15 4
```

```
16 1 1 1 1 1
100016 1 1 1 1 1
```

Each element of `snowflakes` begins as `NULL`, the empty linked list. As we add to `snowflakes`, elements will begin to point at snowflake nodes. The numbers in the first snowflake add up to 21, so it goes into index 21. The second snowflake goes into index 49. The third snowflake goes into index 21. At this point, index 21 is a linked list of *two* snowflakes: `16, 1, 1, 1, 1, 1` followed by `1, 2, 3, 4, 5, 6`.

How about the fourth snowflake? That goes into index 21 again, and now we have a linked list of three snowflakes there. See Figure 1-3 for the hash table that we've built.

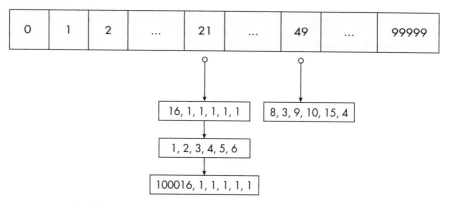

*Figure 1-3: A hash table with four snowflakes*

There are multiple snowflakes in index 21. Does this mean that we have identical snowflakes? No! This emphasizes the fact that a linked list with multiple elements is not sufficient evidence to claim that we have identical snowflakes. We have to compare each pair of those elements to correctly state our conclusion. That's the final piece of the puzzle.

### The New identify_identical Function

We need `identify_identical` to make all pairwise comparisons of snowflakes within each linked list. Listing 1-12 shows the code to do so.

```
void identify_identical(snowflake_node *snowflakes[]) {
  snowflake_node *node1, *node2;
  int i;
  for (i = 0; i < SIZE; i++) {
❶  node1 = snowflakes[i];
    while (node1 != NULL) {
❷    node2 = node1->next;
      while (node2 != NULL) {
        if (are_identical(node1->snowflake, node2->snowflake)) {
          printf("Twin snowflakes found.\n");
          return;
        }
```

```
            node2 = node2->next;
        }
    ❸ node1 = node1->next;
    }
  }
  printf("No two snowflakes are alike.\n");
}
```

*Listing 1-12: Identifying identical snowflakes in linked lists*

We begin with node1 at the first node in a linked list ❶. We use node2 to traverse from the node to the right of node1 ❷ all the way to the end of the linked list. This compares the first snowflake in the linked list to all other snowflakes in that linked list. We then advance node1 to the second node ❸, and we compare that second snowflake to each snowflake to its right. We repeat this until node1 reaches the end of the linked list.

This code is dangerously similar to identify_identical from Solution 1 (Listing 1-7), which made all pairwise comparisons between any two snowflakes. By contrast, our new code only makes pairwise comparisons within a single linked list. But what if someone crafts a test case where all snowflakes end up in the same linked list? Wouldn't the performance then be as bad as in Solution 1? It would, yes, but absent such nefarious data, we're in great shape. Take a minute to submit Solution 2 to the judge and see for yourself. You should see that we've discovered a much more efficient solution! What we've done is use a data structure called a hash table. We'll learn more about hash tables next.

# Hash Tables

A *hash table* consists of two things:

1. An array. Locations in the array are referred to as *buckets*.

2. A *hash function*, which takes an object and returns its code as an index into the array.

The code returned by the hash function is referred to as a *hashcode*; that code determines at which index an object is stored or *hashed*.

Look closely at what we did in Listings 1-10 and 1-11 and you'll see that we already have both of these things. That code function, which took a snowflake and produced its code (a number between 0 and 99,999), is a hash function; and that snowflakes array is the array of buckets, where each bucket contains a linked list.

## Hash Table Design

Designing a hash table involves many design decisions. Let's talk about three of them here.

The first decision concerns size. In Unique Snowflakes, we used an array size of 100,000. We could have instead used a smaller or larger array. A smaller array saves memory. For example, on initialization, a 50,000-element array stores half as many NULL values as does a 100,000-element array. However, a smaller array leads to more objects ending up in the same bucket. When objects end up in the same bucket, we say that a *collision* has occurred. The problem with having many collisions is that they lead to long linked lists. Ideally, all of the linked lists would be short so that we wouldn't have to walk through and do work on many elements. A larger array avoids some of these collisions.

To summarize, we have a memory–time tradeoff here. Make the hash table too small and collisions run rampant. Make the hash table too big and memory waste becomes a concern. In general, try to choose an array size that's a reasonable percentage—such as 20 percent or 50 percent or 100 percent—of the maximum number of elements you expect to insert into the hash table.

In Unique Snowflakes, we used an array size of 100,000 to match the maximum number of snowflakes; had we been constrained to use less memory, smaller arrays would have worked just fine as well.

The second consideration is our hash function. In Unique Snowflakes, our hash function adds up a snowflake's numbers mod 100,000. Importantly, this hash function guarantees that, if two snowflakes are identical, they will end up in the same bucket. (They might also end up in the same bucket if they are not identical, of course.) This is the reason why we can search within linked lists, and not between them, for identical snowflakes.

When solving a problem with a hash table, the hash function that we use should take into account what it means for two objects to be identical. If two objects are identical, then the hash function must hash them to the same bucket. In the case in which two objects must be exactly equal to be considered "identical," we can scramble things so extensively that the mapping between object and bucket is far more intricate than what we did with the snowflakes. Check out the oaat (one-at-a-time) hash function in Listing 1-13 for an example.

```
#define hashsize(n) ((unsigned long)1 << (n))
#define hashmask(n) (hashsize(n) - 1)

unsigned long oaat(char *key, unsigned long len, unsigned long bits) {
  unsigned long hash, i;
  for (hash = 0, i = 0; i < len; i++) {
    hash += key[i];
    hash += (hash << 10);
    hash ^= (hash >> 6);
  }
  hash += (hash << 3);
  hash ^= (hash >> 11);
  hash += (hash << 15);
  return hash & hashmask(bits);
}
```

```
int main(void) { // sample call of oaat
   char word[] = "hello";
   // 2^17 is the smallest power of 2 that is at least 100000
❶ unsigned long code = oaat(word, strlen(word), 17);
   printf("%u\n", code);
   return 0;
}
```

*Listing 1-13: An intricate hash function*

To call oaat ❶ as we do in the main function, we pass three parameters:

key   The data that we want to hash (here, we're hashing the word string)

len   The length of those data (here, the length of the word string)

bits   The number of bits that we want in the resulting hashcode
(here, 17)

The maximum value that a hashcode could have is one less than 2 to the power of bits. For example, if we choose 17, then $2^{17} - 1 = 131,071$ is the maximum that a hashcode could be.

How does oaat work? Inside the for loop, it starts by adding the current byte of the key. That part is similar to what we did when adding up the numbers in a snowflake (Listing 1-10). Those left shifts and exclusive ors are in there to put the key through a blender. Hash functions do this blending to implement an *avalanche effect*, which means that a small change in the key's bits makes a huge change to the key's hashcode. Unless you intentionally created pathological data for this hash function or inserted a huge number of keys, it would be unlikely that you'd get many collisions. This highlights an important point: with a single hash function, there is *always* a collection of data that will lead to collisions galore and subsequently horrible performance. A fancy hash function like oaat can't protect against that. Unless we're concerned about malicious input, though, we can often get away with using a reasonably good hash function and can assume that it will spread the data around.

Indeed, this is why using our hash table solution (Solution 2) for Unique Snowflakes was so successful. We used a good hash function that distributes many nonidentical snowflakes into different buckets. Since we're not securing our code from attack, we don't have to worry about some evil person studying our code and figuring out a way to cause millions of collisions.

For our third and final design decision, we have to think about what we want to use as our buckets. In Unique Snowflakes, we used a linked list as each bucket. Using linked lists like this is known as a *chaining* scheme.

In another approach, known as *open-addressing*, each bucket holds at most one element, and there are no linked lists. To deal with collisions, we search through buckets until we find one that is empty. For example, suppose that we try to insert an object into bucket number 50, but Bucket 50 is already occupied. We might then try Bucket 51, then 52, then 53, stopping when we find an empty bucket. Unfortunately, this simple sequence can lead to poor performance when a hash table has many elements stored in it, so more nuanced search schemes are often used in practice.

Chaining is generally easier to implement than open-addressing, which is why we used chaining for Unique Snowflakes. However, open-addressing does have some benefits, including saving memory by not using linked list nodes.

### Why Use Hash Tables?

Using a hash table turbocharges our solution to Unique Snowflakes. On a typical laptop, a test case with 100,000 elements will take only a fraction of a second to run! No pairwise comparisons of all elements and no sorting is needed, just a little processing on a bunch of linked lists.

Recall that we used an array size of 100,000. The maximum number of snowflakes that can be presented to our program is also 100,000. If we're given 100,000 snowflakes and assume the perfect scenario of each one going into its own bucket, then we'd have only one snowflake per linked list. If we have a little bad luck, then maybe a few of those snowflakes will collide and end up in the same bucket. In the absence of pathological data, though, we expect that each linked list will have at most a few elements. As such, making all pairwise comparisons within a bucket will take only a small, constant number of steps. We expect hash tables to give us a *linear-time* solution, because we take a constant number of steps in each of the $n$ buckets. So we take something like $n$ steps, in comparison to the $n(n - 1)/2$ formula we had for Solution 1. In terms of big O, we'd say that we expect an $O(n)$ solution.

Whenever you're working on a problem and you find yourself repeatedly searching for some element, consider using a hash table. A hash table takes a slow array search and converts it into a fast lookup. For some problems, you may be able to sort an array rather than use a hash table. A technique called binary search (discussed in Chapter 7) could then be used to quickly search for elements in the sorted array. But often—such as in Unique Snowflakes and the problem we'll solve next—that won't work. Hash tables to the rescue!

## Problem 2: Login Mayhem

Let's go through another problem and pay attention to where a naive solution would rely on a slow search. We'll then drop in a hash table to cause a dramatic speedup. We'll go a little more quickly than we did for Unique Snowflakes because now we know what to look for.

This is DMOJ problem coci17c1p3hard.

### The Problem

To log in to your account on a social network website, you'd expect that only your password would work—no one should be able to use a different password to get into your account. For example, let's say that your password is dish. (That's a terribly weak password—don't actually use that anywhere!) To log in to your account, someone would need to enter exactly dish as the password. That's just how logins work.

But now imagine that you are wanting to join a (hopefully theoretical) social network website that has a major security concern: other passwords besides yours can be used to get into your account! Specifically, if someone tries a password that has your password as a substring, then they're in. If your password were dish, for example, then passwords like brandish and radishes would work to get into your account because the string dish is in them. You don't know what password to choose for your account—so at various points you will ask: "If I chose this password, how many current users' passwords would get in to my account?"

We need to support two types of operations:

**Add** Sign up a new user with the given password.

**Query** Given a proposed password $p$, return the number of current users' passwords that could be used to get into an account whose password is $p$.

### Input

The input consists of the following lines:

- A line containing $q$, the number of operations to be performed. $q$ is between 1 and 100,000.

- $q$ lines, each giving one add or query operation to be performed.

Here are the operations that can be performed in those $q$ lines:

- An add operation is specified as the number 1, a space, and then the new user's password. It indicates that a new user has joined with the provided password. This operation doesn't result in any output.

- A query operation is specified as the number 2, a space, and then a proposed password $p$. It indicates that we should output the number of current users' passwords that could be used to get into an account whose password is $p$.

All passwords provided in these operations are between 1 and 10 lowercase characters.

### Output

Output the result of each query operation, one per line.

The time limit for solving the test case is three seconds.

## Solution 1: Looking at All Passwords

Let's work through a test case to make sure that we know exactly what we're being asked to do.

**❶** 6
**❷** 2 dish
1 brandish
1 radishes
1 aaa
**❸** 2 dish
**❹** 2 a

We can tell from the first line **❶** that there are 6 operations for us to perform. The first operation **❷** asks us how many of the existing users' passwords would get into an account whose password is dish. Well, there are no existing users, so the answer is 0!

Next, we add three user passwords, and then we get to our next query operation **❸**. Now we're being asked about dish in the context of these three passwords. You might be thinking that we need to search through the existing passwords to count up the ones that have dish in them. (Hmmm, searching! That's our first inkling that a hash table may be needed here.) If you do that, you'll find that two of the passwords—brandish and radishes—have dish in them. The answer is therefore 2.

And what about the final query **❹**? We're looking for passwords that have an a in them. If you search through the three existing passwords, you'll find that all three of them do! The answer is therefore 3.

We're done! The correct output for the full test case is:

0
2
3

If we implement the solution strategy that we just used, we might arrive at something like Listing 1-14.

```
❶ #define MAX_USERS 100000
   #define MAX_PASSWORD 10

   int main(void) {
     static char users[MAX_USERS][MAX_PASSWORD + 1];
     int num_ops, op, op_type, total, j;
     char password[MAX_PASSWORD + 1];
     int num_users = 0;
     scanf("%d", &num_ops);
     for (op = 0; op < num_ops; op++) {
       scanf("%d%s", &op_type, password);

   ❷   if (op_type == 1) {
         strcpy(users[num_users], password);
         num_users++;
```

```
❸ } else {
    total = 0;
    for (j = 0; j < num_users; j++)
      if (strstr(users[j], password))
        total++;
    printf("%d\n", total);
  }
}
return 0;
}
```

*Listing 1-14: Solution 1*

The problem description says that we'll have at most 100,000 operations. If each is an add operation, then we get 100,000 users ❶, and we can't have any more than that.

For each add operation ❷, we copy the new password into our users array. And for each query operation ❸, we loop through all of the existing user passwords, checking how many of them have the proposed password as a substring.

Like our first solution to Unique Snowflakes, this solution is not fast enough to pass the test cases in time. That's because we have an $O(n^2)$ algorithm here, where $n$ is the number of queries.

We are able to quickly add user passwords to our array—no problem there. What slows us down are the query operations, because each of them has to scan through all existing user passwords. That's where the quadratic-time behavior comes from. Suppose, for example, that a test case starts by adding 50,000 user passwords, and then hammers us with 50,000 queries. Taken together, that would require about $50{,}000 \times 50{,}000 = 2{,}500{,}000{,}000$ steps. That's over 2 billion steps; there's no way that we can do that many in our allowed time limit of three seconds.

## Solution 2: Using a Hash Table

We need to speed up the query operations. And we're going to use a hash table to do so. But how? Isn't it just a fact of life that we need to compare each query password with each existing password? No! Read on as we turn the problem on its head.

### How to Use the Hash Table

For each query operation, it would be nice if we could just look up the needed password in a hash table to determine how many existing user passwords could get into its account. For example, once we add the users with passwords brandish, radishes, and aaa, then it would be nice to be able to look up dish in the hash table and get a value of 2. But while we're adding those three user passwords, how are we supposed to know to be keeping track of what's going on with dish? We don't know which passwords are going to be queried later.

Well, since we don't know the future, let's just add one to the total for every single substring of each user password. That way we'll be ready if we ever need to look any of them up.

Focus on the brandish password. If we consider each substring, then we'll increment the total for b, br, bra, bran, brand, brandi, brandis, brandish, r, ra, and so on. Don't worry: if we process them all, we'll definitely hit dish and increment it. We'll increment dish again when we do the same kind of substring processing on radishes. So, dish will end up with a total of 2, as needed.

You might worry that we're being excessive here, processing a ton of substring passwords, the vast majority of which are not going to be queried. However, remember from the problem description that passwords can be at most 10 characters. Each substring has a starting point and an ending point. In a password of 10 characters, there are only 10 possible starting points and 10 possible ending points, so an upper bound on the number of substrings in a password is $10 \times 10 = 100$. As we have at most 100,000 user passwords, each of which has at most 100 substrings, we'll store at most $100,000 \times 100 = 10,000,000$ substrings in our hash table. That'll take up a few megabytes of memory, for sure, but that's nothing to worry about. We're trading a little memory for the ability to look up any password's total when we need it.

As with Unique Snowflakes, our solution will use a hash table of linked lists. We also need a hash function. We won't use something like the snowflake hash function here, because it would lead to collisions between passwords like cat and act that are anagrams. Unlike in the Unique Snowflakes problem, passwords should be distinguished not just by their letters but by the locations of those letters. Some collisions are inevitable, of course, but we should do what we can to limit their prevalence. To that end, we'll wield that wild oaat hash function from Listing 1-13.

### Searching the Hash Table

We'll use the following node to store passwords in our hash table:

```
#define MAX_PASSWORD 10

typedef struct password_node {
  char password[MAX_PASSWORD + 1];
  int total;
  struct password_node *next;
} password_node;
```

This node is similar to snowflake_node from Unique Snowflakes, but we now also have a total member to keep track of the total count for this password.

Now we can write a helper function to search the hash table for a given password. See Listing 1-15 for the code.

```
#define NUM_BITS 20

password_node *in_hash_table(password_node *hash_table[], char *find) {
  unsigned password_code;
  password_node *password_ptr;
❶ password_code = oaat(find, strlen(find), NUM_BITS);
❷ password_ptr = hash_table[password_code];
  while (password_ptr) {
  ❸ if (strcmp(password_ptr->password, find) == 0)
      return password_ptr;
    password_ptr = password_ptr->next;
  }
  return NULL;
}
```

Listing 1-15: Searching for a password

This in_hash_table function takes a hash table and a password to find in the hash table. If the password is found, the function returns a pointer to the corresponding password_node; otherwise, it returns NULL.

The function works by calculating the hashcode of the password ❶ and using that hashcode to find the appropriate linked list to search ❷. It then checks each password in the list, looking for a match ❸.

### Adding to the Hash Table

We also need a function that will add one to a given password in the hash table. See Listing 1-16 for the code.

```
void add_to_hash_table(password_node *hash_table[], char *find) {
  unsigned password_code;
  password_node *password_ptr;
❶ password_ptr = in_hash_table(hash_table, find);
  if (!password_ptr) {
    password_code = oaat(find, strlen(find), NUM_BITS);
    password_ptr = malloc(sizeof(password_node));
    if (password_ptr == NULL) {
      fprintf(stderr, "malloc error\n");
      exit(1);
    }
    strcpy(password_ptr->password, find);
  ❷ password_ptr->total = 0;
    password_ptr->next = hash_table[password_code];
    hash_table[password_code] = password_ptr;
  }
❸ password_ptr->total++;
}
```

Listing 1-16: Adding one to a password's total

We use our `in_hash_table` function ❶ to determine whether the password is already in the hash table. If it isn't, we add it to the hash table and give it a count of 0 for now ❷. The technique for adding each password to the hash table is the same as for the Unique Snowflakes problem: each bucket is a linked list, and we add each password to the beginning of one of those lists.

Next, whether the password was already in there or not, we increment its total ❸. In that way, a password that we just added will have its total increased from 0 to 1, whereas existing passwords will simply have their total incremented.

### The main Function, Take 1

Ready for the `main` function? Our first attempt is in Listing 1-17.

```
// bugged!
int main(void) {
❶ static password_node *hash_table[1 << NUM_BITS] = {NULL};
  int num_ops, op, op_type, i, j;
  char password[MAX_PASSWORD + 1], substring[MAX_PASSWORD + 1];
  password_node *password_ptr;
  scanf("%d", &num_ops);
  for (op = 0; op < num_ops; op++) {
    scanf("%d%s", &op_type, password);

❷   if (op_type == 1) {
      for (i = 0; i < strlen(password); i++)
        for (j = i; j < strlen(password); j++) {
          strncpy(substring, &password[i], j - i + 1);
          substring[j - i + 1] = '\0';
❸       add_to_hash_table(hash_table, substring);
        }

❹   } else {
❺     password_ptr = in_hash_table(hash_table, password);
❻     if (!password_ptr)
        printf("0\n");
      else
        printf("%d\n", password_ptr->total);
    }
  }
  return 0;
}
```

*Listing 1-17: The main function (bugged!)*

To determine the size of the hash table, we've used this strange bit of code: `1 << NUM_BITS` ❶. We set `NUM_BITS` to 20 in Listing 1-15; `1 << 20` is a shortcut for computing $2^{20}$, which is 1,048,576. (The oaat hash function requires that the hash table have a number of elements that is a power of 2.) Remember that the maximum number of users we'll have is 100,000; the hash table size that I chose is about 10 times this maximum to account for the fact that we insert multiple strings for each password. Smaller or larger hash tables would have worked fine, too.

For each add operation ❷, we increment the total for each substring by using our add_to_hash_table helper function ❸. And for each query operation ❹, we use our in_hash_table helper function ❺ to retrieve the total for the password; if the password isn't in the hash table ❻ then we output 0.

Put all of our functions together and let's try running our code! Remember this test case?

```
6
2 dish
1 brandish
1 radishes
1 aaa
2 dish
2 a
```

The output is supposed to be:

```
0
2
3
```

Unfortunately, our code gives this instead:

```
0
2
5
```

Wait, 5? Where's that 5 coming from?

Look at the password aaa. How many a substrings are in there? There are three! And we're going to find each of them, resulting in three increments to the total for a. But that doesn't make sense: aaa should be able to bump up the total for a at most once, not multiple times. After all, aaa is only one password.

### The main Function, Take 2

What we need to do is make sure that, for each password, each of its substrings counts only once. To do that, we'll maintain an array of all of the substrings that we've generated for the current password. Prior to using a substring, we'll search to make sure that we haven't used that substring yet.

We're introducing a new search here, so it's worth thinking about whether we need a new hash table of substrings. While we could indeed add another hash table for that, we don't need to: as we already argued, each password won't have too many substrings, so a *linear search* (that is, an element-by-element search) through them is going to be fast enough.

Check out Listing 1-18 for the finishing touch.

```
❶ int already_added(char all_substrings[][MAX_PASSWORD + 1],
                     int total_substrings, char *find) {
    int i;
    for (i = 0; i < total_substrings; i++)
      if (strcmp(all_substrings[i], find) == 0)
        return 1;
    return 0;
  }

  int main(void) {
    static password_node *hash_table[1 << NUM_BITS] = {NULL};
    int num_ops, op, op_type, i, j;
    char password[MAX_PASSWORD + 1], substring[MAX_PASSWORD + 1];
    password_node *password_ptr;
    int total_substrings;
    char all_substrings[MAX_PASSWORD * MAX_PASSWORD][MAX_PASSWORD + 1];
    scanf("%d", &num_ops);
    for (op = 0; op < num_ops; op++) {
      scanf("%d%s", &op_type, password);

      if (op_type == 1) {
        total_substrings = 0;
        for (i = 0; i < strlen(password); i++)
          for (j = i; j < strlen(password); j++) {
            strncpy(substring, &password[i], j - i + 1);
            substring[j - i + 1] = '\0';
❷         if (!already_added(all_substrings, total_substrings, substring)) {
              add_to_hash_table(hash_table, substring);
              strcpy(all_substrings[total_substrings], substring);
              total_substrings++;
            }
          }

      } else {
        password_ptr = in_hash_table(hash_table, password);
        if (!password_ptr)
          printf("0\n");
        else
          printf("%d\n", password_ptr->total);
      }
    }
    return 0;
  }
```

*Listing 1-18: A new helper function and fixed main function*

We have a new `already_added` helper function here ❶ that we'll use to tell us whether the `find` substring is already in the `all_substrings` array for the current password.

In the `main` function itself, notice now that we check whether we've seen the current substring ❷. If we have not, only then do we add it to the hash table.

It's time to submit our code to the judge. Go for it! As with Unique Snowflakes, the speedup from using a hash table amounts to an improvement from $O(n^2)$ to $O(n)$, which is plenty fast for the three-second time limit.

# Problem 3: Spelling Check

Sometimes, problems look like they can be solved in a particular way because they bear resemblance to other problems. Here's a problem where it seems that a hash table is appropriate, but on further reflection we see that hash tables vastly overcomplicate what is required.

This is Codeforces problem 39J (Spelling Check). (The easiest way to find it is to search online for *Codeforces 39J*.)

## The Problem

In this problem, we are given two strings where the first string has one more character than the second. Our task is to determine the number of ways in which one character can be deleted from the first string to arrive at the second string. For example, there is one way to get from favour to favor: we can remove the u from the first string.

There are three ways to get from abcdxxxef to abcdxxef: we can remove any of the x characters from the first string.

The context for the problem is a spellchecker. The first string might be bizzarre (a misspelled word) and the second might be bizarre (a correct spelling). In this case, there are two ways to fix the misspelling—by removing either one of the two zs from the first string. The problem is more general, though, having nothing to do with actual English words or spelling mistakes.

### Input

The input is two lines, with the first string on the first line and the second string on the second line. Each string can be up to one million characters.

### Output

If there is no way to remove a character from the first string to get the second string, output 0. Otherwise, output two lines:

- On the first line, output the number of ways in which a character can be deleted from the first string to get the second string.

- On the second line, output a space-separated list of the indices of the characters in the first string that can be removed to get the second string. The problem requires we index a string from 1, not 0. (That's a bit annoying, but we'll be careful.)

For example, for this input:

---

abcdxxxef
abcdxxef

---

we would output:

---

3
5 6 7

---

The 5 6 7 are the indices of the three x characters in the first string, since we are counting from one (not zero).

The time limit for solving the test cases is two seconds.

## *Thinking About Hash Tables*

I spent a truly embarrassing number of hours searching for the problems that drive the chapters in this book. The problems dictate what I can teach you about the relevant data structure or algorithm. I need the problem solutions to be algorithmically complex, but the problems themselves need to be sufficiently simple so that we can understand what is being asked and keep the relevant details at hand. I really thought I had found exactly that kind of hash table problem I needed for this section. Then I went to solve it.

In Problem 2, Login Mayhem, we were given the passwords as part of the input. That was nice, because we just jammed each substring from the passwords into a hash table and then used the hash table to search for them as needed. Here, in Problem 3, we're not given any such list of strings to insert. Unfazed, when I first tried solving this problem, I created a hash table and I inserted into it each prefix of the second (that is, shorter) string. For example, for the word abc, I would have inserted a, ab, and abc. I also created another hash table for the suffixes of the second string. For the word abc, I would have inserted c, bc, and abc. Armed with those hash tables, I proceeded to consider each character of the first string. Removing each character is tantamount to splitting the string into a prefix and a suffix. We can just use the hash tables to check whether both the prefix and suffix are present. If they are, then removing that character is one of the ways in which we can transform the first string into the second.

This technique is tempting, right? Want to give it a try?

The thing I had failed to keep in mind was that each string could be up to a million characters long. We certainly can't store all of the prefixes and suffixes themselves in the hash table—that would take up way too much memory. I played around with using pointers in the hash table to point to both the start and end of the prefixes and suffixes. That solves the concerns of memory use, but it doesn't free us from having to compare these extra-long strings whenever we perform a search using the hash table. In Unique Snowflakes and Login Mayhem, the elements in the hash table were small:

6 integers for a snowflake and 10 characters for a password. That's nothing. However, here, the situation is different: we might have strings of a million characters! Comparing such long strings is very time-consuming.

Another timesink here is computing the hashcode of prefixes and suffixes of these strings. We might call oaat on a string of length 900,000, and then call it again on a string with one additional character. That duplicates all of the work from the first oaat call, when all we wanted was to incorporate one more character into the string being hashed.

Yet, I persisted. I had it in my mind that a hash table was the way to go here, and I failed to consider alternatives. At this point, I probably should have taken a fresh look at the problem. Instead, I learned about *incremental hash functions*, hash functions that are very fast when generating the hashcode for an element that is very similar to the previously hashed element. For example, if I already have the hashcode for abcde, then computing the hashcode for abcdef using an incremental hash function will be very fast, because it can lean on the work already done for abcde rather than starting from scratch.

Another insight was that, if it is too costly to compare extra-long strings, we should try to avoid comparing them at all. We could just hope that our hash function is good enough and that we're lucky enough with the test cases so that no collisions occur. If we look for some element in the hash table, and we find a match . . . well, let's hope it was an actual match and not us getting unlucky with a false positive. If we're willing to make this concession, then we can use a structure that's simpler than the hash table array that we used up to this point in the chapter. In array prefix1, each index i gives the hashcode for the prefix of length i from the first string. In array prefix2, each index i gives the hashcode for the prefix of length i from the second string. In each of two other arrays, we can do similarly for the suffixes of the first string and suffixes of the second string.

Here is some code that shows how the prefix1 array can be built:

```
// long long is a very large integer type in C99
unsigned long long prefix1[1000001];
prefix1[0] = 0;
for (i = 1; i <= strlen(first_string); i++)
❶ prefix1[i] = prefix1[i - 1] * 39 + first_string[i];
```

The other arrays can be built similarly.

It's important that we use unsigned integers here. In C, overflow is well defined on unsigned integers but not signed integers. If a word is long enough, we'll definitely get overflow, so we don't want to allow undefined behavior.

Now we can use these arrays to determine whether prefixes or suffixes match. For example, to determine whether the first i characters of the first string equal the first i characters of the second string, just check whether prefix1[i] and prefix2[i] are equal.

Note how little work it takes to calculate the hashcode for prefix1[i] given the hashcode for prefix1[i - 1]: it's just a multiplication, followed by adding the new character ❶. Why multiply by 39 and add the character? Why not use something else for the hash function? Honestly, because what I chose didn't lead to any collisions in the Codeforces test cases. Yes, I know, it's unsatisfying.

Not to worry, though: there's a better way! To get there, we'll stare at the problem a little more closely, instead of just jumping to a hash table solution.

## An Ad Hoc Solution

Let's think more carefully through an earlier example:

---

abcdxxxef

abcdxxef

---

Suppose that we remove the f from the first string (index 9). Does this make the first string equal the second? No, so 9 will not show up in our space-separated list of indices. The strings have a long prefix of matching characters. There are six such characters to be exact: abcdxx. After that, the two strings diverge, where the first string has an x and the second has an e. If we don't fix that, then we have no hope that the two strings will be equal. The f is too far to the right for its deletion to produce equal strings.

That leads to our first observation: if the length of the *longest common prefix* (in our example, six, the length of abcdxx) is $p$, then our only options for deleting characters are those with indices of $\leq p + 1$. In our example, we should consider deleting the characters whose indices are $\leq 7$: a, b, c, d, the first x, the second x, and the third x. Deleting anything to the right of index $p + 1$ doesn't fix the diverging character at index $p + 1$ and hence can't make the strings equal.

Notice that only some of these deletions actually work. For example, deleting the a, b, c, or d from the first string does not give us the second string. Only each of the three deletions of x gives us the second string. So, while we've got an upper bound for indices to consider ($\leq p + 1$), we also need a lower bound.

To think about a lower bound, consider removing the a from the first string. Does that make the two strings equal? Nope. The reasoning is similar to that in the previous paragraph: there are diverging characters to the right of the a that can't possibly be fixed by removing the a. If the length of the *longest common suffix* (in our example, four, the length of xxef) is $s$, then we should consider deleting each of the final $s + 1$ characters of the first string. In terms of indices, we're interested only in those that are $\geq n - s$, where $n$ is the length of the first string. In our example, this tells us to consider only indices that are $\geq 9 - 4 = 5$. In the above paragraph, we argued that we should look at only indices that are $\leq 7$. Together, we see that indices 5, 6, and 7 are the ones whose deletion transforms the first string into the second. As can be seen in Figure 1-4, what matters here are the indices that are included in both the prefixes and suffixes: each of those characters is a valid deletion.

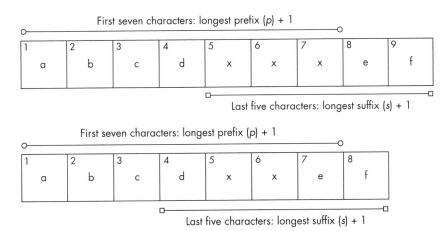

Figure 1-4: Overlap between the longest prefix and longest suffix

In general, the indices of interest go from $n - s$ to $p + 1$. For any index in this range, we know from $p + 1$ that the two strings are the same prior to the index. We also know from $n - s$ that the two strings are the same after the index. Therefore, once we remove the index, the two strings are identical. If the range is empty, then there are *no* indices whose deletion transforms the first string into the second, so 0 is output in this case. Otherwise, we use a for loop to loop through the indices and printf to produce the space-separated list. Let's take a look at the code!

### Longest Common Prefix

We have a helper function in Listing 1-19 to calculate the length of the longest common prefix of two strings.

```
int prefix_length(char s1[], char s2[]) {
  int i = 1;
  while (s1[i] == s2[i])
    i++;
  return i - 1;
}
```

Listing 1-19: Calculating the longest common prefix

Here s1 is the first string and s2 is the second string. We use 1 as the starting index of the strings. Starting at index 1, the loop continues as long as corresponding characters are equal. (In a case such as abcde and abcd, the e will fail to match the null terminator at the end of abcd, so i will correctly end up with value 5.) When the loop terminates, index i is the index of the first mismatched character; therefore, i - 1 is the length of the longest common prefix.

### Longest Common Suffix

Now, to calculate the longest common suffix, we use Listing 1-20.

```
int suffix_length(char s1[], char s2[], int len) {
  int i = len;
  while (i >= 2 && s1[i] == s2[i - 1])
    i--;
  return len - i;
}
```

Listing 1-20: Calculating the longest common suffix

The code is quite similar to Listing 1-19. This time, however, we compare from right to left, rather than left to right. For this reason, we need the len parameter, which gives us the length of the first string. The final comparison that we're allowed to make is i == 2. If we had i == 1, then we'd be accessing s2[0], which is not a valid element of the string!

### The main Function

Finally, we have our main function in Listing 1-21.

```
#define SIZE 1000000

int main(void) {
❶ static char s1[SIZE + 2], s2[SIZE + 2];
  int len, prefix, suffix, total;
❷ gets(&s1[1]);
❸ gets(&s2[1]);

  len = strlen(&s1[1]);
  prefix = prefix_length(s1, s2);
  suffix = suffix_length(s1, s2, len);
❹ total = (prefix + 1) - (len - suffix) + 1;
❺ if (total < 0)
❻   total = 0;

❼ printf("%d\n", total);
❽ for (int i = 0; i < total; i++) {
    printf("%d", i + len - suffix);
    if (i < total - 1)
      printf(" ");
    else
      printf("\n");
  }
  return 0;
}
```

Listing 1-21: The main function

We use SIZE + 2 as the size of our two character arrays ❶. The maximum number of characters that we're required to read is one million, but we need an extra element for the null terminator. And we need one element on top of that because we start indexing our strings at index 1, "wasting" index 0.

We read the first ❷ and second string ❸. Notice we pass a pointer to index 1 of each string: gets therefore starts storing characters at index 1 rather than index 0. After calling our helper functions, we calculate the number of indices that can be deleted from s1 to give us s2 ❹. If this number is negative ❺, then we set it to 0 ❻. This makes the printf call correct ❼. We use a for loop ❽ to print the correct indices. We want to start printing at len - suffix, so we add len - suffix to each integer i.

When submitting to the judge, you may need to choose GNU G++ rather than GNU GCC.

There we have it: a linear-time solution. We had to perform some tough analysis, but after that we were able to proceed without complex code and without the need for a hash table. Before considering a hash table, ask yourself, is there anything about the problem that would make hash tables unwieldy? Is a search really necessary, or are there features of the problem that obviate such searching in the first place?

## Summary

A hash table is a data structure: a way to organize data so that certain operations are fast. Hash tables speed up the search for some specified element. To speed up other operations, we need other data structures. For example, in Chapter 8, we'll learn about a heap, which is a data structure that can be used when we need to quickly identify the maximum or minimum element in an array.

Data structures are general approaches to organizing and manipulating data. Hash tables apply to all kinds of problems beyond what is shown here; I hope that you now have good intuition for when a hash table can be used. Be on the lookout for other problems where otherwise efficient solutions are hampered by repeated, slow searches.

## Notes

Unique Snowflakes is originally from the 2007 Canadian Computing Olympiad.

Login Mayhem is based on a problem from the 2017 Croatian Open Competition in Informatics, Round 1.

Spelling Check is originally from the 2010 School Team Contest #1, hosted by Codeforces. The prefix-suffix solution (used after I finally gave up on a hash table solution) originates from a note posted at *https://codeforces.com/blog/entry/786*.

In our hash table code, we used malloc to allocate nodes of our linked lists. It's sometimes possible to avoid using malloc and node structures altogether. See "Unique Snowflakes: Implicit Linked Lists" in Appendix B if you're interested in how that can be done.

The oaat hash function is by Bob Jenkins (see *http://burtleburtle.net/bob/hash/doobs.html*).

For additional information about hash table applications and implementations, see *Algorithms Illuminated (Part 2): Graph Algorithms and Data Structures* by Tim Roughgarden (2018).

# 2

## TREES AND RECURSION

In this chapter, we'll look at two problems that will require processing and answering questions about hierarchical data. The first problem is about collecting candy from a neighborhood. The second concerns queries on family trees. Because loops are a natural means to process collections of data, we'll try them first. We'll soon see, though, that these problems push against what we can easily express with loops, and this will motivate a shift in the way we think about and solve such problems. You'll leave this chapter knowing about recursion, a problem-solving technique that applies whenever the solution to a problem involves solutions to simpler, smaller problems.

## Problem 1: Halloween Haul

This is DMOJ problem dwite12c1p4.

## The Problem

It's Halloween, a holiday that often involves getting dressed up, candy from neighbors, and a stomachache. In this problem, you want to collect all the candy from a particular neighborhood as efficiently as possible. The neighborhood has a rigid, though strange, shape. Figure 2-1 shows a sample neighborhood.

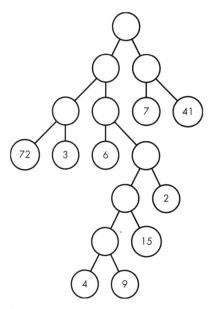

*Figure 2-1: A sample neighborhood*

The circles with numbers in them are houses. Each number gives the amount of candy you'll get by visiting that house. Candy values are at most two digits. The circle at the top is your starting location. The circles without numbers are intersections between streets, where you choose which way to walk next. The lines that connect circles are the streets. Moving from one circle to another corresponds to walking one street.

Let's think about how you could move through this neighborhood. Begin at the top circle. If you walk down the street on the right, you get to an intersection. If you then walk down the street on the right from that circle, you end up at a house and collect 41 pieces of candy. You could then walk back up the two streets to the top to return to your starting location. You'll have thus walked a total of four streets and collected 41 pieces of candy.

However, your goal is to collect *all* of the candy and to do so by walking the minimum number of streets. You're allowed to end your walk as soon as you've collected all of the candy; there's no requirement to get back to the top circle.

### Input

The input consists of exactly five lines, where each line is a string of at most 255 characters that describes a neighborhood.

How can a string encode a diagram? This isn't like the Unique Snowflakes problem from Chapter 1, where each snowflake was just six integers. Here we have circles, lines connecting circles, and candy values in some of those circles.

As with the Unique Snowflakes problem, we can simplify things by initially ignoring some of the complexities of the full problem. For that reason, I'll defer the way that the input is provided until later. Here's a teaser, though: there's a quite clever and compact way to represent these diagrams as strings. Stay tuned.

### Output

Our output will be five lines of text, with each line corresponding to one of the five input lines. Each line of output contains two integers separated by a space: the minimum number of streets walked to obtain all of the candy and the total amount of candy obtained.

The time limit for solving the test case is two seconds.

### Binary Trees

In Figure 2-2, I've augmented the neighborhood from Figure 2-1 to include letters in the nonhouse circles. These letters have nothing to do with the problem and won't affect our code, but they allow us to uniquely refer to each circle.

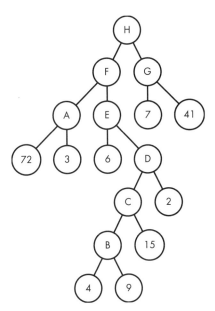

Figure 2-2: A sample neighborhood with letter labels

The particular shape of the neighborhoods in our Halloween Haul problem is known as a *binary tree*. Both *binary* and *tree* are important words here. Let's unpack their definitions, starting with tree.

### Defining Tree

A *tree* is a structure that consists of *nodes* (the circles) and *edges* between nodes (the lines representing streets). The node at the top—the H circle—is referred to as the *root*. You'll often see the term *vertex* used synonymously with node; in this book, I'll stick to "node."

The nodes in the tree have a parent-child relationship. For example, we say that H is the *parent* of F and G, because there is an edge from H to F and an edge from H to G. We also say that F and G are *children* of H. More specifically, F is the *left child* of H, and G is the *right child* of H. Any node that has no children is referred to as a *leaf*. In the current problem, the nodes with candy values (the houses) are leaves.

Much of the terminology that computer scientists use when discussing trees is familiar from the notion of family trees. For example, F and G are *siblings*, because they have the same parent. E is an example of a *descendant* of H, because E is reachable by moving down the tree from H.

The *height* of a tree is determined by the largest number of edges that we can traverse on a downward path from the root to a leaf. What is the height of our sample tree? Well, here's one downward path we could traverse: H to G to 7. That path has two edges (H to G and G to 7), giving us a height of at least two. However, we can find a much longer downward path! Here's one such longest downward path: H to F to E to D to C to B to 4. That path has six edges on it. Convince yourself that there is no longer downward path here. The height of this tree is six.

Trees have a very regular, repeatable structure, which helps us process them. For example, if we remove the root H, along with the edges from H to F and from H to G, we end up with two *subtrees* (Figure 2-3).

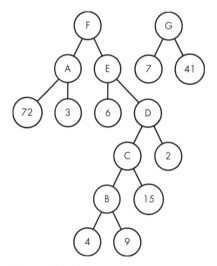

*Figure 2-3: A tree split in two*

Notice that each of the two subtrees is a legitimate tree on its own: it has a root, nodes and edges, and the proper structure. We could further split these trees into even smaller pieces, and each of those pieces would be a tree. A tree can be thought of as consisting of smaller trees, each of which consists of even smaller trees, and so on.

### Defining Binary

In the context of trees, *binary* simply means that each node in our trees has at most two children. A given node in a binary tree can have zero children, or one child, or two children, but no more. The binary trees in our current problem are in fact a little more constrained than that: each node is required to have exactly zero or two children—you'll never see a node with exactly one child. Such a binary tree, where every nonleaf node has exactly two children, is referred to as a *full* binary tree.

## Solving the Sample Instance

Let's go ahead and solve the Halloween Haul problem on our sample tree (Figure 2-2). We're required to return both the minimum number of streets we have to walk to get all of the candy and the total amount of candy. We'll start with the latter, because it's the easier of the two to calculate.

We can calculate the total amount of candy by hand: just add up all of the candy values in the house nodes. If we do that, we get 7 + 41 + 72 + 3 + 6 + 2 + 15 + 4 + 9 = 159.

Now, let's figure out the minimum number of streets that you must walk to collect all of the candy. Does it even matter how we traverse the tree? After all, you have to visit every house—maybe your quickest route is simply to avoid visiting the same house multiple times.

Let's traverse the tree by visiting left children before right children. By using this strategy, here is the order in which you visit the nodes: H, F, A, 72, A, 3, A, F, E, 6, E, D, C, B, 4, B, 9, B, C, 15, C, D, 2, D, E, F, H, G, 7, G, 41. Note how your final stop is the 41 house and not H: you're not required to return to your starting location once you're finished collecting the candy. There are 30 edges in that path. (There are 31 nodes in the path, and the number of edges in a path is always the number of nodes minus one.) Is walking 30 streets the best you can do?

In fact, you can do better: the most efficient route involves walking only 26 streets. Spend some time now trying to find this more optimized traversal. As in the 30-street traversal, you'll have to visit the nonhouse nodes multiple times and you want to visit each house exactly once, but you can save four street-walks by being strategic about the *final* house that you visit.

## Representing Binary Trees

To create a solution in code, we'll need to find a way to represent neighborhood trees. As you'll see, it's convenient to convert the strings from the input that represent trees to explicit tree structures that represent relationships between nodes. In this section, I'll provide those tree structures. We won't yet be able to read the strings and convert them to trees, but we'll be able to hardcode trees. That gives us the foothold we need to start solving the problem.

### Defining Nodes

When solving the Unique Snowflakes problem in the last chapter, we used a linked list to store a chain of snowflakes. Each snowflake node contained the snowflake itself, and it also contained a pointer to the next snowflake in the chain:

```
typedef struct snowflake_node {
  int snowflake[6];
  struct snowflake_node *next;
} snowflake_node;
```

We can use a similar struct to represent a binary tree. In our neighborhood trees, the houses have candy values and the other nodes do not. Even though we have these two kinds of nodes, we'll be okay with just one node structure. We'll just make sure that house nodes have correct candy values; we won't even initialize the candy values of nonhouse nodes, because we won't look at those values anyway.

That gives us this starting point:

```
typedef struct node {
  int candy;
  // ... what else should we add?
} node;
```

In a linked list, each node points to the next node in the chain (or is NULL if there is no next node). From one node, we can move to exactly one other node. In contrast, in a tree, a single next pointer per node will not suffice, because a nonleaf node will have both a left child and a right child. We need two pointers per node, as in Listing 2-1.

```
typedef struct node {
  int candy;
  struct node *left, *right;
} node;
```

*Listing 2-1: The node struct*

It's apparent that the parent is not included here. Should we throw in a *parent as well, letting us access the parent of a node in addition to its children? This would be useful for some problems, but it is not required for Halloween Haul. We will need a way to move up the tree (from child to parent), but we can do so implicitly, without explicitly following parent pointers. You'll see more about this later.

## Building a Tree

With this node type in hand, we can now build sample trees. We work bottom-up, uniting subtrees until we reach the root. Let's demonstrate the start of this process on our sample tree.

We'll start with the 4 and 9 nodes at the bottom of our sample tree. Then we can combine those under a new parent to create the subtree whose root is B.

Here's the 4 node:

```
node *four = malloc(sizeof(node));
four->candy = 4;
four->left = NULL;
four->right = NULL;
```

This is a house node, so we remember to give it a candy value. It's also important to set its left and right children to NULL. If we don't do that, they'll remain uninitialized, pointing to unspecified memory, and that'll mean trouble if we try to access it.

Now consider the 9 node. This is another house, so the code is structurally identical:

```
node *nine = malloc(sizeof(node));
nine->candy = 9;
nine->left = NULL;
nine->right = NULL;
```

We now have two nodes. They're not yet part of a tree. They're hanging out by themselves. We can unite them under a common parent, like this:

```
node *B = malloc(sizeof(node));
B->left = four;
B->right = nine;
```

This B node is given a left pointer to the 4 house and a right pointer to the 9 house. It's candy member is not initialized, which is fine because non-house nodes have no sensible candy value anyway.

Figure 2-4 depicts what we've generated so far.

Figure 2-4: The first three nodes
in our hardcoded tree

Before powering ahead and producing the C subtree, let's do a little cleanup. Creating a house node involves four things: allocating the node, setting the candy value, setting the left child to NULL, and setting the right child to NULL. Similarly, creating a nonhouse node involves doing three things: allocating the node, setting the left child to some existing subtree, and setting the right child to some other existing subtree. We can capture these steps in helper functions rather than typing them out each time, as shown in Listing 2-2.

```c
node *new_house(int candy) {
  node *house = malloc(sizeof(node));
  if (house == NULL) {
    fprintf(stderr, "malloc error\n");
    exit(1);
  }
  house->candy = candy;
  house->left = NULL;
  house->right = NULL;
  return house;
}

node *new_nonhouse(node *left, node *right) {
  node *nonhouse = malloc(sizeof(node));
  if (nonhouse == NULL) {
    fprintf(stderr, "malloc error\n");
    exit(1);
  }
  nonhouse->left = left;
  nonhouse->right = right;
  return nonhouse;
}
```

Listing 2-2: Helper functions for creating nodes

Let's rewrite our earlier four, nine, B code to use these helper functions, and add the 15 and C nodes while we're at it:

```c
node *four = new_house(4);
node *nine = new_house(9);
node *B = new_nonhouse(four, nine);
node *fifteen = new_house(15);
node *C = new_nonhouse(B, fifteen);
```

Figure 2-5 depicts our five-node tree.

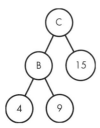

Figure 2-5: The first five nodes in
our hardcoded tree

Notice that node C has a left child that is a nonhouse node (B in our code) and a right child that is a house node (fifteen in our code). Our new_nonhouse function allows this asymmetry (one nonhouse child and one house child): each is just a node. We can mix and match nonhouse nodes and house nodes at will.

At this point, we have a five-node subtree rooted at node C. We should be able to use that C node to access the candy values stored in the tree. (We could also use B, four, nine, and fifteen to access parts of the tree, because building a tree piecewise leaves a residue of node variables in our wake, but later we'll build a function for converting a string to a tree that will furnish us with only the tree's root, so let's not cheat by using those variables here.)

Here's a quick exercise: What does this print?

```
printf("%d\n", C->right->candy);
```

If you said 15, you'd be correct! We access C's right child, which is the fifteen house node, and then we access fifteen's candy value.

How about this?

```
printf("%d\n", C->left->right->candy);
```

That should output 9: a left and then a right takes us from C to nine. Now try this:

```
printf("%d\n", C->left->left);
```

Yikes! On my laptop, I'm getting the value 10752944. Why? The reason is that we're printing a pointer value, not a candy value. We will have to be careful here.

Finally, what would this print?

```
printf("%d\n", C->candy);
```

This gives us a useless number. Here we're printing the candy member for a nonhouse node, but only houses have meaningful values of candy.

We're now ready to start tackling this problem. Finish up the code to build the sample tree and we'll be on our way.

## Collecting All the Candy

We have two main tasks: calculating the minimum number of streets required to collect all of the candy and calculating the total amount of candy in the tree. We'll write a helper function for each task, starting with calculating the total amount of candy, the easier of the two tasks. The helper function will have the following signature:

```
int tree_candy(node *tree)
```

The function takes a pointer to a node that is the root of the tree and returns an integer that will be the total amount of candy in the tree.

If we were dealing with linked lists, we could use a loop like we did when solving the Unique Snowflakes problem. The body of the loop would process the current node and then use the next member of the node to advance to the next node. At each step, there's only one place to go: further down the linked list. However, the structure of binary trees is more complex. Each nonleaf node has a left and a right subtree. Each must be traversed; otherwise, we'll miss processing part of the tree!

To show a tree traversal in action, we will return to our sample tree (Figure 2-2): Beginning at node H, where should we go first? We could move right to G and then move right again to 41, collecting 41 pieces of candy there. Then what? We're at a dead end, and there's a lot more candy to collect. Remember that each nonleaf node stores pointers only to its left and right children, not to its parent. Once at 41, we have no way to get back up to G.

Starting again, we need to move from H to G and to record that we must later process the F subtree—otherwise, we'll have no way to return to the F subtree.

Once at G, we similarly need to move to 41 and to record that we must later process the 7 subtree. When we're at 41, we see that there are no subtrees to process, and we have recorded two subtrees (F and 7) that we still need to process.

Perhaps next we choose to process the 7 subtree, giving us a total candy value of 41 + 7 = 48. After that, we'll process the F subtree. Making any one decision about where to go from F leaves a whole subtree unprocessed, so we also need to record that.

That is, if we use a loop, for each nonleaf node we must do two things: choose one of its subtrees to process first and record that the other subtree is pending to be processed. Choosing one of the subtrees amounts to following the left or right pointer—there is no problem there. Recording information so that we can visit the other subtree later, however, will be trickier. We'll need a new tool.

### Storing Pending Subtrees on a Stack

At any moment, we can have multiple subtrees pending for us to visit later. We need to be able to add another subtree to that collection and to remove and return subtrees when we're ready to process them.

We can use an array to manage this bookkeeping. We'll define a large array that can hold as many references to pending subtrees as needed. To tell us how many subtrees are pending, we'll keep a highest_used variable that will track the highest index being used in the array. For example, if highest_used is 2, it means that indices 0, 1, and 2 hold references to pending subtrees and that the rest of the array is currently unused. If highest_used is 0, it means that only index 0 is being used. To signify that no part of the array is being used, we set highest_used to -1.

The easiest spot to add to the array is at index highest_used + 1. If we tried to add an element anywhere else, we'd first have to move existing elements to the right; otherwise, we'd overwrite one of the existing elements! Similarly, the easiest element to remove from the array is highest_used. Using any other index would necessitate moving elements to the left to fill the vacancy left by the removed element.

Using this scheme, suppose we first add a reference to subtree F and then add a reference to subtree 7. This places the F subtree at index 0 and the 7 subtree at index 1. The value of highest_used is currently 1. Now, when we remove an element from this array, which subtree do you think gets removed: the F subtree or the 7 subtree?

The 7 subtree gets removed! In general, the element that was most recently added is the one that is removed.

Computer scientists refer to this as *last-in, first-out (LIFO)* access. Collections of data that provide LIFO access are referred to as *stacks*. Adding an element to a stack is known as a *push*, and removing an element from a stack is known as a *pop*. The *top* of the stack refers to the element that would next be popped from the stack; that is, the top of the stack is the most recently pushed item.

There are real-life stacks all over the place. Say you have some plates that have just been washed, and you put them away on a shelf in a cupboard, one after the other. The last one that you add (push) to the shelf will be at the top of the stack, and it will be the first plate that you remove (pop) when retrieving a plate from the cupboard. This is LIFO.

A stack also powers the undo functionality in your word processor. Suppose you type a word, then a second word, then a third word. Now you hit undo. The third word goes away, since it was the last one that you entered.

### Implementing a Stack

Let's implement the stack. To begin, we package both the array and highest _used into a struct. This keeps the stack's variables together and also allows us to create as many stacks as we wish. (In Halloween Haul, we need only one stack, but you might use this code in other settings where multiple stacks are required.) Here's our definition:

```
#define SIZE 255

typedef struct stack {
  node * values[SIZE];
```

```
    int highest_used;
} stack;
```

Recall that each input line is at most 255 characters. Each character will represent at most one node. Each tree that we deal with will thus have at most 255 nodes, and this is why our `values` array has space for 255 elements. Also, notice that each element in `values` is of type `node *`, a pointer to `node`. We could have stored nodes in there directly, rather than pointers to nodes, but that would be less memory efficient because the nodes from the tree would be duplicated when added to the stack.

We'll create a function for each operation on a stack. First, we need a `new_stack` function that creates a new stack. Next, we need `push_stack` and `pop_stack` functions to add to and remove from the stack, respectively. Finally, we'll have an `is_empty_stack` function that tells us whether the stack is empty.

The `new_stack` function is provided in Listing 2-3.

```
stack *new_stack(void) {
❶ stack *s = malloc(sizeof(stack));
   if (s == NULL) {
     fprintf(stderr, "malloc error\n");
     exit(1);
   }
❷ s->highest_used = -1;
   return s;
}
```

*Listing 2-3: Creating a stack*

First, we allocate memory for the stack ❶. Then, we set `highest_used` to -1 ❷; recall that -1 here means an empty stack. Notice that we don't do anything to initialize the elements of `s->values` here: our stack is empty, so its values are irrelevant.

I've put `stack_push` and `stack_pop` together in Listing 2-4 to highlight the symmetry of their implementation.

```
void push_stack(stack *s, node *value) {
❶ s->highest_used++;
❷ s->values[s->highest_used] = value;
}

node * pop_stack(stack *s) {
❸ node * ret = s->values[s->highest_used];
❹ s->highest_used--;
❺ return ret;
}
```

*Listing 2-4: Push and pop on a stack*

In push_stack, we first make room for a new element ❶, and then place value in that free location ❷.

Our pop_stack function is responsible for removing the element at index highest_used. If it did just that, however, then the function wouldn't be all that useful: we'd be able to call it and it would pop the element for us, but it wouldn't tell us what was popped! To remedy that, we store in ret the element from the stack that we are about to remove ❸. We then remove the element from the stack by decreasing highest_used by one ❹. Finally, we return the element that was removed ❺.

I have not included error checking in push_stack or pop_stack. Notice that push_stack would fail if you tried to push more than the maximum number of elements—but we're safe, because we've made the stack as big as any input we'll be provided. Likewise, pop_stack would fail if you tried to pop from an empty stack—but we'll be careful to check that the stack is nonempty before we pop. Of course, general-purpose stacks should be made more robust!

We'll determine whether a stack is empty using is_empty_stack (shown in Listing 2-5), which uses == to check whether highest_used is -1.

```
int is_empty_stack(stack *s) {
  return s->highest_used == -1;
}
```

Listing 2-5: Determining whether a stack is empty

Before we calculate the total amount of candy in a tree, let's exercise our stack code with a small, standalone example, as given in Listing 2-6. I encourage you to take a few minutes to trace the example on your own. Predict what will happen! Then, run the code and check whether the output matches what you expected.

```
int main(void) {
  stack *s;
  s = new_stack();
  node *n, *n1, *n2, *n3;
  n1 = new_house(20);
  n2 = new_house(30);
  n3 = new_house(10);
  push_stack(s, n1);
  push_stack(s, n2);
  push_stack(s, n3);
  while (!is_empty_stack(s)) {
    n = pop_stack(s);
    printf("%d\n", n->candy);
  }
  return 0;
}
```

Listing 2-6: An example of using a stack

Let's figure out what this example does. First we create a new stack called s. We then create three house nodes: n1 has 20 pieces of candy, n2 has 30 pieces of candy, and n3 has 10 pieces of candy.

We push these (single-node) subtrees onto the stack: first n1 is pushed, then n2, then n3. As long as the stack is nonempty, we pop an element from the stack and print its candy value. The elements come off the stack in the opposite order in which they were pushed, so we get 10, 30, 20 as the result of the printf calls.

### A Stack Solution

We now have a means of keeping track of pending subtrees: whenever we make a choice of which subtree to process, we put the other one on the stack. What's important for calculating the total amount of candy is that the stack gives us a way to push a subtree (to help us remember that subtree) and pop a subtree (to help us process a subtree when we're ready to do so).

We could also have used a *queue*, a data structure to give us elements in *first-in, first-out (FIFO)* order, which would change the order in which subtrees are visited and the order in which we add candy to our total, but it would give us the same end result. I chose a stack because it's easier to implement than a queue.

We're now ready to implement tree_candy using a stack. We need to handle two cases: the first is what we do when looking at a nonhouse node, and the second is what we do when looking at a house node.

To know whether our current node is a nonhouse node, we can check its left and right pointers. For a nonhouse, both will be non-null, because they point to subtrees. If we confirm we're looking at a nonhouse node, we store the pointer to the left subtree in the stack, and we proceed down the right subtree. The code for the nonhouse-node case goes like this:

```
if (tree->left && tree->right) {
  push_stack(s, tree->left);
  tree = tree->right;
}
```

Otherwise, if left and right are NULL, then we're looking at a house node. House nodes have candy, so the first thing we should do is add that house's candy value to our total amount of candy:

```
total = total + tree->candy;
```

It's a house, so there's no further down in the tree we can go. If the stack is empty, we're done: an empty stack means that there are no more pending trees to process. If the stack is not empty, then we need to pop a subtree from the stack and process that subtree. Here's the code for processing a house:

```
total = total + tree->candy;
if (is_empty_stack(s))
  tree = NULL;
```

```
else
    tree = pop_stack(s);
```

The complete code for tree_candy, using a stack, is given in Listing 2-7.

```
int tree_candy(node *tree) {
  int total = 0;
  stack *s = new_stack();
  while (tree != NULL) {
    if (tree->left && tree->right) {
      push_stack(s, tree->left);
      tree = tree->right;
    } else {
      total = total + tree->candy;
      if (is_empty_stack(s))
        tree = NULL;
      else
        tree = pop_stack(s);
    }
  }
  return total;
}
```

*Listing 2-7: Calculating the total amount of candy using a stack*

Let $n$ be the number of nodes in a tree. Each time through the while loop, tree is a different node. We therefore visit each node just once. Each node is also pushed to and popped from the stack at most once. In all, each node is involved in a constant number of steps, so we have a linear-time, or $O(n)$, algorithm here.

## A Completely Different Solution

Our tree_candy function works, but it isn't the simplest solution. We had to write an implementation of a stack. We had to keep track of pending trees. We had to backtrack to a pending tree whenever we hit a dead end. For two reasons, using a stack in the way we have done may not be the ideal solution strategy when writing functions on trees:

1.  Whenever we have to go one way but return later to go the other way, we're stuck using this kind of stack code. Tree-processing is rife with problems that require this pattern.

2.  The complexity of stack-based code scales with the complexity of the problem. Adding up all of the candy in a tree isn't so bad, but other related problems that we solve later in this chapter are more challenging. Those problems require not only a stack of pending trees but control flow information for tracking the processing that we need to perform on each tree.

We'll rewrite our code so it's able to work at a higher level of abstraction, eliminating stacks completely from both our code and our thought processes.

### Recursive Definitions

Our stack-based `tree_candy` function is concerned with the *particular steps* needed to solve the problem: push this on the stack, move that way in the tree, pop from the stack when we hit a dead end, stop when we've processed the entire tree. I will now give you another solution that focuses on the *structure* of the problem. This method solves the main problem in terms of solutions to smaller subproblems. The solution comprises two rules:

**Rule 1**   If the root of the tree is a house node, then the total amount of candy in the tree equals the amount of candy at that house.

**Rule 2**   If the root of the tree is a nonhouse node, then the total amount of candy in the tree equals the total amount of candy in the left subtree plus the total amount of candy in the right subtree.

This is called a *recursive* definition. A definition is recursive if it offers a solution to a problem by referring to solutions to subproblems. Rule 2 is where we see this in action. We care about solving the original problem of calculating the total amount of candy in the tree. That total can be calculated, according to Rule 2, by adding up the solutions to two smaller problems: the total amount of candy in the left subtree and the total amount of candy in the right subtree.

It's at about this time that students in my classes start blanching all over the place. How is this description going to solve anything? Even if it does, how can this kind of thing be written in code? The problem is aggravated by books and tutorials that imbue recursive definitions with a mystical quality that is to be trusted but not understood. However, there is no leap of faith or temerity required.

Let's work through a small example to get a feel for why this recursive definition is correct.

Consider this tree consisting of a single house with four pieces of candy:

Rule 1 immediately tells us that the answer for this tree is four. Whenever we see this tree later, just remember that the answer is four.

Now, consider this tree consisting of a single house with nine pieces of candy:

Again, Rule 1 applies, telling us that the answer is nine: when we see this tree later, we'll just respond that the answer is nine.

Now, let's solve the problem for a bigger tree:

This time, Rule 1 does not apply: the root of the tree is a nonhouse node, not a house node. However, we are rescued by Rule 2, which tells us that the total amount of candy here is the total amount of candy in the left subtree plus the total amount of candy in the right subtree. We already know that the total amount of candy in the left subtree is four: it is a tree that we have seen before. Similarly, we know that the total amount of candy in the right subtree is nine: we have seen that tree before, too. By Rule 2, therefore, the entire tree has 4 + 9 = 13 pieces of candy. Remember this for when we see this tree again!

Let's go a little further. Here's another one-house tree, this one with 15 pieces of candy:

Rule 1 tells us this tree has a total of 15 pieces of candy. Remember that! Now consider a five-node tree:

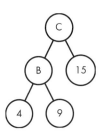

Rule 2 applies here, because the root is a nonhouse node. We need the total amount of candy in the left subtree and the total amount of candy in the right subtree. We already know the total amount of candy in the left subtree, as we remember our earlier answer of 13. There's no point going into that left subtree and recalculating anything: we already know the answer. Similarly, we already know the total amount of candy in the right subtree, as it was 15. By Rule 2, then, we have a total of 13 + 15 = 28 pieces of candy in the tree.

You can keep using this logic to find the total amount of candy in bigger and bigger trees. As we did in the example here, solve smaller subtrees before larger subtrees. In doing so, Rule 1 or Rule 2 will always apply, and answers for smaller subtrees will be known when they are needed.

Let's encode Rule 1 and Rule 2 as a C function; see Listing 2-8.

```
int tree_candy(node *tree) {
❶ if (!tree->left && !tree->right)
    return tree->candy;
❷ return tree_candy(tree->left) + tree_candy(tree->right);
}
```

*Listing 2-8: Calculating the total amount of candy using recursion*

Notice how Rule 1 and Rule 2 are directly represented here. We have an if statement whose condition is true when the left and right subtrees are NULL ❶. No subtrees means that tree is a house node. We should therefore apply Rule 1, which is exactly what we do. Specifically, we return the amount of candy in the house node tree. If Rule 1 does not apply, we know that tree is a nonhouse node, and we can implement Rule 2 and return the candy in the left subtree plus the candy in the right subtree ❷ ... but here we pause.

How does Rule 2 work here? The total amount of candy in the left subtree is obtained by calling tree_candy on the left subtree. This is the same as for the right subtree: to obtain the total amount of candy in the right subtree, we're calling tree_candy on the right subtree. But we're already in tree_candy!

Calling a function from inside itself is known as a *recursive call*. A function that makes a recursive call is said to be using *recursion*. One of the biggest mistakes you can make at this point is to try to trace what's going on in the computer when this recursion happens. I'm going to refrain from giving the low-level details on how the computer organizes these recursive calls. (Suffice it to say that it uses a stack to keep track of pending function calls. It's very similar to how we earlier used a stack in our code to solve tree_candy! For that reason, our recursive code, much like our stack-based code, is an *O(n)* solution.)

Over and over, I've seen the quagmire that can result from trying to manually trace recursive calls. It's the wrong level of abstraction. Let the computer execute it in the same way that, without a second thought, you let it execute your loops or function calls.

Here's how I suggest thinking through what the recursive code is doing:

- If the root of the tree is a house, return its amount of candy.

- Otherwise, the root of the tree is a nonhouse. Return the total amount of candy in the left subtree plus the total amount of candy in the right subtree.

It's easy to err when writing recursive code. One common mistake is to inadvertently throw information away when in fact it should be returned. The following flawed implementation exhibits this error:

```
// bugged!
int tree_candy(node *tree) {
  if (!tree->left && !tree->right)
    return tree->candy;
```

```
❶ tree_candy(tree->left) + tree_candy(tree->right);
}
```

Our bug is that we return nothing from the recursive calls ❶, as there is no return keyword. We're supposed to return the sum, not throw it away.

Another common mistake is to make a recursive call on something that's not a smaller subproblem of the current problem. Here's an example:

```
// bugged!
int tree_candy(node *tree) {
  if (!tree->left && !tree->right)
    return tree->candy;
❶ return tree_candy(tree);
}
```

Look at the second return statement ❶. If I told you that the total amount of candy in a tree is obtained by calculating the total amount of candy in the tree, I think you'd be quite vexed—but that's exactly the rule that it embodies. This function will not work on a tree whose root is a nonhouse node: it will continue to use up memory with pending function calls until the program crashes.

### Practicing Recursion

Before proceeding with solving the Halloween Haul problem, let's practice with recursion by writing two more functions in the spirit of tree_candy.

First, given a pointer to the root of a full binary tree, let's return the number of nodes in the tree. If the node is a leaf, then there is only one node in the tree, so 1 is the correct return value. Otherwise, we're looking at a nonleaf, and the number of nodes in the tree is one (this node) plus the number of nodes in the left subtree plus the number of nodes in the right subtree. That is, the two rules are as follows:

**Rule 1**   If the root of the tree is a leaf node, then the number of nodes in the tree equals 1.

**Rule 2**   If the root of the tree is a nonleaf node, then the number of nodes in the tree equals 1 plus the number of nodes in the left subtree plus the number of nodes in the right subtree.

A rule like Rule 1 is known as a *base case*, because it can be solved directly, without using recursion. A rule like Rule 2 is known as a *recursive case*, because its solution requires that smaller subproblems be recursively solved. Every recursive function requires at least one base case and at least one recursive case: the base case tells us what to do when the problem is easy, and the recursive case tells us what to do when the problem is not.

Converting these rules to code yields the function in Listing 2-9.

```
int tree_nodes(node *tree) {
  if (!tree->left && !tree->right)
    return 1;
```

```
  return 1 + tree_nodes(tree->left) + tree_nodes(tree->right);
}
```

*Listing 2-9: Calculating the number of nodes*

Second, let's write a function to return the number of leaves in a tree. If the node is a leaf, we return 1. If the node is a nonleaf, then that node is *not* a leaf, so it doesn't count; what does count is the number of leaves in the left subtree and the number of leaves in the right subtree. The code is given in Listing 2-10.

```
int tree_leaves(node *tree) {
  if (!tree->left && !tree->right)
    return 1;
  return tree_leaves(tree->left) + tree_leaves(tree->right);
}
```

*Listing 2-10: Calculating the number of leaves*

The only difference between this code and that in Listing 2-9 is the lack of the 1 + in the last line. Recursive functions are often very similar to each other but can compute very different things!

## Walking the Minimum Number of Streets

I've gone on and on and on, so you might want to revisit the problem description to reorient yourself. We know how to produce the total amount of candy now, but that's only one of the two required outputs. We also need to output the minimum number of streets that must be walked to obtain all of the candy. No candy for guessing that we'll nail this using recursion!

### Calculating the Number of Streets

Earlier, I provided a 30-street walk for the tree in Figure 2-2. I also asked you to find an even better—and in fact optimal—26-street walk. This optimal walk saves four streets by taking advantage of the fact that we can end the walk as soon as the final piece of candy has been collected. There's no requirement in the problem description to walk back to the root of the tree.

What if we *did* return to the root of the tree as part of the walk? It's true that we'd get the wrong answer, because we'd walk more streets than required. It's also true, though, that returning to the root greatly simplifies the problem. We don't have to be concerned with the thorny issue of how to cleverly do the walk to minimize the number of streets. (After all, we'll end up back at the root, so we don't have to orchestrate things so that the final house we visit is a good choice.) Perhaps we'll be able to overshoot the minimum (by returning to the root) and then subtract off the extra streets that we walked? That's our gambit!

Let's follow the same plan as for tree_candy and define a base case and a recursive case.

What do we do if the root of the tree is a house—how many streets do we walk starting from that house and getting back to that house? The answer is zero! No streets are required.

What do you do if the root is a nonhouse? Return to Figure 2-3, where I split the tree in two. Suppose we knew the number of streets required to walk the F subtree and the number of streets required to walk the G subtree. We can calculate those recursively. Then, add H and its two edges back in. How many more streets must we walk now? We have to walk one street from H to F and then walk one street from F back to H after we finish with the F subtree. We have to do similarly for G: walking from H to G and then from G back to H after we finish with the G subtree. That's four additional streets, beyond those that we get from the recursion.

Here are our two rules:

**Rule 1**    If the root of the tree is a house node, then the number of streets we walk is zero.

**Rule 2**    If the root of the tree is a nonhouse node, then the number of streets we walk is the number of streets we walk for the left subtree plus the number of streets we walk for the right subtree plus 4.

At this stage, you should be getting a little more comfortable converting such rules into code. Listing 2-11 supplies an implementation.

```
int tree_streets(node *tree) {
  if (!tree->left && !tree->right)
    return 0;
  return tree_streets(tree->left) + tree_streets(tree->right) + 4;
}
```

*Listing 2-11: Calculating the number of streets getting back to the root*

If you perform a walk in Figure 2-2 starting at H, collecting all the candy, and ending at H, you will walk 32 streets. No matter how you walk the tree, as long as you visit each house once and don't unnecessarily rewalk streets, you'll get 32. The minimum number of streets we can walk, with no requirement to return to the root, is 26. Since 32 − 26 = 6, by ending at the root we overshoot the correct answer by six.

Because there's no requirement to return to the root, it makes sense to arrange our walk so that the last house that we visit is as far away as possible from the root. For example, ending at the house with 7 pieces of candy is a bad move, because we're only two streets from H anyway—but look at those gloriously distant 4 and 9 houses way at the bottom. It would be wonderful to end our walk at one of those houses. If we end our walk at 9, for example, then we'd save six streets: 9 to B, B to C, C to D, D to E, E to F, and F to H.

The plan, then, is to end our walk at a house that is located the maximum number of streets away from the root. If that house is six streets from the root, it means that there is a path of six edges from the root to some leaf. This is exactly the definition of the height of a tree! If we can calculate the height of a tree—recursively, I'll bet—then we can subtract the height from what tree_streets gives us. That leaves us off at a house furthest from the root, thereby saving us the maximum number of streets.

As a quick aside, there's actually no reason to know which house is the furthest, or even to know how to perform a walk to make that house be last. All we have to do is convince ourselves that we *can* construct a walk to make that house be last. I'll give a quick argument using Figure 2-2 that I hope convinces you. Starting at H, compare the heights of the F and G subtrees, and completely walk whichever has smaller height—G, in this case. Then, repeat this process using F's subtrees. Compare the heights of the A and E subtrees, and completely walk the A subtree (because it's height is smaller than that of E). Keep doing this until all subtrees have been walked; the final house that you visit will be a house furthest from H.

## Calculating Tree Height

Let's now move on to tree_height and another manifestation of our Rule 1–Rule 2 recursive approach.

The height of a tree consisting of a single house is zero, because there are no edges at all that we can traverse.

For a tree whose root is a nonhouse, consult Figure 2-3 again. The F subtree has a height of five, and the G subtree has a height of one. We can solve these subproblems recursively. The height of the original tree, with H in there, is one more than the maximum of five and one, because an edge from H increases the number of edges to each leaf by one.

That analysis gives us these two rules:

**Rule 1**   If the root of the tree is a house node, then the tree's height is zero.

**Rule 2**   If the root of the tree is a nonhouse node, then the tree's height is one more than the maximum of the left subtree's height and the right subtree's height.

See Listing 2-12 for the code. We have a little max helper function to tell us the maximum of two numbers; otherwise, tree_height holds no surprises.

```
int max(int v1, int v2) {
  if (v1 > v2)
    return v1;
  else
    return v2;
}

int tree_height(node *tree) {
  if (!tree->left && !tree->right)
    return 0;
  return 1 + max(tree_height(tree->left), tree_height(tree->right));
}
```

*Listing 2-12: Calculating the height of the tree*

We now have `tree_candy` to calculate the total amount of candy and tree
_streets and `tree_height` to calculate the minimum number of streets. Putting
those three together gives us a function that solves the problem given a tree;
see Listing 2-13.

```
void tree_solve(node *tree) {
  int candy = tree_candy(tree);
  int height = tree_height(tree);
  int num_streets = tree_streets(tree) - height;
  printf("%d %d\n", num_streets, candy);
}
```

Listing 2-13: Solving the problem, given a tree

Try calling this function on the trees you built in "Building a Tree" on
page 43.

## Reading the Input

We are now ever so close, but we're not quite there. Yes, we can solve the
problem if we have a tree in hand, but recall that the input to the problem
is lines of text, not trees. We'll have to convert each of those lines to a tree
before we can unleash `tree_solve` on it. At last, we're finally ready to unveil
the way in which trees are represented as text.

### Representing a Tree as a String

I'll show you the correspondence between a line of text and its tree by pro-
gressing through several examples.

First, a tree of a single house node is represented simply as the text of
the candy value. For example, this tree (whose node's candy value is four):

is represented as follows:

```
4
```

A tree whose root is a nonhouse node is represented (recursively!) by
the following, in order: an opening parenthesis, a first smaller tree, a space,
a second smaller tree, and a closing parenthesis. The first smaller tree in
there is the left subtree, and the second smaller tree is the right subtree. For
example, this three-node tree

is represented like this:

---

(4 9)

---

Similarly, here is a five-node tree:

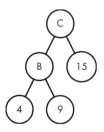

This five-node tree is represented like this:

---

((4 9) 15)

---

Here, the left subtree is (4 9) and the right subtree is 15.

Written as rules, we have the following:

**Rule 1**   If the text is the digits of integer c, then the tree is a single house node with c candy.

**Rule 2**   If the text starts with an opening parenthesis, then the root of the tree is a nonhouse node. After the opening parenthesis, the text contains the tree's left subtree, a space, the tree's right subtree, and a closing parenthesis.

### Reading in a Nonhouse Node

Our goal is to write function read_tree with this signature:

---

```
node *read_tree(char *line)
```

---

It takes a string, and it returns the corresponding tree.

Let's start by implementing Rule 2, since Rule 1 involves some subtle work to convert characters to integers.

Rule 2, the recursive rule, requires us to make two calls to read_tree: one to read the left subtree and one to read the right subtree. Let's see how far we get:

---

```
node *tree;
tree = malloc(sizeof(node));
if (line[0] == '(') {
❶ tree->left = read_tree(&line[1]);
❷ tree->right = read_tree(???);
  return tree;
}
```

---

After allocating memory for the root of our tree, we make a recursive call to read the left subtree ❶. We pass a pointer to index 1 of line so that the recursive call receives the string not including the opening parenthesis at index 0. However, in the next line, we're in trouble ❷. Where do we start reading the right subtree? Equivalently, how many characters are in the left subtree? We don't know! We could write a separate function to figure out where the left subtree ends. For example, we could count the number of opening and closing parentheses until they're equal, except that this seems wasteful: If read_tree successfully read the left subtree, surely that recursive call knew where that subtree ended? If only there were a way to communicate that information back to the original read_tree call, it could use that to determine what part of the string to pass to the second recursive call.

Adding a parameter to a recursive function is a general and powerful way to solve this kind of problem. Whenever a recursive call has information not conveyed through what it returns, or it needs information that is not passed, consider adding a parameter. If that parameter is a pointer, it can be used to both pass additional information to recursive calls and receive information back.

For our purposes, we want to be able to tell a recursive call where its string starts. Also, we want the recursive call to be able to tell us, when it's finished, where we should continue processing the string. To do this, we'll add an integer pointer parameter pos. However, we don't want to add that parameter to read_tree, because the caller of read_tree has no business or interest knowing about this extra parameter. The caller of read_tree should be able to just pass a string, not caring about this pos parameter that is internal to our implementation.

We'll keep the signature of read_tree as before, with only the line parameter. Then read _tree will call read_tree_helper, and it's read_tree_helper that has this pos parameter and induces the recursion.

Listing 2-14 gives the read_tree code. It passes a pointer to 0 to read_tree _helper, because index 0 (the start of the string) is where we want to start processing.

```
node *read_tree(char *line) {
  int pos = 0;
  return read_tree_helper(line, &pos);
}
```

*Listing 2-14: Calling our helper, with a pointer to int*

We're now ready to try again with our implementation of Rule 2:

```
node *tree;
tree = malloc(sizeof(node));
if (line[*pos] == '(') {
❶ (*pos)++;
  tree->left = read_tree_helper(line, pos);
❷ (*pos)++;
  tree->right = read_tree_helper(line, pos);
```

```
❸ (*pos)++;
  return tree;
}
```

The function will be called with pos referring to the first character of a tree, so we first advance pos by one character to skip over the opening parenthesis ❶. Now pos is perfectly positioned at the start of the left subtree. We then make the recursive call to read the left subtree. That recursive call will update pos to the index of the character following the left subtree. Because a space follows the left subtree, we skip over that space ❷. Now we're positioned at the start of the right subtree; we recursively grab that right subtree and then skip over the closing parenthesis ❸, the one that closes the opening parenthesis that we skipped over initially ❶. Skipping the closing parenthesis is important, because this function is responsible for processing the entire subtree, including its closing parenthesis. If we left out this final skip, whoever called the function may be left staring at a closing parenthesis when they expected a space. After skipping that closing parenthesis, the only thing left to do is return our tree.

### Reading in a House Node

With Rule 2 out of the way, let's tackle Rule 1. Before we can make much progress, we'll need to be able to convert part of a string to an integer. Let's write a small, separate program to make sure that we can do this. It will take a string that we assume represents a house node and print its candy value. Surprisingly, if we're not careful, we may get baffling results. Be advised: we are not careful in Listing 2-15.

```
#define SIZE 255

// bugged!
int main(void) {
  char line[SIZE + 1];
  int candy;
  gets(line);
  candy = line[0];
  printf("%d\n", candy);
  return 0;
}
```

Listing 2-15: Reading a candy value (bugged!)

Run that program and enter the number 4.

You'll likely see 52 as the output. Run it again and enter the number 9. You're likely to see 57. Now run it with 0. You'll likely see 48. Finally, run it with each value from 0 to 9. You should see that each output is offset by the output that 0 produced. If 0 outputs 48, then 1 will output 49, 2 will output 50, 3 will output 51, and so on.

What we're seeing here is the character code for each digit. The crucial point is that the codes for integers are consecutive. We can therefore subtract the character code for zero to put our integers in the proper range. With this fix, we get the code in Listing 2-16. Try it!

```
#define SIZE 255

int main(void) {
  char line[SIZE + 1];
  int candy;
  gets(line);
  candy = line[0] - '0';
  printf("%d\n", candy);
  return 0;
}
```

*Listing 2-16: Reading a candy value*

This little program works for single-digit integers. The description of Halloween Haul, though, requires that we also accommodate candy integers that are two digits. Suppose we read digit 2 and then digit 8. We want to combine these and end up with the integer 28. What we can do is multiply the first digit by 10 (that gives us 20 here) and then add the 8 (for a total of 28). Listing 2-17 is another little test program to enable us to check that we've got this right. Here we assume that a string of two digits will be typed.

```
#define SIZE 255

int main(void) {
  char line[SIZE + 1];
  int digit1, digit2, candy;
  gets(line);
  digit1 = line[0] - '0';
  digit2 = line[1] - '0';
  candy = 10 * digit1 + digit2;
  printf("%d\n", candy);
  return 0;
}
```

*Listing 2-17: Reading a candy value with two digits*

That's all we need for Rule 1, and we can write this:

```
--snip--
  tree->left = NULL;
  tree->right = NULL;
❶ tree->candy = line[*pos] - '0';
❷ (*pos)++;
  if (line[*pos] != ')' && line[*pos] != ' ' &&
    line[*pos] != '\0') {
❸   tree->candy = tree->candy * 10 + line[*pos] - '0';
```

❹ (*pos)++;
}
return tree;

We begin by setting the left and right subtrees to NULL; we're creating a house node, after all. We then take a character and convert it to a digit ❶ and then skip over that digit ❷. Now, if this candy value is only one digit, then we have correctly stored its value. If it is two digits, then we need to multiply the first digit by 10 and add the second digit. We therefore determine whether the candy value is one or two digits. If we're not looking at a closing parenthesis, or a space, or the null terminator at the end of the string, then we must be looking at a second digit. If a second digit is present, we incorporate it into our candy value ❸ and move past the digit ❹.

Listing 2-18 puts together our code for Rules 2 and 1.

```
node *read_tree_helper(char *line, int *pos) {
  node *tree;
  tree = malloc(sizeof(node));
  if (tree == NULL) {
    fprintf(stderr, "malloc error\n");
    exit(1);
  }
  if (line[*pos] == '(') {
    (*pos)++;
    tree->left = read_tree_helper(line, pos);
    (*pos)++;
    tree->right = read_tree_helper(line, pos);
    (*pos)++;
    return tree;
  } else {
    tree->left = NULL;
    tree->right = NULL;
    tree->candy = line[*pos] - '0';
    (*pos)++;
    if (line[*pos] != ')' && line[*pos] != ' ' &&
        line[*pos] != '\0') {
      tree->candy = tree->candy * 10 + line[*pos] - '0';
      (*pos)++;
    }
    return tree;
  }
}
```

Listing 2-18: Converting a string to a tree

All that's left is to construct a tidy main function to read each test case and solve it! Listing 2-19 is all it takes.

```
#define SIZE 255
#define TEST_CASES 5

int main(void) {
  int i;
  char line[SIZE + 1];
  node *tree;
  for (i = 0; i < TEST_CASES; i++) {
    gets(line);
    tree = read_tree(line);
    tree_solve(tree);
  }
  return 0;
}
```

Listing 2-19: The main function

We've successfully used recursion to solve this problem, as you should be able to verify by submitting our solution to the judge.

## Why Use Recursion?

It's not always easy to know whether recursion will offer a clean solution to a problem. Here's the telltale sign: whenever a problem can be solved by combining solutions to smaller subproblems, you should try recursion. In all of our recursive code in this chapter, we have solved exactly two subproblems in order to solve the larger problem. These two-subproblem problems are very common, but a problem may require solving three or four or more subproblems.

How do you know that breaking a problem into subproblems can help you solve the original problem, and how do you know what those subproblems are in the first place? We'll revisit these questions in Chapter 3, when we build on what we've learned here to study memoization and dynamic programming. In the meantime, think about whether you could easily solve a given problem if someone told you the solutions to smaller subproblems. For example, think back to calculating the total amount of candy in the tree. This is not an easy problem. What if someone told you the total amount of candy in the left subtree and the total amount of candy in the right subtree? That would make the problem easier. A problem made easier by virtue of knowing its subproblem solutions is a strong clue that recursion applies.

Let's move on to another problem where recursion is useful. As you read the problem description, try to identify where and why recursion will come into play.

## Problem 2: Descendant Distance

We'll now move away from binary trees to general trees in which nodes can have many children.

This is DMOJ problem ecna05b.

### The Problem

In this problem, we are given a family tree and a specified distance $d$. The score for each node in the tree is the number of descendants it has at distance $d$. Our task is to output the nodes with high scores; I'll explain exactly how many nodes that is in the Output section. To see what I mean by descendants at a specified distance, look at the family tree in Figure 2-6.

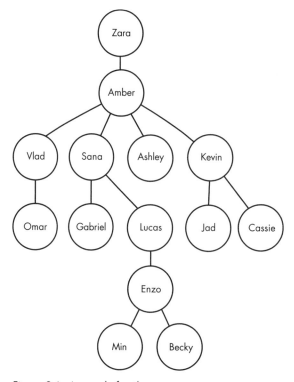

*Figure 2-6: A sample family tree*

Consider the Amber node. Amber has four children, so she has four descendants at a distance of one. Amber also has five grandchildren: five nodes at a distance of two. Generalizing, we can say that, for any node, the number of descendants at distance $d$ is the number of nodes that are exactly $d$ edges down the tree from that node.

### Input

The first line of input gives the number of test cases that will follow. Each test case consists of the following lines:

- A line containing two integers, *n* and *d*, where *n* tells us how many more lines there are for this test case and *d* specifies the descendant distance of interest.

- *n* lines used to build the tree. Each of these lines consists of the name of a node, an integer *m*, and *m* node names giving the children of this node. Each name is at most 10 characters long. These lines can come in any order—there's no requirement that parent lines come before their descendant lines.

There are at most 1,000 nodes in any test case.

Here is a possible input to generate the sample tree in Figure 2-6, asking for the nodes with the most descendants at a distance of two:

```
1
7 2
Lucas 1 Enzo
Zara 1 Amber
Sana 2 Gabriel Lucas
Enzo 2 Min Becky
Kevin 2 Jad Cassie
Amber 4 Vlad Sana Ashley Kevin
Vlad 1 Omar
```

**Output**

The output for each test case has two parts.

First, output the following line:

```
Tree i:
```

where *i* is 1 for the first test case, 2 for the second test case, and so on.

Then, output information for the nodes with high scores (where the score for a node is the number of descendants it has at distance *d*), sorted from most to least. Output the names that are tied for the number of descendants at distance *d* in alphabetical order.

Use the following rules to determine how many names to output:

- If there are three or fewer names with descendants at distance *d*, output them all.

- If there are more than three names with descendants at distance *d*, start by outputting those with the top three scores, starting from the highest score. Then, output each other name whose score is the same as the third score from the top. For example, if we have names with eight, eight, two, two, two, one, and one descendants at distance *d*, we would output information for five names: those with eight, eight, two, two, and two descendants at distance *d*.

For each name that we're required to output, we output a line consisting of the name, followed by a space, followed by its number of descendants at distance $d$.

Output for each test case is separated from the next by a blank line. Here is the output for the above sample input:

```
Tree 1:
Amber 5
Zara 4
Lucas 2
```

The time limit for solving the test cases is 0.6 seconds.

## Reading the Input

One interesting difference between this problem and the Halloween Haul problem is that we're no longer dealing with binary trees. Here, a node can have any number of children. We'll have to change our node structure, since `left` and `right` pointers are not going to work for us anymore. Instead, we'll use an array `children` of children and an integer `num_children` to record the number of children stored in the array. We'll also have a `name` member to store the node's name (Zara, Amber, and so on) and a `score` member for when we calculate the number of descendants at distance $d$. Our `node` struct is given in Listing 2-20.

```
typedef struct node {
  int num_children;
  struct node **children;
  char *name;
  int score;
} node;
```

Listing 2-20: The node struct

In Halloween Haul, the trees started as recursively defined expressions, from which we could recursively read off the left and right subtrees. This is not the case here: nodes can come in any order. For example, we might see

```
Zara 1 Amber
Amber 4 Vlad Sana Ashley Kevin
```

where we learn about Zara's child, Amber, before we learn about Amber's children. However, we could equally well see

```
Amber 4 Vlad Sana Ashley Kevin
Zara 1 Amber
```

where we learn about Amber's children before Zara's!

We know that the nodes and parent-child relationships we read from the file will, by the time we're done, form a single tree. Nonetheless, there's no guarantee that we have a single tree as we process the lines. For example, we might read the lines

```
Lucas 1 Enzo
Zara 1 Amber
```

This tells us that Enzo is a child of Lucas and that Amber is a child of Zara, but so far that's all we know. We have two disconnected subtrees here, and it will take future lines to connect these subtrees.

For these reasons, maintaining a single, connected tree as we read the lines is hopeless. Instead, we'll maintain an array of pointers to nodes. Every time we see a name we haven't seen before, we create a new node and add a pointer to that node to the array. It will therefore prove valuable to have a helper function that searches the array and tells us whether we have seen a name before.

### Finding a Node

Listing 2-21 implements a find_node function. The nodes parameter is an array of pointers to nodes, num_nodes gives the number of pointers in the array, and name is the name that we're searching for.

```
node *find_node(node *nodes[], int num_nodes, char *name) {
  int i;
  for (i = 0; i < num_nodes; i++)
    if (strcmp(nodes[i]->name, name) == 0)
      return nodes[i];
  return NULL;
}
```

*Listing 2-21: Finding a node*

A *linear search* is an element-by-element search of an array. Inside our function, we use a linear search to search through nodes, and ... but wait! Aren't we searching through an array? This is tailor-made hash table territory right here (see Chapter 1). I encourage you to swap in a hash table on your own and compare the performance. To keep things simple, and because there are at most only 1,000 nodes, we'll proceed with this (slow) linear search.

We do a string comparison between each name in the array and the desired name. If strcmp returns 0, it means that the strings are equal, so we return the pointer to the corresponding node. If we reach the end of the array without finding the name, we return NULL to signal that the name was not found.

### Creating a Node

When a name is not found in the array, we'll have to create a node with that name. This will involve a call to malloc, and we'll see that malloc will be required elsewhere in the program as well. So, I've written a helper function, malloc_safe, that we can call whenever we need it. See Listing 2-22: it's just a regular malloc, but with error checking added:

```
void *malloc_safe(int size) {
  char *mem = malloc(size);
  if (mem == NULL) {
    fprintf(stderr, "malloc error\n");
    exit(1);
  }
  return mem;
}
```

Listing 2-22: The malloc_safe function

The new_node helper function in Listing 2-23 uses malloc_safe to create a new node.

```
node *new_node(char *name) {
  node *n = malloc_safe(sizeof(node));
  n->name = name;
  n->num_children = 0;
  return n;
}
```

Listing 2-23: Creating a node

We allocate the new node and then set the node's name member. Then, we set the node's number of children to 0. The reason we use zero here is because we may not know how many children the node has. For example, suppose that the first line that we read for the tree is

```
Lucas 1 Enzo
```

We know that Lucas has one child, but we have no idea how many children Enzo has. The caller of new_node can set the number of children to a new value once that information is available. That happens immediately for Lucas here, but not for Enzo.

### Building a Family Tree

Now we're ready to read and build the tree. Listing 2-24 gives the function. Here nodes is an array of pointers to nodes, with space allocated by the caller of this function; num_lines indicates the number of lines to read.

```
#define MAX_NAME 10

int read_tree(node *nodes[], int num_lines) {
  node *parent_node, *child_node;
  char *parent_name, *child_name;
  int i, j, num_children;
  int num_nodes = 0;
❶ for (i = 0; i < num_lines; i++) {
```

```
      parent_name = malloc_safe(MAX_NAME + 1);
      scanf("%s", parent_name);
      scanf("%d", &num_children);
❷    parent_node = find_node(nodes, num_nodes, parent_name);
      if (parent_node == NULL) {
        parent_node = new_node(parent_name);
        nodes[num_nodes] = parent_node;
        num_nodes++;
      }
      else
❸      free(parent_name);

❹    parent_node->children = malloc_safe(sizeof(node) * num_children);
❺    parent_node->num_children = num_children;
      for (j = 0; j < num_children; j++) {
        child_name = malloc_safe(MAX_NAME + 1);
        scanf("%s", child_name);
        child_node = find_node(nodes, num_nodes, child_name);
        if (child_node == NULL) {
          child_node = new_node(child_name);
          nodes[num_nodes] = child_node;
          num_nodes++;
        }
        else
          free(child_name);
❻      parent_node->children[j] = child_node;
      }
    }
    return num_nodes;
}
```

*Listing 2-24: Converting lines into a tree*

The outer for loop ❶ iterates once for each of the num_lines lines of input. Each line has the name of a parent and one or more names for children; we deal with the parent first. We allocate memory, read the parent's
name, and read the parent's number of children. Then, we use our find_node
helper function to determine whether we have seen this node before ❷. If
we have not, we use our new_node helper function to create a new node, store
a pointer to the new node in the nodes array, and increment the number of
nodes. If the node is already in the nodes array, we free the memory for the
parent name since it will not be used ❸.

We next allocate memory for the parent's child pointers ❹, and we store
the number of children ❺. We then process the child nodes; each child is
processed similarly to the parent node. Once the child node exists and has
its members set, we store a pointer to it in the parent's children array ❻. Notice that there is no child code that allocates any memory or sets the number
of children, like we had for the parent. If we have seen a child name before,

then its children were already set when this name was encountered the first time. If this is the first time we're seeing the name, then we'll set its children when we later learn about its children; if this child is a leaf, its number of children will remain at its initialized value of 0.

We end by returning the number of nodes in the tree. We'll need this when we want to process each node.

## Number of Descendants from One Node

We need to calculate the number of descendants at distance $d$ for each node, so we can find the nodes with the most such descendants. A more modest goal, and the goal for this section, is to calculate the number of descendants at distance $d$ from a single node. We'll write the function with this signature:

```
int score_one(node *n, int d)
```

where n is the node whose number of descendants at distance d we'd like to calculate.

If d is 1, then we want to know the number of children of n. That we can do: we have stored a num_children member with each node. All we have to do is return that:

```
if (d == 1)
  return n->num_children;
```

If d is greater than 1, then what? It may be worth thinking about this first in the more familiar context of binary trees. Here's the binary tree from Halloween Haul (Figure 2-2) again:

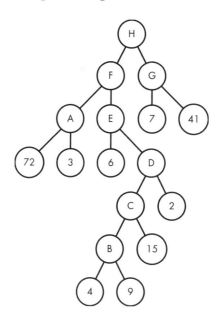

Suppose we had a node of a binary tree and we wanted to know its number of descendants at some specified distance. If we knew how many descendants at that distance were in the left subtree and how many were in the right subtree, would that help?

Not quite. Suppose, for example, that we wanted to know the number of descendants of H at a distance of two. We calculate the number of descendants of F at a distance of two and the number of descendants of G at a distance of two. That doesn't help, because each of those descendants is at a distance of three from H! We don't care about nodes at a distance of three.

How do we fix this? We calculate the number of descendants of F at a distance of one and G at a distance of one! Each of those nodes is at a distance of two from H.

To calculate the number of descendants at any distance $d$, then, we calculate the number of descendants at distance $d - 1$ in the left subtree and number of descendants at distance $d - 1$ in the right subtree.

In the context of family trees, where a node can have more than two children, we generalize this slightly: the number of descendants at distance $d$ is the sum of the number of descendants at distance $d - 1$ in each subtree. And how are we going to find the number of descendants at distance $d - 1$ in each subtree? It's recursion time!

Here are some rules for us to use. Given a node $n$:

**Rule 1**    If $d$ equals one, then the number of descendants at distance $d$ equals the number of children of $n$.

**Rule 2**    If $d$ is greater than one, then the number of descendants at distance $d$ equals the sum of the number of descendants at distance $d - 1$ in each subtree of $n$.

The corresponding code is given in Listing 2-25.

```
int score_one(node *n, int d) {
  int total, i;
  if (d == 1)
    return n->num_children;
  total = 0;
  for (i = 0; i < n->num_children; i++)
    total = total + score_one(n->children[i], d - 1);
  return total;
}
```

*Listing 2-25: The number of descendants from one node*

## Number of Descendants from All Nodes

To calculate the number of descendants at distance $d$ for all nodes, we simply put score_one in a loop (Listing 2-26).

```
void score_all(node **nodes, int num_nodes, int d) {
  int i;
```

```
  for (i = 0; i < num_nodes; i++)
    nodes[i]->score = score_one(nodes[i], d);
}
```

*Listing 2-26: The number of descendants from all nodes*

Here is where we use the score member in each node struct: after this function runs, score holds the number of descendants of interest for each node. Now we just have to figure out which nodes have the highest scores!

### Sorting Nodes

In our ill-fated attempt to sort snowflakes (see "Diagnosing the Problem" on page 9), we came across the C qsort function. We can bring qsort to bear here to sort our nodes. We're required to sort by number of descendants at distance *d*, from highest to lowest. If nodes are tied for the number of descendants at distance *d*, then we sort those alphabetically.

To use qsort, we're tasked with writing a comparison function that takes pointers to two elements and returns a negative integer if the first element is less than the second, 0 if they are equal, and a positive integer if the first is greater than the second. Our comparison function is given in Listing 2-27.

```
int compare(const void *v1, const void *v2) {
  const node *n1 = *(const node **)v1;
  const node *n2 = *(const node **)v2;
  if (n1->score > n2->score)
    return -1;
  if (n1->score < n2->score)
    return 1;
  return strcmp(n1->name, n2->name);
}
```

*Listing 2-27: A comparison function for sorting*

Any qsort comparison function, like this one, has the same signature: it takes two void pointers. These pointers are const to signify that we should not make any changes to the elements that they point to.

Void pointers must be cast before we can perform comparisons or otherwise access the underlying elements. Remember that qsort calls compare with pointers to two elements from our array, but, because our array is an array of pointers, what gets passed to compare is two pointers to pointers to elements. Therefore, we first cast the void pointers to type const node**, and then we apply * to give us values for n1 and n2 that are of type const node*. Now we can use n1 and n2 as pointers to nodes.

We begin by comparing the scores that are stored in each node. These scores will have already been calculated as the number of descendants at the distance *d*. If n1 has more such descendants than n2, we return -1 to indicate that n1 should sort before n2. Similarly, if n1 has fewer descendants at distance *d* than n2, we return 1 to indicate that n1 should sort after n2.

The only way to get to the final line, then, is if n1 and n2 have the same number of descendants at distance *d*. It's here where we want to break the tie by sorting on the nodes' names. We do this using strcmp, which returns a negative number, zero, or positive number if the first string is alphabetically less than, equal to, or greater than the second string, respectively.

## Outputting the Information

After we sort the nodes, the names to output are those at the beginning of the nodes array. Listing 2-28 gives the function that produces this output:

```
void output_info(node *nodes[], int num_nodes) {
  int i = 0;
❶ while (i < 3 && i < num_nodes && nodes[i]->score > 0) {
    printf("%s %d\n", nodes[i]->name, nodes[i]->score);
    i++;
  ❷ while (i < num_nodes && nodes[i]->score == nodes[i - 1]->score) {
      printf("%s %d\n", nodes[i]->name, nodes[i]->score);
      i++;
    }
  }
}
```

*Listing 2-28: Outputting the nodes*

The variable i counts the number of nodes that we have outputted. The outer while loop ❶ is controlled by three conditions that together determine whether we are allowed to output more nodes. If all three conditions are true, we know that more output is required, so we enter the body of that while loop. We then print information for the current node and increase i so that we look at the next node. Now, as long as this new node is tied with the previous node, we want to keep outputting nodes, with no heed to the "maximum of three nodes" rule. The conditions on the inner while loop ❷ encode this logic: if there are more nodes and the current node's score is tied with the previous node, then we enter the body of the inner while loop and print information for the relevant node.

## The main Function

All that remains is to glue our functions together and add the logic to process the test cases. We do this in Listing 2-29.

```
#define MAX_NODES 1000

int main(void) {
  int num_cases, case_num;
  int n, d, num_nodes;
❶ node **nodes = malloc_safe(sizeof(node) * MAX_NODES);
  scanf("%d", &num_cases);
```

```
  for (case_num = 1; case_num <= num_cases; case_num++) {
❷   printf("Tree %d:\n", case_num);
    scanf("%d %d", &n, &d);
    num_nodes = read_tree(nodes, n);
    score_all(nodes, num_nodes, d);
    qsort(nodes, num_nodes, sizeof(node*), compare);
    output_info(nodes, num_nodes);
❸   if (case_num < num_cases)
      printf("\n");
  }
  return 0;
}
```

*Listing 2-29: The main function*

We begin by allocating pointers for the maximum number of nodes that can make up a test case ❶. We then read the number of test cases and loop once for each test case. Recall that each test case requires two pieces of output: information about the test case number and information about the relevant nodes. The first is handled by a single call of printf ❷. For the second, we start leaning on our earlier functions: we read the tree, solve the problem for each node, sort the nodes, and then output the required information.

There's a check at the bottom of the code to tell whether or not we're in the final test case ❸; this is so we can output a blank line between tests.

## Summary

Recursive solutions are virtuous, simple, clean, easy to devise, easy to understand, and easy to prove correct...

Well, at least, that's the sense you'd get if you read enough about recursion and talked to enough recursion enthusiasts. It's clear what the experts think. Through my students, however, I've observed a disconnect between the way that recursion is touted and the way it is learned. It takes time and practice to appreciate the expert perspective. Don't worry if you find recursive solutions tough to devise and trust. Keep at it! Many teachers and writers have their own approaches and examples for introducing recursion. More than for any other topic in the book, I encourage you to seek out additional material on recursion to complement what I have offered here.

In the next chapter, we'll keep going with recursion, optimizing it for a different class of problems.

## Notes

Halloween Haul is originally from the 2012 DWITE Programming Competition, Round 1. Descendant Distance is originally from the 2005 East Central North America Regional Programming Contest. For a book-length treatment of recursion, check out *Thinking Recursively with Java* by Eric Roberts (2005).

# 3

## MEMOIZATION AND DYNAMIC PROGRAMMING

In this chapter, we'll study three problems that appear to be solvable using recursion. As you'll see, while in theory we can use recursion, in practice it leads to an explosion of work that renders the problems unsolvable. Not to worry: you'll learn two powerful, related techniques, called memoization and dynamic programming, that will lead to shocking performance increases, morphing runtimes from hours or days to seconds. In the next chapter, we'll level up and solve two even more challenging problems using these techniques. Once you get the hang of this stuff, you'll be able to solve hundreds of other programming problems as well. If you're going to read one chapter in this book, read this one.

# Problem 1: Burger Fervor

This is UVa problem 10465.

## The Problem

A man named Homer Simpson likes to eat and drink. He has $t$ minutes that he'll spend eating burgers and drinking beer. There are two kinds of burgers. One of them takes $m$ minutes to eat, and the other takes $n$ minutes to eat.

Homer likes burgers more than beer, so he'd like to spend the entire $t$ minutes eating burgers. However, doing so isn't always possible. For example, if $m = 4$, $n = 9$, and $t = 15$, then no combination of the 4-minute and 9-minute burgers can take him exactly 15 minutes to eat. In such a case, he'll spend as much time as possible eating burgers and then fill the rest of the time drinking beer. Our task is to determine the number of burgers that Homer can eat.

### Input

We read test cases until there is no more input. Each test case is represented by a line of three integers: $m$, the number of minutes it takes to eat the first kind of burger; $n$, the number of minutes it takes to eat the second kind of burger; and $t$, the number of minutes that Homer will spend eating burgers and drinking beer. Each $m$, $n$, and $t$ value is less than 10,000.

### Output

For each test case:

- If Homer can spend exactly $t$ minutes eating burgers, then output the maximum number of burgers that he can eat.

- Otherwise, output the maximum number of burgers that Homer can eat when maximizing his time eating burgers, a space, and the number of remaining minutes (during which he'll drink beer).

The time limit for solving the test cases is three seconds.

## Forming a Plan

Let's start by thinking about a few different test cases. Here's the first one:

---

4 9 22

---

Here, the first kind of burger takes 4 minutes to eat ($m = 4$), the second kind of burger takes 9 minutes to eat ($n = 9$), and Homer has 22 minutes to spend ($t = 22$). This is an example in which Homer can fill the entire time by eating burgers. The maximum number of burgers that Homer can eat here is three, so 3 is the correct output for this test case.

The three burgers that Homer should eat are one 4-minute burger and two 9-minute burgers. This takes him $1 \times 4 + 2 \times 9 = 22$ minutes, as required.

Notice, though, that we are *not* being asked to indicate the number of each kind of burger he should eat. All we're asked to do is output the total number of burgers. When I provide the number of each kind of burger below, I do so only to offer evidence that the proposed output makes sense.

Here's another test case:

---

4 9 54

---

Again, Homer can fill the entire time with burgers. The correct output here is 11, obtained by eating nine 4-minute burgers and two 9-minute burgers. Unlike the 4 9 22 test case, here Homer has multiple ways to spend exactly 54 minutes eating burgers. For example, he could eat six 9-minute burgers—that fills up the 54 minutes, too—but, remember, if we can fill the entire t minutes, then we want to output the *maximum* number of burgers.

As noted in the problem description, it's not always possible for Homer to completely fill the *t* minutes by eating burgers. Let's study the example that I gave there as our next test case:

---

4 9 15

---

How many burgers should Homer eat here? He can eat a maximum of three burgers by eating three 4-minute burgers. By doing so, Homer would spend 12 minutes eating burgers, and he would have to spend the remaining 15 – 12 = 3 minutes drinking beer. So, he eats three burgers and has three minutes' beer-drinking time, making the output 3 3. Have we solved this test case?

We have not! Carefully reread the problem description and zone in on this: "output the maximum number of burgers that Homer can eat when maximizing his time eating burgers." That is, when Homer cannot fill the entire time by eating burgers, we want to maximize the *time* that he spends eating burgers and then the maximum number of burgers he can eat in that time. The correct output for 4 9 15 is in fact 2 2: the first 2 means that he eats two burgers (one 4-minute burger and one 9-minute burger, for a total of 13 minutes) and the second 2 means that he has to spend 2 minutes (15 – 13) drinking beer.

In the 4 9 22 and 4 9 54 test cases, we're asked to solve the problem for 22 and 54 minutes, respectively. We found that there is indeed a way to spend the entire time eating burgers, so we can report the maximum number of burgers as our solution. However, in the 4 9 15 case, we found that there is no way to completely fill the 15 minutes by eating burgers. Thinking ahead to our code, how are we going to handle this? How will we be able to conclude that the answer is 2 2?

One idea is that we can next try to fill exactly 14 minutes with the 4-minute and 9-minute burgers. If we succeed, then we have our answer: we report the maximum number of burgers that Homer can eat in exactly 14 minutes, followed by 1, the number of minutes Homer spends drinking beer. This would maximize the amount of time that Homer can spend eating burgers. We already know that eating burgers for exactly 15 minutes is impossible, so 14 minutes is the next best option.

Let's see if 14 minutes works. Can we fill exactly 14 minutes with the 4-minute and 9-minute burgers? No! Like the 15-minute case, this will be impossible.

We can, though, fill exactly 13 minutes by eating two burgers: one 4-minute burger and one 9-minute burger. That leaves Homer two minutes for drinking beer. This justifies 2 2 as the correct output.

In summary, our plan is to determine whether Homer can eat burgers for exactly $t$ minutes. If he can, then we're done: we report the maximum number of burgers he can eat. If he can't, then we next determine whether Homer can eat burgers for exactly $t - 1$ minutes. If he can, then we're done, and we report the maximum number of burgers he can eat and the number of minutes spent drinking beer. If he can't, then we will move on to trying $t - 2$ minutes, then $t - 3$ minutes, and so on, stopping when the time can be completely filled by eating burgers.

### Characterizing Optimal Solutions

Consider the 4 9 22 test case. Whatever combination of burgers and beer we propose as the solution better take exactly 22 minutes, and it better actually be doable using the 4-minute and 9-minute burgers. Such a solution, which adheres to the rules of a problem, is called a *feasible* solution. A solution attempt that does not follow the rules is called an *infeasible* solution. For example, having Homer spend 4 minutes eating burgers and 18 minutes drinking beer is feasible. Having Homer spend 8 minutes eating burgers and 18 minutes drinking beer is infeasible, because 8 + 18 is not 22. Having Homer spend 5 minutes eating burgers and 17 minutes drinking beer is also infeasible, because there's no way we can use the 4-minute and 9-minute burgers to get a total of 5 minutes of burger time.

Burger Fervor is an *optimization problem*. An optimization problem involves choosing the best—that is, *optimal*—solution out of all feasible solutions. There may be many feasible solutions of varying quality. Some will be really poor, such as drinking beer for 22 minutes. Others will be close to but not quite optimal—maybe they're off by one or two. And, of course, some of them will be optimal. Our goal is to identify an optimal solution among all possible solutions.

Suppose we're solving a case where the first kind of burger takes $m$ minutes to eat, the second kind of burger takes $n$ minutes to eat, and we want to try to spend *exactly* $t$ minutes eating burgers.

If $t = 0$, then the correct output is 0, because we can fill the entire 0 minutes by eating zero burgers. As we continue, we'll therefore focus on what to do when $t$ is greater than 0.

Let's think about what an optimal solution for $t$ minutes must look like. Of course, we can't possibly know anything specific, such as "Homer eats a 4-minute burger, then a 9-minute burger, then another 9-minute burger, then..." We haven't done anything yet to solve the problem, so obtaining this level of detail is wishful thinking.

There is, however, something we can say that's not wishful thinking. It's at once so inane that you'd be forgiven for wondering why I am stating it at all and so powerful that at its core lies a solution strategy for a bewildering number of optimization problems.

Here it is: Suppose that Homer can fill exactly $t$ minutes by eating burgers. (If this supposition ends up being wrong, then we'll try it again with $t - 1$ minutes, then $t - 2$ minutes, and so on.) The final burger that he eats, the one that finishes off his $t$ minutes, must be an $m$-minute burger or an $n$-minute burger.

How could that final burger be anything else? Homer can only eat $m$-minute and $n$-minute burgers, so there are only two choices for the last burger that he eats and so two choices for what the end of the optimal solution must look like.

If we know that the final burger that Homer eats in an optimal solution is an $m$-minute burger, we know he has $t - m$ minutes left to spend. There must be a way to fill those $t - m$ minutes with burgers, without drinking any beer: remember that we are assuming that Homer can spend the entire $t$ minutes by eating burgers. If we could spend those $t - m$ minutes optimally, with Homer eating the maximum number of burgers, then we'd have an optimal solution to the original problem of $t$ minutes. We'd take the number of burgers that he can eat in $t - m$ minutes and add one $m$-minute burger to fill the remaining $m$ minutes.

Now, what if we knew that the final burger that Homer eats in an optimal solution is an $n$-minute burger? Then he has $t - n$ minutes left to spend. Again, by virtue of the entire $t$ minutes being spent eating burgers, we know that it must be possible for Homer to eat burgers for the first $t - n$ of those minutes. If we could spend those $t - n$ minutes optimally, then we'd have an optimal solution to the original problem of $t$ minutes. We'd take the number of burgers that he can eat in $t - n$ minutes and add one $n$-minute burger to fill the remaining $n$ minutes.

Now we seem to be squarely in farce territory. We just assumed that we knew what the final burger was! However, there's no way we could know this. We do know that the final burger is an $m$-minute burger $or$ an $n$-minute burger. We definitely don't know which it is.

The wonderful truth is that we don't need to know. We can assume the final burger is an $m$-minute burger and solve the problem optimally given that choice. We then make the other choice—assume that the final burger is an $n$-minute burger—and solve the problem optimally given that choice. In the first case, we have a subproblem of $t - m$ minutes to solve optimally; in the second case, we have a subproblem of $t - n$ minutes to solve optimally. Whenever we have characterized a solution to a problem in terms of solutions to subproblems, we would do well to try a recursive approach as we did in Chapter 2.

## Solution 1: Recursion

Let's attempt a recursive solution. We'll begin by writing a helper function to solve for exactly $t$ minutes. Once we're done, we'll rely on it to write a function that solves for exactly $t$ minutes, $t - 1$ minutes, $t - 2$ minutes, and so on, until we can completely fill some number of minutes with burgers.

### The Helper Function: Solving for the Number of Minutes

To solve each problem and subproblem instance, we need three things: $m$ and $n$ from the test case and the $t$ value for the current instance. We'll therefore write the body of the following function:

```
int solve_t(int m, int n, int t)
```

If Homer can spend exactly t minutes eating burgers, then we'll return the maximum number of burgers he can eat. If he can't spend exactly t minutes eating burgers—meaning he must spend at least one minute drinking beer—then we'll return -1. A return value of 0 or more means that we've solved the problem using burgers alone; a return value of -1 means that the problem cannot be solved using burgers alone.

If we call solve_t(4, 9, 22), we expect to get 3 as the return value: three is the maximum number of burgers that Homer can eat in exactly 22 minutes. If we call solve_t(4, 9, 15), we expect to get -1 as the return value: there's no combination of 4-minute and 9-minute burgers that gives us exactly 15 minutes.

We've already settled on what to do when $t = 0$: in this case, we have 0 minutes to spend, and we do so by having Homer eat zero burgers:

```
if (t == 0)
  return 0;
```

That's the base case of our recursion. To implement the rest of this function, we need the analysis from the last section. Remember that, to solve the problem for exactly $t$ minutes, we think about the final burger that Homer eats. Maybe it's an $m$-minute burger. To check that possibility, we solve the subproblem for exactly $t - m$ minutes. Of course, the final burger can only be an $m$-minute burger if we've got at least $m$ minutes to spend. This logic can be coded as follows:

```
int first;
if (t >= m)
  first = solve_t(m, n, t - m);
else
  first = -1;
```

We use first to store the optimal solution to the t - m subproblem, with -1 indicating "no solution." If t >= m, then there's a chance that an $m$-minute burger is the final one, so we make a recursive call to compute the optimal number of burgers that Homer can eat in exactly t - m minutes. That recursive call will return a number greater than -1 if it can be solved exactly or -1 if it can't. If t < m, then there's no recursive call to make: we set first = -1 to signify that an $m$-minute burger isn't the final burger and that it can't participate in an optimal solution for exactly t minutes.

Now, what about when an $n$-minute burger is the final burger? The code for this case is analogous to the $m$-minute burger case, this time storing the result in the variable second instead of first:

```
int second;
if (t >= n)
  second = solve_t(m, n, t - n);
else
  second = -1;
```

Let's summarize our current progress:

- The variable first is the solution to the t - m subproblem. If it's -1, then we can't completely fill t - m minutes with burgers. If it's anything else, then it gives the optimal number of burgers that Homer can eat in exactly t - m minutes.

- The variable second is the solution to the t - n subproblem. If it's -1, then we can't completely fill t - n minutes with burgers. If it's anything else, then it gives the optimal number of burgers that Homer can eat in exactly t - n minutes.

There's a chance that both first and second have values of -1. A value of -1 for first means that an *m*-minute burger can't be the final burger. A value of -1 for second means that an *n*-minute burger can't be the final burger. If the final burger can't be an *m*-minute burger and can't be an *n*-minute burger, then we're out of options and have to conclude that there's no way to solve the problem for exactly t minutes:

```
if (first == -1 && second == -1)
  return -1;
```

Otherwise, if first or second or both are greater than -1, then we can build at least one solution for exactly t minutes. In this case, we start with the maximum of first and second to choose the better subproblem solution. If we add one to that maximum, thereby incorporating the final burger, then we obtain the maximum for the original problem of exactly t minutes:

```
return max(first, second) + 1;
```

The full function is given in Listing 3-1.

```
int max(int v1, int v2) {
  if (v1 > v2)
    return v1;
  else
    return v2;
}

int solve_t(int m, int n, int t) {
  int first, second;
  if (t == 0)
    return 0;
  if (t >= m)
```

```
❶  first = solve_t(m, n, t - m);
   else
     first = -1;
   if (t >= n)
❷  second = solve_t(m, n, t - n);
   else
     second = -1;
   if (first == -1 && second == -1)
❸  return -1;
   else
❹  return max(first, second) + 1;
}
```

*Listing 3-1: Solving for exactly t minutes*

It's worth spending a few minutes getting a feel for what the function does—even if you're already convinced of its correctness.

Let's begin with solve_t(4, 9, 22). The recursive call for first ❶ solves the subproblem for 18 minutes (22 − 4). That recursive call returns 2, because two is the maximum number of burgers that Homer can eat in exactly 18 minutes. The recursive call for second ❷ solves the subproblem for 13 minutes (22 − 9). That recursive call returns 2 as well, because two is the maximum number of burgers that Homer can eat in exactly 13 minutes. That is, both first and second are 2 in this case; tacking on the final four-minute or nine-minute burger gives a solution of 3 ❹ for the original problem of exactly 22 minutes.

Let's now try solve_t(4, 9, 20). The recursive call for first ❶ solves the subproblem for 16 minutes (20 − 4) and yields 4 as a result, but what about the recursive call for second ❷? Well, that one is asked to solve the subproblem for 11 minutes (20 − 9), but there is no way to spend exactly 11 minutes by eating 4-minute and 9-minute burgers! Thus this second recursive call returns -1. The maximum of first and second is therefore 4 (the value of first), and so we return 5 ❹.

So far we've seen an example where the two recursive calls both give subproblem solutions with the same number of burgers and an example where only one recursive call gives a subproblem solution. Now let's look at a case where each recursive call returns a subproblem solution, but where one is better than the other! Consider solve_t(4, 9, 36). The recursive call for first ❶ yields 8, the maximum number of burgers that Homer can eat in exactly 32 minutes (36 − 4). The recursive call for second ❷ yields 3, the maximum number of burgers that Homer can eat in exactly 27 minutes (36 − 9). The maximum of 8 and 3 is 8, and so we return 9 as the overall solution ❹.

Finally, try solve_t(4, 9, 15). The recursive call for first ❶ is asked to solve for exactly 11 minutes (15 − 4) and, since this is impossible with these kinds of burger, returns -1. The result for the second recursive call ❷ is similar: solving for exactly 6 minutes (15 − 9) is impossible, so it also returns -1. There is therefore no way to solve for exactly 15 minutes, so we return -1 ❸.

### The solve and main Functions

Recall from "Forming a Plan" on page 78 that if we can fill exactly *t* minutes by eating burgers, then we output the maximum number of burgers. Otherwise, Homer has to spend at least one minute drinking beer. To figure out the number of minutes that he must spend drinking beer, we try to solve for exactly *t* − 1 minutes, *t* − 2 minutes, and so on, until we find a number of minutes that can be filled by eating burgers. Happily, with our solve_t function, we can set the t parameter to whatever we want. We can start at the given value of t and then, as needed, make calls on t - 1, t - 2, and so on. We effect this plan in Listing 3-2.

```
void solve(int m, int n, int t) {
  int result, i;
❶ result = solve_t(m, n, t);
  if (result >= 0)
❷   printf("%d\n", result);
  else {
    i = t - 1;
❸   result = solve_t(m, n, i);
    while (result == -1) {
      i--;
❹     result = solve_t(m, n, i);
    }
❺   printf("%d %d\n", result, t - i);
  }
}
```

*Listing 3-2: Solution 1*

First, we solve the problem for exactly t minutes ❶. If our result is at least zero, then we output the maximum number of burgers ❷ and stop.

If it wasn't possible for Homer to eat burgers for the entire t minutes, we set i to t - 1, since t - 1 is the next-best number of minutes that we should try. We then solve the problem for this new value of i ❸. If we don't get a value of -1, we're successful and the while loop is skipped. If we're not successful, the while loop executes until we successfully solve a subproblem. Inside the while loop, we decrement the value of i and solve that smaller subproblem ❹. The while loop will eventually terminate; for example, we can certainly fill zero minutes with burgers. Once we escape the while loop, we've found the largest number of minutes, i, that can be filled by burgers. At that point, result will hold the maximum number of burgers, and t - i is the number of minutes that remain, so we output both values ❺.

That's that. We use recursion in solve_t to solve for t exactly. We tested solve_t on different kinds of test cases, and everything looked good. Not being able to solve for exactly t poses no problem: we use a loop inside of solve to try the minutes one by one, from largest to smallest. All we need now is a main function to read the input and call solve; Listing 3-3 provides the code.

```
int main(void) {
  int m, n, t;
  while (scanf("%d%d%d", &m, &n, &t) != -1)
    solve(m, n, t);
  return 0;
}
```

Listing 3-3: The main function

Ah, a harmonious moment. We're now ready to submit Solution 1 to the judge. Please do that now. I'll wait . . . and wait . . . and wait.

## Solution 2: Memoization

Solution 1 fails, not because it's incorrect, but because it's too slow. If you submit Solution 1 to the judge, you'll receive a "Time-Limit Exceeded" error. Remember the "Time-Limit Exceeded" error we received in Solution 1 of the Unique Snowflakes problem in Chapter 1? There, the inefficiency was emblematic of doing unnecessary work. Here, as we'll soon see, the inefficiency does not lie in doing unnecessary work, but in doing necessary work over and over and over.

The problem description says that $t$ can be any number of minutes less than 10,000. Surely, then, the following test case should pose no problem at all:

4 2 88

The $m$ and $n$ values, 4 and 2, are very small. Relative to 10,000, the $t$ value of 88 is very small as well. You may be surprised and disappointed that our code on this test case may not run within the three-second problem time limit. On my laptop, it takes about 10 seconds. That's 10 seconds on a puny 88 test case. While we're at it, let's try this slightly bigger test case:

4 2 90

All we did was increase t from 88 to 90, but this small increase has a disproportionate effect on runtime: on my laptop, this test case takes about 18 seconds—almost double what the 88 test case takes! Testing with a t value of 92 just about doubles the runtime again, and so on and so on. No matter how fast the computer, you're unlikely to ever make it to a t value of even 100. By extrapolating from this trend, we can see that it's unfathomable how much time it would take to run our code on a test case where t is in the thousands. This kind of algorithm, in which a fixed increment in problem size leads to a doubling of runtime, is called an *exponential-time algorithm*.

We have established that our code is slow—but why? Where is the inefficiency?

## Counting the Function Calls

I'm going to take Solution 1 and add some code that counts the number of times that solve_t is called; see Listing 3-4 for the new solve_t and solve functions. We now have a global variable total_calls that is initialized to 0 on entry to solve and is increased by 1 on every call of solve_t. That variable is of type long long; long or int simply isn't big enough to capture the explosion of function calls.

```
unsigned long long total_calls;

int solve_t(int m, int n, int t) {
  int first, second;
❶ total_calls++;
  if (t == 0)
    return 0;
  if (t >= m)
    first = solve_t(m, n, t - m);
  else
    first = -1;
  if (t >= n)
    second = solve_t(m, n, t - n);
  else
    second = -1;
  if (first == -1 && second == -1)
    return -1;
  else
    return max(first, second) + 1;
}

void solve(int m, int n, int t) {
  int result, i;
❷ total_calls = 0;
  result = solve_t(m, n, t);
  if (result >= 0)
    printf("%d\n", result);
  else {
    i = t - 1;
    result = solve_t(m, n, i);
    while (result == -1) {
      i--;
      result = solve_t(m, n, i);
    }
    printf("%d %d\n", result, t - i);
  }
❸ printf("Total calls to solve_t: %llu\n", total_calls);
}
```

*Listing 3-4: Solution 1, instrumented*

At the start of solve_t, we increase total_calls by 1 ❶ to count this function call. In solve, we initialize total_calls to 0 ❷ so that the count of calls is reset before each test case is processed. For each test case, the code prints the number of times that solve_t was called ❸.

If we give it a go with this input:

```
4 2 88
4 2 90
```

we get this as output:

```
44
Total calls to solve_t: 2971215072
45
Total calls to solve_t: 4807526975
```

We've made billions of calls!

Consider a given *m*, *n*, *t* test case. Our solve_t function has three parameters, but only the third parameter *t* ever changes. There are, therefore, only *t* + 1 different ways that solve_t can be called. For example, if *t* in a test case is 88, then the only calls that can be made to solve_t are those with *t* values of 88, 87, 86, and so on. Once we know the answer for some *t* value, such as 86, there's no reason to ever compute that answer again.

Of those billions of calls, only about 88 or 90 of them can be distinct. We conclude that the same subproblems are being solved a staggering number of times.

### Remembering Our Answers

Here's some intuition for the staggering number of calls we make. If we call solve_t(4, 2, 88), it makes two recursive calls: one to solve_t(4, 2, 86) and the other to solve_t(4, 2, 84). So far, so good. Now consider what will happen for the solve_t(4, 2, 86) call. It will make two recursive calls of its own, the first of which is solve_t(4, 2, 84)—exactly one of the recursive calls made by solve_t(4, 2, 88)! That solve_t(4, 2, 84) work will therefore be performed twice. Once would have been enough!

However, the imprudent duplication is only just beginning. Consider the two solve_t(4, 2, 84) calls. By reasoning as in the previous paragraph, we see that each call eventually leads to two calls of solve_t(4, 2, 80), for a total of four. Again, once would have been enough!

Well, it would have been enough if we had somehow remembered the answer from the first time we computed it. If we remember the answer to a call of solve_t the first time we compute it, we can just look it up later when we need that answer again.

*Remember, don't refigure.* That's the maxim of the *memoization* technique. Memoization comes from the word *memoize*, which means to store as if on a memo. It is a clunky word, sure, but one that's in widespread use.

Using memoization involves three steps:

1. Declare an array large enough to hold the solutions to all possible subproblems. In Burger Fervor, t is less than 10,000, so an array of 10,000 elements suffices. This array is typically given the name memo.

2. Initialize the elements of memo to a value reserved to mean "unknown value."

3. At the start of the recursive function, add code to check whether the subproblem solution has already been solved. This involves checking the corresponding index of memo: if the "unknown value" is there, then we have to solve this subproblem now; otherwise, the answer is already stored in memo and we simply return it, without doing any further recursion. Whenever we solve a new subproblem, we store its solution in memo.

Let's augment Solution 1 with memoization.

### Implementing Memoization

The appropriate place to declare and initialize the memo array is in solve, since that's the function that first gets triggered for each test case. We'll use a value of -2 to represent an unknown value; we can't use positive numbers because those would be confused with numbers of burgers, and we can't use -1 because we're already using -1 to mean "no solution possible." The updated solve function is given in Listing 3-5.

```
#define SIZE 10000

void solve(int m, int n, int t) {
  int result, i;
❶ int memo[SIZE];
  for (i = 0; i <= t; i++)
    memo[i] = -2;
  result = solve_t(m, n, t, memo);
  if (result >= 0)
    printf("%d\n", result);
  else {
    i = t - 1;
    result = solve_t(m, n, i, memo);
    while (result == -1) {
      i--;
      result = solve_t(m, n, i, memo);
    }
    printf("%d %d\n", result, t - i);
  }
}
```

*Listing 3-5: Solution 2, with memoization implemented*

We declare the memo array using the maximum possible size for any test case ❶. Then we loop from 0 to t and set each element in the range to -2.

There's also a small but important change in our calls to solve_t. Now we're passing in memo along with the other arguments; in this way, solve_t can check memo to determine whether the current subproblem has already been solved and update memo if it has not.

The updated solve_t code is given in Listing 3-6.

```
int solve_t(int m, int n, int t, int memo[]) {
  int first, second;
❶ if (memo[t] != -2)
    return memo[t];
  if (t == 0) {
    memo[t] = 0;
    return memo[t];
  }
  if (t >= m)
    first = solve_t(m, n, t - m, memo);
  else
    first = -1;
  if (t >= n)
    second = solve_t(m, n, t - n, memo);
  else
    second = -1;
  if (first == -1 && second == -1) {
    memo[t] = -1;
    return memo[t];
  } else {
    memo[t] = max(first, second) + 1;
    return memo[t];
  }
}
```

Listing 3-6: Solving for exactly t minutes, with memoization implemented

The game plan is the same as it was in Solution 1, Listing 3-1: if t is 0, solve the base case; otherwise, solve for t - m minutes and t - n minutes and use the better one.

To this structure we fasten memoization. The huge reduction in time is realized when we check if a solution for t is already in the memo array ❶, returning that stored result if it is. There is no fussing over whether the final burger takes *m* or *n* minutes. There is no further recursion. All we have is an immediate return from the function.

If we don't find a solution in memo, then we have work to do. The work is the same as before—except that, whenever we're about to return the solution, we first store it in the memo. Before each of our return statements, we store the value we're about to return in memo so that our program maintains a memory of it.

## Testing Our Memoization

I demonstrated that Solution 1 was doomed by showing you two things: that small test cases took far too long to run and that the slowness was caused by making an exorbitant number of function calls. How does Solution 2 fare in terms of these metrics?

Try Solution 2 with the input that bested Solution 1:

```
4 2 88
4 2 90
```

On my laptop, the time taken is imperceptibly small.

How many function calls are made? I encourage you to instrument Solution 2 in the way that we did for Solution 1 (Listing 3-4). If you do that and run it with the above input, you should get this output:

```
44
Total calls to solve_t: 88
45
Total calls to solve_t: 90
```

88 calls when t is 88. 90 calls when t is 90. The difference between Solution 2 and Solution 1 is like night and a few billion days. We've gone from an exponential-time algorithm to a linear-time algorithm. Specifically, we now have an $O(t)$ algorithm, where $t$ is the number of Homer's minutes.

It's judge time. If you submit Solution 2, you'll see that we pass all of the test cases.

This is certainly a milestone, but it is not the last word on Homer and his burgers. We'll be able to use something called dynamic programming to eliminate the recursion from our code.

## Solution 3: Dynamic Programming

We'll bridge our way from memoization to dynamic programming by making explicit the purpose of recursion in Solution 2. Consider the solve_t code in Listing 3-7; it's the same as the code in Listing 3-6 except that I'm now highlighting just the two recursive calls.

```
int solve_t(int m, int n, int t, int memo[]) {
  int first, second;
  if (memo[t] != -2)
    return memo[t];
  if (t == 0) {
    memo[t] = 0;
    return memo[t];
  }
  if (t >= m)
❶ first = solve_t(m, n, t - m, memo);
  else
    first = -1;
```

```
  if (t >= n)
❷ second = solve_t(m, n, t - n, memo);
  else
    second = -1;
  if (first == -1 && second == -1) {
    memo[t] = -1;
    return memo[t];
  } else {
    memo[t] = max(first, second) + 1;
    return memo[t];
  }
}
```

*Listing 3-7: Solving for exactly t minutes, focusing on recursive calls*

At the first recursive call ❶, one of two very different things will happen. The first is that the recursive call finds its subproblem solution in the memo and returns immediately. The second is that the recursive call does not find the subproblem solution in the memo, in which case it carries out its own recursive calls. All of this is true of the second recursive call ❷ as well.

When we make a recursive call and it finds its subproblem solution in the memo, we have to wonder why we made the recursive call at all. The only thing that the recursive call will do is check the memo and return; we could have done that ourselves. If the subproblem solution is not in the memo, however, then the recursion is really necessary.

Suppose that we could orchestrate things so that the memo array always holds the next subproblem solution that we need to look up. We want to know the optimal solution when t is 5? It's in memo. What about when t is 18? That's in memo, too. By virtue of always having the subproblem solutions in the memo, we'll never require a recursive call; we can just look up the solution right away.

Here we have the difference between memoization and dynamic programming. A function that uses memoization makes a recursive call to solve a subproblem. Maybe the subproblem was already solved, maybe it wasn't— regardless, it will be solved when the recursive call returns. A function that uses *dynamic programming* organizes the work so that a subproblem is already solved by the time we need it. We then have no reason to use recursion: we just look up the solution.

Memoization uses recursion to ensure that a subproblem is solved; dynamic programming ensures that the subproblem is already solved and therefore has no use for recursion.

Our dynamic-programming solution dispenses with the solve_t function and systematically solves for all values of t in solve. Listing 3-8 gives the code.

```
void solve(int m, int n, int t) {
  int result, i, first, second;
  int dp[SIZE];
❶ dp[0] = 0;
```

```
  for (i = 1; i <= t; i++) {
❷ if (i >= m)
  ❸ first = dp[i - m];
    else
      first = -1;
❹ if (i >= n)
    second = dp[i - n];
    else
    second = -1;
    if (first == -1 && second == -1)
  ❺ dp[i] = -1;
    else
  ❻ dp[i] = max(first, second) + 1;
  }

❼ result = dp[t];
  if (result >= 0)
    printf("%d\n", result);
  else {
    i = t - 1;
    result = dp[i];
    while (result == -1) {
      i--;
  ❽ result = dp[i];
    }
    printf("%d %d\n", result, t - i);
  }
}
```

*Listing 3-8: Solution 3, with dynamic programming*

The canonical name for a dynamic-programming array is dp. We could have called it memo, since it serves the same purpose as a memo table, but we call it dp to follow convention. Once we declare the array, we solve the base case, explicitly storing the fact that the optimal solution for zero minutes is to eat zero burgers ❶. Then we have the loop that controls the order in which the subproblems are solved. Here, we solve the subproblems from smallest number of minutes (1) to largest number of minutes (t). The variable i determines which subproblem is being solved. Inside our loop, we have the familiar check of whether it makes sense to test the m-minute burger as the final burger ❷. If so, we look up the solution to the i - m subproblem in the dp array ❸.

Notice how we just look up the value from the array ❸, without using any recursion. We can do that because we know, by virtue of the fact that i - m is less than i, that we've already solved subproblem i - m. This is precisely why we solve subproblems in order, from smallest to largest: larger subproblems will require solutions to smaller subproblems, so we must ensure that those smaller subproblems have already been solved.

The next `if` statement ❹ is analogous to the previous one ❷ and handles the case when the final burger is an $n$-minute burger. As before, we look up the solution to a subproblem using the `dp` array. We know for sure that the `i - n` subproblem has already been solved, because the `i - n` iteration took place before this `i` iteration.

We now have the solutions to both of the required subproblems. All that's left to do is store the optimal solution for `i` in `dp[i]` ❺ ❻.

Once we've built up the `dp` array, solving subproblems 0 to t, we can look up subproblem solutions at will. We thus simply look up the solution to subproblem t ❼, printing it if there's a solution and looking up solutions to progressively smaller subproblems if there's not ❽.

Like our memoized solution, this is a linear-time solution. In general, the dynamic-programming and memoized solutions of a problem will have the same efficiency, but, that efficiency may be easier to identify in dynamic-programming solutions because they use a loop rather than recursion.

Let's see one example `dp` array before moving on. For the test case that follows:

---

4 9 15

---

the final contents of the `dp` array are:

| Index | 0 | 1 | 2 | 3 | 4 | 5 | 6 | 7 | 8 | 9 | 10 | 11 | 12 | 13 | 14 | 15 |
|-------|---|----|----|----|---|----|----|----|---|---|----|----|----|----|----|----|
| Value | 0 | -1 | -1 | -1 | 1 | -1 | -1 | -1 | 2 | 1 | -1 | -1 | 3  | 2  | -1 | -1 |

We can trace the code in Listing 3-8 to confirm each of these subproblem solutions. For example, `dp[0]`, the maximum number of burgers that Homer can eat in zero minutes, is 0 ❶. `dp[1]` is -1 because both checks ❷ ❹ fail, meaning we store -1 ❺.

As a final example, we're going to reverse-engineer how `dp[12]` got its value of 3. Since 12 is greater than 4, the first check passes ❷. We then set `first` to `dp[8]` ❸, which has a value of 2. Similarly, 12 is greater than 9, so the second check passes ❹, and we set `second` to `dp[3]`, which has a value of -1. The maximum of `first` and `second` is therefore 2, so we set `dp[12]` to 3, one more than that maximum ❻.

Please feel free to submit our dynamic programming solution to the judge. It should pass all test cases just like our memoization solution did. Is one of these solutions better than the other? And when should we be using memoization and dynamic programming, anyway? Read on to find out.

## Memoization and Dynamic Programming

We solved Burger Fervor in four steps. First, we characterized what an optimal solution must look like; second, we wrote a recursive solution; third, we added memoization; and fourth, we eliminated the recursion by explicitly solving subproblems from smallest to largest. These four steps offer a general plan for tackling many other optimization problems.

## Step 1: Structure of Optimal Solutions

The first step is to show how to decompose an optimal solution to a problem into optimal solutions for smaller subproblems. In Burger Fervor, we did this by reasoning about the final burger that Homer eats. Is it an $m$-minute burger? That leaves the subproblem of filling $t - m$ minutes. What if it is an $n$-minute burger? That leaves the problem of filling $t - n$ minutes. We don't know which it is, of course, but we can simply solve these two subproblems to find out.

It's critical that our subproblems really are *smaller* than the original problem. If they are not, then we will fail to eventually reach a base case. The problems in Chapter 5 serve as examples of what we need to do when subproblems cannot be easily ordered by size.

We also require that an optimal solution to a problem contains within it not just some solutions to the smaller subproblems but *optimal* solutions to those subproblems. Let's make this point explicit here.

In Burger Fervor, when supposing that the final burger in an optimal solution is an $m$-minute burger, we argued that a solution to the $t - m$ subproblem was part of the solution to the overall $t$ problem. Moreover, an optimal solution for $t$ must include the optimal solution for $t - m$: if it didn't, then the solution for $t$ wouldn't be optimal after all, since we could improve it by using the better solution for $t - m$! A similar argument can be used to show that, if the last burger in an optimal solution is an $n$-minute burger, then the remaining $t - n$ minutes should be filled with an optimal solution for $t - n$.

Let me unpack this a little through an example. Suppose that $m = 4$, $n = 9$, and $t = 54$. The value of an optimal solution is 11. There is an optimal solution $S$ where the final burger is a 9-minute burger. My claim is that $S$ must consist of this 9-minute burger along with an optimal solution for 45 minutes. The optimal solution for 45 minutes is 10 burgers. If $S$ used some suboptimal solution for the first 45 minutes, then $S$ wouldn't be an example of an optimal 11-burger solution. For example, if $S$ used a suboptimal five-burger solution for the first 45 minutes, then it would use a total of only six burgers for the full 54 minutes!

If an optimal solution to a problem is composed of optimal solutions to subproblems, we say that the problem has *optimal substructure*. If a problem has optimal substructure, the techniques from this chapter are likely to apply.

I've read and heard people claim that solving optimization problems using memoization or dynamic programming is formulaic, that once you've seen one such problem, you've seen them all, and you can just turn the crank when a new problem arises. I don't think so. That perspective belies the challenges of both characterizing the structure of optimal solutions and identifying that this will be fruitful in the first place.

For example, when discussing the structure of an optimal solution for Burger Fervor, I made a big deal about focusing on *exactly* $t$ minutes. As a result, in our code we couldn't necessarily look up the answer in one shot—we needed to check for a solution to exactly $t$ minutes, then exactly $t - 1$ minutes, then exactly $t - 2$ minutes, and so on, until we found a solution. But couldn't we have found a way to characterize the optimal solution so that we didn't need to search like that? Well, we could have, but that would have led to an overall trickier solution for this problem. (We'll see this alternate kind of approach as an effective way to solve Problem 3 later in this chapter.)

My point here is simply that discovering what an optimal solution looks like can be surprisingly tricky. The sheer breadth of problems that can be solved using memoization and dynamic programming means that practicing with and generalizing from as many problems as possible is the only way forward.

## Step 2: Recursive Solution

Step 1 not only suggests to us that memoization and dynamic programming will lead to a solution, but also leaves in its wake a recursive approach for solving the problem. To solve the original problem, try each of the possibilities for an optimal solution, solving subproblems optimally using recursion. In Burger Fervor, we argued that an optimal solution for exactly $t$ minutes might consist of an $m$-minute burger and an optimal solution for exactly $t - m$ minutes or an $n$-minute burger and an optimal solution for exactly $t - n$ minutes. Solving the $t - m$ and $t - n$ subproblems is therefore required and, as these are smaller subproblems than $t$, we used recursion to solve them. In general, the number of recursive calls depends on the number of available candidates competing to be the optimal solution.

## Step 3: Memoization

If we succeed with Step 2, then we have a correct solution to the problem. As we saw with Burger Fervor, though, such a solution may require an absolutely unreasonable amount of time to execute. The culprit is that the same subproblems are being solved over and over, as a result of a phenomenon known as *overlapping subproblems*. Really, if we didn't have overlapping subproblems, then we could stop right here: recursion would be fine on its own. Think back to Chapter 2 and the two problems we solved there. We solved those successfully with recursion alone, and that worked because each subproblem was solved only once. In Halloween Haul, for example, we calculated the total amount of candy in a tree. The two subproblems were finding the total amounts of candy in the left and right subtrees. Those problems are independent: there's no way that solving the subproblem for the left subtree could somehow require information about the right subtree, or vice versa.

If there's no subproblem overlap, we can just use recursion. When there is subproblem overlap, however, it's time for memoization. As we learned when solving Burger Fervor, memoization means that we store the solution to a subproblem the first time we solve it. Then, whenever that subproblem solution is needed in the future, we simply look it up rather than recalculate it. Yes, the subproblems still overlap, but now they are solved only once, just like in Chapter 2.

### Step 4: Dynamic Programming

Very likely, the solution resulting from Step 3 will be fast enough. Such a solution still uses recursion, but without the risk of duplicating work. As I'll explain in the next paragraph, sometimes we want to eliminate the recursion. We can do so as long as we systematically solve smaller subproblems before larger subproblems. This is dynamic programming: the use of a loop in lieu of recursion, explicitly solving all subproblems in order from smallest to largest.

So what's better: memoization or dynamic programming? For many problems, they are roughly equivalent and, in those cases, you should use what you find more comfortable. My personal choice is memoization. We'll see an example (Problem 3 later in this chapter) where the memo and dp tables have multiple dimensions. In such problems, I often have trouble getting all of the base cases and bounds for the dp table correct.

Memoization solves subproblems on an as-needed basis. For example, consider the Burger Fervor test case where we have a kind of burger that takes 2 minutes to eat, a kind of burger that takes 4 minutes to eat, and 90 minutes of time. A memoized solution will never solve for odd numbers of minutes, such as 89 or 87 or 85, because those subproblems do not result from subtracting multiples of 2 and 4 from 90. Dynamic programming, by contrast, solves all subproblems on its way up to 90. The difference here seems to favor memoized solutions; indeed, if huge swaths of the subproblem space are never used, then memoization may be faster than dynamic programming. This has to be balanced against the overhead inherent in recursive code, though, with all of the calling and returning from functions. If you're so inclined, it wouldn't hurt to code up both solutions to a problem and see which is faster!

You'll commonly see people refer to memoized solutions as *top-down* solutions and dynamic-programming solutions as *bottom-up* solutions. It's called "top-down" because, to solve large subproblems, we recurse down to small subproblems. In "bottom-up" solutions, we start from the bottom—the smallest subproblems—and work our way to the top.

Memoization and dynamic programming are captivating to me. They can solve so many types of problems; I don't know another algorithm design technique that even comes close. Many of the tools that we learn in this book, such as hash tables in Chapter 1, offer valuable speedups. The truth is that, even without those tools, we could solve many problem instances—not in time to have such solutions accepted by the judge, but perhaps still in time to be practically useful. However, memoization and dynamic programming are different. They vivify recursive ideas, turning algorithms that are astonishingly slow into those that are astonishingly fast. I hope I can pull you into the fold with this chapter and the next and that you won't stop when these chapters do.

# Problem 2: Moneygrubbers

In Burger Fervor, we were able to solve each problem by considering only two subproblems. Here, we'll see an example where each problem may require solving many more subproblems.

This is UVa problem 10980.

## *The Problem*

You want to buy apples, so you go to an apple store. The store has a price for buying one apple—for example, $1.75. The store also has *m* pricing schemes, where each pricing scheme gives a number *n* and a price *p* for buying *n* apples. For example, one pricing scheme might state that three apples cost a total of $4.00; another might state that two apples cost a total of $2.50. You want to buy *at least k* apples and do so as cheaply as possible.

### Input

We read test cases until there's no more input. Each test case consists of the following lines:

- A line containing the price for buying one apple, followed by the number *m* of pricing schemes for this test case. *m* is at most 20.

- *m* lines, each of which gives a number *n* and total price *p* for buying *n* apples. *n* is between 1 and 100.

- A line containing integers, where each integer *k* is between 0 and 100 and gives the desired number of apples to buy.

Each price in the input is a floating-point number with exactly two decimal digits.

In the problem description, I gave an example price of one apple as $1.75. I also gave two example pricing schemes: three apples for $4.00 and two apples for $2.50. Using that data, suppose we wanted to determine the minimum price for buying at least one apple and at least four apples, respectively. Here's the input for this test case:

---

```
1.75 2
3 4.00
2 2.50
1 4
```

---

### Output

For each test case, output the following:

- A line containing Case *c*:, where *c* is the number of the test case starting at 1.

- For each integer *k*, a line containing Buy *k* for $*d*, where *d* is the cheapest cost for which we can buy at least *k* apples.

Here's the output for the above sample input:

```
Case 1:
Buy 1 for $1.75
Buy 4 for $5.00
```

The time limit for solving the test cases is three seconds.

## Characterizing Optimal Solutions

The problem description specifies that we want to buy *at least* $k$ apples as cheaply as possible. This means that buying exactly $k$ apples is only one option; we can buy more than $k$ apples if it's cheaper that way. We're going to start by trying to solve for exactly $k$ apples, much as we solved for exactly $t$ minutes in Burger Fervor. Back then, we found a way when necessary to move from exactly $t$ minutes to smaller numbers of minutes. The hope is that we can do something similar here, starting with $k$ apples and finding the cheapest cost for $k$, $k + 1$, $k + 2$, and so on. If it ain't broke...

Before just recalling the title of this chapter and diving headlong into memoization and dynamic programming, let's make sure that we really do need those tools.

What's better: buying three apples for a total of $4.00 (Scheme 1) or two apples for a total of $2.50 (Scheme 2)? We can try to answer this by calculating the cost per apple for each of these pricing schemes. In Scheme 1, we have $4.00/3 = $1.33 per apple, and in Scheme 2 we have $2.50/2 = $1.25 per apple. It looks like Scheme 2 is better than Scheme 1. Let's also suppose that we can buy one apple for $1.75, which looks even worse than the two schemes. We therefore have the cost per apple, from cheapest to most expensive, as follows: $1.25, $1.33, $1.75.

Now, suppose that we want to buy *exactly* $k$ apples. How's this for an algorithm: at each step, use the cheapest cost per apple, until we've bought $k$ apples?

If we wanted to buy exactly four apples for the above case, then we'd start with Scheme 2, because it lets us buy apples with the best price per apple. Using Scheme 2 once costs us $2.50 for two apples, and it leaves us with two apples to buy. We can then use Scheme 2 again, buying two more apples (for a total now of four apples) for another $2.50. We'd have spent $5.00 for the four apples and, indeed, we cannot do better.

Note that just because an algorithm is intuitive or works on one test case does not mean that it is correct in general. This algorithm of using the best-available price per apple is flawed, and there are test cases that prove it. Try to find such a test case before continuing!

Here's one: suppose that we want to buy exactly three apples, not four. We'd start with Scheme 2 again, giving us two apples for a total of $2.50. Now we have only one apple to buy—and the only choice is to pay $1.75 for the one apple. The total cost is $4.25—but there is a better way. Namely, we should simply have used Scheme 1 once, costing us $4.00: yes, it has a higher cost per apple than Scheme 2, but it makes up for that by freeing us from paying for one apple that has a still higher cost per apple.

It's tempting to start affixing extra rules to our algorithm to try to fix it; for example, "if there's a pricing scheme for exactly the number of apples that we need, then use it." Suppose, however, we want to buy exactly three apples. We can easily break this augmented algorithm by adding a scheme in which the store sells three apples for $100.00.

When using memoization and dynamic programming, we try all the available options for an optimal solution and then pick the best one. In Burger Fervor, should Homer end with an $m$-minute burger or an $n$-minute burger? We don't know, so we try both. By contrast, a *greedy algorithm* is an algorithm that tries just one option: the one that looks like the best choice at the time.

Using the best price per apple, as we did above, is an example of a greedy algorithm, because at each step it chooses what to do without considering other options. Sometimes greedy algorithms work. Moreover, since they often run faster than dynamic-programming algorithms and are easier to implement , a working greedy algorithm may be better than a working dynamic-programming algorithm. For this problem, it appears that greedy algorithms—whether the one above or others that might come to mind—are not sufficiently powerful.

In Burger Fervor, we reasoned that, if it's possible to spend $t$ minutes eating burgers, then the final burger in an optimal solution must be an $m$-minute burger or an $n$-minute burger. For the present problem, we want to say something analogous: that an optimal solution for buying $k$ apples must end in one of a small number of ways. Here's a claim: if the available pricing schemes are Scheme 1, Scheme 2, ..., Scheme $m$, then the final thing we do must be to use one of these $m$ pricing schemes. There can't be anything else that we could do, right?

Well, this is not quite true. The final thing that we do in an optimal solution might be buying one apple. We always have that as an option. Rather than solve two subproblems as in Burger Fervor, we solve $m + 1$ subproblems: one for each of the $m$ pricing schemes and one for buying one apple.

Suppose that an optimal solution for buying $k$ apples ends with us paying $p$ dollars for $n$ apples. We then need to optimally buy $k - n$ apples and add that cost to $p$. We need to establish that the overall optimal solution for $k$ apples contains within it an optimal solution for $k - n$ apples. This is the optimal substructure requirement of memoization and dynamic programming. As with Burger Fervor, optimal substructure does hold. If a solution for $k$ didn't use an optimal solution for $k - n$, then that solution for $k$ cannot be optimal after all: it's not as good as what we'd get if we built it on the optimal solution for $k - n$.

Of course, we don't know what to do at the end of the solution to make it optimal. Do we use Scheme 1, use Scheme 2, use Scheme 3, or just buy one apple? Who knows? As in any memoization or dynamic-programming algorithm, we simply try them all and choose the best one.

Before we look at a recursive solution, note that, for any number $k$, we can always find a way to buy exactly $k$ apples. Whether one apple, two apples, five apples, whatever, we can buy that many. The reason is that we always have the option of buying one apple, and we can do that as many times as we like. Compare this to Burger Fervor, where there were values of $t$ such that $t$ minutes could not be filled by the available burgers. As a consequence of this difference, here we won't have to worry about the case where a recursive call on a smaller subproblem fails to find a solution.

## Solution 1: Recursion

Like in Burger Fervor, the first thing to do is write a helper function to solve for a specific number of apples.

### The Helper Function: Solving for the Number of Apples

Let's write the function solve_k, whose job will be analogous to the solve_t functions that we wrote for Burger Fervor. The function signature is as follows:

```
double solve_k(int num[], double price[], int num_schemes,
           double unit_price, int num_apples)
```

Each of these parameters except for the last comes directly from the current test case. Here's what each parameter is for:

num An array of numbers of apples, with one element per pricing scheme. For example, if we have two pricing schemes, the first for three apples and the second for two apples, then this array would be [3, 2].

price An array of prices, one element per pricing scheme. For example, if we have two pricing schemes, the first with cost 4.00 and the second with cost 2.50, then this array would be [4.00, 2.50]. Notice that num and price together give us all of the information about the pricing schemes.

num_schemes The number of pricing schemes. It's the m value from the test case.

unit_price The price for one apple.

num_apples The number of apples that we want to buy.

The solve_k function returns the minimum cost for buying exactly num_apples apples.

The code for solve_k is given in Listing 3-9. In addition to studying this code on its own, I strongly encourage you to compare it to the solve_t function from Burger Fervor (Listing 3-1). What differences do you notice? Why are these differences present? Memoization and dynamic-programming solutions share a common code structure. If we can nail that structure, then we can focus on what's different in and specific to each problem.

```
❶ double min(double v1, double v2) {
    if (v1 < v2)
      return v1;
    else
      return v2;
  }

  double solve_k(int num[], double price[], int num_schemes,
                 double unit_price, int num_apples) {
    double best, result;
    int i;
❷ if (num_apples == 0)
❸   return 0;
    else {
❹   result = solve_k(num, price, num_schemes, unit_price,
                     num_apples - 1);
❺   best = result + unit_price;
      for (i = 0; i < num_schemes; i++)
❻     if (num_apples - num[i] >= 0) {
❼       result = solve_k(num, price, num_schemes, unit_price,
                         num_apples - num[i]);
❽       best = min(best, result + price[i]);
        }
        return best;
    }
  }
```

*Listing 3-9: Solving for exactly num_apples apples*

We start with a little min function ❶: we'll need that for comparing solutions and picking the smaller one. In Burger Fervor, we used a similar max function, because we wanted the maximum number of burgers. Here, we want the minimum cost. Some optimization problems are *maximization problems* (Burger Fervor) and others are *minimization problems* (Moneygrubbers)—carefully read problem statements to make sure you're optimizing in the right direction!

What do we do if asked to solve for 0 apples ❷? We return 0 ❸, because the minimum cost to buy zero apples is exactly $0.00. That's a base case, just like filling zero minutes in Burger Fervor. As with recursion in general, at least one base case is required for any optimization problem.

If we're not in the base case, then num_apples will be a positive integer, and we need to find the optimal way to buy exactly that many apples. The variable best is used to track the best (minimum-cost) option that has been found so far.

One option is to optimally solve for num_apples - 1 apples ❹ and add the cost of the final apple ❺.

We now hit the big structural difference between this problem and Burger Fervor: a loop inside of the recursive function. In Burger Fervor, we didn't need a loop, because we only had two subproblems to try. We just tried the first one and then tried the second one. Here, though, we have one subproblem per pricing scheme, and we have to go through all of them. We check whether the current pricing scheme can be used at all ❻: if its number of apples is no larger than the number that we need, then we can try it. We make a recursive call to solve the subproblem resulting from removing the number of apples in this pricing scheme ❼. (It's similar to the earlier recursive call where we subtracted one for the single apple ❹.) If that subproblem solution plus the price of the current scheme is our best option so far, then we update best accordingly ❽.

### The solve Function

We've optimally solved for exactly *k* apples, but there's this detail from the problem statement that we haven't addressed yet: "You want to buy *at least k* apples and to do so as cheaply as possible." Why does the difference between exactly *k* apples and at least *k* apples matter in the first place? Can you find a test case where it's cheaper to buy more than *k* apples than it is to buy *k* apples?

Here's one for you. We'll say that one apple costs $1.75. We have two pricing schemes: Scheme 1 is that we can buy four apples for $3.00, and Scheme 2 is that we can buy two apples for $2.00. Now, we want to buy at least three apples. This test case in the form of problem input is as follows:

```
1.75 2
4 3.00
2 2.00
3
```

The cheapest way to buy exactly three apples is to spend $3.75: one apple for $1.75 and two apples using Scheme 2 for $2.00. However, we can spend less money by in fact buying four apples, not three. The cheapest way to buy four apples is to use Scheme 1 once, which costs us only $3.00. That is, the correct output for this test case is:

```
Case 1:
Buy 3 for $3.00
```

(This output is a bit confusing, because we're actually buying four apples, not three, but it is correct to output Buy 3 here. We always output the number of apples that we're asked to buy, whether or not we buy more than that to save money.)

What we need is a solve function like the one we had for Burger Fervor in Listing 3-2. There, we tried smaller and smaller values until we found a solution. Here, we'll try larger and larger values, keeping track of the minimum solution as we go. Here's a first crack at the code:

```
double solve(int num[], double price[], int num_schemes,
             double unit_price, int num_apples) {
  double best;
```

```
    int i;
❶ best = solve_k(num, price, num_schemes,
                 unit_price, num_apples);
❷ for (i = num_apples + 1; i < ???; i++)
     best = min(best, solve_k(num, price, num_schemes,
                              unit_price, i));
   return best;
}
```

We initialize best to the optimal solution for buying exactly num_apples apples ❶. Then, we use a for loop to try larger and larger numbers of apples ❷. The for loop stops when . . . uh-oh. How do we know when it's safe to stop? Maybe we're being asked to buy 3 apples, but the cheapest thing to do is to buy 4 or 5 or 10 or even 20. We didn't have this problem in Burger Fervor, because there we were making our way downward, toward zero, rather than upward.

We can find a game-saving observation from the problem input specification: it says that the number of apples in a given pricing scheme is at most 100. How does this help?

Suppose we're being asked to buy at least 50 apples. Might it be best to buy exactly 60 apples? Sure! Maybe the final pricing scheme in an optimal solution for 60 apples is for 20 apples. Then we could combine those 20 apples with an optimal solution for 40 apples to get a total of 60 apples.

Suppose again that we're buying 50 apples. Could it make sense for us to buy exactly 180 apples? Well, think about an optimal solution for buying exactly 180 apples. The final pricing scheme that we use gives us at most 100 apples. Before using that final pricing scheme, we'd have bought at least 80 apples and had done so more cheaply than we did for 180 apples. Crucially, 80 is still greater than 50! Therefore, buying 80 apples is cheaper than buying 180 apples. Buying 180 apples cannot be the optimal thing to do if we want at least 50 apples.

In fact, for 50 apples, the maximum number of apples we should even consider buying is 149. If we buy 150 or more apples, then removing the final pricing scheme gives us a cheaper way to buy 50 or more apples.

The problem input specification not only limits the number of apples per pricing scheme to 100, it also limits the number of apples to buy to 100. In the case in which we are asked to buy 100 apples, then, the maximum number of apples we should consider buying is 100 + 99 = 199. Incorporating this observation leads to the solve function in Listing 3-10.

```
#define SIZE 200

double solve(int num[], double price[], int num_schemes,
             double unit_price, int num_apples) {
  double best;
  int i;
  best = solve_k(num, price, num_schemes, unit_price, num_apples);
  for (i = num_apples + 1; i < SIZE; i++)
```

```
        best = min(best, solve_k(num, price, num_schemes,
                                  unit_price, i));
    return best;
}
```

*Listing 3-10: Solution 1*

Now all we need is a main function and we can start submitting stuff to the judge.

## The main Function

Let's get a main function written. See Listing 3-11. It's not completely self-contained, but all we'll need is one helper function, get_number, that I'll describe shortly.

```
#define MAX_SCHEMES 20

int main(void) {
    int test_case, num_schemes, num_apples, more, i;
    double unit_price, result;
    int num[MAX_SCHEMES];
    double price[MAX_SCHEMES];
    test_case = 0;
❶  while (scanf("%lf%d ", &unit_price, &num_schemes) != -1) {
        test_case++;
        for (i = 0; i < num_schemes; i++)
❷          scanf("%d%lf ", &num[i], &price[i]);
        printf("Case %d:\n", test_case);
        more = get_number(&num_apples);
❸      while (more) {
            result = solve(num, price, num_schemes, unit_price, num_apples);
            printf("Buy %d for $%.2f\n", num_apples, result);
            more = get_number(&num_apples);
        }
❹      result = solve(num, price, num_schemes, unit_price, num_apples);
        printf("Buy %d for $%.2f\n", num_apples, result);
    }
    return 0;
}
```

*Listing 3-11: The main function*

We begin by using scanf to try to read the first line of the next test case from the input ❶. The next scanf call ❷ is in a nested loop, and it reads the number of apples and price for each pricing scheme.

Notice that each of the scanf format strings ends with a space, which ensures that we're always positioned at the start of each line. This becomes important once we get to the line containing the numbers of apples that we are asked to buy, because we're going to use a helper function that assumes we're at the start of the line.

Why do we need a helper function? Well, we can't just airily keep calling scanf to read those numbers of apples, because we have to be able to stop at a newline. That's why we use my get_number helper function instead, described further below. It returns 1 if there are more numbers to read and 0 if this is the last number on the line. We call this function to read each number in the loop ❸ that solves the test cases. We also need some code below the loop ❹: when the loop terminates because it has read the final number on the line, we still need to solve that final test case.

The code for get_number is given in Listing 3-12.

```
int get_number(int *num) {
    int ch;
    int ret = 0;
    ch = getchar();
❶  while (ch != ' ' && ch != '\n') {
        ret = ret * 10 + ch - '0';
        ch = getchar();
    }
❷  *num = ret;
❸  return ch == ' ';
}
```

Listing 3-12: The function to get an integer

This function reads an integer value using an approach reminiscent of Listing 2-17. The loop continues as long as we haven't yet hit a space or newline character ❶. When the loop terminates, we store what was read in the pointer parameter passed to this function call ❷. We use that pointer parameter, rather than return the value, because the return value has another role: to indicate whether or not this is the last number on the line ❸. That is, if get_number returns 1 (because it found a space after the number that it read), it means that there are more numbers on this line; if it returns 0, then this is the final number on this line.

We've got a complete solution now, but its performance is glacial. Even test cases that look small will take ages, because we're going all the way up to 299 apples no matter what.

Oh well. Let's memoize the heck out of this thing.

## Solution 2: Memoization

We introduced the memo array in solve (Listing 3-5) when memoizing Burger Fervor. That was because each call of solve was for an independent test case. However, in Moneygrubbers, we have that line where each integer specifies a number of apples to buy, and we have to solve each one. It would be wasteful to throw away the memo array before we've completely finished with the test case!

We're therefore going to declare and initialize memo in main. The updated main function is in Listing 3-13.

```c
int main(void) {
  int test_case, num_schemes, num_apples, more, i;
  double unit_price, result;
  int num[MAX_SCHEMES];
  double price[MAX_SCHEMES];
❶ double memo[SIZE];
  test_case = 0;
  while (scanf("%lf%d ", &unit_price, &num_schemes) != -1) {
    test_case++;
    for (i = 0; i < num_schemes; i++)
      scanf("%d%lf ", &num[i], &price[i]);
    printf("Case %d:\n", test_case);
❷  for (i = 0; i < SIZE; i++)
❸    memo[i] = -1;
    more = get_number(&num_apples);
    while (more) {
      result = solve(num, price, num_schemes, unit_price, num_apples, memo);
      printf("Buy %d for $%.2f\n", num_apples, result);
      more = get_number(&num_apples);
    }
    result = solve(num, price, num_schemes, unit_price, num_apples, memo);
    printf("Buy %d for $%.2f\n", num_apples, result);
  }
  return 0;
}
```

Listing 3-13: The main function, with memoization implemented

We declare the memo array ❶, and we set each element of memo to -1 ("unknown" value) ❷ ❸. Notice that the initialization of memo occurs just once per test case. The only other change is that we add memo as a new parameter to the solve calls.

The new code for solve is given in Listing 3-14.

```c
double solve(int num[], double price[], int num_schemes,
            double unit_price, int num_apples, double memo[]) {
  double best;
  int i;
  best = solve_k(num, price, num_schemes, unit_price, num_apples, memo);
  for (i = num_apples + 1; i < SIZE; i++)
    best = min(best, solve_k(num, price, num_schemes, unit_price, i, memo));
  return best;
}
```

Listing 3-14: Solution 2, with memoization implemented

In addition to adding `memo` as a new parameter at the end of the parameter list, we pass `memo` to the `solve_k` calls. That's it.

Finally, let's take a look at the changes required to memoize `solve_k`. We will store in `memo[num_apples]` the minimum cost of buying exactly `num_apples` apples. See Listing 3-15.

```
double solve_k(int num[], double price[], int num_schemes,
               double unit_price, int num_apples, double memo[]) {
  double best, result;
  int i;
❶ if (memo[num_apples] != -1)
    return memo[num_apples];
  if (num_apples == 0) {
    memo[num_apples] = 0;
    return memo[num_apples];
  } else {
    result = solve_k(num, price, num_schemes, unit_price,
                     num_apples - 1, memo);
    best = result + unit_price;
    for (i = 0; i < num_schemes; i++)
      if (num_apples - num[i] >= 0) {
        result = solve_k(num, price, num_schemes, unit_price,
                         num_apples - num[i], memo);
        best = min(best, result + price[i]);
      }
      memo[num_apples] = best;
      return memo[num_apples];
  }
}
```

*Listing 3-15: Solving for exactly num_apples apples, with memoization implemented*

Remember that the first thing we do when solving with memoization is check whether the solution is already known ❶. If any value besides -1 is stored for the `num_apples` subproblem, we return it. Otherwise, as with any memoized function, we store a new subproblem solution in `memo` before returning it.

We've now reached a natural stopping point for this problem: this memoized solution can be submitted to the judge and should pass all test cases. If you'd like more practice with dynamic programming, though, here's a perfect opportunity for you to convert this memoized solution into a dynamic-programming solution! Otherwise, we'll put this problem on ice.

## Problem 3: Hockey Rivalry

Our first two problems used a one-dimensional `memo` or `dp` array. Let's look at a problem whose solution dictates using a two-dimensional array.

I live in Canada, so I suppose we weren't getting through this book without some hockey. Hockey is a team sport like soccer ... but with goals.

This is DMOJ problem cco18p1.

## The Problem

The Geese played $n$ games, each of which had one of two outcomes: a win for the Geese (W) or a loss for the Geese (L). (There are no tie games.) For each of their games, we know whether they won or lost and we know the number of goals that they scored. For example, we might know that their first game was a win (W) and that they scored four goals in that game. (Their opponent, whoever it was, must therefore have lost and scored fewer than four goals.) The Hawks also played $n$ games and, the same as the Geese, each game was a win or loss for the Hawks. Again, for each of their games, we know whether they won or lost and we know the number of goals that they scored.

Some of the games that these teams played may have been against each other, but there are other teams, too, and some of the games may have been against these other teams.

We have no information about who played whom. We might know that the Geese won a certain game and that they scored four goals in that game, but we don't know who their opponent was—their opponent could have been the Hawks, but it also could have been some other team.

A *rivalry game* is a game where the Geese played the Hawks.

Our task is to determine the maximum number of goals that could have been scored in rivalry games.

### Input

The input contains one test case, the information for which is spread over five lines as follows:

- The first line contains $n$, the number of games that each team played. $n$ is between 1 and 1,000.

- The second line contains a string of length $n$, where each character is a W (win) or L (loss). This line tells us the outcome of each game played by the Geese. For example, WLL means that the Geese won their first game, lost their second game, and lost their third game.

- The third line contains $n$ integers, giving the number of goals scored in each game by the Geese. For example, 4 1 2 means that the Geese scored four goals in their first game, one goal in their second game, and two goals in their third game.

- The fourth line is like the second, but it tells us the outcome of each game for the Hawks.

- The fifth line is like the third, but it tells us the number of goals scored in each game by the Hawks.

### Output

The output is a single integer: the maximum number of goals scored in possible rivalry games.

The time limit for solving the test case is 0.6 seconds.

## About Rivalries

Before jumping to the structure of optimal solutions, let's be sure that we understand exactly what's being asked by working through some test cases.

We'll start with this one:

---

```
3
WWW
2 5 1
WWW
5 7 8
```

---

There can't be *any* rivalry games at all here. A rivalry game, like any game, requires that one team win and the other lose—but the Geese won all their games and the Hawks won all their games, so the Geese and Hawks could not have played each other. Since there are no rivalry games possible, there are no goals scored in rivalry games. The correct output is 0.

Let's now have the Hawks lose all their games:

---

```
3
WWW
2 5 1
LLL
5 7 8
```

---

Are there any rivalry games now? The answer is still no! The Geese won their first game by scoring two goals. For that game to be a rivalry game, it must be with a game where the Hawks lost and where the Hawks scored fewer than two goals. Since the fewest goals scored by the Hawks was five, though, none of those games can be a rivalry game with the Geese's first game. Similarly, the Geese won their second game by scoring five goals, but there is no loss for the Hawks where they scored four goals or fewer. That is, there is no rivalry involving the Geese's second game. The same kind of analysis shows that the Geese's third game also cannot be part of a rivalry. Again, 0 is the correct output.

Let's move past these zero cases. Here's one:

---

```
3
WWW
2 5 1
LLL
4 7 8
```

---

We've changed the first Hawks game so that they scored four goals instead of five, and this is enough to produce a possible rivalry game! Specifically, the second game played by the Geese, where the Geese won and scored five goals, could be a rivalry game with the first game by the Hawks, where the Hawks lost and scored four goals. That game had nine goals scored in it. As there are no other rivalry games that we can include, there are no other goals that we can add to our total. The correct output here is 9.

Now consider this one:

---

```
2
WW
6 2
LL
8 1
```

---

Look at the final game that each team played: the Geese won and scored two goals, and the Hawks lost and scored one goal. That could be a rivalry game, with a total of three goals. The first game played by each team cannot be a rivalry game (the Geese won with six goals, and the Hawks could not have lost the same game with eight goals), so we can't add any more goals. Is 3 the correct output?

It is not! We chose poorly, matching those final games. What we should have done is match the first game played by the Geese with the second game played by the Hawks. That could be a rivalry game, and it has seven goals. This time we've got it: the correct output is 7.

Let's look at one more example. Try to figure out the maximum total before reading my answer:

---

```
4
WLWW
3 4 1 8
WLLL
5 1 2 3
```

---

The correct output is 20, witnessed by having two rivalry games: the second Geese game with the first Hawks game (9 goals there) and the fourth Geese game with the fourth Hawks game (11 goals there).

Did you predict instead that the correct output would be 25? If so, we're not allowed to add a rivalry of the first Geese game with the third Hawks game. Call that pair $x$. Each team's games are played in order, so if we used $x$ as a rivalry game, then we wouldn't be allowed to also pair the second Geese game (played after $x$) with the first Hawks game (played before $x$).

## Characterizing Optimal Solutions

Consider an optimal solution to this problem: a solution that maximizes the number of goals scored in rivalry games. What might this optimal solution look like? Assume that the games for each team are numbered from 1 to $n$.

## Option 1

One option is that the optimal solution uses the final game $n$ played by the Geese and the final game $n$ played by the Hawks as a rivalry game. That game has a certain number of goals scored in it: call that $g$. We can then strip out both of these games and optimally solve the smaller subproblem on the Geese's first $n-1$ games and the Hawks' first $n-1$ games. That subproblem solution, plus $g$, is the optimal solution overall. Note, though, that this option is only available if the two $n$ games can really be a rivalry game. For example, if both teams have a W for that game, then this cannot be a rivalry game and Option 1 cannot apply.

Remember this test case from the prior section?

---

```
4
WLWW
3 4 1 8
WLLL
5 1 2 3
```

---

That's an example of Option 1: we match the two rightmost scores, 8 and 3, and then optimally solve the subproblem for the remaining games.

## Option 2

Another option is that the optimal solution has nothing to do with these final games at all. In that case, we strip out game $n$ played by the Geese and game $n$ played by the Hawks, and we optimally solve the subproblem on the Geese's first $n-1$ games and the Hawks' first $n-1$ games.

Here's a test case from the prior section that is an example of Option 2:

---

```
3
WWW
2 5 1
LLL
4 7 8
```

---

The 1 and 8 at the right are not part of an optimal solution. The optimal solution for the other games is the optimal solution overall.

So far we've covered the case where both game $n$ scores are used and the case where neither game $n$ score is used. Are we done?

To see that we are not done, consider this test case from the previous section:

---

```
2
WW
6 2
LL
8 1
```

---

Option 1, matching the 2 and 1, leads to a maximum of three goals in rivalry games. Option 2, throwing away both the 2 and 1, leads to a maximum of zero goals in rivalry games. However, the maximum overall here is seven. Our coverage of types of optimal solutions, using only Option 1 and Option 2, is therefore spotty.

What we need to be able to do here is drop a game from the Geese but not from the Hawks. Specifically, we'd like to drop the Geese's second game and then solve the subproblem consisting of the Geese's first game and *both* of the Hawks' games. For symmetry, we should also be able to drop the second Hawks game and solve the resulting subproblem on the first Hawks game and both Geese games. Let's get these two additional options in there.

**Option 3**

Our third option is that the optimal solution has nothing to do with the Geese's game $n$. In that case, we strip out game $n$ played by the Geese, and we optimally solve the subproblem on the Geese's first $n - 1$ games and the Hawks' first $n$ games.

**Option 4**

Our fourth and final option is that the optimal solution has nothing to do with the Hawks' game $n$. In that case, we strip out game $n$ played by the Hawks, and we optimally solve the subproblem on the Geese's first $n$ games and the Hawks' first $n - 1$ games.

Options 3 and 4 induce a change in the structure of a solution to this problem—whether that solution uses recursion, memoization, or dynamic programming. In the previous problems of this chapter, our subproblems were characterized by only one varying parameter: $t$ for Burger Fervor and $k$ for Moneygrubbers. Without Options 3 and 4, we'd have gotten away with a single parameter, $n$, for the Hockey Rivalry problem, too. That $n$ parameter would have reflected the fact that we were solving a subproblem for the first $n$ games played by the Geese and the first $n$ games played by the Hawks. With Options 3 and 4 in the mix, however, these $n$ values are no longer yoked: one can change when the other does not. For example, if we're solving a subproblem concerning the first five games played by the Geese, this does not mean that we're stuck looking at the first five games played by the Hawks. Symmetrically, a subproblem concerning the first five games played by the Hawks doesn't tell us anything about the number of games played by the Geese.

We therefore need two parameters for our subproblems: $i$, the number of games played by the Geese, and $j$, the number of games played by the Hawks.

For a given optimization problem, the number of subproblem parameters could be one, two, three, or more. When confronting a new problem, I suggest beginning with one subproblem parameter. Then, think about the possible options for an optimal solution. Perhaps each option can be solved by solving one-parameter subproblems, in which case additional parameters are not required. However, sometimes it will be that one or more options require the solution to a subproblem that cannot be pinned down by one parameter. In these cases, a second parameter can often help.

The benefit of adding additional subproblem parameters is the larger subproblem space in which to couch our optimal solutions. The cost is the responsibility of solving more subproblems. Keeping the number of parameters small—one, two, or perhaps three—is key for designing fast solutions to optimization problems.

Before we move on, I want to highlight an important difference between the way that we solved Burger Fervor and Moneygrubbers and the way that we're solving Hockey Rivalry. In the two earlier problems, we focused on solving for exactly $t$ minutes or exactly $k$ apples. Here, by contrast, we're not forcing our subproblems to use any specific game. For example, a subproblem involving the first $i$ games played by the Geese isn't forced to use Geese game $i$. The difference arose as a byproduct of our analysis of the structure of optimal solutions. Each time we use dynamic programming, we need to choose whether to use "exactly." If we had chosen to use "exactly" for Hockey Rivalry, then we would have ended up with comparably slower and more complicated code. I've included that code in the online resources for this book—check it out once you're done here!

If you're struggling to relate a problem to smaller subproblems, or struggling to solve subproblems efficiently, it's worth adding or removing "exactly" and trying again. We'll continue to practice identifying subproblems in the next chapter.

### Solution 1: Recursion

It's now time for our recursive solution. Here's the signature for the solve function that we'll write this time:

```
int solve(char outcome1[], char outcome2[], int goals1[],
          int goals2[], int i, int j)
```

The first four parameters come directly from the current test case, while the fifth and sixth are the subproblem parameters. Here are brief descriptions of the parameters:

outcome1    The array of W and L characters for the Geese

outcome2    The array of W and L characters for the Hawks

goals1    The array of goals scored for the Geese

goals2    The array of goals scored for the Hawks

i    The number of Geese games that we're considering in this subproblem

j    The number of Hawks games that we're considering in this subproblem

The last two parameters—the ones specific to the current subproblem—are the only parameters that change on recursive calls.

If we started each of the arrays at index 0, as is standard for C arrays, then we'd have to keep in our minds that information for some game k was not at index k but at index k - 1. For example, information about game four would be at index 3. To avoid this, we'll store information about games starting at index 1, so information about game four will be at index 4. This leaves us with one less mistake to make! In addition, it frees up the value 0 to characterize zero games played.

The code for the recursive solution is given in Listing 3-16.

```
❶ int max(int v1, int v2) {
     if (v1 > v2)
       return v1;
     else
       return v2;
   }

   int solve(char outcome1[], char outcome2[], int goals1[],
             int goals2[], int i, int j) {
❷   int first, second, third, fourth;
❸   if (i == 0 || j == 0)
       return 0;
❹   if ((outcome1[i] == 'W' && outcome2[j] == 'L' &&
          goals1[i] > goals2[j]) ||
         (outcome1[i] == 'L' && outcome2[j] == 'W' &&
          goals1[i] < goals2[j]))
❺     first = solve(outcome1, outcome2, goals1, goals2, i - 1, j - 1) +
               goals1[i] + goals2[j];
     else
       first = 0;
❻   second = solve(outcome1, outcome2, goals1, goals2, i - 1, j - 1);
❼   third = solve(outcome1, outcome2, goals1, goals2, i - 1, j);
❽   fourth = solve(outcome1, outcome2, goals1, goals2, i, j - 1);
❾   return max(first, max(second, max(third, fourth)));
   }
```

*Listing 3-16: Solution 1*

This is a maximization problem: we want to maximize the number of goals scored in rivalry games. We start with a max function ❶—we'll use that when we need to determine which of the options is best. We then declare four integer variables, one for each of the four options ❷.

Let's begin with base cases: What do we return if both i and j are 0? This subproblem is for the first zero Geese games and zero Hawks games. Since there are no games, there are certainly no rivalry games, and since there are no rivalry games, there are no goals scored in rivalry games. We should therefore return 0 here.

That isn't the only base case, though. For example, consider the subproblem where the Geese play zero games (i = 0) and the Hawks play three games (j = 3). As with the case in the prior paragraph, there can't be any rivalry games here, because the Geese don't have any games! A similar situation arises when the Hawks play zero games: even if the Geese play some games, none of them can be against the Hawks.

That captures all of the base cases. That is to say, if i has value 0 *or* j has value 0, then we have zero goals scored in rivalry games ❸.

With the base cases out of the way, we must now try the four possible options for an optimal solution and choose the best one.

**Option 1**

Recall that this option is valid only when the final Geese game and final Hawks game can be a rivalry game. There are two ways for this game to be a rivalry game:

1. The Geese win, the Hawks lose, and the Geese score more goals than the Hawks.
2. The Geese lose, the Hawks win, and the Geese score fewer goals than the Hawks.

We encode these two possibilities ❹. If the game can be a rivalry game, we compute the optimal solution for this option ❺: it consists of the optimal solution for the first i - 1 Geese games and j - 1 Hawks games plus the total goals scored in the rivalry game.

**Option 2**

For this one, we solve the subproblem for the first i - 1 Geese games and j - 1 Hawks games ❻.

**Option 3**

Here, we solve the subproblem for the first i - 1 Geese games and j Hawks games ❼. Notice that i changes but j does not. This is exactly why we need two subproblem parameters here, not one.

**Option 4**

We solve the subproblem for the first i Geese games and j - 1 Hawks games ❽. Again, one subproblem parameter changes but the other does not; it's a good thing there's no need for us to keep them at the same value!

There we go: first, second, third, and fourth—those are the only four possibilities for our optimal solution. We want the maximum of these, and that is what we compute and return ❾. The innermost max call calculates the maximum of third and fourth. Working outward, the next max call calculates the maximum of that winner and second. Finally, the outermost call calculates the maximum of that winner and first.

We're just about there. All we need now is a main function that reads the five lines of input and calls solve. The code is given in Listing 3-17.

```
#define SIZE 1000

int main(void) {
```

```
  int i, n, result;
❶ char outcome1[SIZE + 1], outcome2[SIZE + 1];
❷ int goals1[SIZE + 1], goals2[SIZE + 1];
❸ scanf("%d ", &n);
  for (i = 1; i <= n; i++)
    scanf("%c", &outcome1[i]);
  for (i = 1; i <= n; i++)
    scanf("%d ", &goals1[i]);
  for (i = 1; i <= n; i++)
    scanf("%c", &outcome2[i]);
  for (i = 1; i <= n; i++)
    scanf("%d", &goals2[i]);
  result = solve(outcome1, outcome2, goals1, goals2, n, n);
  printf("%d\n", result);
  return 0;
}
```

*Listing 3-17: The main function*

We declare the outcome (W and L) ❶ and goals-scored arrays ❷. The + 1 there is because of our choice to begin indexing at 1. If we had used just SIZE, then valid indices would go from zero to 999, when what we need is to include index 1,000.

We then read the integer on the first line ❸, which gives the number of games played by the Geese and Hawks. There's a space right after the %d and before the closing quote. That space causes scanf to read whitespace following the integer. Crucially, this reads the newline character at the end of the line, which otherwise would be included when we use scanf to read individual characters . . . which we do next!

We read the W and L information for the Geese and then read the goals-scored information for the Geese. We then do the same for the Hawks. Finally, we call solve. We want to solve the problem considering all *n* Geese games and all *n* Hawks games, which explains why the last two arguments are n. We know exactly how to call solve to get our answer in one shot; unlike for our solutions to Burger Fervor and Moneygrubbers, we don't need to search for it.

Any chance you'll submit this solution to the judge? The "Time-Limit Exceeded" error should come as no surprise.

### Solution 2: Memoization

In Burger Fervor and Moneygrubbers, we used a one-dimensional array for the memo. That's because our subproblems had but one parameter: the number of minutes and number of apples, respectively. In contrast, the subproblems in Hockey Rivalry have two parameters, not one. We'll correspondingly need a memo array with two dimensions, not one. Element memo[i][j] is used to hold the solution to the subproblem on the first i Geese games and the first j Hawks games. Other than switching from one to two dimensions in the memo, the technique remains as before: return the solution if it's already stored; calculate and store it if it's not.

The updated `main` function is given in Listing 3-18.

```
int main(void) {
  int i, j, n, result;
  char outcome1[SIZE + 1], outcome2[SIZE + 1];
  int goals1[SIZE + 1], goals2[SIZE + 1];
  static int memo[SIZE + 1][SIZE + 1];
  scanf("%d ", &n);
  for (i = 1; i <= n; i++)
    scanf("%c", &outcome1[i]);
  for (i = 1; i <= n; i++)
    scanf("%d ", &goals1[i]);
  for (i = 1; i <= n; i++)
    scanf("%c", &outcome2[i]);
  for (i = 1; i <= n; i++)
    scanf("%d", &goals2[i]);
  for (i = 0; i <= SIZE; i++)
    for (j = 0; j <= SIZE; j++)
      memo[i][j] = -1;
  result = solve(outcome1, outcome2, goals1, goals2, n, n, memo);
  printf("%d\n", result);
  return 0;
}
```

*Listing 3-18: The main function, with memoization implemented*

Notice that the `memo` array is huge—over 1,000 elements in each dimension and therefore over 1 million elements in all—so we make the array static as in Listing 1-8.

The memoized `solve` function is given in Listing 3-19.

```
int solve(char outcome1[], char outcome2[], int goals1[],
          int goals2[], int i, int j, int memo[SIZE + 1][SIZE + 1]) {
  int first, second, third, fourth;
  if (memo[i][j] != -1)
    return memo[i][j];
  if (i == 0 || j == 0) {
    memo[i][j] = 0;
    return memo[i][j];
  }
  if ((outcome1[i] == 'W' && outcome2[j] == 'L' &&
       goals1[i] > goals2[j]) ||
      (outcome1[i] == 'L' && outcome2[j] == 'W' &&
       goals1[i] < goals2[j]))
    first = solve(outcome1, outcome2, goals1, goals2, i - 1, j - 1, memo) +
            goals1[i] + goals2[j];
```

```
      else
        first = 0;
      second = solve(outcome1, outcome2, goals1, goals2, i - 1, j - 1, memo);
      third = solve(outcome1, outcome2, goals1, goals2, i - 1, j, memo);
      fourth = solve(outcome1, outcome2, goals1, goals2, i, j - 1, memo);
      memo[i][j] = max(first, max(second, max(third, fourth)));
      return memo[i][j];
}
```

*Listing 3-19: Solution 2, with memoization implemented*

This solution passes all test cases and does so quickly. If we just wanted to solve this problem, we would stop right now, but here we have the opportunity to plumb further and learn more about dynamic programming as we do so.

## Solution 3: Dynamic Programming

We just saw that to memoize this problem we needed a two-dimensional memo array, not a one-dimensional array. To develop a dynamic-programming solution, we'll correspondingly need a two-dimensional dp array. We declared the memo array as follows in Listing 3-18:

```
static int memo[SIZE + 1][SIZE + 1];
```

and we'll do likewise for the dp array:

```
static int dp[SIZE + 1][SIZE + 1];
```

As in the memo array, element dp[i][j] will hold the subproblem solution for the first i Geese games and first j Hawks games. Our task, then, is to solve each of these subproblems and return dp[n][n] once we're done.

In memoized solutions to optimization problems, it's not our responsibility to determine an order in which to solve the subproblems. We make our recursive calls, and those calls return to us the solutions for their corresponding subproblems. In dynamic-programming solutions, however, it *is* our responsibility to determine an order in which to solve the subproblems. We can't just solve them in any order we want, because then a subproblem solution might not be available when we need it.

For example, suppose we wanted to fill in dp[3][5]—that's the cell for the first three Geese games and the first five Hawks games. Take another look back at the four options for an optimal solution.

- Option 1 requires us to look up dp[2][4].
- Option 2 also requires us to look up dp[2][4].
- Option 3 requires us to look up dp[2][5].
- Option 4 requires us to look up dp[3][4].

We must arrange it so that these elements of dp are already stored by the time we want to store dp[3][5].

For subproblems with only one parameter, you generally solve those subproblems from smallest index to largest index. For subproblems with more than one parameter, things are not so simple, as there are many more orders in which the array can be filled. Only some of these orders maintain the property that a subproblem solution is available by the time we need it.

For the Hockey Rivalry problem, we can solve dp[i][j] if we've already stored dp[i - 1][j - 1] (Option 1 and Option 2), dp[i - 1][j] (Option 3), and dp[i][j - 1] (Option 4). One order we can use is to solve all of the dp[i - 1] subproblems before solving any of the dp[i] subproblems. For example, this would result in dp[2][4] being solved before dp[3][5], which is exactly what we need to satisfy Options 1 and 2. It would also result in dp[2][5] being solved before dp[3][5], which is what we need for Option 3. That is, solving row i - 1 before row i satisfies Options 1 to 3.

To satisfy Option 4, we can solve the dp[i] subproblems from smallest j index to largest j index. That, for example, would solve dp[3][4] before dp[3][5].

In summary, we solve all of the subproblems in row 0 from left to right, then all of the subproblems in row 1 from left to right, and so on, until we have solved all subproblems in row n.

The solve function is given in Listing 3-20.

```
int solve(char outcome1[], char outcome2[], int goals1[],
          int goals2[], int n) {
  int i, j;
  int first, second, third, fourth;
  static int dp[SIZE + 1][SIZE + 1];
  for (i = 0; i <= n; i++)
    dp[0][i] = 0;
  for (i = 0; i <= n; i++)
    dp[i][0] = 0;
❶ for (i = 1; i <= n; i++)
  ❷ for (j = 1; j <= n; j++) {
      if ((outcome1[i] == 'W' && outcome2[j] == 'L' &&
          goals1[i] > goals2[j]) ||
          (outcome1[i] == 'L' && outcome2[j] == 'W' &&
          goals1[i] < goals2[j]))
        first = dp[i - 1][j - 1] + goals1[i] + goals2[j];
      else
        first = 0;
      second = dp[i - 1][j - 1];
      third = dp[i - 1][j];
      fourth = dp[i][j - 1];
      dp[i][j] = max(first, max(second, max(third, fourth)));
    }
❸ return dp[n][n];
}
```

*Listing 3-20: Solution 3, with dynamic programming*

We begin by initializing the base case subproblems, which are those in which at least one of the indices is 0. Then, we hit the double for loop ❶ ❷, which controls the order in which the non-base-case subproblems are solved. We first range over the rows ❶ and then the elements in each row ❷, which, as we have argued, is a valid order for solving the subproblems. Once we have filled in the table, we return the solution for the original problem ❸.

We're solving $n^2$ subproblems here, each of which takes us a constant number of steps. Therefore, we've achieved an $O(n^2)$ solution.

We can visualize the array produced by a two-dimensional dynamic-programming algorithm as a table. This is helpful for getting a feel for how the elements of the array are filled in. Let's look at the final array for the following test case:

---

4
WLWW
3 4 1 8
WLLL
5 1 2 3

---

Here's the resulting array:

| 4 | 0 | 9 | 18 | 19 | 20 |
|---|---|---|----|----|----|
| 3 | 0 | 9 | 9 | 9 | 9 |
| 2 | 0 | 9 | 9 | 9 | 9 |
| 1 | 0 | 0 | 4 | 5 | 5 |
| 0 | 0 | 0 | 0 | 0 | 0 |
|   | 0 | 1 | 2 | 3 | 4 |

Consider, for example, the computation for the element in row 4, column 2 or, in terms of the dp table, dp[4][2]. This is the subproblem for the first four Geese games and first two Hawks games. Looking at the Geese's game four and the Hawks' game two, we see that the Geese won with eight goals and the Hawks lost with one goal, so this game could be a rivalry game. Option 1 is therefore a possible option. Nine goals were scored in this game. To that nine, we add the value at row 3, column 1, which is nine again. This gives us a total of 18. That's our maximum so far—now we have to try Options 2 to 4 to see whether they are better. If you do that, you should observe that they all happen to have the value nine. We therefore store 18, the maximum of all available options, in dp[4][2].

The only quantity of real interest here, of course, is that in the topmost, rightmost cell, corresponding to the subproblem allowing the full n games for the Geese and n games for the Hawks. That value, 20, is what we return as the optimal solution. The other quantities in the table are only useful insofar as they help us make progress toward calculating that 20.

In terms of the main function, we make one small change to the code of Listing 3-17: the only thing to do is remove the second n passed to solve, resulting in:

```
result = solve(outcome1, outcome2, goals1, goals2, n);
```

## A Space Optimization

I mentioned in "Step 4: Dynamic Programming" on page 97 that memoization and dynamic programming are roughly equivalent. *Roughly*, because sometimes there are benefits to be had by choosing one or the other. The Hockey Rivalry problem furnishes an example of a typical optimization that we can perform when using dynamic programming but not when using memoization. The optimization is not one of speed but of space.

Here's the key question: When solving a subproblem in row i of the dp array, which rows do we access? Look back at the four options. The only rows used are i - 1 (the previous row) and i (the current row). There's no i - 2 or i - 3 or anything else in there. As such, keeping the entire two-dimensional array in memory is wasteful. Suppose we're solving subproblems in row 500. All we need is access to row 500 and row 499. We might as well not have row 498 or 497 or 496 or any other row in memory, because we'll never look at these again.

Rather than a two-dimensional table, we can pull through with only two one-dimensional arrays: one for the previous row and one for the current row we are solving.

Listing 3-21 implements this optimization.

```
int solve(char outcome1[], char outcome2[], int goals1[],
          int goals2[], int n) {
  int i, j, k;
  int first, second, third, fourth;
  static int previous[SIZE + 1], current[SIZE + 1];
❶ for (i = 0; i <= n; i++)
❷   previous[i] = 0;
  for (i = 1; i <= n; i++) {
    for (j = 1; j <= n; j++) {
      if ((outcome1[i] == 'W' && outcome2[j] == 'L' &&
           goals1[i] > goals2[j]) ||
          (outcome1[i] == 'L' && outcome2[j] == 'W' &&
           goals1[i] < goals2[j]))
        first = previous[j - 1] + goals1[i] + goals2[j];
      else
        first = 0;
      second = previous[j - 1];
      third = previous[j];
      fourth = current[j - 1];
      current[j] = max(first, max(second, max(third, fourth)));
```

```
    }
❸ for (k = 0; k <= SIZE; k++)
    ❹ previous[k] = current[k];
  }
  return current[n];
}
```

*Listing 3-21: Solution 3, with space optimization implemented*

We initialize previous to all zeros ❶ ❷, thereby solving all subproblems in row 0. In the rest of the code, whenever we previously referred to row i - 1, we now use previous. In addition, whenever we previously referred to row i, we now use current. Once a new row has been fully solved and stored in current, we copy current into previous ❸ ❹ so that current can be used to solve the next row.

## Summary

I've presented what I think of as the core of memoization and dynamic programming: explicating the structure of an optimal solution, developing a recursive algorithm, speeding it up through memoization, and optionally replacing the recursion by filling a table.

There's more to learn, though. What if I showed you how to crack some nasty dynamic-programming problems merely through a change in perspective? What if I told you that we can work with three or more dimensions to solve the toughest dynamic-programming problems?

In the next chapter, you'll learn all that and more. See you there!

## Notes

Hockey Rivalry is originally from the 2018 Canadian Computing Olympiad.

Sometimes, you need to know not only the value of an optimal solution, but the decisions that you should make to achieve that solution. Check out "Burger Fervor: Reconstructing a Solution" in Appendix B for an example of how to do this.

Many algorithm textbooks delve deeper into the theory and application of memoization and dynamic programming. My favorite treatment is *Algorithm Design* by Jon Kleinberg and Éva Tardos (2006).

# 4

## ADVANCED MEMOIZATION AND DYNAMIC PROGRAMMING

In this chapter, we're going to continue with memoization and dynamic programming. You don't need to read this chapter to continue through the book. But there's more to learn if you'd like to deepen your understanding. We'll see how to make a dynamic-programming problem easier through a change in perspective, work with more than two dimensions in our subproblem arrays, and stretch our skills to go beyond the "optimize the solution" problems we've seen thus far. We'll also get a bit more practice with the fundamentals. You'll be a dynamic-programming rock star after this.

### Problem 1: The Jumper

We'll start this chapter with a dynamic-programming problem that's solvable using what we learned in Chapter 3. As in that chapter, we'll be able to solve the problem by focusing on what the end of the optimal solution must look like. We'll see, though, that this isn't the only way to do it. In particular, we'll see that we can instead focus not on the *end* of the optimal solution, but on its *beginning*. You may find this second approach more intuitive than the first, if not for this problem then perhaps for other problems. And once you learn this change in perspective, you'll have two approaches to throw at your next dynamic-programming problem.

This is DMOJ problem crci07p2.

## The Problem

Nikola is playing a game on a row of *n* squares. The leftmost square is Square 1 and the rightmost square is Square *n*. Nikola starts on Square 1 and wants to get to Square *n*. To do so, she makes one or more jumps. Her first jump is required to be from Square 1 to Square 2. After that, the jumping rules are as follows:

- Nikola can jump to the right by exactly one more than the number of squares on her previous jump. For example, if Nikola jumped 3 squares on her previous jump, then she can jump to the right by 4 squares now.

- Nikola can jump to the left by exactly the same number of squares as on her previous jump. For example, if Nikola jumped 3 squares on her previous jump, then she can jump 3 squares to the left now.

I'll use the term *jump distance* to refer to the number of squares moved on a given jump.

The valid squares here are those from 1 to *n*. Therefore, if a jump would take Nikola to the left of square 1 or to the right of square *n*, that jump is not allowed.

Each square has an entry cost. Whenever Nikola jumps, she pays the entry cost of the square in which she lands.

We want to determine the minimum total cost for Nikola to get from Square 1 to Square *n*.

### Input

The input consists of the following lines:

- A line containing *n*, the number of squares in the row. *n* is between 2 and 1,000.

- *n* lines, each giving the entry cost for a square. The first of these lines is the entry cost for Square 1, the second is the entry cost for Square 2, and so on. Each entry cost is an integer between 1 and 500.

### Output

Output the minimum total cost for Nikola to get from Square 1 to Square *n*.

The time limit for solving the test case is 0.6 seconds.

## Working Through an Example

Let's work through one test case to make sure we know exactly what we are being asked to do. Here it is:

```
7
3
5
1
9
7
2
3
```

Nikola starts on Square 1 and has to get to Square 7. Remembering that the first jump has to be to Square 2, here's one possible route:

**Square 1 to Square 2**
    Cost 5.
    Most recent jump distance is now 1.

**Square 2 to Square 4**
    Cost 9.
    Most recent jump distance is now 2.

**Square 4 to Square 7**
    Cost 3.
    Most recent jump distance is now 3.

We made it to Square 7! The total cost is 5 + 9 + 3 = 17. This is *not* the minimum total cost, though. Try to find it before continuing.

Here's how we can get the minimum total cost:

**Square 1 to Square 2**
    Cost 5.
    Most recent jump distance is now 1.

**Square 2 to Square 1**
    Cost 3.
    Most recent jump distance remains 1.

**Square 1 to Square 3**
    Cost 1.
    Most recent jump distance is now 2.

**Square 3 to Square 6**
    Cost 2.
    Most recent jump distance is now 3.

**Square 6 to Square 3**
    Cost 1.
    Most recent jump distance remains 3.

**Square 3 to Square 7**

Cost 3.

Most recent jump distance is now 4.

The total cost this time is $5 + 3 + 1 + 2 + 1 + 3 = 15$.

## Solution 1: Backward Formulation

Before we can write any code, we need to settle on our subproblems and how to use these subproblems to characterize the structure of an optimal solution.

### Finding the Subproblems

How many subproblem parameters do we need? Could we get away with just one?

If we have only one subproblem parameter, then we could use it to keep track of which square Nikola is on. But then how would we know which jumps were allowed for a given subproblem? Think about the end of an optimal solution for getting from Square 1 to Square 4. To get closer to a base case, we'd need to know which square Nikola was on prior to Square 4 so that we could make a recursive call to that earlier square. For example, if we knew that Nikola used a jump distance of 2 to get to Square 4, then we would know that prior to Square 4 she must have been on Square 2 or Square 6. But we don't know the jump distance that Nikola used—it's not one of our subproblem parameters. This isn't going to work.

Let's try one more time with just one subproblem parameter. What if we use it to keep track of the most recent jump distance? Well, then we won't have a subproblem parameter available to tell us which square Nikola is on! And without knowing where Nikola is, we won't have a way to know when we've reached the base case square.

It looks like we need two subproblem parameters: one to tell us the square that Nikola is on and one to tell us the jump distance that she used to get to that square.

For each of these parameters, we need to decide whether to use "exactly." In Chapter 3, we saw examples of using "exactly" subproblems when we solved Burger Fervor and Moneygrubbers. We also saw an example of *not* using "exactly" when we solved Hockey Rivalry. Had we used "exactly" in Hockey Rivalry, our subproblems would have forced specific games to be matched as rivalry games, which wasn't needed for that problem.

Here, it makes sense that we'd want to know *exactly* which square Nikola is on. We could use that to figure out exactly which square she was on prior to the most recent jump... well, not quite. We'd also need to know *exactly* the jump distance that she used to get to the current square. We could then use both the current square and jump distance to figure out exactly where Nikola must have come from. That is, we need "exactly" for both subproblem parameters.

The problem description specifies that we have no choice for the first jump: it has to be from Square 1 to Square 2. Instead of worrying about maintaining that condition in our subproblems, we'll just ignore it: our subproblems will tell us the minimum cost to get from Square 2 to some other square. Later, we'll add the cost of jumping from Square 1 to Square 2, and that'll give us our final solution.

We can't use any old sequence of jumps from Square 2, though. Think about what would happen if our solution from Square 2 started with a jump of distance 3. We need to jump from Square 1 to Square 2 first and, uh-oh, a jump distance of 3 is not allowed to follow that! We need to ensure that our subproblems solve only for solutions that are feasible given that we'll prepend the jump from Square 1 to Square 2. We'll call such solutions *connectible*.

Okay, now we're ready for the subproblems! The subproblem with parameters $i$ and $j$ will tell us the minimum cost of a connectible solution from Square 2 to exactly Square $i$ using a final jump distance of exactly $j$.

That subproblem definition is quite a mouthful. Let's use the test case from the prior section to nail down a few examples of how the definition works.

What is the solution for the subproblem when $i = 7$ and $j = 3$? This is asking us for the best connectible solution that starts at Square 2, ends at Square 7, and has a final jump distance of 3. The answer is 12, witnessed by Nikola jumping from Square 2 to Square 4 (cost 9), to Square 7 (cost 3). (Remember we're ignoring the cost of jumping from Square 1 to Square 2 in these subproblems.)

What about the solution for the subproblem with $i = 7$ and $j = 4$? The answer is 10: Nikola can jump from Square 2 to Square 1 (cost 3), then to Square 3 (cost 1), to Square 6 (cost 2), to Square 3 (cost 1), and finally to Square 7 (cost 3).

What about $i = 7$ and $j = 2$? Try it, and you should find that achieving this is impossible: there's no way to find a connectible solution that gets from Square 2 to Square 7 with a final jump distance of 2.

One more: $i = 2$ and $j = 1$. We're already at Square 2 here. Furthermore, $j = 1$ means that we need a jump of distance 1 to get us to Square 2. No problem: the jump from square 1 to Square 2 that we're going to prepend is exactly this kind of jump! The answer here is therefore 0. Hmm, I think we may have just found a base case.

### Characterizing Optimal Solutions

Consider a subproblem with some value of $i$ and some value of $j$. What might the optimal solution look like for this subproblem?

### Option 1

One option is that this optimal solution ends with a jump to the right. The $j$ value gives us the distance of this jump, so we know that this jump must have been from Square $i - j$. In order to jump to the right by $j$, Nikola must have gotten to her previous square with a jump distance of $j - 1$. (Why $j - 1$? Because a jump to the right is required to have a jump distance that's one more than the jump distance of the previous jump.) So the solution for this option is the solution to the subproblem for Square $i - j$ and jump distance $j - 1$, plus the entry cost of Square $i$.

Yikes—it can be confusing thinking about the solution backward like this! For example, we're talking about jumping to the right, yet we're using a Square $i - j$ that's to the left. But remember: we're looking for the square that Nikola came from, so if she jumped to the right from that square, then she indeed came from a smaller-numbered square.

### Option 2

Our second option is that this optimal solution ends with a jump to the left. The $j$ value gives us the distance of this jump, so we know that this jump must have been from Square $i + j$. In order to jump to the left by $j$, Nikola must have gotten to her previous square with a jump distance of $j$. So the solution for this option is the solution to the subproblem for Square $i + j$ and jump distance $j$, plus the entry cost of Square $i$.

### Solving One Subproblem

Let's skip the bare recursive solution and work on a memoized solution. To do so, we'll start by writing the code for the following solve_ij function signature:

```
int solve_ij(int cost[], int n, int i, int j,
             int memo[SIZE + 1][SIZE + 1])
```

This function solves the subproblem for the given values of i and j. Here's what each parameter is for:

cost    The array of entry costs. The entry cost for Square 1 is cost[1], the entry cost for Square 2 is cost[2], and so on.

n    The number of squares in the row.

i    The ending square for this subproblem.

j    The final jump distance for this subproblem.

memo    The memoization array.

The code for this function is given in Listing 4-1.

```
#define SIZE 1000

int min(int v1, int v2) {
  if (v1 < v2)
    return v1;
  else
    return v2;
}

int solve_ij(int cost[], int n, int i, int j, int memo[SIZE + 1][SIZE + 1]) {
  int first, second;
❶ if (memo[i][j] != -2)
```

```
    return memo[i][j];
❷ if (i ==  2 && j == 1) {
    memo[i][j] = 0;
    return memo[i][j];
  }
❸ if (i - j >= 1 && j >= 2)
    first = solve_ij(cost, n, i - j, j - 1, memo);
  else
    first = -1;
❹ if (i + j <= n)
    second = solve_ij(cost, n, i + j, j, memo);
  else
    second = -1;
❺ if (first == -1 && second == -1) {
    memo[i][j] = -1;
    return memo[i][j];
  } else if (second == -1) {
    memo[i][j] = first + cost[i];
    return memo[i][j];
  } else if (first == -1) {
    memo[i][j] = second + cost[i];
    return memo[i][j];
  } else {
    memo[i][j] = min(first, second) + cost[i];
    return memo[i][j];
  }
}
```

*Listing 4-1: Solving one subproblem*

As we did when solving Burger Fervor in Chapter 3, we use -2 in the memo array ❶ to indicate that a subproblem hasn't been solved yet. The typical value to use here would be -1, but we'll use -1 to indicate that we've already tried to solve a subproblem but that it has no solution.

As we discovered in the previous section, an important base case is when we're on square 2 and need to get to that square with a jump of distance 1 ❷. In this case, we return 0: there's no cost to get from Square 2 to Square 2!

Next we try each of the two options for an optimal solution. We use the variable first to hold the value for Option 1 and second to hold the value for Option 2.

**Option 1**

This is the option where Nikola jumps to the right to get to Square i. To use this option, we need to ensure that Nikola would have come from a valid square. We also need to ensure that j is at least 2 ❸, which guarantees that she got to the previous square with a jump distance of at least 1. After all, it wouldn't make sense to say that Nikola got to a prior square using a jump of distance 0!

## Option 2

This is the option where Nikola jumps to the left to get to Square i. As in the previous option, we need to ensure that Nikola came from a valid square ❹.

It's possible for one or both options to fail to find a solution; in those cases we use a value of -1. If both options fail, then we return -1 ❺. The rest of the code determines which of the two options is best, and returns that plus cost[i] as the solution.

### Where's the Optimal Solution?

Now we can solve any subproblem we want. So, what call of solve_ij should we make to find the solution to the original problem?

Trick question: one call won't be enough! We're going to need to do some searching, much as we did when we solved Burger Fervor and Money-grubbers in Chapter 3. But why?

We know for sure that we need to end exactly on Square n, so we don't need any searching there. What we *don't* know is the jump distance that we should have used as the final jump. Should we have ended with a jump distance of 2? 3? 4? Who knows? We need to try them all and pick the best one. See Listing 4-2 for the code to do this.

```
int solve(int cost[], int n) {
  int i, j, best, result;
❶ static int memo[SIZE + 1][SIZE + 1];
  for (i = 1; i <= SIZE; i++)
    for (j = 1; j <= SIZE; j++)
      memo[i][j] = -2;
❷ best = -1;
❸ for (j = 1; j <= n; j++) {
    result = solve_ij(cost, n, n, j, memo);
    if (result != -1) {
      if (best == -1)
      ❹ best = cost[2] + result;
      else
      ❺ best = min(best, cost[2] + result);
    }
  }
  return best;
}
```

*Listing 4-2: Solution 1*

This function is where we set up the memo array ❶ so that it's shared across all calls to solve_ij.

The best variable holds the best solution that we've found thus far. It begins at -1 ❷ and is updated whenever we find a better solution ❹ ❺. Be careful: we need to add cost[2] here in order to reincorporate the jump from Square 1 to Square 2.

Notice that we're looping through the final jump distances between 1 and n ❸. There's no point trying any final distance larger than n because they can't lead to a valid square. That is, we're guaranteed to find the best final jump distance because we're trying all of the valid possibilities.

### The main Function

It's time to wrap up this solution. All we need is a main function to read the input and call solve. The code is in Listing 4-3.

```
int main(void) {
  int i, n;
  int cost[SIZE + 1];
  scanf("%d ", &n);
  for (i = 1; i <= n; i++)
    scanf("%d", &cost[i]);
  printf("%d\n", solve(cost, n));
  return 0;
}
```

*Listing 4-3: The main function*

If you submit our code to the judge, you should pass all test cases within the time limit.

But we can still do better.

## Solution 2: Forward Formulation

Let's first talk about why Solution 1 is fast, and then discuss why we can still improve it.

### How Fast is Solution 1?

Solution 1 is an $O(n^2)$ algorithm. It'd be easier to see that from a bottom-up dynamic-programming solution, with its telltale two nested loops, but we can still make an argument using our memoized solution. Our solve_ij function (Listing 4-1) fills in each of the $n^2$ elements of memo at most once. To fill in each such element, our code makes two recursive calls. We can therefore say that our code makes at most $2n^2$ recursive calls. Beyond that, each recursive call of solve_ij performs a constant number of steps to decide whether to use first or second in the optimal solution. So solve_ij takes $O(n^2)$ time throughout all recursive calls.

The maximum number of squares in a row is 1,000. Our $O(n^2)$ algorithm is therefore performing something like $1,000^2 = 1,000,000$ steps. We can do that easily within our 0.6-second time limit.

All right, so Solution 1 is fast. What could we possibly want to improve, then?

## Backward vs. Forward

Perhaps you've been bothered by an incongruity between the way that Nikola's jumps are described in the problem description and the way that we thought about jumps in our memoized solution. The problem description tells us what Nikola can do on each jump starting from the first jump. That is, it focuses on where Nikola is right now and what she can do next. Our memoized solution, by contrast, focuses on where Nikola got to and how she got there. For example, rather than thinking, "Nikola jumped from Square 2 to Square 4," we have to think, "Nikola got to Square 4 by jumping from Square 2." We have to think about the problem backward!

In addition to those extra mental gymnastics, our backward formulation has a consequence on the amount of code we have to write as well. Remember how we had to search through all possible final jump distances in Listing 4-2? The reason we needed that is because we don't know how the optimal solution ends. Maybe it ends with a jump distance of 2, or a jump distance of 3, or a jump distance of 4, and so on. But we *do* know exactly how it begins: with a jump distance of 1 from Square 1 to Square 2! As long as we keep track of the most recent jump distance, we'll never have to guess what it might be. That is, if we solve the problem forward (keeping track of where we are) rather than backward (keeping track of where we ended up), we'll be able to entirely avoid the jump-distance search. We'll get to the end of the optimal solution with whatever we need the final jump distance to be.

## Finding the Subproblems, Again

We'll stick with our earlier idea of using two subproblem parameters. That's because we need one to tell us the square that Nikola is on and one to tell us the jump distance that she used to get to that square.

This time, the subproblem with parameters $i$ and $j$ is going to tell us the minimum cost of a solution from exactly Square $i$ to Square $n$ given that Square $i$ was reached with a jump distance of exactly $j$.

We need some examples of this! We'll again use the test case from "Working Through an Example" on page 127.

Let's start with the subproblem with $i = 2$ and $j = 1$. This is asking us for the best solution that starts at Square 2, ends at Square 7, and got to Square 2 using a jump distance of 1. (Notice that we don't care at all about the jump distance that ultimately takes us to Square $n$. It could be anything!) The answer here is 10: Nikola can jump from Square 2 to Square 1 (cost 3), to Square 3 (cost 1), to Square 6 (cost 2), to Square 3 (cost 1), to Square 7 (cost 3). Hey, that's the same answer as for the $i = 7$, $j = 4$ subproblem from the backward formulation! But in the backward formulation, we would have to try all final jump distances to confirm that this is the optimal one. No longer.

Now think about any subproblem with $i = n$. What's the answer? It's 0: we're already on square $n$! We don't care what $j$ is, because we don't care how we got to Square $n$. We've found our base case again.

## Characterizing Optimal Solutions, Again

We need to redo our optimal substructure work from Solution 1.

### Option 1

One option is that Nikola next makes a jump to the right. The $j$ value gives us the jump distance to the current square. The jump to the right will have distance $j + 1$, and Nikola will therefore land on Square $i + j + 1$. So the solution for this option is the entry cost of Square $i + j + 1$, plus the solution to the subproblem for Square $i + j + 1$ and jump distance $j + 1$.

### Option 2

Our second option is that Nikola next makes a jump to the left. That jump to the left will have distance $j$, and Nikola will therefore land on Square $i - j$. So the solution for this option is the entry cost of Square $i - j$, plus the solution to the subproblem for Square $i - j$ and jump distance $j$.

### Solving the Needed Subproblem

Now we can write a solve function that solves a subproblem of our choice. See Listing 4-4 for the code.

```
int solve(int cost[], int n, int i, int j,
          int memo[SIZE + 1][SIZE + 1]) {
  int first, second;
  if (memo[i][j] != -2)
    return memo[i][j];
  if (i == n) {
    memo[i][j] = 0;
    return memo[i][j];
  }
❶ if (i + j + 1 <= n)
    first = solve(cost, n, i + j + 1, j + 1, memo);
  else
    first = -1;
❷ if (i - j >= 1)
    second = solve(cost, n, i - j, j, memo);
  else
    second = -1;
  if (first == -1 && second == -1) {
    memo[i][j] = -1;
    return memo[i][j];
  } else if (second == -1) {
    memo[i][j] = cost[i + j + 1] + first;
    return memo[i][j];
  } else if (first == -1) {
    memo[i][j] = cost[i - j] + second;
    return memo[i][j];
  } else {
    memo[i][j] = min(cost[i + j + 1] + first, cost[i - j] + second);
```

```
    return memo[i][j];
  }
}
```

*Listing 4-4: Solution 2*

As in our backward formulation (Listing 4-1), we need to implement each of the two options for an optimal solution. In each case, we first check that the next square is a valid square ❶ ❷ prior to considering the jump.

### The main Function

What call of solve should we make in order to find the solution to the original problem?

That's not a trick question this time—we know exactly which subproblem we need to solve! We need to solve the subproblem with $i = 2$ (starting on square 2) and $j = 1$ (getting to square 2 with a jump of distance 1). We can incorporate this in our main function that reads the input. Check out the code in Listing 4-5.

```
int main(void) {
  int i, j, n, result;
  int cost[SIZE + 1];
  static int memo[SIZE + 1][SIZE + 1];
  scanf("%d ", &n);
  for (i = 1; i <= n; i++)
    scanf("%d", &cost[i]);
  for (i = 1; i <= SIZE; i++)
    for (j = 1; j <= SIZE; j++)
      memo[i][j] = -2;
  result = cost[2] + solve(cost, n, 2, 1, memo);
  printf("%d\n", result);
  return 0;
}
```

*Listing 4-5: The main function*

For this problem, I prefer the forward solution, but you may instead prefer the backward solution—it's an individual choice!

When I'm working on a memoization or dynamic-programming solution, I always start by trying to formulate a backward solution. Backward solutions often feel more natural to me because they more closely model the way that I think about recursion. If I get stuck for too long, though, or when there's friction between the forward nature of the problem description and the backward formulation, I'll give it a whirl with a forward solution. Keep both of these complementary approaches in your dynamic-programming toolbox!

### What About Dynamic Programming?

We have a perfectly good forward memoized solution for this problem. Still, you might want to develop a dynamic-programming solution. If you do, there's a bit of a surprise waiting in there!

Think back to how we solved Hockey Rivalry in Chapter 3 with dynamic programming. In "Solution 3: Dynamic Programming" on page 119, we learned that we need to figure out the order in which to solve the subproblems. In Hockey Rivalry, we did this by solving all of the subproblems in row 0 from left to right, then all of the subproblems in row 1 from left to right, and so on.

But that order won't work for us now.

What do we need in order to solve dp[i][j]? From Option 1, we need to have already solved dp[i + j + 1][j + 1]; that is, we need something from a higher-numbered column. From Option 2, we need to have already solved dp[i - j][j]; that is, we need something from a lower-numbered row in the current column. Taken together, we need to solve all of the subproblems in column n, then all of the subproblems in column n - 1, and so on. And within each column, we need to solve the subproblem in row 1, then row 2, and so on.

Here's the double for loop that we can use to solve the subproblems in the right order:

```
for (j = n; j >= 1; j--)
  for (i = 1; i < n; i++) {
    code to fill in dp[i][j]
}
```

Always be careful with the order that you solve the subproblems!

If you'd like to see the full dynamic-programming solution, please check the online resources for this book. Otherwise, we're ready to continue here with another dynamic-programming problem. A real doozy. You're so ready for this.

# Problem 2: Ways to Build

The four dynamic-programming problems that we've solved so far (three in Chapter 3 and one in this chapter) asked us to maximize (Burger Fervor and Hockey Rivalry) or minimize (Moneygrubbers and The Jumper) the value of a solution. I'd like to end this chapter with a problem of a slightly different flavor: rather than find an optimal solution, we'll count the number of possible solutions.

One other difference that will arise is in the number of dimensions of our subproblem array. In the four earlier problems, we used a one- or two-dimensional array of subproblem solutions. We're going to need more dimensions than that to solve this one.

This is DMOJ problem noip15p5.

### The Problem

We're given a source string $a$, a target string $b$, and an integer $k$. We want to build $b$ from $a$ by putting together $k$ substrings of $a$.

There are some rules that we need to follow:

- We have to use the substrings of $a$ in the same order that they occur in $a$.

- We're not allowed to use any empty substrings—each one has to have at least one character.

- We're not allowed to use substrings that overlap: if we use some character from $a$ in one of our substrings, then we are not allowed to use that character in some other substring.

- We have to use exactly $k$ substrings of $a$ to build $b$.

For example, let's say that $a$ is xxyzxyz, $b$ is xxyz, and $k$ is 3. One way to build $b$ by putting together three substrings of $a$ is to take the x from the beginning of $a$, the xy to the right of that, and the z from the end of $a$. Putting those substrings together gives us xxyz, exactly the string $b$ that we need.

Now, there may be many different ways to build $b$ from $a$. But notice that as long as we follow the rules it doesn't matter how we build $b$—each way is just as good as the others. It therefore doesn't make sense to talk about the optimal way to build $b$. What we're asked to determine for this problem, then, is not the best way to build $b$, but the total number of ways that we can build $b$. In the previous example, there are 11 ways. Can you find them all?

### Input

The input contains one test case, the information for which is spread over three lines as follows:

- The first line contains three numbers: the length of String $a$, the length of String $b$, and the integer $k$ giving the number of substrings that we must take from $a$ to build $b$. The length of String $a$ is between 1 and 1,000, the length of String $b$ is between 1 and 200, and $k$ is between 0 and 200.

- The second line contains the String $a$.

- The third line contains the String $b$.

### Output

Output the number of ways we can build $b$ using exactly $k$ substrings of $a$.

This number may be huge. To spare us from integer overflow worries, the problem specifies that we output this number mod 1,000,000,007.

The time limit for solving the test case is two seconds.

## Working Through an Example

Were you able to find all 11 ways to build $b$ for the example that I gave in the problem description? Let's make sure you have them all, as we'll be using this as a running example for this problem.

Here is the example in the form of a test case:

---

7 4 3
xxyzxyz
xxyz

---

For quick reference, here are the indices for the characters of $a$:

| Index | 0 | 1 | 2 | 3 | 4 | 5 | 6 |
|-------|---|---|---|---|---|---|---|
| Value | x | x | y | z | x | y | z |

How can we build xxyz from xxyzxyz using exactly three substrings? In the following, I'll indicate each substring of $a$ using a range of indices; for example, 0-0 refers to the substring of $a$ that consists of the character at index 0, and 1-2 refers to the substring of $a$ consisting of the characters at indices 1 and 2.

Here are five ways to do it:

- 0-1 (xx), 5-5 (y), 6-6 (z)
- 1-1 (x), 4-5 (xy), 6-6 (z)
- 0-0 (x), 4-5 (xy), 6-6 (z)
- 0-1 (xx), 2-2 (y), 6-6 (z)
- 0-0 (x), 1-2 (xy), 6-6 (z)

Notice in each of these ways that our final substring is the final character z from $a$. That is, we've fixed the final substring to be that z and then searched for ways to take two substrings from xxyzxy to build xxy. We are starting to see how we can find solutions to the initial problem by finding solutions to smaller subproblems.

There are six remaining ways. Let's get those down:

- 1-1 (x), 4-4 (x), 5-6 (yz)
- 0-0 (x), 4-4 (x), 5-6 (yz)
- 0-0 (x), 1-1 (x), 5-6 (yz)
- 0-1 (xx), 2-2 (y), 3-3 (z)
- 0-0 (x), 1-2 (xy), 3-3 (z)
- 0-0 (x), 1-1 (x), 2-3 (yz)

Adding up the five ways from before, we now have a total of 5 + 6 = 11 ways to solve the problem.

## Solution 1: Using "Exactly" Subproblems

We need to identify our subproblems and then use them to find all optimal solutions. We'll try for a backward formulation.

### Finding the Subproblems

How many subproblem parameters will we need this time?

We need to keep track of where we are in String $a$ and keep track of where we are in String $b$. That's a good start, but it isn't quite enough. We also need a subproblem parameter to tell us how many more substrings to take. For the first time, we're going to use three subproblem parameters!

We did well using "exactly" subproblem parameters when we solved The Jumper earlier in this chapter. As usual, we need to decide whether to use it for each of our subproblem parameters here. It makes sense to use "exactly" for the parameter that tracks how many more substrings to take, because we need to use exactly that number of substrings (not, for instance, at most that number of substrings). It's less clear what to do for the subproblem parameters that keep track of where we are in $a$ and where we are in $b$. Let's just start with "exactly" parameters for those, too, and see what happens. In what follows, we'll use the notation $s[i..j]$ to refer to the characters from index $i$ up to and including index $j$ of String $s$.

The subproblem with parameters $i, j$, and $k$ is going to tell us the number of ways that we can choose exactly $k$ substrings from $a[0..i]$ to build exactly $b[0..j]$, with the restriction that the rightmost substring ends with exactly the character $a[i]$.

Let's return to our running example to clarify how these subproblems work. What's our answer for the subproblem with $i = 6, j = 3$, and $k = 3$? (Don't answer "11" too quickly!)

Since $a[0..6]$ is all of $a$, and $b[0..3]$ is all of $b$, this subproblem is asking about the full $a$ and $b$ strings. So we're looking for all ways to choose exactly three substrings from $a$ to build $b$, with the restriction that the rightmost substring ends with exactly the z at $a[6]$.

The answer is 8! Here they are—the first five are the ones that use the final z in $a$ as its own substring, and the remaining three use the final yz in $a$ as its own substring:

- 0-1 (xx), 5-5 (y), 6-6 (z)
- 1-1 (x), 4-5 (xy), 6-6 (z)
- 0-0 (x), 4-5 (xy), 6-6 (z)
- 0-1 (xx), 2-2 (y), 6-6 (z)
- 0-0 (x), 1-2 (xy), 6-6 (z)
- 1-1 (x), 4-4 (x), 5-6 (yz)
- 0-0 (x), 4-4 (x), 5-6 (yz)
- 0-0 (x), 1-1 (x), 5-6 (yz)

But why can't we include the missing solutions, like 0-1 (xx), 2-2 (y), and 3-3 (z)? Shouldn't those count?

The reason we can't use them here is because they don't use that final z at $a[6]$. They don't satisfy the requirements of the type of "exactly" subproblem that we're using.

That said, we have eight ways so far, and we do need to get to 11. Looking at the $i = 6, j = 3, k = 3$ subproblem therefore isn't enough. We can find the three missing ways by looking at the subproblem $i = 3, j = 3, k = 3$. Those ways are as follows:

- 0-1 (xx), 2-2 (y), 3-3 (z)

- 0-0 (x), 1-2 (xy), 3-3 (z)

- 0-0 (x), 1-1 (x), 2-3 (yz)

As in our backward formulation of The Jumper in this chapter and Burger Fervor and Moneygrubbers in Chapter 3, we'll need to do some post-processing to find what we need. In those other problems, we searched the relevant subproblems to discover the optimal one; here, we'll search the relevant subproblems to find all possible solutions.

### Characterizing the Ways

Consider an $i, j, k$ subproblem as described in the previous section. There are two categories of ways to satisfy this subproblem. In each category, we require that $a[i]$ is the same character as $b[j]$—if it isn't, then the requirements of the subproblem are not met and the answer is zero.

### Category 1

One category of ways involves using $a[i]$ as the final substring. If we use up one substring on $a[i]$, then we have $k - 1$ substrings to go, so we'll continue by solving subproblems with $k - 1$ as the third parameter. Similarly, we'll continue with $j - 1$ as the second parameter, because we just used character $b[j]$.

What about the first parameter—what do we do there? Do we just do the same thing that we did with $j$ and $k$ and continue with $i - 1$?

Not necessarily! It's true that continuing with $i - 1$ is one possibility, but there are others. We need to be able to skip some characters from $a$ and continue at an earlier point. That is, we might want to match $b[j - 1]$ with $a[i - 2]$ or $a[i - 3]$ or some even earlier character. We're going to need a loop in here that tries all values of the first parameter up to $i - 1$, while fixing $j - 1$ for the second parameter and $k - 1$ for the third parameter.

Using our running example, consider again the subproblem with $i = 6, j = 3$, and $k = 3$. We know that the answer for this subproblem is 8. Of those 8, there are 5 that fall into Category 1. We get 3 of those 5 from the subproblem with $i = 5, j = 2$, and $k = 2$ and the other 2 from the subproblem with $i = 2, j = 2$, and $k = 2$.

### Category 2

The other category of ways involves using at least two characters for the final substring.

There's a neat trick that we can use for this one. Imagine that we solve the subproblem with parameters $i - 1, j - 1$, and $k$ (that's right: the third parameter is $k$, not $k - 1$!). It turns out that this is the only subproblem that we need to solve!

That subproblem uses all $k$ substrings to find solutions that end by matching $a[i - 1]$ with $b[j - 1]$. But each of those solutions can be extended to a solution that matches $a[i]$ with $b[j]$ by just tacking $a[i]$ (or $b[j]$—they're the same) on to the final substring. Similarly, any solution in this category that matches $a[i]$ with $b[j]$ and uses $k$ substrings corresponds to a solution to the subproblem that matches $a[i - 1]$ with $b[j - 1]$ and uses $k$ substrings. In conclusion, the number of solutions here is exactly the same as it is for the $i - 1, j - 1, k$ subproblem.

In our running example, the subproblem with $i = 6, j = 3$, and $k = 3$ has three solutions in this category. We get that by looking up the answer to the subproblem with $i = 5, j = 2$, and $k = 3$.

Notice that there can not be any other categories besides these two. Category 1 uses the single-character string $a[i]$ as the final substring; Category 2 uses a longer string that ends with $a[i]$ as the final substring. There can't be anything else.

### Solving One Subproblem

As we did when solving The Jumper earlier in this chapter, we'll skip the unadorned recursive solution and jump right to a memoized one. We need a function to tell us the answer for the subproblem with the given i, j, and k values. That function will have the following signature:

```
int solve_ijk(char a[], char b[], int i, int j, int k,
              int memo[MAX_A][MAX_B][MAX_K + 1])
```

Here, a is the source string; b is the target string; i, j, and k are the three subproblem parameters; and memo is the memoization array.

The code for this function is given in Listing 4-6.

```
#define MAX_A 1000
#define MAX_B 200
#define MAX_K 200
#define MOD 1000000007

int solve_ijk(char a[], char b[], int i, int j, int k,
              int memo[MAX_A][MAX_B][MAX_K + 1]) {
  int total, q;
  if (memo[i][j][k] != -1)
    return memo[i][j][k];
❶ if (j == 0 && k == 1 && a[i] == b[j]) {
    memo[i][j][k] = 1;
    return memo[i][j][k];
  }
```

```
❷ if (i == 0 || j == 0 || k == 0) {
     memo[i][j][k] = 0;
     return memo[i][j][k];
   }
❸ if (a[i] != b[j]) {
     memo[i][j][k] = 0;
     return memo[i][j][k];
   }
   total = 0;
❹ for (q = 0; q < i; q++)
   ❺ total = (total + solve_ijk(a, b, q, j - 1, k - 1, memo)) % MOD;
❻ total = (total + solve_ijk(a, b, i - 1, j - 1, k, memo)) % MOD;
   memo[i][j][k] = total;
   return memo[i][j][k];
}
```

*Listing 4-6: Solving one subproblem*

When we solved Hockey Rivalry in Chapter 3, we started indexing our arrays at 1 rather than 0, and that simplified our solution a little. Here, however, I've decided to index starting at 0. You could indeed use the Hockey Rivalry indexing trick here as well; I've chosen not to in order to spare us the trouble of defining what subproblems mean when the empty string is in play.

Let's work through the code, starting with the base cases.

Our first base case is when j is 0, k is 1, and a[i] and b[j] are the same character ❶. What we're being asked for here is the number of ways to build the one-character string b[0] using a[i] given that a[i] matches b[0]. The answer is 1, because we can use a[i] as a match!

Now, in any other case where i is 0, or j is 0, or k is 0 ❷, the answer is 0. For example, if i is 0 and j is greater than 0, then we're being asked to choose substrings from a one-character string to build a string with more than one character. That would be impossible!

There's actually one more base case here ❸, and it kicks in when characters a[i] and b[j] are not equal. In this case, we return 0 right away, because there's no way to use that final character a[i] to match b[j].

Now we arrive at the code for implementing each of the two categories. Each one adds its contribution to the total variable.

For Category 1, we need a loop ❹ that tries each relevant ending point of a, adding the subproblem answers to total ❺. We use the mod operator here as required by the problem description.

For Category 2, we don't need a loop: we just solve the one subproblem that directly gives us the answer ❻.

### Collecting the Solutions

We need to call solve_ijk using all values of i. That's because any character of a might match the rightmost character of b. The code that calls solve_ijk in the needed ways is in Listing 4-7.

```
int solve(char a[], char b[], int a_length, int b_length,
          int num_substrings) {
  int i, j, k, result;
  static int memo[MAX_A][MAX_B][MAX_K + 1];
  for (i = 0; i < a_length; i++)
    for (j = 0; j < b_length; j++)
      for (k = 0; k <= num_substrings; k++)
        memo[i][j][k] = -1;
  result = 0;
  for (i = 0; i < a_length; i++) {
    result = result + solve_ijk(a, b, i, b_length - 1, num_substrings, memo);
    result = result % MOD;
  }
  return result;
}
```

*Listing 4-7: Solution 1*

In our prior dynamic-programming problems, we used min or max to find the best solution. But notice in Listing 4-6 and Listing 4-7 that we're not doing that. Instead, because we want to find the total number of solutions, we are adding everything together using +.

### The main Function

The main function for this solution is in Listing 4-8.

```
int main(void) {
  int a_length, b_length, num_substrings;
  char a[MAX_A + 1], b[MAX_B + 1];
  scanf("%d%d%d", &a_length, &b_length, &num_substrings);
  scanf("%s", a);
  scanf("%s", b);
  printf("%d\n", solve(a, b, a_length, b_length, num_substrings));
  return 0;
}
```

*Listing 4-8: The main function*

Now we have a complete solution to this problem. Feel free to submit to the judge.

Prepare to be disappointed.

## Solution 2: Adding More Subproblems

For the first time in this book, we have received a "Time-Limit Exceeded" error when using memoization. The thing is, even if we use memoization or dynamic programming, we may still have to be concerned with the efficiency of our algorithm. Some problems admit multiple such solutions that, while faster than exponential time, may still differ from each other in terms of their efficiency.

## Runtime of Solution 1

Let's use $m$ for the length of the source string, $n$ for the length of the target string, and $k$ for the number of substrings we need to take. There are a total of about $mnk$ subproblems that our solution may end up solving. For each, we get hammered by Category 1 solutions, which require that we loop through the source string, adding another factor of $m$ to our runtime. What we have, then, is an algorithm that takes a number of steps proportional to $m^2nk$. To see how bad this is, let's substitute the maximum values for these variables here: 1,000 for $m$, 200 for $n$, and 200 for $k$. This will give us $1,000^2 \times 200 \times 200 = 40,000,000,000$. Forty billion! And we need to get all of this done with a two-second time limit? Not gonna happen. We need to do better. As we'll see, we'll be able to drop one of the factors of $m$ and solve this thing in just $O(mnk)$ time.

There are two general strategies we might consider at this point. The first is to throw our existing subproblems away and try again with new subproblems. I tried doing that; you can check the online resources for this book to see what I came up with. It didn't help.

Throwing those subproblems away in this case is a needlessly drastic move. After all, we have a correct and reasonably efficient solution; the only hitch is the loop that we need for each subproblem in Category 1.

The second strategy, and the one that we will succeed with here, is to add new subproblems to our existing subproblems. This second strategy may seem counterintuitive. You might reason that if our program is already too slow, adding and solving more subproblems would just slow us down even further. But what if our new subproblems in fact helped us solve our existing subproblems faster? In particular, what if they gave us a way to solve subproblems from Category 1 without the need of a loop? And what if we could also solve those new subproblems efficiently? Then we'd be golden! We'll be solving more subproblems, yes, but we'll make up for it bigtime with how efficiently we can solve each subproblem. Let's try!

## The New Subproblems

Remember this bit of code from Listing 4-6?

```
for (q = 0; q < i; q++)
  total = (total + solve_ijk(a, b, q, j - 1, k - 1, memo)) % MOD;
```

That's the loop that adds up all of the ways in Category 1. It's the loop we need to eliminate.

This q loop keeps j - 1 and k - 1 fixed, and varies the first subproblem parameter from 0 to i - 1. That is, it solves the $0, j-1, k-1$ subproblem, then the $1, j-1, k-1$ subproblem, then the $2, j-1, k-1$ subproblem, and so on.

How awesome would it be if we could look up, in one shot, the sum of all of these subproblem answers? Then we wouldn't need the q loop at all. This is what our new subproblems are going to do for us. For example, a new subproblem with parameters $i = 4$, $j$, and $k$ will be the sum of five of our old subproblems: the ones with the same $j$ and $k$ values, but where $i$ is 0, 1, 2, 3, or 4. That is, the new subproblems drop the requirement that $a[i]$ is the same character as $b[j]$. Here are the definitions for both our old and new subproblems.

### Old

The old subproblem with parameters $i$, $j$, and $k$ is going to tell us the number of ways that we can choose exactly $k$ substrings from $a[0..i]$ to build exactly $b[0..j]$, with the restriction that the rightmost substring ends with exactly the character $a[i]$.

### New

The new subproblem with parameters $i$, $j$, and $k$ is going to tell us the number of ways that we can choose exactly $k$ substrings from $a[0..i]$ to build exactly $b[0..j]$.

Now, with these new subproblems, let's return to our running example. What's our answer for the new subproblem with $i = 6$, $j = 3$, and $k = 3$? This time it really is 11! The subproblem is asking, with no restrictions, for all the ways that we can choose exactly three substrings from $a$ to build $b$. And we know that there are 11 of them. Notice, as a nice side bonus here, that we no longer need to solve multiple subproblems as in Listing 4-7. All we need is the answer to one subproblem: the one that includes all characters of $a$, all characters of $b$, and the number of substrings $k$.

### Solving the Needed Subproblem

Let's jump to the new code. For each triple of values i, j, and k, we're going to store answers not for one, but for two subproblems. We'll use a C struct to collect both:

```
typedef struct pair {
  int end_at_i;
  int total;
} pair;
```

The end_at_i member will store the number of solutions for our old subproblems (the ones from Solution 1), and the total member will store the number of solutions for our new subproblems. Our memo array stays as a three-dimensional array, with each element now consisting of both end_at_i and total. Other possible designs include two separate three-dimensional memo arrays or a four-dimensional array where the new dimension is of length 2.

Now we can write the code that will solve both our old and new subproblems.

In all of our memoization and dynamic-programming code thus far, we had to figure out one answer for each setting of the subproblem parameters. But here we need to figure out two, one for each member of the struct. Look out for that as you read through the code. Check it out in Listing 4-9.

```
pair solve(char a[], char b[], int i, int j, int k,
           pair memo[MAX_A][MAX_B][MAX_K + 1]) {
  int total, end_at_i;
  if (memo[i][j][k].total != -1)
    return memo[i][j][k];
  if (j == 0 && k == 1) {
❶ if (a[i] != b[j]) {
      if (i == 0)
        total = 0;
      else
      ❷ total = solve(a, b, i - 1, j, k, memo).total;
    ❸ memo[i][j][k] = (pair){0, total};
    } else {
      if (i == 0)
        total = 1;
      else
        total = 1 + solve(a, b, i - 1, j, k, memo).total;
      memo[i][j][k] = (pair){1, total};
    }
    return memo[i][j][k];
  }
  if (i == 0 || j == 0 || k == 0) {
    memo[i][j][k] = (pair){0, 0};
    return memo[i][j][k];
  }
  if (a[i] != b[j])
    end_at_i = 0;
  else {
  ❹ end_at_i = (solve(a, b, i - 1, j - 1, k - 1, memo).total +
          ❺ solve(a, b, i - 1, j - 1, k, memo).end_at_i);
    end_at_i = end_at_i % MOD;
  }
❻ total = (end_at_i + solve(a, b, i - 1, j, k, memo).total) % MOD;
  memo[i][j][k] = (pair){end_at_i, total};
  return memo[i][j][k];
}
```

*Listing 4-9: Solution 2*

As in Solution 1, a critical case here is when j is 0 and k is 1. There are
two important subcases to consider.

Let's begin with the one where a[i] and b[j] are different characters ❶.
We know that the end_at_i number of solutions is 0 here, as it would be in
Solution 1. But the total number of solutions might not be 0. For example,
if i were 4 and each of the first three characters of a were the same as b[0],
then our answer would be 3 here. To get them all, we make a recursive call
to find the total number of matches using the characters from a up to index

i - 1 ❷. We then store in our memo array both the total answer that we calculated and the end_at_i answer of 0 ❸.

Our handling of the subcase where a[i] and b[j] are the same character is similar; we just need to add 1 to both end_at_i and total to account for the match between a[i] and b[j].

Now let's work on how to solve the current end_at_i subproblem. Recall that Category 1 involves using *a*[*i*] as the final substring, and Category 2 involves using at least two characters for the final substring.

It's easier to talk through Category 2, so let's do that one first. That code is nearly the same as before: we retrieve the number of end_at_i solutions using the subproblem parameters i - 1, j - 1, and k ❺.

What about our new code for Category 1? This is our moment of victory, because we can solve such a subproblem in a single step ❹ by looking up the needed total subproblem directly!

There's one final thing that we need to do. After all, we have those new total subproblems now. It's our responsibility to solve those, too, so that they're correct when we look them up. Fortunately, we'll be able to solve each total subproblem quickly as well. To do it, we make use of the fact that we just found the number of solutions that use a[i]. We can just add that to the old total for i - 1 to get our final total ❻.

There's a nice interplay here between the end_at_i subproblems and the total subproblems in that we use each to efficiently solve the other. This is the core reason why adding our new total subproblems helped us: they speed up the computation of the end_at_i subproblems and, having quickly solved the relevant end_at_i subproblem, we can repay the favor and quickly solve the total subproblem as well.

### The main Function

All we need now is our main function. See the code in Listing 4-10.

```
int main(void) {
  int a_length, b_length, num_substrings, i, j, k, result;
  char a[MAX_A + 1];
  char b[MAX_B + 1];
  static pair memo[MAX_A][MAX_B][MAX_K + 1];
  scanf("%d%d%d", &a_length, &b_length, &num_substrings);
  scanf("%s", a);
  scanf("%s", b);
  for (i = 0; i < a_length; i++)
    for (j = 0; j < b_length; j++)
      for (k = 0; k <= num_substrings; k++)
        memo[i][j][k] = (pair){-1, -1};
  result = solve(a, b, a_length - 1, b_length - 1, num_substrings, memo).total;
  printf("%d\n", result);
  return 0;
}
```

*Listing 4-10: The main function*

If you submit this solution to the judge, you should be able to pass all test cases in time.

## Summary

In this chapter, we've learned that dynamic-programming problems can be solved forward or backward, and that sometimes it matters a great deal which we choose. We've also learned that our initial solution approach may not be fast enough, at which point we need to reconsider our subproblems or add new subproblems.

Can't get enough of this? You may be happy to know that ideas related to dynamic programming often make cameos in other algorithms. In the next chapter, for example, you'll see that we'll once again store results for later lookup. And in Chapter 7, you'll see a problem in which dynamic programming plays a supporting role, speeding up computation required by the main algorithm of interest.

## Notes

The Jumper is originally from the 2007 Croatian Regional Competition in Informatics. Ways to Build is originally from the 2015 National Olympiad in Informatics in Provinces.

# 5

## GRAPHS AND BREADTH-FIRST SEARCH

In this chapter, we'll study three problems in which we're asked to solve puzzles in the minimum number of moves. How quickly can a knight catch a pawn? How quickly can a student climb a rope in gym class? How cheaply can we translate a book written in one language to other target languages? Breadth-first search (BFS) is the unifying algorithm here. BFS dispatches these problems, and it applies more generally whenever we want to solve a puzzle with the minimum number of moves. Along the way, we'll learn about graphs, a powerful way to model and solve problems that involve objects and connections between those objects.

## Problem 1: Knight Chase

This is DMOJ problem ccc99s4.

### The Problem

This problem concerns two players, a pawn and a knight, playing a board game. (Don't worry: you don't need to know anything about chess.)

The board has $r$ rows, with row 1 at the bottom and row $r$ at the top. The board has $c$ columns, with column 1 at the left and column $c$ at the right.

The pawn and knight each start on their own square of the board. The pawn moves first, then the knight moves, then the pawn, then the knight, and so on, until the game ends. For each turn, a move must be made: remaining at the current square is not an option.

The pawn has no choice on what move to make: for each of its turns, it moves up one square.

The knight, by contrast, has up to eight choices for each move:

- Up 1, right 2
- Up 1, left 2
- Down 1, right 2
- Down 1, left 2
- Up 2, right 1
- Up 2, left 1
- Down 2, right 1
- Down 2, left 1

I say "up to eight choices," not "exactly eight choices," because moves that bring the knight outside of the board are not allowed. For example, if the board has 10 columns and the knight is in column 9, then no move that takes the knight two columns to the right is allowed.

The following diagram shows the knight's available moves:

|   |   |   |   |   |   |   |
|---|---|---|---|---|---|---|
|   |   | f |   | e |   |   |
|   | b |   |   |   | a |   |
|   |   |   | K |   |   |   |
|   | d |   |   |   | c |   |
|   |   | h |   | g |   |   |
|   |   |   |   |   |   |   |

Here, the knight is represented as K, and each letter from a to h represents one of its possible moves.

The game ends when one of three things happens: the knight wins, the game is a stalemate (that is, a tie), or the knight loses.

**Win**  The knight wins if the knight makes a move and lands on the same square as the pawn before the pawn reaches the top row. To win, the knight has to be the one to make the move; if the pawn makes a move and lands on the knight, this doesn't count as the knight winning.

**Stalemate**   The game is a stalemate if the knight makes a move and lands on the square above the pawn before the pawn reaches the top row. Again, the knight has to be the one to make this move; the only exception is that the game can start as a stalemate if the knight starts one square above the pawn.

**Loss**   The knight loses if the pawn reaches the top row before the game otherwise ends. That is, if the pawn gets to the top row before the knight lands on the pawn or lands on the square above it, then the knight loses. Once the pawn reaches the top row, the knight is not allowed to move anymore.

The goal is to determine the best-case outcome for the knight and the number of knight moves required to produce that outcome.

### Input

The first line of input gives the number of test cases that will follow. Each test case consists of six lines:

- The number of rows in the board, between 3 and 99

- The number of columns in the board, between 2 and 99

- The starting row of the pawn

- The starting column of the pawn

- The starting row of the knight

- The starting column of the knight

It's guaranteed that the pawn and knight will have different starting positions and that the knight starts at a position where it has at least one available move.

### Output

For each test case, output a line with one of three messages:

- If the knight can win, output `Win in m knight move(s)`.

- If the knight cannot win but can cause a stalemate, output `Stalemate in m knight move(s)`.

- If the knight cannot win or cause a stalemate, output `Loss in m knight move(s)`.

Here, $m$ is the minimum number of moves made by the knight.
   The time limit for solving the test cases is one second.


## *Moving Optimally*

A true two-player game, such as tic-tac-toe or chess, gives each player a choice of what move to make next. However, here, only the knight has a choice. The pawn's moves are all fixed, and we'll know exactly where the pawn is at all times. It's a good thing, too, because this problem would be significantly more difficult if both players had choices.

There may be various ways for the knight to win or cause a stalemate. Suppose that the knight can win. Each way that the knight can win requires some number of moves; we want to identify the minimum number of moves.

## Exploring the Board

Let's explore a little through this input:

---

1

7

7

1

1

4

6

---

The board for this test case has seven rows and seven columns. The pawn starts at row 1, column 1, and the knight starts at row 4, column 6.

Moving optimally, the knight can win here in three moves. The following diagram shows how the knight can do this:

| | 1 | 2 | 3 | 4 | 5 | 6 | 7 |
|---|---|---|---|---|---|---|---|
| 7 | | | | | | | |
| 6 | | K2 | | | | | |
| 5 | | | | K1 | | | |
| 4 | K3 P3 | | | | | K | |
| 3 | P2 | | | | | | |
| 2 | P1 | | | | | | |
| 1 | P | | | | | | |

Here, K is used for the knight's starting position and P for the pawn's starting position. K1, K2, and K3 give the location of the knight after move 1, move 2, and move 3, respectively; P1, P2, and P3 do likewise for the pawn.

The coordinates $(x, y)$ refer to row $x$, column $y$. As expected, the pawn simply marches up its column, from $(1, 1)$, to $(2, 1)$, to $(3, 1)$, and finally to $(4, 1)$. The knight, however, moves as follows:

1. Starting at $(4, 6)$, it moves up one and left two to $(5, 4)$. The pawn is at $(2, 1)$.

2. From $(5, 4)$, it moves up one and left two to $(6, 2)$. The pawn is at $(3, 1)$.

3. From $(6, 2)$, it moves down two and left one to $(4, 1)$. That's where the pawn is!

There are other ways for the knight to win. For example, here's what can happen if the knight goofs off a little:

| 7 |       |    |    |    |   |   |   |
|---|-------|----|----|----|---|---|---|
| 6 |       | K2 |    |    |   |   |   |
| 5 | K4 P4 |    |    | K1 |   |   |   |
| 4 | P3    |    | K3 |    |   | K |   |
| 3 | P2    |    |    |    |   |   |   |
| 2 | P1    |    |    |    |   |   |   |
| 1 | P     |    |    |    |   |   |   |
|   | 1     | 2  | 3  | 4  | 5 | 6 | 7 |

The knight catches the pawn after four moves, not three. Though the knight still wins, this is *not* the fastest way that it can do so. We need to report a minimum of three moves here, not four.

Suppose that we had an algorithm to determine the minimum number of moves that the knight can take from its starting point to some destination. We could then determine the number of knight moves required to get to each pawn location; if the knight can get there at the same time as the pawn, then the knight wins. If the knight cannot win, then we could do similarly for stalemates. That is, we could determine the number of knight moves required to get to the square above each pawn location; if at any point the knight can land on the square above the pawn, we have a stalemate.

To design such an algorithm, we can explore the board from the knight's starting point. There's only one square on the board that is reachable in zero moves: the knight's starting point itself. From there, we can discover those squares that are reachable in one move. From those squares that are one move away, we can discover those squares that are reachable in two moves. We can use those squares reachable in two moves to find those reachable in three moves, and so on. We stop when we find the desired destination; at that point, we'll know the minimum number of moves that it takes to get there.

Let's demonstrate this procedure using the same test case as before: seven rows and seven columns, with the knight starting at $(4, 6)$. (We'll ignore the pawn for now.) To confirm our answer of three moves that we arrived at by hand, we'll calculate the minimum number of moves for the knight to get from $(4, 6)$ to $(4, 1)$.

In the following diagrams, numbers in the squares indicate the minimum distance from the knight's starting point. As mentioned above, the only square reachable in zero moves is the knight's starting point itself, $(4, 6)$. We'll call this round 0 of the exploration:

From $(4, 6)$, we try all eight possible moves to identify the squares reachable in one move. We can't move up one and right two or down one and right two, because those would take us beyond the right edge of the board. That leaves six squares that are one move away. This is round 1:

| | 1 | 2 | 3 | 4 | 5 | 6 | 7 |
|---|---|---|---|---|---|---|---|
| **7** | | | | | | | |
| **6** | | | | | 1 | | 1 |
| **5** | | | | 1 | | | |
| **4** | | | | | | 0 | |
| **3** | | | | 1 | | | |
| **2** | | | | | | 1 | 1 |
| **1** | | | | | | | |

We haven't found $(4, 1)$ yet, so we keep going. We explore from each of those six new squares that we discovered in round 1; that will yield the squares that are two moves away. For example, consider square $(6, 5)$; the squares reachable from there are as follows:

- Up 1, right 2: $(7, 7)$
- Up 1, left 2: $(7, 3)$
- Down 1, right 2: $(5, 7)$
- Down 1, left 2: $(5, 3)$
- Up 2, right 1: (which is not valid)
- Up 2, left 1: (which is not valid)
- Down 2, right 1: $(4, 6)$
- Down 2, left 1: $(4, 4)$

These squares are two moves away from the starting point—except for $(4, 6)$, whose value $(0)$ we filled in before! Looking at all valid moves from all squares that are one move away brings us to round 2, the squares that are two moves away.

| 7 | | | 2 | | 2 | | 2 |
|---|---|---|---|---|---|---|---|
| 6 | | 2 | | | 1 | 2 | 1 |
| 5 | | | 2 | 1 | 2 | | 2 |
| 4 | | 2 | | 2 | | 0 | |
| 3 | | | 2 | 1 | 2 | | 2 |
| 2 | | 2 | | | 1 | 2 | 1 |
| 1 | | | 2 | | 2 | | 2 |
| | **1** | **2** | **3** | **4** | **5** | **6** | **7** |

Notice that there cannot be any other squares that are two moves away. Every square that is two moves away must emanate from a square that is one move away, and we explored all possible moves from all possible squares that are one move away.

There is still no (4, 1), so we keep going. Exploring from all squares that are two moves away gives us round 3, the squares that are three moves away:

| 7 | | 3 | 2 | 3 | 2 | 3 | 2 |
|---|---|---|---|---|---|---|---|
| 6 | 3 | 2 | 3 | | 1 | 2 | 1 |
| 5 | | 3 | 2 | 1 | 2 | 3 | 2 |
| 4 | 3 | 2 | 3 | 2 | 3 | 0 | 3 |
| 3 | | 3 | 2 | 1 | 2 | 3 | 2 |
| 2 | 3 | 2 | 3 | | 1 | 2 | 1 |
| 1 | | 3 | 2 | 3 | 2 | 3 | 2 |
| | **1** | **2** | **3** | **4** | **5** | **6** | **7** |

There we have it: square (4, 1) is filled in with a value of 3. It therefore takes a minimum of three moves to get from (4, 6) to (4, 1). Had we not found (4, 1) here, we'd continue: we could proceed to find squares that are four moves away, then five moves away, and so on.

This technique—finding all squares that are zero moves away, then one move away, then two moves away, and so on—is called *breadth-first search*, or BFS for short. The word *breadth* refers to a full range. BFS is so named because we explore the full range of what is reachable from each square before moving on to other squares. BFS is fast, memory efficient, and clean to implement. It's an absolute power move to invoke BFS whenever you want the minimum distance from one location to another location. Let's go for it!

### Implementing Breadth-First Search

Let's start with a couple of type definitions that clean up our code a little. First, each board position is composed of a row and a column, so let's package those together using a struct:

```
typedef struct position {
  int row, col;
} position;
```

A board is a two-dimensional array, and we can make a type definition for that too. We'll let it hold integers, which will correspond to numbers of moves. We have a maximum of 99 rows and 99 columns, but we allocate one extra row and column so we can start indexing rows and columns at 1, not 0:

```
#define MAX_ROWS 99
#define MAX_COLS 99

typedef int board[MAX_ROWS + 1][MAX_COLS + 1];
```

Finally, let's make an array type for holding the positions that we discover during the BFS. We'll make it big enough that it can hold every possible square on the board:

```
typedef position positions[MAX_ROWS * MAX_COLS];
```

Now we're ready for the BFS itself. We need a function to determine the minimum number of knight moves to get from its starting point to some destination that we specify. (Recall that our plan is to find the minimum number of moves needed to catch the pawn at each pawn location.) Here's the signature for the function we'll implement:

```
int find_distance(int knight_row, int knight_col,
                  int dest_row, int dest_col,
                  int num_rows, int num_cols)
```

The parameters `knight_row` and `knight_col` give the starting location of the knight, and `dest_row` and `dest_col` give the desired destination. The parameters `num_rows` and `num_cols` give, respectively, the number of rows and columns in the board; we'll need those to determine whether a move is valid. The function returns the minimum number of moves for the knight to go from its starting location to the destination. If there's no way for the knight to get to the destination, then we return -1.

There are two key arrays that drive the BFS:

cur_positions   This array holds the positions discovered from the current round of BFS. For example, it might be all of the positions discovered in round 3.

new_positions   This array holds the positions discovered in the next round of BFS. For example, if cur_positions holds the positions discovered in round 3, then new_positions will hold those positions discovered in round 4.

The code is given in Listing 5-1.

```
int find_distance(int knight_row, int knight_col,
                  int dest_row, int dest_col,
                  int num_rows, int num_cols) {
  positions cur_positions, new_positions;
  int num_cur_positions, num_new_positions;
  int i, j, from_row, from_col;
  board min_moves;
  for (i = 1; i <= num_rows; i++)
    for (j = 1; j <= num_cols; j++)
      min_moves[i][j] = -1;
❶ min_moves[knight_row][knight_col] = 0;
❷ cur_positions[0] = (position){knight_row, knight_col};
  num_cur_positions = 1;

❸ while (num_cur_positions > 0) {
    num_new_positions = 0;
    for (i = 0; i < num_cur_positions; i++) {
      from_row = cur_positions[i].row;
      from_col = cur_positions[i].col;
❹    if (from_row == dest_row && from_col == dest_col)
        return min_moves[dest_row][dest_col];

❺    add_position(from_row, from_col, from_row + 1, from_col + 2,
                   num_rows, num_cols, new_positions,
                   &num_new_positions, min_moves);
      add_position(from_row, from_col, from_row + 1, from_col - 2,
                   num_rows, num_cols, new_positions,
                   &num_new_positions, min_moves);
      add_position(from_row, from_col, from_row - 1, from_col + 2,
                   num_rows, num_cols, new_positions,
                   &num_new_positions, min_moves);
```

```
        add_position(from_row, from_col, from_row - 1, from_col - 2,
                     num_rows, num_cols, new_positions,
                     &num_new_positions, min_moves);
        add_position(from_row, from_col, from_row + 2, from_col + 1,
                     num_rows, num_cols, new_positions,
                     &num_new_positions, min_moves);
        add_position(from_row, from_col, from_row + 2, from_col - 1,
                     num_rows, num_cols, new_positions,
                     &num_new_positions, min_moves);
        add_position(from_row, from_col, from_row - 2, from_col + 1,
                     num_rows, num_cols, new_positions,
                     &num_new_positions, min_moves);
        add_position(from_row, from_col, from_row - 2, from_col - 1,
                     num_rows, num_cols, new_positions,
                     &num_new_positions, min_moves);
      }

❻ num_cur_positions = num_new_positions;
   for (i = 0; i < num_cur_positions; i++)
     cur_positions[i] = new_positions[i];
   }
   return -1;
}
```

*Listing 5-1: The minimum number of knight moves using BFS*

The first thing we do is clear out the min_moves array by setting all values to -1; this means that we have not yet computed the number of moves. The only square for which we know the minimum number of moves is the knight's starting square, so we initialize that to 0 ❶. That starting square is also the square that jump-starts the BFS ❷. The while loop then runs as long as the most-recent round of BFS has discovered at least one new square ❸. Inside the while loop, we look at each such square. If we discover the destination square ❹, then we return its minimum number of moves. Otherwise, we keep exploring.

Exploring all eight moves from a given square is accomplished by eight calls to a helper function called add_position, which adds new squares to new_positions and updates num_new_positions accordingly. Focus on the first four arguments: those give the current row and column and the new row and column resulting from one of the eight moves. For example, the first call ❺ is for the move that goes up two and right one. We'll look at the code for add_position shortly.

We've gone through each square in cur_positions and found new squares that are one more move away. That completes one round of BFS. To prepare for the next round, we keep track of the number of new squares ❻ and copy all of the new squares from new_positions to cur_positions. That way, the next iteration of the while loop uses those new squares and finds further new squares from there.

If we reach the bottom of the code and haven't found the destination square, then we return -1—that destination square is not reachable from the knight's starting location.

Now for that add_position helper function; see Listing 5-2.

```
void add_position(int from_row, int from_col,
                  int to_row, int to_col,
                  int num_rows, int num_cols,
                  positions new_positions, int *num_new_positions,
                  board min_moves) {
  struct position new_position;
  if (to_row >= 1 && to_col >= 1 &&
      to_row <= num_rows && to_col <= num_cols &&
      min_moves[to_row][to_col] == -1) {
❶ min_moves[to_row][to_col] = 1 + min_moves[from_row][from_col];
    new_position = (position){to_row, to_col};
    new_positions[*num_new_positions] = new_position;
    (*num_new_positions)++;
  }
}
```

*Listing 5-2: Adding a position*

The if statement has five conditions, all of which must be true for to_row and to_col to be a valid position: the row must be at least one, the column must be at least one, the row must be at most the number of rows, the column must be at most the number of columns, and . . . hmm, that last one, min_moves[to_row][to_col] == -1, what's that doing?

That final condition is there to determine whether we've already seen this square. If we haven't, then it will have a value of -1 and we can go ahead and set its number of moves now. If it already has some other value, then it must have been discovered in an *earlier* round of BFS, and therefore it already has a smaller number of moves than what we could give it now. That is, a value other than -1 means that the minimum number of moves is already set, and we shouldn't mess with it.

If all five conditions pass, then we've discovered a new square. We discovered (from_row, from_col) in the previous round of BFS and (to_row, to_col) in the current round. Therefore, the minimum number of moves to (to_row, to_col) is one more than the minimum moves to (from_row, from_col) ❶. By virtue of (from_row, from_col) coming from the previous round of BFS, we already have its value stored in min_moves, and so we can simply look up its value without recalculating it.

You may see shades of memoization and dynamic programming here. It's true: BFS uses the same trick of looking stuff up rather than recomputing it. However, there's not really a notion of maximizing or minimizing a solution based on subproblem solutions or combining smaller solutions to form a larger solution. Algorithm developers therefore generally don't refer to BFS as a dynamic-programming algorithm, instead classifying it as a search or exploration algorithm.

## Best Knight Outcome

We've got BFS bottled up nicely as the find_distance function. Now let's count the number of moves as the pawn marches up its column and use find_distance to determine whether the knight can ever land on the pawn. For example, if the pawn takes three moves to get somewhere, and the knight can take exactly three moves to get there too, then the knight wins in three moves. If the knight can't win, then we can try a similar technique for stalemates: let the pawn march up its column again, this time checking whether the knight can cause a stalemate. If no stalemates are possible, well, then the knight loses. I've got this logic coded up in Listing 5-3. The function solve takes six parameters: the starting row and column of the pawn, the starting row and column of the knight, and the numbers of rows and columns in the board. It prints one line of output corresponding to whether the knight wins, stalemates, or loses.

```
// bugged!
void solve(int pawn_row, int pawn_col,
           int knight_row, int knight_col,
           int num_rows, int num_cols) {
  int cur_pawn_row, num_moves, knight_takes;

❶ cur_pawn_row = pawn_row;
  num_moves = 0;
  while (cur_pawn_row < num_rows) {
    knight_takes = find_distance(knight_row, knight_col,
                                 cur_pawn_row, pawn_col,
                                 num_rows, num_cols);
❷ if (knight_takes == num_moves) {
      printf("Win in %d knight move(s).\n", num_moves);
      return;
    }
    cur_pawn_row++;
    num_moves++;
  }

❸ cur_pawn_row = pawn_row;
  num_moves = 0;
  while (cur_pawn_row < num_rows) {
    knight_takes = find_distance(knight_row, knight_col,
                                 cur_pawn_row + 1, pawn_col,
                                 num_rows, num_cols);
    if (knight_takes == num_moves) {
      printf("Stalemate in %d knight move(s).\n", num_moves);
      return;
    }
    cur_pawn_row++;
    num_moves++;
```

```
    }

❹  printf("Loss in %d knight move(s).\n", num_rows - pawn_row - 1);
    }
```

*Listing 5-3: The best outcome for the knight (bugged!)*

Let's get a grip on this code by studying it in three chunks.

The first chunk is the code that checks whether the knight can win. We begin by saving the pawn's row in a new variable ❶—we'll mess with the pawn's row to move the pawn up the board, so we need to remember the row in which it originally started. The while loop keeps going as long as the pawn hasn't reached the top row. On each iteration, we calculate the number of moves that the knight needs to get to the same location as the pawn. If the knight can get there at the same time as the pawn ❷, then the knight can win. If the knight can't win, then the pawn will reach the top of the board and we'll continue below the while loop.

That's where the second chunk of code begins ❸. Its task is to determine whether the knight can cause a stalemate. The code is the same as the first chunk, except that in the while loop it checks the number of moves required for the knight to land on the row above the pawn rather than the row of the pawn.

The third chunk is a single line ❹, and it only executes if the knight cannot win or stalemate. This chunk simply outputs the loss message.

That's how we process a single test case. To read and process all of the test cases, we need a little main function; it's as simple as Listing 5-4.

```
int main(void) {
  int num_cases, i;
  int num_rows, num_cols, pawn_row, pawn_col, knight_row, knight_col;
  scanf("%d", &num_cases);
  for (i = 0; i < num_cases; i++) {
    scanf("%d%d", &num_rows, &num_cols);
    scanf("%d%d", &pawn_row, &pawn_col);
    scanf("%d%d", &knight_row, &knight_col);
    solve(pawn_row, pawn_col, knight_row, knight_col, num_rows, num_cols);
  }
  return 0;
}
```

*Listing 5-4: The main function*

Feeling good? We've now got a complete solution. We're using BFS to optimize the number of moves taken by the knight. We're checking for knight wins, stalemates, and losses. Now submit this solution to the judge. Are you still feeling good?

## The Knight Flip-Flop

In earlier chapters, I hit you with some solutions that were correct but too slow to pass the test cases. In contrast, what I've provided here for the Knight Chase problem is *incorrect*: there are test cases for which we produce the wrong output. Our code happens to be unnecessarily slow, too.

Let's fix it all!

### Making Our Code Correct

Our code is incorrect because it does not consider that the knight can sometimes be too fast! That is, it can get to a pawn's location before the pawn gets there. Testing for exactly the same number of pawn and knight moves is therefore too stringent.

A test case will clear this up:

```
1
5
3
1
1
3
1
```

This is a board with five rows and three columns; the pawn starts at row 1, column 1 and the knight starts at row 3, column 1. Here's what our current code outputs for this test case:

```
Loss in 3 knight move(s).
```

(The output is 3, not 4, because the knight is not allowed to move once the pawn reaches the top row.) This means that there is no win or stalemate location for which the minimum number of knight moves is the same as the number of pawn moves. That, at least, is true. However, it's still possible for the knight to win here and to do so in two moves. Take some time to try to identify how the knight can do this!

There's no way for the knight to win in one move if the pawn is at $(2, 1)$. However, after two moves, the pawn is at $(3, 1)$, and it's possible for the knight to land on $(3, 1)$ after two moves, too. Here's what the knight can do:

- Move 1: go from $(3, 1)$ to $(5, 2)$.
- Move 2: go from $(5, 2)$ back to $(3, 1)$.

The minimum number of moves for the knight to get to $(3, 1)$ is zero— it's the knight's starting point, after all. By going to some other square and returning, the knight can land on $(3, 1)$ not only after zero moves but after two moves as well.

Here's a self-check: change the knight's starting point from $(3, 1)$ to $(5, 3)$. Can you figure out how the knight can win now in three moves?

Generalizing, we can say that if the knight can get to a square in a minimum of $m$ moves, then it can also get to that square in $m + 2$ moves, or $m + 4$

moves, and so on. All it has to do is keep going to some other square and returning.

What this means for our solution is that, at each step, there are two ways for the knight to win or stalemate: it can do so because its minimum number of moves matches the number of pawn moves or because its minimum number of moves is an even number larger than the number of pawn moves.

That is, instead of:

```
if (knight_takes == num_moves) {
```

we need this:

```
if (knight_takes >= 0 && num_moves >= knight_takes &&
    (num_moves - knight_takes) % 2 == 0) {
```

Here, we're testing whether the difference between the number of pawn moves and the number of knight moves is a multiple of two.

There are two instances of the incorrect code in Listing 5-3; changing both yields the (correct!) code in Listing 5-5.

```
void solve(int pawn_row, int pawn_col,
           int knight_row, int knight_col,
           int num_rows, int num_cols) {
  int cur_pawn_row, num_moves, knight_takes;

  cur_pawn_row = pawn_row;
  num_moves = 0;
  while (cur_pawn_row < num_rows) {
    knight_takes = find_distance(knight_row, knight_col,
                                 cur_pawn_row, pawn_col,
                                 num_rows, num_cols);
❶  if (knight_takes >= 0 && num_moves >= knight_takes &&
        (num_moves - knight_takes) % 2 == 0) {
      printf("Win in %d knight move(s).\n", num_moves);
      return;
    }
    cur_pawn_row++;
    num_moves++;
  }

  cur_pawn_row = pawn_row;
  num_moves = 0;
  while (cur_pawn_row < num_rows) {
    knight_takes = find_distance(knight_row, knight_col,
                                 cur_pawn_row + 1, pawn_col,
                                 num_rows, num_cols);
❷  if (knight_takes >= 0 && num_moves >= knight_takes &&
        (num_moves - knight_takes) % 2 == 0) {
      printf("Stalemate in %d knight move(s).\n", num_moves);
```

```
        return;
    }
    cur_pawn_row++;
    num_moves++;
}

printf("Loss in %d knight move(s).\n", num_rows - pawn_row - 1);
}
```

*Listing 5-5: The best outcome for the knight*

As promised, all we've done is change two conditions ❶ ❷. Now the code passes the judge.

## A Correctness Argument

If you're suitably convinced of correctness, feel free to skip this section. Otherwise, I'd now like to address a possible concern that you may have at this point.

Suppose that the knight gets to a square an even number of moves ahead of the pawn and that this takes $m$ moves. Also suppose that the knight leaves and revisits this square as many times as it likes, returning to this square after $m + 2$ moves, $m + 4$ moves, and so on, eventually catching the pawn here. It would be scary if the knight could use some other sequence of moves to catch the pawn in $m + 1$ moves, or $m + 3$ moves, and so on, because then adding an odd number of moves could provide us a better minimum than adding an even number of moves. Fortunately, that can't happen.

Try this little experiment: choose a starting point and destination for the knight, and find the minimum number of moves that it takes for the knight to move from the starting point to the destination. That number of moves is $m$. Now try to find a way for the knight to get from that same starting point to that same destination using exactly one more move, or three more moves, and so on. For example, if the fastest way takes two moves, try to find a way to take three moves. You won't be able to do so.

Each knight move changes the row or column number by two and the other by one. For example, it might change the row number from six to four and the column number from four to five. Changing a number by two does not change whether that number is even or odd, but changing a number by one *does* change that number from even to odd or vice versa. That is, in terms of being even or odd, each move leaves one of the two numbers (row or column) alone, and it changes the other one. When a number changes from even to odd or vice versa, we say that its *parity* changes.

Let $k$ be an odd integer. Now we're ready to see why the knight can't take both $m$ moves and $m + k$ moves to get to the same destination. Suppose that the knight can take $m$ moves to get to square $s$, that $m_1$ of those moves change whether the row is even or odd, and that $m_2$ of those moves change whether the column is even or odd.

Let's say that $m_1$ and $m_2$ are both even. As such, the moves don't change the parity of the row or column: if we start with some number and flip its parity an even number of times, its parity doesn't change. If we make some other sequence of moves, and it flips the parity of the row an odd number of times or flips the parity of the column an odd number of times, then that sequence cannot land at $s$, because it will land on a square with different row or column parity than $s$.

Now, $m$, the total number of moves $m_1 + m_2$, is even: adding two even numbers gives an even number. But, $m + k$ is odd, because it's the sum of an even number and an odd number. And, since $m + k$ is odd, it cannot be built from an even number of moves that change the row and an even number of moves that change the column; at least one of them must be odd and therefore change the parity of the row or column. This is why these $m + k$ moves cannot result in the knight landing on $s$! (There are three other cases—$m_1$ even and $m_2$ odd, $m_1$ odd and $m_2$ even, and $m_1$ odd and $m_2$ odd—but I'll skip those. Their analysis is similar.)

## A Time Optimization

Our current solution (Listing 5-5) can make a lot of BFS calls. Each time the pawn moves up a row, we use BFS (by calling find_distance) to determine whether it can be caught there by the knight.

Suppose that the pawn starts at $(1, 1)$. We run a BFS from the knight's starting point to $(1, 1)$, and that explores some of the squares. Suppose that the knight can't catch the pawn here. We then have to run a BFS from the knight's starting point to $(2, 1)$. This explores some of the squares, too. However, $(1, 1)$ and $(2, 1)$ are very close together, to the point that the second BFS probably re-explores many of the squares whose shortest distances were discovered in the first BFS call. Unfortunately, each of our BFS calls is independent, so that second BFS call redoes a lot of the work that the first BFS call did. The third call then duplicates a lot of what the prior two BFS calls did, and on and on.

It's true that BFS is fast, and I'll give more details on why in the next section. Still, it pays to try to reduce the number of invocations of BFS.

I have good news: we can reduce the number of BFS calls to just . . . one! Recall our BFS code in Listing 5-1. We had code ❹ to cut our BFS short if we found the target position. However, if this code is removed, then the BFS will explore the entire board, calculating the shortest distance to each square. Making that change means that we can make one call to BFS and then be done with it. From then on, we just look up what we need in the min_moves array.

Do it! Make the required changes to the code so that BFS is called only one time.

The code we worked through together takes 0.1 seconds when I submit to the judge. With the "only one invocation of BFS" optimization, the code takes only 0.02 seconds, a speedup of 500 percent. More importantly, this optimization shows that BFS can be used not only to find the shortest distance from a starting position to some other position, but also to find the distance from the starting position to *all* other positions. I'll discuss BFS a little more in the next section. And keep reading after that, because I think the flexibility of BFS is going to surprise you.

# Graphs and BFS

BFS is a powerful search algorithm, as we saw in the solution to the Knight Chase problem. To run a BFS, we need what's called a *graph*. We didn't think about graphs when solving the Knight Chase problem—or perhaps didn't know what they were!—but there was indeed a graph underlying the BFS.

## What Are Graphs?

Figure 5-1 is our first example of a graph.

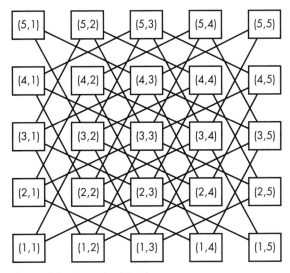

*Figure 5-1: A graph of knight moves*

Like a tree, a graph consists of *nodes* (the boxes) and *edges* between nodes (the lines). In this graph, the edges represent valid knight moves. For example, from the $(5, 1)$ node, the knight can move on an edge to $(4, 3)$ or on an edge to $(3, 2)$. There are no other edges involving $(5, 1)$, so there are no other knight moves from there.

Now I can explain how we implicitly used a graph to solve the Knight Chase problem. Suppose that $(5, 1)$ is the knight's starting position. Our BFS tries all eight moves from there, but six of them lead to a position that is outside of the board; in graph terminology, six of them are not edges from $(5, 1)$. The BFS discovers the two nodes that *are* reachable on an edge from $(5, 1)$: $(4, 3)$ and $(3, 2)$. The exploration then continues with the nodes reachable from each of these two nodes, and so on.

I laid the graph out as a grid to reflect the underlying board, but the way that a graph is drawn carries no meaning. All that matters are the nodes and edges. I could have drawn the graph with the nodes chaotically spread around, and it would have conveyed the same meaning. However, when the graph is rooted in some underlying geometry, it makes sense to display the graph in a corresponding way for easier interpretation.

To solve the Knight Chase problem, we didn't need to explicitly represent the graph in code, because we figured out the available moves (edges) from each node as we explored the board. Sometimes, though, we do need to represent a graph explicitly in code, along the lines of our tree representations in Chapter 2. We'll see how to do that in Problem 3.

### Graphs vs. Trees

Graphs and trees have a lot in common. They're both used to represent relationships between nodes. In fact, every tree is a graph, but there are graphs that are not trees. Graphs are more general, and they can express more than what trees can express.

First, graphs (but not trees) allow cycles. We have a *cycle* in a graph if we can start from a node and get back to it without using any repeated edges or nodes. (The first and last nodes in the cycle are the only ones that repeat.) Look back at Figure 5-1. Here's a cycle in that graph: $(5, 3) \rightarrow (4, 5) \rightarrow (3, 3) \rightarrow (4, 1) \rightarrow (5, 3)$.

Second, graphs (but not trees) can be *directed*. The trees and graph we've seen so far are *undirected*, meaning that if two nodes $a$ and $b$ are connected by an edge, then we can travel both from $a$ to $b$ and from $b$ to $a$. The graph in Figure 5-1 is undirected; for example, we can move from $(5, 3)$ on an edge to $(4, 5)$ and use that same edge to move from $(4, 5)$ to $(5, 3)$. Sometimes, though, we want to allow travel in only one direction, not the other. A *directed* graph is a graph in which each edge indicates the allowed direction of travel. Figure 5-2 depicts a directed graph.

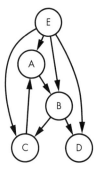

*Figure 5-2: A directed graph*

Note, in Figure 5-2, how it's possible to move from E to each of the other nodes, but it is not possible to move from any of those nodes to E. The edges are one-way edges.

Directed graphs are useful whenever an undirected graph would lead to loss of information. In my Computer Science department, each course has one or more prerequisite courses. For example, we have a C Programming course, which requires that students have already taken our Software Design course. A directed edge Software Design → C Programming captures this relationship. Had we used an undirected edge, we'd still know that the courses were related, but we wouldn't know the order in which the courses must be taken. Figure 5-3 shows a small prerequisite graph.

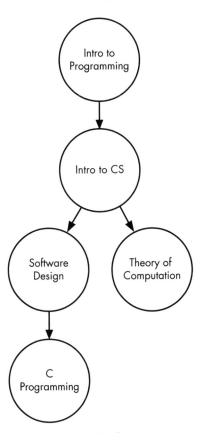

Figure 5-3: A graph of course prerequisites

The third thing that makes graphs more general than trees is that graphs can be *disconnected*. All trees and graphs we have seen to this point are *connected*, which means that you can get from any node to any other node. Now check out the disconnected graph in Figure 5-4.

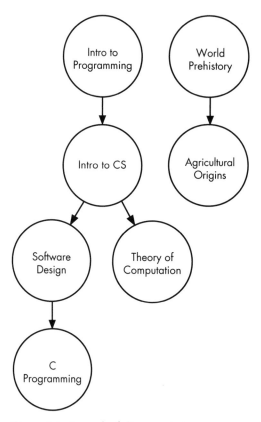

Figure 5-4: A graph of disconnected course prerequisites

It's disconnected because, for example, you can't follow a path from *Intro to Programming* to *World Prehistory*. Disconnected graphs are useful whenever a graph is naturally composed of separate pieces.

## BFS on Graphs

We can run BFS on an undirected graph (as we did for the Knight Chase problem) or a directed graph. The algorithm is the same: we go through the possible moves from the current node and explore them. BFS is known as a *shortest-path* algorithm: among all paths between a starting node and some other node, BFS gives us the shortest one in terms of the number of edges. As long as what we care about is minimizing the number of edges, it solves the *single-source shortest-paths* problem, since it finds shortest paths from a single source (or starting) node.

What we need to control to make BFS fast is not whether the graph is undirected or directed, but the number of times we invoke BFS and the number of edges in the graph. The runtime of a BFS call is proportional to the number of edges reachable from the starting node. That's because BFS looks at each edge once to determine whether it leads to the discovery of a new node. We call BFS a linear-time algorithm, since it does work linear in the number of edges: if 5 edges takes 5 steps for BFS to explore it, then

10 edges will take 10 steps. We'll use the number of edges to estimate the number of steps performed by BFS.

In the Knight Chase problem, we had a board with $r$ rows and $c$ columns. Each node has at most eight edges, so the board has at most $8rc$ edges in total. Therefore, running one BFS takes $8rc$ steps. For the biggest board, $99 \times 99$, this is fewer than 80,000 steps. If we call BFS on the order of $r$ times, as can happen in Listing 5-5, then we're looking at $8r^2c$ steps. Now the $99 \times 99$ board isn't looking so good: it could take over 7 million steps. This is why it helps so much to reduce the number of calls of BFS!

Any time a problem involves a set of objects (board locations, courses, people, websites, and so on) and relationships between those objects, it's a good bet that modeling the problem as a graph will help. Once you model a problem as a graph, you can take advantage of a huge number of fast algorithms on graphs. BFS is one of those algorithms.

### Graphs vs. Dynamic Programming

Sometimes it can be difficult to determine whether to use dynamic programming or a graph to solve a problem. The giveaway is often the presence of a cycle: if you have a cycle, then you need a graph.

None of the problems that we solved in Chapter 3 or Chapter 4 had a cycle. In Burger Fervor we recursed with fewer minutes. In Moneygrubbers we recursed with fewer needed apples. In Hockey Rivalry we recursed with fewer games. We always go down—there's no way to loop back to a higher number of minutes or apples or games to cause a cycle.

It's trickier to see that this is true for The Jumper in Chapter 4, but it is. Think back to our forward formulation. If we jump to the right, then we recurse with a bigger jump distance. If we jump to the left, then we recurse with the same jump distance but a smaller-numbered square. There's no way to start at a given subproblem and get back to it using these jumps. You might try to do that by making some jumps to the left and then making a jump to the right—but your jump to the right will have increased the jump distance by one and there's no way to decrease it by one ever again.

No cycle!

# Problem 2: Rope Climb

In the Knight Chase problem, we were explicitly given a board on which a game takes place. Here, we won't be given the board directly, so we'll have to work it out. Again, the strategy will be to model valid moves using BFS.

This is DMOJ problem wc18c1s3.

### The Problem

Bob is asked to climb a rope in gym class. The rope is infinitely long, but Bob is being asked to get only to a height of at least $h$ meters.

Bob starts at a height of 0. He knows how to jump up by exactly $j$ meters, but that's the only jump he knows how to do—so if $j$ is 5, then he can't jump up four or six meters or any other number of meters except five. In addition, Bob knows how to fall, and he can fall down any number of meters: one, two, three, and so on.

Each jump or fall counts as one move. For example, if Bob jumps up five meters, falls down two meters, jumps up five meters, and falls down eight meters, then Bob will have made four moves.

Now, here's the fun part: Alice has spread itching powder on some segments of the rope. If such a segment goes from height $a$ to height $b$, then the entire segment from $a$ to $b$, including the endpoints $a$ and $b$, has itching powder. The effect that the itching powder has on Bob's moves is as follows:

- Bob cannot jump up $j$ meters if that would land him on itching powder.

- Bob cannot fall down a given number of meters if that would land him on itching powder.

The goal is to determine the minimum number of moves needed for Bob to get to height $h$ or higher.

### Input

The input contains one test case, consisting of the following lines:

- A line containing three integers: $h$, $j$, and $n$. $h$ tells us the minimum height that Bob must reach, $j$ is the distance that Bob can jump up, and $n$ is the number of segments on which Alice has spread itching powder. Each integer is at most 1,000,000, and $j$ is at most $h$.

- $n$ lines, each of which contains two integers. The first integer gives the starting height for a segment of rope with itching powder; the second gives the ending height. Each integer is at most $h - 1$.

### Output

Output the minimum number of moves needed for Bob to reach height $h$ or higher. If there is no way for Bob to reach height $h$ or higher, output -1.

The time limit for solving the test case is 1.8 seconds.

## Solution 1: Finding the Moves

Let's start by making direct comparisons to the Knight Chase problem. Notice in both cases that our goal is to minimize the number of moves. Whether it's a knight on a board or Bob on a rope, the goal is the same. It's true that the knight was moving around a two-dimensional board and Bob is moving around a one-dimensional rope, but that just changes how we'll refer to each position. BFS won't otherwise care about the change from two dimensions to one. If anything, dropping one dimension simplifies things a little!

How about the number of possible moves from each position? The knight had at most eight of those. In contrast, the number of possible moves

Bob can make increases with his position. For example, if Bob is at a height of 4, and he can jump up by 5, then he has five possible moves: jump up by 5, fall down by 1, fall down by 2, fall down by 3, or fall down by 4. If Bob is at a height of 1,000, then he has 1,001 possible moves! So we'll have to take Bob's current position into account when determining the number of available moves.

What about the itching powder? Knight Chase doesn't have anything resembling that. Let's look at a test case to see what we're up against here:

---

```
10 4 1
8 9
```

---

Bob has to get to a height of 10 or higher. He can jump up by four. So, if there were no itching powder, he'd be able to jump from a height of 0 to 4, then to 8, and then to 12. That's three moves.

Bob can't do that, though! He isn't allowed to jump from 4 to 8, because there's itching powder at a height of 8 (as the itching powder goes from 8 to 9). The solution, by factoring in the itching powder, is four moves. For example, Bob can jump from 0 to 4, then fall to 3, then jump to 7, and then jump to 11. That jump from 7 to 11 breezes right past the itching powder.

The move from 4 to 8 seems available based on Bob's ability to jump up by four, but it is actually not available because of the itching powder. This isn't so different than a knight move being unavailable because it would take the knight outside of the board. For those invalid knight moves, we detected them in the BFS and didn't add them to the next round of positions. We'll handle itching powder similarly: any move that would cause Bob to land on itching powder will be disallowed in our BFS code.

Speaking of those invalid knight moves that take the knight outside of the board, do we have to worry about that kind of thing here? The rope is infinitely long, so we won't break any rules by letting Bob climb higher and higher. However, at some point we really do have to stop; otherwise, the BFS will forever be finding and exploring new positions. I'll invoke the insight from Moneygrubbers in Chapter 3 that helped us out of a very similar bind when buying apples. We said there that if we're asked to buy 50 apples, then we should consider buying at most 149 apples, because each pricing scheme gives us at most 100 apples. Here, remember from the problem description that $j$, the distance that Bob jumps up, is at most $h$, the minimum target height. We shouldn't let Bob get to height $2h$ or higher. Think about what it would mean the first time we got Bob to height $2h$ or higher. One move prior, Bob would have been at height $2h - j \geq h$, and that would have taken one move less than getting Bob to height $2h$! Thus, getting Bob to height $2h$ or higher can't be the fastest way to get him to at least height $h$.

### Implementing Breadth-First Search

We'll very closely follow what we did for the Knight Chase problem, making changes only when necessary. Back then, each knight position consisted of both a row and a column, so we created a struct to hold both of those pieces of information. Now, a position on a rope is just an integer, so we don't need a struct for that. We'll make type definitions for the "board" and the positions discovered by BFS:

```
#define SIZE 1000000

typedef int board[SIZE * 2];
typedef int positions[SIZE * 2];
```

It may seem a little weird to call a rope a board, I suppose, but it serves the same purpose as the corresponding type definition in the Knight Chase problem, so let's stick with it.

We're eventually going to make a single call of BFS, and that call is going to calculate the minimum number of moves for Bob to get from a height of zero to each valid position. The code for the BFS is given in Listing 5-6—compare this to the find_distance code in Listing 5-1. (Especially, compare it to the code I hope you wrote after reading "A Time Optimization" on page 168.)

```
void find_distances(int target_height, int jump_distance,
                    int itching[], board min_moves) {
  static positions cur_positions, new_positions;
  int num_cur_positions, num_new_positions;
  int i, j, from_height;
  for (i = 0; i < target_height * 2; i++)
❶   min_moves[i] = -1;
  min_moves[0] = 0;
  cur_positions[0] = 0;
  num_cur_positions = 1;

  while (num_cur_positions > 0) {
    num_new_positions = 0;
    for (i = 0; i < num_cur_positions; i++) {
      from_height = cur_positions[i];

❷     add_position(from_height, from_height + jump_distance,
                  target_height * 2 - 1,
                  new_positions, &num_new_positions,
                  itching, min_moves);
❸     for (j = 0; j < from_height; j++)
        add_position(from_height, j,
                    target_height * 2 - 1,
                    new_positions, &num_new_positions,
                    itching, min_moves);
    }

    num_cur_positions = num_new_positions;
    for (i = 0; i < num_cur_positions; i++)
      cur_positions[i] = new_positions[i];
```

```
    }
}
```

*Listing 5-6: Minimum number of moves for Bob using BFS*

There are four parameters for this find_distances function:

**target_height**  The minimum height that Bob must reach. It's the *h* value from the test case.

**jump_distance**  The distance that Bob can jump up. It's the *j* value from the test case.

**itching**  An array that indicates where itching powder is present. If itching[i] is 0, then there's no itching powder at height i; otherwise, there is. (Looking ahead, we'll have to build this array from the segments of itchy rope given in the test case. But we'll be able to do that, and then we won't have to worry about the particular segments themselves: we can just index this array.)

**min_moves**  The board in which we'll store the minimum number of moves to get to each position.

As in Listing 5-1 for Knight Chase, we initialize each position of the board to -1 ❶, which means that BFS hasn't found this position yet. That initialization, as with any other manipulation of board here, indexes a one-dimensional (not two-dimensional!) array. Other than that, the structure is quite similar to the BFS code for Knight Chase.

There is, however, an interesting structural change to the code that adds positions. Bob has exactly one jump distance, so there's only one jump move to consider ❷: Bob starts at from_height and ends up, if it's a valid position, at from_height + jump_distance. We can use target_height * 2 - 1 to get the maximum height that Bob is allowed to reach. For falling down, we cannot hard-code Bob's available moves; those moves depend on Bob's current height. To handle that, we use a loop ❸ to consider all destination heights from 0 (the ground) up to but not including from_height (Bob's current height). This loop is the only significant change from the Knight Chase BFS.

To wrap up our BFS code, we need to implement the add_position helper function. That code is given in Listing 5-7.

```
void add_position(int from_height, int to_height, int max_height,
                  positions new_positions, int *num_new_positions,
                  int itching[], board min_moves) {
  if (to_height <= max_height && itching[to_height] == 0 &&
      min_moves[to_height] == -1) {
    min_moves[to_height] = 1 + min_moves[from_height];
    new_positions[*num_new_positions] = to_height;
    (*num_new_positions)++;
  }
}
```

*Listing 5-7: Adding a position*

Bob wants to move from from_height to to_height. This move is allowed if it passes three tests. First, Bob can't be jumping above the maximum allowed height. Second, he can't be jumping somewhere that has itching powder. Third, the min_moves board better not have already recorded a number of moves for to_height: if a value is already in there, then it has a faster way to get to to_height. If we passed these tests, then we've found a new, valid position; we set the number of moves to get there and then store this as a position for the next round of BFS.

### Finding the Best Height

There are many possibilities for Bob's final position. It could be the target height $h$ from the test case. However, depending on $j$ and the itching powder, it could be higher than that. We know for each position the minimum number of moves to get there. What we have to do now is check all of the candidate positions, choosing the one that minimizes the number of moves. That code is given in Listing 5-8.

```
void solve(int target_height, board min_moves) {
❶ int best = -1;
  int i;
  for (i = target_height; i < target_height * 2; i++)
  ❷ if (min_moves[i] != -1 && (best == -1 || min_moves[i] < best))
      best = min_moves[i];
  printf("%d\n", best);
}
```

*Listing 5-8: The minimum number of moves*

It's possible that Bob can't get to his target height, so we start best off with a value of -1 ❶. For each candidate height, we then check whether it's possible for Bob to land there. If he can, and doing so is faster than our current minimum number of moves best ❷, then we update best accordingly.

We've now got all the code to process a test case and output the result. All that's left is to read the input. The main function in Listing 5-9 does that.

```
int main(void) {
  int target_height, jump_distance, num_itching_sections;
  static int itching[SIZE * 2] = {0};
  static board min_moves;
  int i, j, itch_start, itch_end;
  scanf("%d%d%d", &target_height, &jump_distance, &num_itching_sections);
  for (i = 0; i < num_itching_sections; i++) {
    scanf("%d%d", &itch_start, &itch_end);
  ❶ for (j = itch_start; j <= itch_end; j++)
    ❷ itching[j] = 1;
  }
  find_distances(target_height, jump_distance, itching, min_moves);
  solve(target_height, min_moves);
```

```
    return 0;
}
```

*Listing 5-9: The main function*

As is typical for large arrays, we have made `itching` and `min_moves` static. The elements of `itching` are initialized to 0, which means that there is no itching powder yet on the rope. For each segment where there is itching powder on the rope, we loop through each integer in the range ❶ and set the corresponding element of `itching` to 1 ❷. Once we're done looping through the itchy segments, each index of `itching` tells us if the rope does (value 1) or does not (value 0) have itching powder there. We no longer care about the individual itchy segments themselves—we have all that we need in `itching`.

That's it. We've got a solution that uses a single call of BFS. It's time to submit to the judge. As some might say, Bob's your uncle . . .

Or, hopefully he will be, but he's not yet. Because you should receive a "Time-Limit Exceeded" error with this code.

## Solution 2: A Remodel

Let's run test cases of increasing size to get a sense of how our runtime is growing. To simplify things, we won't use any itching powder. Here's the first test case:

```
30000 5 0
```

That's a target height of at least 30,000, with a jump distance of 5. On my laptop, that takes about eight seconds. Now let's double the target height:

```
60000 5 0
```

I'm looking at about 30 seconds here. That's nearly four times longer than in the previous case. We've long blown past the 1.8-second time limit, but let's do this one more time, doubling the target height again:

```
120000 5 0
```

That gives a glacially slow 130 seconds, approximately another fourfold increase from the previous test case. That is, it seems that doubling the input size leads to the runtime being multiplied by four. This isn't as catastrophic as what we saw in "Solution 2: Memoization" when solving Burger Fervor in Chapter 3, but it's clearly too slow.

### Too Many Fall Edges

In "BFS on Graphs" on page 172, I warned that we need to keep two things in check when using BFS: the number of times we call BFS and the number of edges in the graph. We're doing as well as possible with the number of BFS calls, as we only call BFS once. To further pursue a solution based on BFS, then, we need a way to reduce the number of edges in the graph.

Let's take a look at the graph for a small example shown in Figure 5-5. We'll then be able to extrapolate to larger examples and see why our code churrs and churrs.

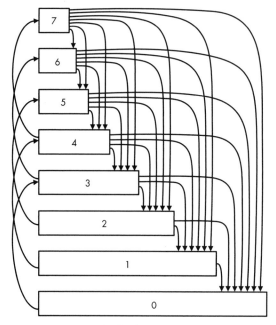

Figure 5-5: A graph of Bob's moves

The graph shows the available moves from a height of 0 to a height of 7, if we assume that Bob can jump up by 3. This is an example of a directed graph; notice, for example, that there is a move from 6 to 5 but not one from 5 to 6.

The graph contains jump edges that encode Bob's possible jumps and fall edges that encode Bob's possible falls. The jump edges go from the bottom to the top and the fall edges go from the top to the bottom. For example, the edge from a height of 0 to a height of 3 is a jump edge; the aforementioned edge from 6 to 5 is a fall edge.

The number of jump edges isn't worrisome at all. We have at most one jump edge per node. If we have $n$ nodes, then we have at most $n$ jump edges. If we decide to model up to a height of 8 instead of 7, then we'd add only one new jump edge.

However, the fall edges proliferate at a much faster rate. Notice that there is one fall edge from a height of 1, two fall edges from 2, three fall edges from 3, and so on. That is, for a rope of height $h$, we have a total of $1 + 2 + 3 + \ldots + h$ fall edges. If we want to know how many fall edges there are for a given rope height, we could add up the integers from 1 to that height. There is, however, a convenient formula that we can use instead to get the answer much faster. It's $h(h + 1)/2$. For a rope height of 50, for example, we'd have $50(51)/2 = 1,275$ fall edges. For a rope height of two million, we'd have over two trillion fall edges.

Back in Chapter 1, we saw a very similar formula in "Diagnosing the Problem" on page 9, when we were counting pairs of snowflakes. Like that one, our formula here is quadratic, being $O(h^2)$, and it's this quadratic growth in fall edges that bests our algorithm.

## Changing the Moves

If we're going to reduce the number of edges in the graph, then we're going to have to change the available moves that the graph encodes. We can't change the rules of the actual game that Bob plays in gym class, but we *can* change the moves in our graph model of the game. Of course, we are only able to change the graph if a BFS on the new graph produces the same answer as a BFS on the old graph.

There's an important lesson here. It's tempting to map the available moves, one for one, from the real-world problem to the graph. We did that for Knight Chase and succeeded in solving the problem. While this might be tempting, it's not a requirement. We can produce a different graph, one with a more desirable number of nodes or edges, as long as that graph can still give us the answer to the original problem.

Suppose that we want to fall some distance from a height of five meters. One possibility might be to fall four meters. Indeed, solving the problem as in Solution 1, there would be a fall edge from a height of 5 down to 1. However, another way to think of this fall is as four falls of one meter each. That is, we can think of Bob falling from 5 to 4, then falling to 3, then falling to 2, and then falling finally to 1. That is, I'm imagining that every fall edge would be exactly one meter long. No more fall edges like those from a height of 5 to 3, or 5 to 2, or 5 to 1, or 5 to 0. There would be just one fall edge from each node, bringing us one meter lower. This should drastically cut down on the number of fall edges!

We have to be careful, though. We can't let each of these mini, one-meter falls count as a move. If Bob falls four meters, using four one-meter-fall edges, then we still have to count it as a single move, not four moves.

Imagine that we have two ropes (0 and 1), not one. Rope 0 is the rope that we've always had. Alice set it up. It might have itching powder. Rope 1 is new, devised by us, for the purposes of modeling. It has no itching powder. In addition, when Bob is on Rope 1, he's not allowed to move upward.

When Bob wants to make a fall move, he will move from Rope 0 to Rope 1. He'll stick with Rope 1, falling, for as long as he wants to fall. Then, at any point where there isn't itching powder on Rope 0, he can end his fall by moving back to Rope 0. Specifically, we have the following moves now:

- When Bob is on Rope 0, he has two possible moves: jump up by $j$ meters or move over to Rope 1. Each costs one move.

- When Bob is on Rope 1, he has two possible moves: fall by one meter or move over to Rope 0. Each costs 0 moves. That's right: these moves are free!

Bob jumps up as before, using Rope 0. When he wants to fall, he moves to Rope 1 (that costs him one move), falls down Rope 1 as much as he likes (that's free), and then moves back to Rope 0 (that's free, too). The whole fall, then, costs Bob just one move. Perfect—this is just as before! No one will know that we're using two ropes instead of one.

Compare Figure 5-5, with its mass of edges, to Figure 5-6, which depicts the two-ropes maneuver.

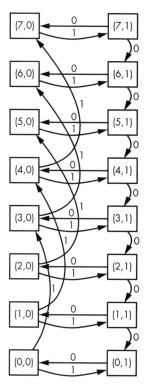

Figure 5-6: A graph of Bob's moves using two ropes

It's true that we've doubled the number of nodes, but that's okay: what we care about for BFS is not the number of nodes but the number of edges. On that front, we're laughing. We have, at most, two edges leaving each node: on Rope 0, we have a jump edge and a move to Rope 1; on Rope 1, we have a fall edge and a move to Rope 0. That is, for height $h$, we have about $4h$ edges. That's linear! We've avoided that messy quadratic $h^2$ business.

I've annotated each edge here with whether it costs a move (1) or doesn't (0). This is our first example of a *weighted* graph, where each edge is given a weight or cost.

### Adding Positions

We've meandered our way back to a two-dimensional board. (Hello, Knight Chase!) We need one dimension for Bob's height and the second for the rope that Bob is on. The standard terminology for that second dimension is a *state*. When Bob is on Rope 0, we'll say he's in state 0, and when Bob is on

Rope 1, we'll say he's in state 1. Let's use "state" from now on instead of "rope."

Here are the new typedefs:

```
typedef struct position {
  int height, state;
} position;

typedef int board[SIZE * 2][2];
typedef position positions[SIZE * 4];
```

Rather than start with find_distances, as we have been doing in this chapter, we'll start with the add_position functions. Yes: functions, plural, because we're going to encode each type of move as its own function. There are four types of moves: a jump up, a fall down, a move from State 0 to State 1, and a move from State 1 to State 0. Hence we'll need four add_position functions.

### Jumping Up

The code for following a jump edge is given in Listing 5-10.

```
void add_position_up(int from_height, int to_height, int max_height,
                     positions pos, int *num_pos,
                     int itching[], board min_moves) {
❶ int distance = 1 + min_moves[from_height][0];
  if (to_height <= max_height && itching[to_height] == 0 &&
❷   (min_moves[to_height][0] == -1 ||
      min_moves[to_height][0] > distance)) {
    min_moves[to_height][0] = distance;
    pos[*num_pos] = (position){to_height, 0};
    (*num_pos)++;
  }
}
```

Listing 5-10: Adding a position: jumping up

This function involves jumping up from from_height to to_height. This kind of move is allowed only in state 0; whenever we index min_moves, we'll therefore use 0 as the second index.

The code is similar to Listing 5-7, but with a few important changes. First, I've changed the name of new_positions to pos and num_new_positions to num_pos. We'll talk about the reason for this change to more generic parameter names after we've gone through the four functions.

Second, to facilitate comparison between the four functions, I've added a distance variable ❶ that indicates the number of moves it takes to get to to_height by using from_height. Here, it's one more move than the minimum number of moves to from_height, because we pay one move for this jump.

Third and finally, I've changed the part of the if condition that checks whether we've found a new position ❷. This is because a position might be discovered by an edge that counts as one move, but it could later be rediscovered by an edge that doesn't count as a move. We want to allow for the possibility that the minimum number of moves is updated and improved by one of those no-cost edges. (Jumping up is not a no-cost edge, so we don't need this change here; but I've kept it in for consistency across the four functions.)

## Falling Down

Let's now take a look at the code for falling down given in Listing 5-11.

```
void add_position_down(int from_height, int to_height,
                       positions pos, int *num_pos,
                       board min_moves) {
❶ int distance = min_moves[from_height][1];
  if (to_height >= 0 &&
      (min_moves[to_height][1] == -1 ||
       min_moves[to_height][1] > distance)) {
    min_moves[to_height][1] = distance;
    pos[*num_pos] = (position){to_height, 1};
    (*num_pos)++;
  }
}
```

Listing 5-11: Adding a position: falling down

Falling down can only happen in state 1; that's why the second index is 1 whenever we access min_moves. Also, there's nothing to do with itching powder here. Bob can fall as much as he likes in State 1 and not have to worry about the itching powder. Finally, a crucial point about the calculated distance is that there's no + 1 added ❶!

Remember: this doesn't count as a move.

## Switching States

There are two more functions to go. First we have the function to move from State 0 to State 1 in Listing 5-12.

```
void add_position_01(int from_height,
                     positions pos, int *num_pos,
                     board min_moves) {
  int distance = 1 + min_moves[from_height][0];
  if (min_moves[from_height][1] == -1 ||
      min_moves[from_height][1] > distance) {
    min_moves[from_height][1] = distance;
    pos[*num_pos] = (position){from_height, 1};
    (*num_pos)++;
  }
}
```

Listing 5-12: Adding a position: moving from state 0 to state 1

Then we have the function to move from state 1 to state 0, shown in Listing 5-13.

```
void add_position_10(int from_height,
                     positions pos, int *num_pos,
                     int itching[], board min_moves) {
  int distance = min_moves[from_height][1];
  if (itching[from_height] == 0 &&
      (min_moves[from_height][0] == -1 ||
       min_moves[from_height][0] > distance)) {
    min_moves[from_height][0] = distance;
    pos[*num_pos] = (position){from_height, 0};
    (*num_pos)++;
  }
}
```

*Listing 5-13: Adding a position: moving from state 1 to state 0*

Moving from State 0 to State 1 costs one move, but moving from State 1 to State 0 does not. Also notice we're only allowed to move from State 1 to State 0 if there's no itching powder at that height. Without that check, we'd be allowed to stop a fall on a segment of the rope with itching powder, and that would be breaking the rules.

## 0-1 BFS

Now it's time to incorporate the state into the find_distances code from Listing 5-6. However, we had better be careful, lest we miscount the moves.

Here's an example. I'll use $(h, s)$ to refer to Bob being at height $h$ in state $s$. Suppose that Bob can jump up by three. Bob starts at $(0, 0)$, and it takes zero moves to get there. Exploring from $(0, 0)$, we will identify $(0, 1)$ as a new position, and record that it takes one move to get there. It'll be added to the positions for the next round of BFS. We'll also find $(3, 0)$ and similarly record that it takes one move to get there. That's another position for the next round of BFS. That's all standard BFS fare.

When exploring out of $(3, 0)$, we'll find the new positions $(3, 1)$ and $(6, 0)$. Both will be added to the next round of BFS, and both will be reachable in a minimum of two moves.

However, we need to be careful with position $(3, 1)$. We know that $(2, 1)$ is reachable from here, so it's tempting to add it to the next round of BFS. If we did that, though, then we wouldn't be doing BFS anymore. We are supposed to put positions in the next round of the BFS when they are exactly one move away from those in the current round. Is $(2, 1)$ one more move away from $(3, 1)$? No! They are the same number of moves from $(0, 0)$, because falling in State 1 is free.

That is, $(2, 1)$ doesn't go in the next round of BFS. It goes in the *current* round of BFS, right along with $(3, 1)$ and everything else whose minimum moves is two.

In summary, whenever we move along an edge that costs us a move, we add the new position to the next round of BFS. That's what we've always done. However, when we move along an edge that is free, then we add it to the current round of BFS so that it can be processed along with the other positions whose distance is the same. This is why we moved away from new_positions and num_new_positions in the add_position functions in "Adding Positions" on page 182. Two of the functions will indeed add moves to the new positions, but the other two will add moves to the current positions.

This variant of BFS is called *0-1 BFS*, because it works on graphs whose edges cost zero moves or one move.

At last, it's time for the BFS. Check it out in Listing 5-14.

```
void find_distances(int target_height, int jump_distance,
                    int itching[], board min_moves) {
  static positions cur_positions, new_positions;
  int num_cur_positions, num_new_positions;
  int i, j, from_height, from_state;
  for (i = 0; i < target_height * 2; i++)
    for (j = 0; j < 2; j++)
      min_moves[i][j] = -1;
  min_moves[0][0] = 0;
  cur_positions[0] = (position){0, 0};
  num_cur_positions = 1;

  while (num_cur_positions > 0) {
    num_new_positions = 0;
    for (i = 0; i < num_cur_positions; i++) {
      from_height = cur_positions[i].height;
      from_state = cur_positions[i].state;

❶     if (from_state == 0) {
        add_position_up(from_height, from_height + jump_distance,
                        target_height * 2 - 1,
                        new_positions, &num_new_positions,
                        itching, min_moves);
        add_position_01(from_height, new_positions, &num_new_positions,
                        min_moves);
      } else {
        add_position_down(from_height, from_height - 1,
                          cur_positions, &num_cur_positions, min_moves);
        add_position_10(from_height,
                        cur_positions, &num_cur_positions,
                        itching, min_moves);
      }
    }

    num_cur_positions = num_new_positions;
    for (i = 0; i < num_cur_positions; i++)
      cur_positions[i] = new_positions[i];
```

```
    }
}
```

*Listing 5-14: The minimum number of moves for Bob using 0-1 BFS*

The new code checks whether the current position is in State 0 or State 1 ❶. In each case, there are two moves to consider. In State 0, the new positions (those for the next round of BFS) are used; in State 1, the current positions are used.

What about the main and solve functions? For main, we can use the same function from Solution 1. For solve, we just need to add State 0 whenever we index min_moves. If you make those changes and submit to the judge, you'll see that we pass all tests with plenty of time to spare.

# Problem 3: Book Translation

In the Knight Chase and Rope Climb problems, there was no explicit graph to read from the input; the BFS incrementally produced the graph as it explored. We'll now see a problem where the graph is presented to us up front.

This is DMOJ problem ecna16d.

## The Problem

You have written a new book in English, and you want to get the book translated into $n$ other target languages. You've found $m$ translators. Each translator knows how to translate between exactly two languages and will do the translation at a given cost. For example, a translator may know how to translate between Spanish and Bengali at a cost of $1,800; this means that you could ask this translator to translate from Spanish to Bengali for $1,800 or Bengali to Spanish for $1,800.

To reach a given target language may require multiple translations. For example, you may want to translate your book from English to Bengali but have no translator between these two languages. You might instead have to translate from English to Spanish and then Spanish to Bengali.

To reduce the number of translation errors, you will minimize the number of translations needed to reach each target language. If there are multiple ways to achieve a minimum number of translations to a target language, then you will choose the cheapest one. Your goal is to minimize the number of translations to each target language; if there are multiple ways to do this, choose the one with minimum total cost.

### Input

The input contains one test case, consisting of the following lines:

- A line containing two integers $n$ and $m$. $n$ is the number of target languages; $m$ is the number of translators. There are at most 100 target languages and at most 4,500 translators.

- A line containing $n$ strings, each naming a target language. English will not be a target language.

- $m$ lines, each giving information for one translator. Each of these lines contains three space-separated tokens: a language, a second language, and the positive integer cost to translate between them. There is at most one translator per pair of languages.

## Output

Output the minimum monetary cost to translate the book into all of the target languages, while minimizing the number of translations to each target language. If there is no way to translate the book into all of the target languages, output Impossible.

The time limit for solving the test case is 0.6 seconds.

## *Reading the Language Names*

Rather than use language names directly—English, Spanish, and so on—I'll associate each language with an integer. English will be language 0, and each target language will be given a unique integer greater than 0. We can then work with integers from here on out, as we did for the other problems in this chapter.

There's one annoyance here: the problem description does not tell us the maximum length of a language name. We therefore cannot hardcode some maximum language name length like 16 or even 100, because we have no control over the input. We therefore use a read_word helper function; see Listing 5-15.

```
/* based on https://stackoverflow.com/questions/16870485 */
char *read_word(int size) {
  char *str;
  int ch;
  int len = 0;
  str = malloc(size);
  if (str == NULL) {
    fprintf(stderr, "malloc error\n");
    exit(1);
  }
❶ while ((ch = getchar()) != EOF && (ch != ' ') && (ch != '\n')) {
    str[len++] = ch;
    if (len == size) {
      size = size * 2;
    ❷ str = realloc(str, size);
      if (str == NULL) {
        fprintf(stderr, "realloc error\n");
        exit(1);
      }
    }
  }
```

```
  }
❸ str[len] = '\0';
  return str;
}
```

*Listing 5-15: Reading a word*

The read_word function takes an initial size that we hope suffices for most
or all of the language names. When we call the function, we will give an
initial size of 16, because that covers most language names we're likely to
see. We can use read_word to read characters ❶ up until the array reaches its
maximum length; if the array fills up and the language name still isn't over,
it then uses realloc to double the array's length ❷, thereby creating more
space to read more characters. We're careful to terminate str with a null
character ❸; otherwise, it wouldn't be a valid string!

## Building the Graph

Now let's turn to building a graph from the input. This will help us explore
the allowable translations from each language.

Let's work with a small test case:

```
3 5
Spanish Bengali Italian
English Spanish 500
Spanish Bengali 1800
English Italian 1000
Spanish Italian 250
Bengali Italian 9000
```

Can you construct the graph? What are the nodes and what are the
edges? Is it undirected or directed? Is it unweighted or weighted?

As always, the edges encode the allowed moves; here, a move corresponds to a translation between two languages. The nodes, then, are the
languages. An edge going from language *a* to language *b* means that there is
a translator between these two languages. The translator can translate from
*a* to *b* or vice versa—so the graph is undirected. It's also weighted, because
each edge (a translation) has a weight (the translation cost). The graph is
shown in Figure 5-7.

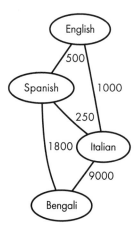

*Figure 5-7: A graph of translations*

The total translation cost for us to reach all of the target languages is $500 for English to Spanish, plus $1,000 for English to Italian, plus $1,800 for Spanish to Bengali. That's $3,300 in all. Don't be taken in by that alluring $250 Spanish–Italian translation: using that would result in a distance of two from English to Italian, but remember that we need the minimum distances, even when that leads to spending more money. Indeed, the reason we'll be able to use BFS here is precisely because we care first about the minimum number of edges for each target language, not its minimum cost overall. For the latter, we'd need more powerful tools, and these will be introduced in Chapter 6.

To store the graph, I'll use what's called an *adjacency list*. (Node *b* is said to be *adjacent* to Node *a* if there is an edge from *a* to *b*; that's where the name "adjacency list" comes from.) This is just an array with one index per node, where each index stores a linked list of the edges involving that node. We use linked lists of edges, rather than arrays of edges, because we don't know in advance the number of edges that involve a given node.

Here are the constants and typedefs:

```
#define MAX_LANGS 101
#define WORD_LENGTH 16

typedef struct edge {
  int to_lang, cost;
  struct edge *next;
} edge;

typedef int board[MAX_LANGS];
typedef int positions[MAX_LANGS];
```

An edge has a to_lang and a cost—that makes sense. However, it doesn't have a from_lang, and that's because we'll already know the from_lang based on which index of the adjacency list the edge is in.

In Chapter 2, when storing trees, we used a struct node rather than a struct edge. The reason for the node-centric focus in Chapter 2 is that the nodes are the entities associated with information, such as candy values and numbers of descendants. In the present problem, we have an edge-centric focus, with the struct edge, because it's the edges (not the nodes) that are associated with information (the translation costs).

It's easiest to add to a linked list at its beginning. One side effect of this choice is that the edges for a node end up in the linked list in the opposite order in which we read them. For example, if we read an edge from Node 1 to Node 2 and then read an edge from Node 1 to Node 3, then in our linked list we will find that the edge to Node 3 shows up *before* the edge to Node 2. Don't let this catch you off guard when tracing through the code.

Now we're ready to see how the graph is built. It's in the main function given in Listing 5-16.

```
int main(void) {
  static edge *adj_list[MAX_LANGS] = {NULL};
  static char *lang_names[MAX_LANGS];
  int i, num_targets, num_translators, cost, from_index, to_index;
  char *from_lang, *to_lang;
  edge *e;
  static board min_costs;
  scanf("%d%d ", &num_targets, &num_translators);
❶ lang_names[0] = "English";

  for (i = 1; i <= num_targets; i++)
❷ lang_names[i] = read_word(WORD_LENGTH);

  for (i = 0; i < num_translators; i++) {
    from_lang = read_word(WORD_LENGTH);
    to_lang = read_word(WORD_LENGTH);
    scanf("%d ", &cost);
    from_index = find_lang(lang_names, from_lang);
    to_index = find_lang(lang_names, to_lang);
    e = malloc(sizeof(edge));
    if (e == NULL) {
      fprintf(stderr, "malloc error\n");
      exit(1);
    }
    e->to_lang = to_index;
    e->cost = cost;
    e->next = adj_list[from_index];
❸ adj_list[from_index] = e;
    e = malloc(sizeof(edge));
    if (e == NULL) {
      fprintf(stderr, "malloc error\n");
      exit(1);
    }
```

```
      e->to_lang = from_index;
      e->cost = cost;
      e->next = adj_list[to_index];
❹   adj_list[to_index] = e;
    }
    find_distances(adj_list, num_targets + 1, min_costs);
    solve(num_targets + 1, min_costs);
    return 0;
}
```

*Listing 5-16: The main function for building the graph*

The lang_names array maps integers (the array indices) to language names. We give English the number 0, as promised ❶. We then map each integer $1, 2, \ldots$, to language names as we read them ❷.

Remember that the graph is undirected: if we add an edge from *a* to *b*, then we had better add the edge from *b* to *a*, too. As such, for each translator, we add two edges to the graph: one from from_index to to_index ❸ and one from to_index to from_index ❹. Those from_index and to_index indices are produced by find_lang, which searches for a language name; see Listing 5-17.

In the calls to the helper functions at the bottom, we use num_targets + 1 rather than num_targets because num_targets gives the number of target languages; the + 1 lets us include English in the count of total languages being processed.

```
int find_lang(char *langs[], char *lang) {
  int i = 0;
  while (strcmp(langs[i], lang) != 0)
    i++;
  return i;
}
```

*Listing 5-17: Finding a language*

## The BFS

The code for add_position in Listing 5-18 is similar to the other add_position functions we've studied earlier in this chapter.

```
void add_position(int from_lang, int to_lang,
                  positions new_positions, int *num_new_positions,
                  board min_moves) {
  if (min_moves[to_lang] == -1) {
    min_moves[to_lang] = 1 + min_moves[from_lang];
    new_positions[*num_new_positions] = to_lang;
```

```
      (*num_new_positions)++;
  }
}
```

*Listing 5-18: Adding a position*

Now we're ready for the BFS itself; see Listing 5-19.

```
void find_distances(edge *adj_list[], int num_langs, board min_costs) {
❶ static board min_moves;
  static positions cur_positions, new_positions;
  int num_cur_positions, num_new_positions;
  int i, from_lang, added_lang, best;
  edge *e;
  for (i = 0; i < num_langs; i++) {
    min_moves[i] = -1;
    min_costs[i] = -1;
  }
  min_moves[0] = 0;
  cur_positions[0] = 0;
  num_cur_positions = 1;

  while (num_cur_positions > 0) {
    num_new_positions = 0;
    for (i = 0; i < num_cur_positions; i++) {
      from_lang = cur_positions[i];
❷    e = adj_list[from_lang];

      while (e) {
        add_position(from_lang, e->to_lang,
                     new_positions, &num_new_positions, min_moves);
        e = e->next;
      }
    }

❸  for (i = 0; i < num_new_positions; i++) {
      added_lang = new_positions[i];
      e = adj_list[added_lang];
      best = -1;
      while (e) {
❹      if (min_moves[e->to_lang] + 1 == min_moves[added_lang] &&
            (best == -1 || e->cost < best))
          best = e->cost;
        e = e->next;
      }
      min_costs[added_lang] = best;
    }

    num_cur_positions = num_new_positions;
```

```
    for (i = 0; i < num_cur_positions; i++)
      cur_positions[i] = new_positions[i];
  }
}
```

*Listing 5-19: Minimum cost of translations using BFS*

For each language, we'll use `min_costs` to store the minimum-cost edge that could have been used to discover that language. Referring back to Figure 5-7, we'd store 500 for Spanish, 1,000 for Italian, and 1,800 for Bengali. In a different function, described soon, we'll add up all of these numbers to get the total cost for all of the translations.

The minimum number of moves is of interest only to this function, not the outside world, so we declare it as a local variable ❶. All the outside world cares about is `min_costs`.

Trying each possible move amounts to traversing the linked list of edges for the current node ❷. That gives us all of the `new_positions`. Now we know which languages are discovered in the next round of the BFS, but we don't yet know the cost of adding each of those languages. The thing is, there could be multiple edges from `cur_positions` that reach the same node in `new_positions`. Consult Figure 5-7 again. Bengali takes two translations, so it's discovered in round 2 of the BFS—but the edge we need is the one from Spanish, not the one from Italian.

We therefore have a new `for` loop ❸, one whose role we haven't seen yet in this chapter. The variable `added_lang` tracks each of the new positions (that is, the positions for the next round of BFS). We find the cheapest edge between `added_lang` and any node discovered in the current round of BFS. Each such language will have a distance of one less than `added_lang`, which explains the first condition in the `if` statement ❹.

### The Total Cost

Once we've got the costs stored, all we do is add them up to get the total cost of translating to all target languages. The code is given in Listing 5-20.

```
void solve(int num_langs, board min_costs) {
  int i, total = 0;
  for (i = 1; i < num_langs; i++)
❶   if (min_costs[i] == -1) {
      printf("Impossible\n");
      return;
    } else {
      total = total + min_costs[i];
    }
❷ printf("%d\n", total);
}
```

*Listing 5-20: The minimum total cost*

The task is impossible if any of the target languages is not reachable ❶. Otherwise, we print the total cost that we accumulated ❷.

Now you're ready to submit to the judge. Sabasa!

## Summary

We wrote gobs of code in this chapter. Of course, I hope that the code offers you a starting point for solving your own graph problems. In the long term, though, what I hope you remember is the importance of modeling as an early step in the problem-solving process. Couching a problem in terms of BFS collapses the domains of knights and ropes and translations into the single domain of graphs. Searching Google for "how to climb a rope" will get you nowhere (except perhaps up a real rope). Searching for "breadth-first search" will instead offer as many code samples and explanations and examples as you're willing to read. If you read comments left by programmers on the judges' websites, you'll see that they communicate on the level of algorithms, not on the level of problem-specific aspects. Often, they'll just say "BFS Problem" to get their point across. You're learning this language of modeling and how to go from the model to working code. There's more graph-modeling coming up in the next chapter, where we tackle weighted graphs in their full generality.

## Notes

Knight Chase is originally from the 1999 Canadian Computing Competition. Rope Climb is originally from the 2018 Woburn Challenge, Online Round 1, Senior Division. Book Translation is originally from the 2016 East Central North America Regional Programming Contest.

There's a trick that we can use to cut down the code we have to write when considering multiple, similar moves in a BFS. Feel free to check out how that works in "Knight Chase: Encoding Moves" in Appendix B.

We learned all about BFS in this chapter, but if you continue with graph algorithms you might like to study *depth-first search* (DFS) as well. I recommend *Algorithms Illuminated (Part 2): Graph Algorithms and Data Structures* by Tim Roughgarden (2018) for more on BFS, DFS, and other graph algorithms.

# 6

## SHORTEST PATHS IN WEIGHTED GRAPHS

This chapter generalizes what we learned in Chapter 5 about finding shortest paths. In Chapter 5, our focus was on finding the minimum number of moves needed to solve a problem. Now, what if we care not about the minimum number of moves but about the minimum amount of time or distance? Think about using a GPS app to get home. Maybe there's a route to get home using only one street that takes 10 minutes. Maybe there's another way that involves using three streets that takes only eight minutes in total. We might prefer using the three streets, since they save us time.

In this chapter, we'll learn *Dijkstra's algorithm* for finding shortest paths in weighted graphs. We'll use it to determine the number of mice that can escape a maze within a time limit and the number of shortest paths between someone's home and their grandma's house. I chose that grandma example in particular to reprise a discovery we made in Chapter 5: that, suitably modified, algorithms such as BFS and Dijkstra's can do much more than "find the shortest path." We're learning algorithms—deservedly famous ones—but also stocking up on flexible problem-solving tools. Let's go!

# Problem 1: Mice Maze

This is UVa problem 1112.

## *The Problem*

A maze consists of cells and passages. Each passage leads from some cell *a* to some other cell *b*, and it takes *t* time units to walk the passage. For example, it may take 5 time units to walk from Cell 2 to Cell 4. Now for the passage going the other way: it may take 70 time units to walk from Cell 4 to Cell 2, or there may be no passage at all from Cell 4 to Cell 2—the $a \rightarrow b$ and $b \rightarrow a$ passages are independent. One of the cells of the maze is designated as the exit cell.

There's a lab mouse in each cell, including the exit cell. The mice have been trained to walk to the exit cell in as little time as possible. Our task is to determine the number of mice that can reach the exit cell within a specified time limit.

### Input

The first line of input gives the number of test cases and is followed by a blank line. There's also a blank line between each pair of test cases. Each test case consists of the following lines:

- A line containing *n*, the number of cells in the maze. Cells are numbered 1 to *n*; *n* is at most 100.

- A line containing *e*, the exit cell. *e* is between 1 and *n*.

- A line containing *t*, the integer time limit for the mice to get to the exit cell. *t* is at least zero.

- A line containing *m*, the number of passages in the maze.

- *m* lines, each describing a passage in the maze. Each such line contains three integers: the first cell *a* (between 1 and *n*), the second cell *b* (between 1 and *n*), and the time (at least zero) it takes to walk from *a* to *b*.

### Output

For each test case, output the number of mice that reach the exit cell *e* within the time limit *t*. The output for each test case is separated from the next by a blank line.

The time limit for solving the test cases—for our code, not the mice—is three seconds.

## Moving On from BFS

There are key similarities between the Mice Maze problem and the three problems in Chapter 5. We can model the Mice Maze as a graph, where the nodes are the maze cells and the edges are the passages. The graph is directed (as in the Rope Climb problem), because a passage from Cell *a* to Cell *b* tells us nothing about the possible passage from *b* to *a*.

The workhorse for the three problems in Chapter 5 was breadth-first search. The killer feature of BFS is that it finds shortest paths. Not coincidentally, we want shortest paths for our Mice Maze, too. They'll let us determine how long it takes each mouse to reach the exit cell.

However, all this talk of similarities is obscuring a crucial difference: the Mice Maze graph is *weighted*: on each edge, we have an arbitrary integer giving the time required to traverse that edge. See Figure 6-1 for an example.

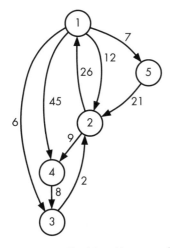

Figure 6-1: The Mice Maze graph

Let's say that the exit cell is Cell 4. What's the minimum amount of time taken by the mouse in Cell 1 to get to Cell 4? There's an edge directly from Cell 1 to Cell 4, so if we were counting edges (as in BFS), then the answer would be 1. However, we are not interested in the number of edges here: instead, we want the shortest path in terms of the sum of its edge weights. The weight of the $1 \rightarrow 4$ edge is 45. That is not the shortest path. The shortest path from Cell 1 to Cell 4 is the three-edge path that goes from Cell 1 to Cell 3 (six units of time), then from Cell 3 to Cell 2 (two units of time), and finally from Cell 2 to Cell 4 (nine units of time). That's 6 + 2 + 9 = 17 in all. It is because of this focus on edge weights, not edge counts, that BFS is out of its element here and we'll need a different algorithm.

 Hold on, though: there were some weighted graphs in Chapter 5, and we used BFS on those. What gives? Look back at Figure 5-6, a Rope Climb graph where some of the edges had weight 1 and others had weight 0. We managed to use a variant of BFS there, but only because the edge weights were so constrained. Now look back at Figure 5-7, a Book Translation graph. That's a full-blown weighted graph with arbitrary edge weights. We managed to use BFS there, too, but that's because the primary distance measure was the number of edges. Once a node's edge distance was determined by BFS, only then did the edge weights come into play, helping us add the node as cheaply as possible.

However, in no way does the Mice Maze have anything to do with the number of edges. A path from *a* to *b* might have 100 edges and a total time of 5 units. A different path from *a* to *b* might have only 1 edge with a time of 80 units. BFS would discover that second path, when what we want is the first.

## Finding Shortest Paths in Weighted Graphs

BFS operates by progressively identifying nodes that are further and further away, in terms of edge count, from the starting node. The algorithm that I'll present in this section operates similarly: it identifies the shortest path for nodes further and further away, in terms of total edge weight, from the starting node.

BFS organizes its work in rounds, where the nodes discovered in the next round are one edge more distant than the nodes in the current round. We aren't going to be able to use that rounds idea to find shortest paths in weighted graphs, because the shortest paths that we discover most recently are not necessarily those that will help us find the shortest path for a new node. We'll have to work a little harder to find the next shortest path.

To demonstrate, let's find the shortest paths from Node 1 to each node in the graph using Figure 6-1. That will tell us how long it takes the mouse in cell 1 to get to the exit cell.

For each node, we'll maintain two pieces of information:

*done*  This is a true/false variable. If it's false, it means that we haven't found the shortest path for this node yet; if it's true, then we have. Once a node's *done* value is true, we're done with it: its shortest path will never change again.

*min_time*  This is the shortest path distance from the starting node to this node, in terms of total time, using a path whose other nodes are all done. As more and more nodes become done, *min_time* can decrease, because we have more options for paths to this node.

The shortest path from Node 1 to Node 1 is 0: there's nowhere to go and no edge to take. Let's start there, with a *min_time* for Node 1 of 0 and no *min_time* information for the other nodes:

| node | done | min_time |
|------|------|----------|
| 1 | false | 0 |
| 2 | false | |
| 3 | false | |
| 4 | false | |
| 5 | false | |

We next set Node 1 to done, and then we set the *min_time* for each other node based on the edge weights from Node 1. Here's our next snapshot:

| node | done | min_time |
|------|------|----------|
| 1 | true | 0 |
| 2 | false | 12 |
| 3 | false | 6 |
| 4 | false | 45 |
| 5 | false | 7 |

Now, here's a claim that's at the heart of what we're doing here: the shortest path from Node 1 to Node 3 is 6, and there's no way we can ever do better than 6. I chose Node 3 in my claim because it has the smallest *min_time* value of any node that is not done.

Claiming that the answer is 6 right now might seem brazen. What if there were some other path to Node 3 that was shorter, maybe another path that goes through some other nodes before eventually making its way to Node 3?

Here's why that can't happen, and why our claim of 6 is safe. Imagine that there were some shorter path $p$ from Node 1 to Node 3. That path must start at Node 1 and leave Node 1 on some edge $e$. Then it must take zero or more other edges and arrive at Node 3. Check it out: $e$ already takes at least 6 time units, because 6 is the minimum time it takes to go from Node 1 to some other node. Any other edges that are on $p$ only add to this, so there's no way that $p$ could have a total time of less than 6 units!

So, Node 3 is done: we know its shortest path. Now we will have to use Node 3 to check whether we can improve any of the shortest paths for nodes that are not yet done. Remember that the *min_time* values give the shortest path using done nodes. It takes 6 time units to get to Node 3, and there's an edge from Node 3 to Node 2 that takes 2 time units, so we now have a way to get from Node 1 to Node 2 in only 8 time units. We therefore update the *min_time* value for Node 2 from 12 to 8. Here's where that leaves us:

| node | done | min_time |
|------|------|----------|
| 1 | true | 0 |
| 2 | false | 8 |
| 3 | true | 6 |
| 4 | false | 45 |
| 5 | false | 7 |

Nodes 2, 4, and 5 are not yet done. Which one can we doneify now? The answer is Node 5: it's got the minimum *min_time*. Can we use Node 5 to update any of our other shortest paths? Node 5 does have an outgoing edge to Node 2, but getting from Node 1 to Node 5 (7 time units) and then taking the edge from Node 5 to Node 2 (21 time units) takes more time (7 + 21 = 28) than our old path from Node 1 to Node 2 (8 time units). So we leave Node 2's *min_time* alone. The only change in the next snapshot, then, is to set Node 5 to done.

| node | done | min_time |
|------|------|----------|
| 1 | true | 0 |
| 2 | false | 8 |
| 3 | true | 6 |
| 4 | false | 45 |
| 5 | true | 7 |

There are two nodes to go. Node 2 has a *min_time* of 8, and Node 4 has a *min_time* of 45. As always, we choose the smaller, finalizing the shortest path distance from Node 1 to Node 2 as 8. Again, there can be no shorter path to Node 2 than 8. Any shorter path *p* from Node 1 to Node 2 must begin with some done nodes and will at some point cross for the first time on an edge from a done node to one that is not done. Call that edge $x \rightarrow y$, where *x* is done and *y* is not. So that's how *p* gets from Node 1 to Node *y*. It can then do whatever it wants to get from Node *y* to Node 2 . . . but it's all frivolous. Getting from Node 1 to Node *y* already takes at least 8 time units: if it were less, then *y*'s *min_time* value would be less than 8 and we'd have chosen to set *y* to done rather than Node 2. Whatever *p* does to get from Node *y* to Node 2 can only add even more time. So *p* can't be shorter than 8.

Adding Node 2 gives us two edges to check for shorter paths. There's an edge from Node 2 to Node 1, but that won't help us because Node 1 is already done. There's an edge of 9 time units from Node 2 to Node 4. That one does help us! Getting from Node 1 to Node 2 takes 8 time units, and then the $2 \rightarrow 4$ edge takes 9 time units, for a total of 17 time units. That's better than our old path from Node 1 to Node 4 that took 45 time units. Here's the next snapshot:

| node | done | min_time |
|------|------|----------|
| 1 | true | 0 |
| 2 | true | 8 |
| 3 | true | 6 |
| 4 | false | 17 |
| 5 | true | 7 |

There's only one node, Node 4, that's not done. As all other nodes are done, we've found all of their shortest paths. Node 4, therefore, can't help us find any new, shorter paths. We can set Node 4 to done and conclude:

| node | done | min_time |
|------|------|----------|
| 1 | true | 0 |
| 2 | true | 8 |
| 3 | true | 6 |
| 4 | true | 17 |
| 5 | true | 7 |

It takes 17 time units for the mouse in Cell 1 to get to the exit cell 4. We could repeat the process for each other node to find out how long each other mouse takes to get to the exit cell, then count the mice that get there in time.

This algorithm is known as Dijkstra's algorithm, after Edsger W. Dijkstra, a pioneering and influential computer scientist. Given a starting node $s$ and a weighted graph, it calculates the shortest path from $s$ to each node in the graph. It's exactly what we need to solve the Mice Maze problem. Let's read the input to build the graph and then see how Dijkstra's algorithm can be implemented.

## Building the Graph

With all of your experience building trees and graphs to this point, there won't be many surprises here. We'll build the graph like we built it for the Book Translation problem in the previous chapter (see "Building the Graph" on page 189). The only difference is that the graphs there were undirected and our graphs here are directed. In more good news, we're given the node numbers directly and don't have to map between language names and integers.

Just so we have something on which to test, here's an input corresponding to Figure 6-1:

---

```
1

5
4
❶ 12
9
1 2 12
1 3 6
2 1 26
1 4 45
1 5 7
3 2 2
2 4 9
4 3 8
5 2 21
```

---

That 12 ❶ gives the time limit for the mice to get to the exit. (You can verify that three mice can get to the exit within this time limit; those mice are the ones in Cells 2, 3, and 4.)

As in Book Translation, we'll use an adjacency list representation of the graph. Each edge maintains the cell to which it points, the length of time required to walk the edge, and a next pointer.

Here's the needed constant and typedef:

---

```
#define MAX_CELLS 100

typedef struct edge {
```

```
    int to_cell, length;
    struct edge *next;
  } edge;
```

The graphs are read by the main function in Listing 6-1.

```
int main(void) {
  static edge *adj_list[MAX_CELLS + 1];
  int num_cases, case_num, i;
  int num_cells, exit_cell, time_limit, num_edges;
  int from_cell, to_cell, length;
  int total, min_time;
  edge *e;

  scanf("%d", &num_cases);
  for (case_num = 1; case_num <= num_cases; case_num++) {
    scanf("%d%d%d", &num_cells, &exit_cell, &time_limit);
    scanf("%d", &num_edges);
❶   for (i = 1; i <= num_cells; i++)
      adj_list[i] = NULL;
    for (i = 0; i < num_edges; i++) {
      scanf("%d%d%d", &from_cell, &to_cell, &length);
      e = malloc(sizeof(edge));
      if (e == NULL) {
        fprintf(stderr, "malloc error\n");
        exit(1);
      }
      e->to_cell = to_cell;
      e->length = length;
      e->next = adj_list[from_cell];
❷     adj_list[from_cell] = e;
    }

    total = 0;
    for (i = 1; i <= num_cells; i++) {
❸     min_time = find_time(adj_list, num_cells, i, exit_cell);
❹     if (min_time >= 0 && min_time <= time_limit)
        total++;
    }
    printf("%d\n", total);
    if (case_num < num_cases)
      printf("\n");
  }
  return 0;
}
```

Listing 6-1: The main function for building the graph

The input specification says that a blank line follows the number of test cases and that a blank line sits between each pair of test cases. However, using scanf, we don't have to worry about that: when reading a number, scanf skips leading whitespace (including newlines) that it encounters.

The first thing we do for each test case is to clear the adjacency list by setting each cell's edge list to NULL ❶. Not doing that results in a horrible bug where each test case includes edges from prior test cases. (I would know: I made that mistake, and three hours later it was three hours later.) It's our responsibility to clear things for each test case!

Upon initializing each edge, we add it to the linked list for from_cell ❷. We don't add anything to the linked list for to_cell, because the graph is directed (not undirected).

The problem requires that we find the shortest path from each cell to the exit cell. For each cell, then, we call find_time ❸, a helper function that implements Dijkstra's algorithm. We'll write that function next. Given a starting cell i and target cell exit_cell, it returns -1 if there's no path at all or else returns the shortest path time. Each cell that takes time_limit units of time or less to get to the exit cell results in total being incremented by one ❹. Once each cell's shortest path has been considered, total is output.

### Implementing Dijkstra's Algorithm

Now it's time to implement Dijkstra's algorithm, following the outline provided in "Finding Shortest Paths in Weighted Graphs" on page 200. Here's the signature for the function that we'll implement:

```
int find_time(edge *adj_list[], int num_cells,
              int from_cell, int exit_cell)
```

The four parameters correspond to the adjacency list, number of cells, starting cell, and exit cell, respectively. Dijkstra's algorithm will calculate the shortest path time from the starting cell to all other cells, including the exit cell. Once we're done, we can return the shortest path time to the exit cell. That may seem extravagant, calculating the shortest path to all cells only to throw everything away except the shortest path to the exit cell. There are various optimizations that we can perform, and we'll turn to those in the next subsection. For now, let's settle in with a working, unadorned implementation.

The body of Dijkstra's algorithm is implemented by two nested for loops. The outer for loop runs once per cell; each iteration sets one cell to done and updates shortest paths using that new cell. The inner for loop is a minimum computation: it finds the cell whose min_time value, among all cells that are not done, is minimum. See Listing 6-2 for the code.

```
int find_time(edge *adj_list[], int num_cells,
              int from_cell, int exit_cell) {
  static int done[MAX_CELLS + 1];
  static int min_times[MAX_CELLS + 1];
```

```
     int i, j, found;
     int min_time, min_time_index, old_time;
     edge *e;
❶ for (i = 1; i <= num_cells; i++) {
       done[i] = 0;
       min_times[i] = -1;
     }
❷ min_times[from_cell] = 0;

     for (i = 0; i < num_cells; i++) {
       min_time = -1;
❸   found = 0;
❹   for (j = 1; j <= num_cells; j++) {
❺     if (!done[j] && min_times[j] >= 0) {
❻       if (min_time == -1 || min_times[j] < min_time) {
           min_time = min_times[j];
           min_time_index = j;
           found = 1;
         }
       }
     }
❼   if (!found)
       break;
     done[min_time_index] = 1;

     e = adj_list[min_time_index];
     while (e) {
       old_time = min_times[e->to_cell];
❽     if (old_time == -1 || old_time > min_time + e->length)
         min_times[e->to_cell] = min_time + e->length;
       e = e->next;
     }
   }
❾ return min_times[exit_cell];
 }
```

*Listing 6-2: The shortest path to the exit cell using Dijkstra's algorithm*

The purpose of the done array is to indicate whether each cell is done: a 0 means "not done" and a 1 means "done." The purpose of the min_times array is to store the shortest path distance from the starting cell to each cell.

We use a for loop ❶ to initialize these two arrays: it sets all done values to 0 (false) and min_times values to -1 (not found). We then set min_times for from_cell to 0 ❷ to indicate that the shortest path distance from the starting cell to itself is zero.

The found variable tracks whether a new cell can be discovered by Dijkstra's algorithm. On each iteration of the outer for loop, it starts off as 0 (false) ❸ and gets set to 1 (true) if a cell can be found—but how could a cell not be found? For example, earlier in this chapter, we found all of the cells. However, there may be graphs where there is *no* path between a starting cell and some other cell. On those graphs, there will be cells that Dijkstra's algorithm does not find; when no new cell can be found, it's time to stop.

Now we arrive at the inner for loop ❹, whose task is to identify the cell whose shortest path will be found next. This loop will leave min_time_index with the index of the cell whose shortest path has been found and min_time with the shortest path time itself. The eligible cells are those that are both not done and have a min_times value that's at least 0 (that is, not -1) ❺. We need the cell to be not done, because done cells already have their shortest paths finalized. We also need the min_times value to be at least 0: if it's -1, then the cell hasn't been found yet, so we have no idea what its shortest path is. If we had no eligible cell yet or the current cell has a shorter path than our shortest thus far ❻, we update min_time and min_time_index and set found to 1 to flag that we successfully found a cell.

If no cell was found, then we stop ❼. Otherwise, we set the identified cell to done and loop through its outgoing edges to find shorter paths. For each edge e, we check whether the cell provides a shorter path to e->to_cell ❽. That possible shorter path is min_time (the time taken to get from from_cell to min_time_index) plus the time taken to walk edge e (from min_time_index to e->to_cell).

When looking at edge e, shouldn't we first be verifying that e->to_cell is not done before checking whether we've found a shorter path ❽? Although we could add that check, it would have no effect. Done cells already have their finalized shortest paths; there's no way that some shorter path can be found.

Having computed shortest paths to all cells, we've certainly computed the shortest path to the exit cell. The final thing to do is return that time ❾.

That's a wrap! Go ahead and submit to the judge. The code should pass all of the test cases.

## Two Optimizations

There are a few things that can be done to speed up Dijkstra's algorithm. The most widely applicable and dramatic speedup is wrought by a data structure called a *heap*. In our current implementation, it's very expensive to find the next node to set to done, as we need to scan through all nodes that are not done to find the one with the shortest path. A heap uses a tree to convert this slow, linear search into a fast search. As heaps are useful in many contexts beyond Dijkstra's algorithm, I'll discuss them later, in Chapter 8. Here, I'll offer a couple of optimizations more specific to the Mice Maze problem.

Recall that as soon as a cell is done, we never change its shortest path again. As such, once we set the exit cell to done, we have its shortest path. After that, there's no reason to find shortest paths for other cells. We may as well terminate Dijkstra's algorithm early.

We can still do better, though. For a maze of *n* cells, we invoke Dijkstra's algorithm *n* times, once for each cell. For Cell 1, we compute all shortest paths—and then keep only the shortest path to the exit cell. We do the same for Cell 2, Cell 3, and so on, throwing out all of the shortest paths we found except for those that involve the exit cell.

Instead, consider running Dijkstra's algorithm just once, with the exit cell as the starting cell. Dijkstra's algorithm would then find the shortest path from the exit cell to Cell 1, the exit cell to Cell 2, and so on. However, that's not quite what we want, because the graph is directed: the shortest path from the exit cell to Cell 1 is *not* necessarily the shortest path from Cell 1 to the exit cell.

Here again is Figure 6-1:

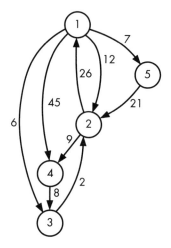

As we discovered earlier, the shortest path from Cell 1 to Cell 4 is 17, but the shortest path from Cell 4 to Cell 1 is 36.

The shortest path from Cell 1 to Cell 4 uses the edges $1 \rightarrow 3, 3 \rightarrow 2$, and $2 \rightarrow 4$. If we intend on starting Dijkstra's algorithm from Cell 4, then we need it to find edges $4 \rightarrow 2, 2 \rightarrow 3$, and $3 \rightarrow 1$. Each of these edges is the *reverse* of an edge in the original graph. Figure 6-2 shows the *reversed graph*.

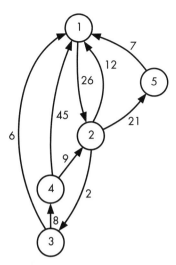

*Figure 6-2: A reversed version of the graph in Figure 6-1*

Now we can run Dijkstra's algorithm—just one invocation of it!—from Cell 4 to recover shortest paths to all nodes.

In terms of implementation, we would need to produce the reversed graph instead of the original graph. This can be done in the main function (Listing 6-1), when reading the graph. Instead of:

```
e->to_cell = to_cell;
e->length = length;
e->next = adj_list[from_cell];
adj_list[from_cell] = e;
```

we want this:

```
e->to_cell = from_cell;
e->length = length;
e->next = adj_list[to_cell];
adj_list[to_cell] = e;
```

That is, the edge now points to from_cell, and it gets added to the linked list for to_cell. If you make this change and adapt the code so that it invokes Dijkstra's algorithm just once (from the exit cell), you'll end up with a much faster program. Give it a try!

# Dijkstra's Algorithm

Dijkstra's algorithm takes over where BFS leaves off. BFS finds shortest paths in terms of numbers of edges in an unweighted graph; Dijkstra's algorithm finds shortest paths in terms of edge weights in a weighted graph.

Like BFS, Dijkstra's algorithm takes a starting node, and it finds shortest paths from there to each node in the graph. Like BFS, it then solves the *single-source shortest-paths* problem, except on weighted graphs rather than unweighted graphs.

To be fair, Dijkstra's algorithm *can* find shortest paths in unweighted graphs, too. Just take the unweighted graph and give each edge a weight of one. Now, when Dijkstra's algorithm finds the shortest paths, it will have minimized the number of edges in the path, precisely what BFS does.

Why not hammer every shortest-path problem, unweighted or weighted, with Dijkstra's algorithm, then? Indeed, there are problems where it's difficult to decide between BFS and Dijkstra's algorithm. For example, I suspect that many people would have chosen Dijkstra's algorithm over (modified) BFS to solve the Rope Climb problem in Chapter 5. When the task is clearly to minimize the number of moves, BFS should still get the call: it's generally easier to implement than Dijkstra's algorithm and runs a little faster, too. By no means, however, is Dijkstra's algorithm slow.

## Runtime of Dijkstra's Algorithm

Let's characterize the runtime of Dijkstra's algorithm as seen in Listing 6-2. We'll use $n$ to refer to the number of nodes in the graph.

The initialization loop ❶ iterates $n$ times, doing a constant number of steps per iteration, so it does total work proportional to $n$. The next bit of initialization ❷ is a single step. Whether we say that the initialization takes $n$ steps or $n + 1$ steps changes nothing, so we'll ignore this 1 and say that it takes $n$ steps.

The real work done by Dijkstra's algorithm starts now. Its outer for loop iterates up to $n$ times. For each such iteration, the inner for loop does $n$ iterations to find the next node. The inner for loop, then, iterates a total of $n^2$ times. Each such iteration does a constant amount of work, so the inner for loop does total work proportional to $n^2$.

The other work that Dijkstra's algorithm does is to iterate through the edges of each node. There are a total of $n$ nodes, so certainly each node has no more than $n$ edges leaving it. We therefore take $n$ steps to iterate through the edges of one node, and we have to do this for each of the $n$ nodes. That's another $n^2$ steps.

Summarizing, we've got $n$ work in the initialization, $n^2$ work in the inner for loop, and $n^2$ work checking the edges. The biggest exponent there is 2, so this is an $O(n^2)$, or quadratic, algorithm.

In Chapter 1, we sneezed at a quadratic-time algorithm for Unique Snowflakes, tossing it away in favor of a linear-time algorithm. In that sense, the implementation of Dijkstra's algorithm that we have developed is not too impressive. In another sense, though, it is, because in $n^2$ time it's solving not one but $n$ problems, one for each shortest path from the starting node.

I've chosen to present Dijkstra's algorithm in this book, but there are many other shortest-paths algorithms. Some find the shortest path between all pairs of nodes in the graph in one fell swoop. Doing so solves the *all-pairs shortest-paths* problem. One such algorithm is called the *Floyd–Warshall algorithm*, and it runs in $O(n^3)$ time. Interestingly, we can find all-pairs shortest paths with Dijkstra's algorithm, too, and just as quickly. We can run Dijkstra's algorithm $n$ times, once from each starting node. That's $n$ invocations of an $n^2$ algorithm, for a total of $O(n^3)$ work.

Weighted or unweighted, single-source or all-pairs, Dijkstra's algorithm can do it. Is it simply unstoppable? Negative!

## Negative-Weight Edges

We've made an implicit assumption to this point in the chapter: edge weights are nonnegative. In the Mice Maze, for example, edge weights represent times to walk edges; walking an edge surely can't cause time to go backward, so no edge weight was negative. Similarly, in many other graphs, edges with negative weights don't arise simply because they don't make sense. For example, consider a graph where the nodes are cities and edges are flight costs between cities. No airline is going to pay us for taking their flights, so each edge will be a nonnegative dollar cost.

Now consider a game in which some moves give us points, and other moves take points away. Those latter moves correspond to *negative-weight edges*. Thus negative-weight edges do appear from time to time. How does Dijkstra's algorithm respond? Let's find out using the sample graph in Figure 6-3.

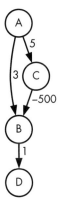

*Figure 6-3: A graph with a negative-weight edge*

Let's try to find shortest paths from Node A. As always, Dijkstra's algorithm begins by assigning a shortest path of 0 to Node A and setting Node A to done. The distance to B from A is 3, the distance to C from A is 5, but the distance to D from A is not defined (and has been left blank):

| node | done | min_distance |
| --- | --- | --- |
| A | true | 0 |
| B | false | 3 |
| C | false | 5 |
| D | false | |

Dijkstra's algorithm then decides to finalize the shortest path to Node B at 3, and it sets B to done. It also updates the shortest path to D:

| node | done | min_distance |
| --- | --- | --- |
| A | true | 0 |
| B | true | 3 |
| C | false | 5 |
| D | false | 4 |

By virtue of B being done, we're claiming that 3 is the shortest path from A to B, but that spells trouble, because 3 is *not* the shortest path that we can find from A to B. The shortest path is $A \rightarrow C \rightarrow B$, with a total weight of −495. For kicks, let's continue under these fishy circumstances and see what Dijkstra's algorithm would do anyway. The next node that's done is D:

| node | done | min_distance |
| --- | --- | --- |
| A | true | 0 |
| B | true | 3 |
| C | false | 5 |
| D | true | 4 |

That shortest path to D is wrong, too! It should be −494. As all nodes are done except for C, there's nothing that C can do:

| node | done | min_distance |
| --- | --- | --- |
| A | true | 0 |
| B | true | 3 |
| C | true | 5 |
| D | true | 4 |

Even if we let Dijkstra's algorithm change the shortest path to B here, from 3 to −495, then the shortest path to D will still be wrong. We'd have to somehow process B again, even though B is done. We'd need some way of saying, "Hey, I know that I said B was done, but I'm changing my mind." In any event, the classical Dijkstra's algorithm as I've presented it gets this example wrong.

In general, Dijkstra's algorithm does not work when graph edges can be negative. For that, you may wish to explore the *Bellman–Ford algorithm* or the aforementioned Floyd–Warshall algorithm.

Let's proceed here with another problem where we don't have to worry about negative-weight edges. We'll use Dijkstra's algorithm again, or, rather, we'll adapt Dijkstra's algorithm to solve a new kind of problem about shortest paths.

# Problem 2: Grandma Planner

Sometimes, we'll be asked for not only the shortest path distance but also further information about the shortest paths. This problem is just such an example.

This is DMOJ problem saco08p3.

## The Problem

Bruce is planning a trip to his grandma's house. There are $n$ towns, numbered 1 to $n$. Bruce starts in Town 1, and his grandma lives in Town $n$. Between each pair of towns is a road, and we're given the length (distance) of each road.

Bruce wishes to arrive at his grandma's with a box of cookies, so he must buy it along the way. Some of the towns have cookie stores; Bruce is required to hit at least one of these cookie towns on his way to his grandma's.

Our task is twofold. First, we must determine the minimum distance needed for Bruce to get from his starting point to his grandma's house, picking up a box of cookies along the way. That minimum distance does not tell us how many options Bruce has for getting to his grandma's. Maybe there's only one way that he can do it, with all other routes requiring greater distance, or maybe there are several routes all with the same minimum distance. So, second, we're asked to determine the number of these minimum-distance routes.

### Input

The input contains one test case, consisting of the following lines:

- A line containing $n$, the number of towns. Towns are numbered 1 to $n$. There are between 2 and 700 towns.

- $n$ lines, each containing $n$ integers. The first of these lines gives the road distance from Town 1 to each town (Town 1, then Town 2, and so on); the second of these lines gives the road distance from Town 2 to each town; and so on. The distance from a town to itself is zero; each other distance is at least one. The distance from Town $a$ to Town $b$ is the same as the distance from Town $b$ to Town $a$.

- A line containing $m$, the number of towns that have a cookie store. $m$ is at least one.

- A line containing *m* integers, each giving the number of a town with a cookie store.

## Output

Output the following on a single line:

- The minimum distance to get from Town 1 to Town *n* (picking up a box of cookies along the way)
- A space
- The number of minimum-distance routes, mod 1,000,000

The time limit for solving the test case is one second.

## Adjacency Matrix

The way that the graph is represented here differs from that of the Mice Maze and that of the Book Translation problem in Chapter 5. In those two problems, each edge was supplied as one node, the other node, and the edge weight. For example, consider the following:

---
1 2 12
---

This means that there's an edge from Node 1 to Node 2 with weight 12.

In the Grandma Planner problem, the graph is presented as an *adjacency matrix*, which is a two-dimensional array of numbers where a given row, column coordinate gives us the weight of the edge at that row and column.

Here's a sample test case:

---
4
0 3 8 2
3 0 2 1
8 2 0 5
2 1 5 0
1
2
---

The 4 at the top tells us that there are four towns. The next four lines are the adjacency matrix. Let's focus on the first of those lines:

---
0 3 8 2
---

This single line gives all of the edges leaving Town 1. There's an edge from Town 1 to Town 1 of weight 0, from Town 1 to Town 2 of weight 3, from Town 1 to Town 3 of weight 8, and from Town 1 to Town 4 of weight 2.

The next line,

---
3 0 2 1
---

does similarly for Town 2, and so on.

Notice that there's an edge between any pair of towns; that is, there are no missing edges. Such a graph is called a *complete graph*.

This adjacency matrix has some redundancy. For example, it says in row 1, column 3 that there's an edge from Town 1 to Town 3 of weight 8. However, since the problem specifies that the road from Town *a* to Town *b* is the same distance as that of the road from Town *b* to Town *a*, we see this 8 again in row 3, column 1. (We're therefore dealing with undirected graphs.) We also have 0's along the diagonal, which explicitly state that the distance from some town to itself is zero. We'll just ignore those.

## Building the Graph

This problem is ultimately going to demand our creativity not once, but twice. First, we'll need to force our paths through a town with a cookie store. Among those paths, we want the shortest one. Second, we'll need to keep track not only of the shortest path but also of the number of ways we can realize that shortest path. Double the fun, I say!

Let's begin by reading the test case from the input and building the graph. We're well positioned to do that at this point. With our graph in hand, we'll then be ready for what lies ahead.

The plan is to read the adjacency matrix, building our adjacency lists as we go. We'll have to keep track of the town indices ourselves, since the adjacency matrix doesn't explicitly provide them.

It's possible to read in and use the adjacency matrix directly, avoiding the adjacency list representation altogether. Each row *i* gives the distance to each town, so we could just loop through row *i* in Dijkstra's algorithm instead of looping through *i*'s adjacency list. Since the graph is complete, we wouldn't even have to waste time skipping over edges that don't exist. We'll use adjacency lists here, however, for continuity with what we've already done.

Here's a constant and edge struct that we'll use:

```
#define MAX_TOWNS 700

typedef struct edge {
  int to_town, length;
  struct edge *next;
} edge;
```

The code for reading the graph is given in Listing 6-3.

```
int main(void) {
  static edge *adj_list[MAX_TOWNS + 1] = {NULL};
  int i, num_towns, from_town, to_town, length;
  int num_stores, store_num;
  static int store[MAX_TOWNS + 1] = {0};
  edge *e;
```

```
    scanf("%d", &num_towns);
❶ for (from_town = 1; from_town <= num_towns; from_town++)
    for (to_town = 1; to_town <= num_towns; to_town++) {
      scanf("%d", &length);
❷    if (from_town != to_town) {
        e = malloc(sizeof(edge));
        if (e == NULL) {
          fprintf(stderr, "malloc error\n");
          exit(1);
        }
        e->to_town = to_town;
        e->length = length;
        e->next = adj_list[from_town];
        adj_list[from_town] = e;
      }
    }

❸ scanf("%d", &num_stores);
  for (i = 1; i <= num_stores; i++) {
    scanf("%d", &store_num);
    store[store_num] = 1;
  }
  solve(adj_list, num_towns, store);
  return 0;
}
```

*Listing 6-3: The main function for building the graph*

After reading the number of towns, we use a double for loop to read the adjacency matrix. Each iteration of the outer for loop ❶ is responsible for reading one row, specifically, the row for from_town. To read that row, we have an inner for loop, which reads one length value for each to_town. So now we know where the edge starts, where the edge ends, and the length of the edge. We then want to add the edge, but only if it's not one of those 0-weight edges that go from a town back to itself. If the edge is between distinct towns ❷, then we add it to the adjacency list for from_town. Because the graph is undirected, we must also ensure that eventually this edge is added to the adjacency list for to_town. We had to do that explicitly in Listing 5-16 when solving the Book Translation problem. We don't have to do that here, though, because it'll get added later without us doing anything special when we process the row for to_town. For example, if from_town is 1 and to_town is 2, then the $1 \rightarrow 2$ edge will be added now. Later, when from_town is 2 and to_town is 1, then the $2 \rightarrow 1$ edge will be added.

All that's left is to read the information about which towns have cookie stores, starting with the number of such towns ❸. To keep track of these towns, we use array store, where store[i] is 1 (true) if Town i has a cookie store and 0 (false) if it does not.

## Working Through a Weird Test Case

Let's get a feel for the problem by working through the test case from "Adjacency Matrix" on page 214. The corresponding graph is provided in Figure 6-4, where **c** represents a cookie town.

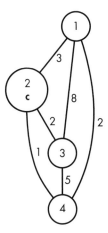

*Figure 6-4: The grandma graph*

Bruce starts in Town 1 and has to get to Town 4. Town 2 is the only town with a cookie store. What's the shortest-distance path? While it's true that Bruce can zip from Town 1 directly to Town 4 along the edge of distance 2, that isn't a feasible solution to the problem. Remember that we need to ensure that a town with a cookie store is included in any proposed shortest path. For this particular graph, this means that we must include Town 2. (In other test cases, there could be multiple towns that have cookie stores; what we'd need to do is include one or more of them.)

Here's a path from Town 1 to Town 4 that *is* feasible: 1 → 2 (distance 3) → 4 (distance 1). That's a total distance of 4, and it is indeed a shortest path from Town 1 to Town 4 that passes through Town 2.

That's not the only optimal path, though. There's one more, and here it is: 1 → 4 (distance 2) → 2 (distance 1) → 4 (distance 1). What's a little weird about this path is that we visit Town 4, grandma's house, *twice*. We start by going from Town 1 to Town 4, but we cannot end the path there because we don't have the box of cookies yet. Then we go from Town 4 to Town 2, where we pick up the box of cookies. Finally, we go from Town 2 to Town 4, which is our second visit to Town 4, but this time we arrive with the box of cookies, and so we have a feasible path.

It does seem that this path is cyclic, since we get to Town 4 once and then get to Town 4 again. Viewed in a different light, however, there is no cycle at all. When we visited Town 4 the first time, we had no box of cookies; when we visited Town 4 again, we had a box of cookies. These two visits are therefore not repeats: it's true that Town 4 was visited twice, but it is also true that the state (not carrying a box of cookies versus carrying a box of cookies) differs each time.

Now we see that the same town can't possibly be visited more than twice. If a town is visited three times, for example, then two of those visits must be in the same state. Perhaps Visit 1 and Visit 2 were both in the "not carrying a box of cookies" state. Then that really is a cycle, and it costs us some distance to traverse the cycle, so removing it gives a shorter path.

It's not sufficient, then, to know which town we're in. We also need to know whether or not a box of cookies has been picked up.

We've wrestled with this kind of problem once before, when solving Rope Climb in Chapter 5. There, we discussed adding a second rope to produce a more suitable model of the problem. We're going to reprise that idea here, by adding a state that tells us whether or not a box of cookies is being carried. In State 0, no box of cookies is being carried; in State 1, a box of cookies is being carried. A feasible path, then, is any path that arrives at grandma's house in State 1. Arriving at grandma's house in State 0 cannot be the end of a feasible path.

Take a look at Figure 6-5, which introduces a cookie state to Figure 6-4. Again, **c** represents a cookie town. The edges with no arrows are undirected, but now we have some directed edges, too.

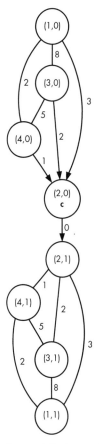

Figure 6-5: A grandma graph
with a cookie state

Here's what we do to create this graph:

- Add four new town nodes, one for each original town in the graph. The original nodes are in State 0; the new nodes are in Sate 1.

- Keep all of the original edges, except for those leaving Town 2 (the town with the cookie store). If we reach Town 2 in State 0, then we've transitioned to State 1, so the only edge leaving (2,0) is the directed edge to (2,1). It's a 0-weight edge, because changing state takes no time. While Dijkstra's algorithm can't be trusted on graphs with negative-weight edges (see "Negative-Weight Edges" on page 211), 0-weight edges are okay.

- Connect nodes in State 1 using exactly the same edges that originally connected nodes in State 0.

When we're in State 0 and reach a town with a cookie store, we buy a box of cookies and end up in State 1. Once we're in State 1, the graph gives us no way to return to State 0, because there's no way to lose the box of cookies.

We start in Town 1, State 0. We must arrive in Town 4, State 1. This requires that we eventually move from State 0 to State 1 and then go to Town 4 using the State-1 edges. When there are multiple towns with cookie stores, the problem becomes increasingly tricky, because then we have to choose exactly which cookie town takes us from State 0 to State 1. Well, it might be tricky for us, but not for Dijkstra's algorithm, because we're just asking for a shortest path in a graph.

## Task 1: Shortest Paths

So far, we've talked about how to model the problem as a graph and find the shortest path distance, but not how to find the *number* of shortest paths. I'll take these two subtasks in turn. At the end of this subsection, we'll have solved half of the problem, correctly printing the shortest path distance. We won't be printing anything for the number of paths, though, so we'll still fail all of the test cases. Don't worry: in the next subsection, we'll work out how to coax the number of paths out of our code, too. It's Dijkstra time!

With our new model (using the States 0 and 1), the graph that we read from the input no longer corresponds to the graph that we'll explore with Dijkstra's algorithm. One idea is to produce the adjacency list representation of the new graph from the adjacency list for the original graph. That is, start with an empty graph that has twice the number of nodes and add all of the required edges. That can be done, but I think it's easier to leave the graph alone, logically adding the state to the code for Dijkstra's algorithm. (When solving the Rope Climb problem in Chapter 5, we didn't have much of a choice of what to do, because the input did not contain a graph.)

We'll write the function with the following signature:

```
void solve(edge *adj_list[], int num_towns, int store[])
```

Here, adj_list is the adjacency list, num_towns is the number of towns (and the number of grandma's town), and store tells us for any given i whether town i has a cookie store.

Now we'll proceed just as we did with the Mice Maze (Listing 6-2). At each step, however, we ask what effect the state has on our code and we make appropriate modifications. Let's walk through the code, which is given in Listing 6-4. Compare this code to Listing 6-2 to highlight the similarities.

```
void solve(edge *adj_list[], int num_towns, int store[]) {
  static int done[MAX_TOWNS + 1][2];
  static int min_distances[MAX_TOWNS + 1][2];
  int i, j, state, found;
  int min_distance, min_town_index, min_state_index, old_distance;
  edge *e;

❶ for (state = 0; state <= 1; state++)
    for (i = 1; i <= num_towns; i++) {
      done[i][state] = 0;
      min_distances[i][state] = -1;
    }
❷ min_distances[1][0] = 0;

❸ for (i = 0; i < num_towns * 2; i++) {
    min_distance = -1;
    found = 0;
    for (state = 0; state <= 1; state++)
      for (j = 1; j <= num_towns; j++) {
        if (!done[j][state] && min_distances[j][state] >= 0) {
          if (min_distance == -1 || min_distances[j][state] < min_distance) {
            min_distance = min_distances[j][state];
            min_town_index = j;
            min_state_index = state;
            found = 1;
          }
        }
      }
    if (!found)
      break;
❹   done[min_town_index][min_state_index] = 1;

❺   if (min_state_index == 0 && store[min_town_index]) {
      old_distance = min_distances[min_town_index][1];
      if (old_distance == -1 || old_distance > min_distance)
        min_distances[min_town_index][1] = min_distance;
    } else {
❻     e = adj_list[min_town_index];
      while (e) {
        old_distance = min_distances[e->to_town][min_state_index];
```

```
        if (old_distance == -1 || old_distance > min_distance + e->length)
          min_distances[e->to_town][min_state_index] = min_distance +
                                                        e->length;

        e = e->next;
      }
    }
  }
❼ printf("%d\n", min_distances[num_towns][1]);
}
```

*Listing 6-4: The shortest path to grandma's using Dijkstra's algorithm*

Right from the start, we see the influence of the state on our arrays, as done and min_distances are now two-dimensional arrays. The first dimension is indexed by the town number, and the second is indexed by the state. In our initialization ❶, we're careful to initialize the elements of both states.

Our starting point is Town 1, State 0, so that's the distance that we initialize to 0 ❷.

As always, we want to continue running Dijkstra's algorithm until no new nodes can be found. We have num_towns towns, but each one exists in both State 0 and State 1, so we have a maximum of num_towns * 2 nodes to find ❸.

The nested state and j loops together find the next node. When these loops are done ❹, two important variables will be set: min_town_index gives the index of the town, and min_state_index gives the index of the state.

Our next step depends on which state we're in and whether the town has a cookie store. If we're in State 0 and at a town with a cookie store ❺, then we ignore adj_list and consider only the transition to State 1. Remember that the transition from [min_town_index][0] to [min_town_index][1] has distance 0, so our new path to [min_town_index][1] has the same distance as the shortest path to [min_town_index][0]. In typical Dijkstra fashion, we update the shortest path if our new path is shorter.

Otherwise, we're in State 0 but not at a town with a cookie store, or we're in State 1. The available edges here are exactly those in the input graph from the current town, so we examine all edges from min_town_index ❻. Now we're in Mice Maze territory, looking for new shorter paths using edge e. Just be careful to use min_state_index everywhere, since none of these edges changes the state.

The final thing to do is print the shortest path distance ❼. We use num_towns as the first index (that's grandma's town) and 1 as the second index (so that a box of cookies is being carried).

If you run our program on the test case from "Adjacency Matrix" on page 214, you should get the correct output of 4. Indeed, for any test case, we'll output the shortest path. Now, let's move on to the number of shortest paths.

## Task 2: Number of Shortest Paths

It takes just a few changes to beef up Dijkstra's algorithm so that it finds not only the shortest path distance, but also the number of shortest paths. Those changes are subtle, so I'll begin by working a few steps of an example to give you some intuition about why what we're doing makes sense. I'll then show the new code before giving a more detailed correctness argument.

### Working Through an Example

Let's trace Dijkstra's algorithm on Figure 6-5 from node (1,0). In addition to tracking whether each node is done and the minimum distance to each node, we'll also keep *num_paths*, giving the number of shortest paths of minimum distance to the node. We'll see that those paths counted by *num_paths* get thrown away whenever a shorter path is found.

To begin, we initialize the state for the starting node (1, 0). We set its minimum distance to 0 and set it to be done. As there's exactly one path of distance 0 from the starting node to itself (the path of no edges), we set its number of paths to 1. We use the edges from the starting node to initialize the other nodes, and we set each of them to have one path (the path from the starting node). This gives us our first snapshot:

| node | done | min_distance | num_paths |
|------|------|------------|-----------|
| (1,0) | true | 0 | 1 |
| (2,0) | false | 3 | 1 |
| (3,0) | false | 8 | 1 |
| (4,0) | false | 2 | 1 |
| (1,1) | false | | |
| (2,1) | false | | |
| (3,1) | false | | |
| (4,1) | false | | |

Now what? Well, as always with Dijkstra's algorithm, we scan through the nodes that are not done and choose one with minimum *min_distance* value. We therefore choose node (4,0). Dijkstra's algorithm guarantees that this node has its shortest path set, so we can set it to done. Then, we must check the edges leaving (4,0) to see whether we can find shorter paths to other nodes. We can indeed find a shorter path to (3,0): before it was 8, but now it's 7, because we can get to (4,0) with distance 2, and then from (4,0) to (3,0) with distance 5. What do we put for the number of shortest paths to (3,0)? Well, it used to be 1, so it's tempting to make it 2. However, 2 is wrong, because that would count the path of distance 8, and that's no longer a shortest path. The answer is 1, because there's only one path of distance 7.

There's an edge from (4,0) to (2,0) that we shouldn't dismiss too quickly. The old shortest path to (2,0) was 3. What does the edge from (4,0) to (2,0) do for us? Does it give us a shorter path? Well, the distance to (4,0) is 2, and the edge from (4,0) to (2,0) has distance 1, so we have a new way to get to (2,0) with distance 3. That's not a shorter path, but it is *another* shortest path! That is, getting to (4,0) and then using the edge to (2,0) gives us new ways to get to (2,0). The number of new ways is the number of shortest paths to (4,0), which is just one. That gives us 1 + 1 = 2 shortest paths to get to (2,0).

This is all summarized in the next snapshot:

| node | done | min_distance | num_paths |
|------|------|--------------|-----------|
| (1,0) | true | 0 | 1 |
| (2,0) | false | 3 | 2 |
| (3,0) | false | 7 | 1 |
| (4,0) | true | 2 | 1 |
| (1,1) | false | | |
| (2,1) | false | | |
| (3,1) | false | | |
| (4,1) | false | | |

The next node that's done is (2,0). There's an edge of weight 0 from (2,0) to (2,1), and it takes distance 3 to get to (2,0), so we have a shortest path of distance 3 to (2,1) as well. There are two ways to get to (2,0) with that minimum distance, so there are two ways to get to (2,1) as well. Here's what we've got now:

| node | done | min_distance | num_paths |
|------|------|--------------|-----------|
| (1,0) | true | 0 | 1 |
| (2,0) | true | 3 | 2 |
| (3,0) | false | 7 | 1 |
| (4,0) | true | 2 | 1 |
| (1,1) | false | | |
| (2,1) | false | 3 | 2 |
| (3,1) | false | | |
| (4,1) | false | | |

The next node that's done is (2,1), and it is this node that finds the shortest path distance to our destination (4,1). There are two shortest paths to (2,1), so there are two shortest paths to (4,1) as well. Node (2,1) also finds new shortest paths to (1,1) and (3,1). Here's what we've got now:

| node | done | min_distance | num_paths |
|------|------|--------------|-----------|
| (1,0) | true | 0 | 1 |
| (2,0) | true | 3 | 2 |
| (3,0) | false | 7 | 1 |
| (4,0) | true | 2 | 1 |
| (1,1) | false | 6 | 2 |
| (2,1) | true | 3 | 2 |
| (3,1) | false | 5 | 2 |
| (4,1) | false | 4 | 2 |

Node (4,1) is the next one out, so we have our answer: the shortest path is 4 and the number of shortest paths is 2. (In our code we won't have a stopping criterion here at the destination, so Dijkstra's algorithm would keep going, finding shortest paths and number of shortest paths for other nodes. I encourage you to persevere with this example until the end.)

That's how the algorithm works. It can be summarized by two rules:

**Rule 1** Suppose that we use Node $u$ to find a shorter path to Node $v$. Then the number of shortest paths to $v$ is the number of shortest paths to $u$. (All of the old paths to $v$ are invalidated and no longer count, because we now know that they are not shortest paths.)

**Rule 2** Suppose that we use Node $u$ to find a path to Node $v$ that's the same distance as the current shortest path to $v$. Then the number of paths to $v$ is the number of shortest paths that we already had for $v$, plus the number of shortest paths to $u$. (All of the old paths to $v$ still count.)

Suppose that we focus on some node $n$ and watch what happens to its minimum distance and number of shortest paths as it runs. We don't know what the shortest path to $n$ will be: we might have its shortest path now, or Dijkstra's algorithm might find a shorter one later. If we have its shortest path now, then we had better accumulate the number of shortest paths to $n$, since we may ultimately need that value to compute the number of shortest paths for other nodes. If we don't have its shortest path now, then in retrospect we'll have pointlessly accumulated its number of shortest paths. That's okay, though, because we'll just reset the number of shortest paths anyway when we find a shorter path.

### The Code

To solve this task, we can start with Listing 6-4 and make the changes necessary to find the number of shortest paths. The updated code is given in Listing 6-5.

```
#define MOD 1000000

void solve(edge *adj_list[], int num_towns, int store[]) {
  static int done[MAX_TOWNS + 1][2];
  static int min_distances[MAX_TOWNS + 1][2];
❶ static int num_paths[MAX_TOWNS + 1][2];
  int i, j, state, found;
  int min_distance, min_town_index, min_state_index, old_distance;
  edge *e;

  for (state = 0; state <= 1; state++)
    for (i = 1; i <= num_towns; i++) {
      done[i][state] = 0;
      min_distances[i][state] = -1;
    ❷ num_paths[i][state] = 0;
    }
```

```
        min_distances[1][0] = 0;
❸ num_paths[1][0] = 1;

    for (i = 0; i < num_towns * 2; i++) {
      min_distance = -1;
      found = 0;
      for (state = 0; state <= 1; state++)
        for (j = 1; j <= num_towns; j++) {
          if (!done[j][state] && min_distances[j][state] >= 0) {
            if (min_distance == -1 || min_distances[j][state] < min_distance) {
              min_distance = min_distances[j][state];
              min_town_index = j;
              min_state_index = state;
              found = 1;
            }
          }
        }
      if (!found)
        break;
      done[min_town_index][min_state_index] = 1;

      if (min_state_index == 0 && store[min_town_index]) {
        old_distance = min_distances[min_town_index][1];
❹      if (old_distance == -1 || old_distance >= min_distance) {
          min_distances[min_town_index][1] = min_distance;
❺        if (old_distance == min_distance)
            num_paths[min_town_index][1] += num_paths[min_town_index][0];
          else
            num_paths[min_town_index][1] = num_paths[min_town_index][0];
❻        num_paths[min_town_index][1] %= MOD;
        }
      } else {
        e = adj_list[min_town_index];
        while (e) {
          old_distance = min_distances[e->to_town][min_state_index];
          if (old_distance == -1 ||
              old_distance >= min_distance + e->length) {
            min_distances[e->to_town][min_state_index] = min_distance +
                                                         e->length;
❼          if (old_distance == min_distance + e->length)
              num_paths[e->to_town][min_state_index] +=
                  num_paths[min_town_index][min_state_index];
            else
              num_paths[e->to_town][min_state_index] =
                  num_paths[min_town_index][min_state_index];
❽          num_paths[e->to_town][min_state_index] %= MOD;
          }
```

```
        e = e->next;
      }
    }
  }
❾ printf("%d %d\n", min_distances[num_towns][1], num_paths[num_towns][1]);
}
```

*Listing 6-5: The shortest path and number of shortest paths to grandma's*

I added a num_paths array that tracks the number of paths that we've found for each node ❶ and set all of its elements to 0 ❷. The only nonzero element in num_paths is for our starting node (1,0), which has one path of distance 0 (the path that begins at the starting node and follows no edges) ❸.

The remaining new work is to update num_paths. As we've discussed, there are two cases. If we find a shorter path, then the old number of paths no longer counts. If we find another way to reach a node using its current path distance, then we add to the old number of paths. It's that second case that can trip us up if we're not careful, because we need to include an equality check in addition to a greater-than check ❹. If we used exactly the code that we've used throughout the chapter,

```
if (old_distance == -1 || old_distance > min_distance) {
```

then the number of paths to a node would only be updated when a shorter path was found; there would be no way to accumulate shortest paths from multiple sources. Instead, we use >= rather than >

```
if (old_distance == -1 || old_distance >= min_distance) {
```

so that we can find more shortest paths, even if the shortest path itself does not change.

Now we can implement exactly the two cases that we've discussed for updating the number of paths. We have to do these cases twice, because there are two places in the code where Dijkstra's algorithm can find shortest paths. The first addition ❺ is to the code that follows a 0-weight edge from State 0. If the shortest path is the same as before, we add; if there's now a new shorter path, we reset. The second addition of essentially the same code ❼ is added to the code for looping through the edges leaving the current node. In both cases, we use the mod operator ❻ ❽ to keep us under 1,000,000 shortest paths.

The final required change is to update the printf call at the end ❾, now also printing the number of shortest paths to grandma's.

You're ready to submit to the judge. Let's discuss a little bit about correctness before we wrap up for good.

### Algorithm Correctness

There are no negative-weight edges in our Grandma Planner graphs, so we know that Dijkstra's algorithm will correctly find all shortest path distances. There are some 0-weight edges—one from each cookie town in State 0 to the corresponding town in State 1—but Dijkstra's algorithm copes just fine with those when finding shortest paths.

However, we must carefully think through the implications of 0-weight edges on finding the *number* of shortest paths. If we allow arbitrary 0-weight edges, then there may be an *infinite* number of shortest paths. Take a look at Figure 6-6, where we have 0-weight edges from A to B, B to C, and C to A. The shortest path from A to C, for example, is 0, and we have an infinite number of such paths: A → B → C, A → B → C → A → B → C, and so on.

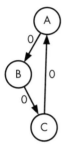

Figure 6-6: A graph with
an infinite number of
shortest paths

Luckily, cycles of 0-weight edges cannot actually present themselves in Grandma Planner graphs. Remember that all road distances are at least one. Suppose that there were a 0-weight edge from Node $u$ to Node $v$. This means that $u$ is in State 0 and $v$ is in State 1. We can never get from $v$ back to $u$, because our graphs provide no way to move from State 1 back to State 0.

I'll end by arguing the following: once a node is set to done, we have found its total number of shortest paths. Consider a run of our algorithm where it gives the wrong number of shortest paths. Our algorithm hums along, finding shortest paths and the number of shortest paths... and then, boom, it makes a mistake for the first time. It sets some node $n$ to done, but it's missed finding some of its shortest paths. We need to argue that this mistake cannot arise.

Suppose that some shortest paths to $n$ end with some edge $m \rightarrow n$. If $m \rightarrow n$ has a weight greater than 0, then the shortest path to $m$ is shorter than the shortest path to $n$. (It's the shortest path to $n$ minus the weight of $m \rightarrow n$.) Dijkstra's algorithm works by finding nodes that are further and further from the starting node, so Node $m$ must be done by this point. When Dijkstra's algorithm set $m$ to done, it would have gone through all edges from $m$, including $m \rightarrow n$. Since $m$'s number of paths was set correctly ($m$ is done, and Dijkstra's algorithm hadn't made its mistake yet), Dijkstra's algorithm includes all of those paths in $n$'s path count.

Now, what if $m \rightarrow n$ is a 0-weight edge? We need $m$ to be done before $n$; otherwise, $m$'s number of paths cannot be trusted when exploring the edges that leave $m$. We know that 0-weight edges go from a node in State 0 to a node in State 1, so $m$ must be in State 0 and $n$ must be in State 1. The shortest path to $m$ must be the same as the shortest path to $n$, since the 0-weight edge adds nothing to $m$'s shortest path. At some point, then, at the time when $m$ and $n$ are not done, Dijkstra's algorithm will have to choose which of the two to next set to done. It had better choose $m$; and it will, because, as I've written the code, when there is a tie it chooses a node from State 0 rather than State 1.

We need to tread lightly: we're really getting away with something here. Here's a test case that exemplifies why we have to process State-0 nodes before State-1 nodes:

---

```
4
0 3 1 2
3 0 2 1
1 2 0 5
2 1 5 0
2
2 3
```

---

Trace our modified Dijkstra's algorithm on this example. If you have a choice of which node to next set to done, choose one from State 0. If you do that, you'll get the correct answer: a shortest path distance of four and four shortest paths. Then, trace the algorithm again, only this time break ties by choosing a node from State 1. You'll still get the correct shortest path distance of four, because Dijkstra's algorithm is not sensitive to how ties are broken. But our modified Dijkstra's algorithm is, witnessed by the fact that you should get two shortest paths rather than four.

## Summary

Dijkstra's algorithm is designed to find shortest paths in graphs. We've seen in this chapter how to model a problem instance as a suitable weighted graph and then use Dijkstra's algorithm. Moreover, Dijkstra's algorithm, like BFS in Chapter 5, can serve as a guide for solving related but distinct problems. In the Grandma Planner problem, we found the number of shortest paths by a suitable modification to Dijkstra's algorithm. We didn't have to start from scratch. We're not always literally going to be asked for the shortest path. If Dijkstra's algorithm were resolute, finding shortest paths and nothing else, then it would offer no help when contexts shift. Indeed, we'd have learned a powerful algorithm, but one of an all-or-nothing flavor. Fortunately, Dijkstra's algorithm applies more broadly. If you continue with graph algorithms beyond what I've included in this book, you'll likely see ideas from Dijkstra's algorithm appear again. While there may be millions of problems out there, there are far fewer algorithms. The best algorithms are often the ones that rest on ideas so flexible that they can ooze beyond their intended purpose.

# Notes

Mice Maze is originally from the 2001 Southwestern Europe Regional Contest. Grandma Planner is originally from the 2008 South African Programming Olympiad, Final Round.

For more about graph search and its many applications to competitive programming problems, I recommend *Competitive Programming 4* by Steven Halim and Felix Halim (2020).

# 7

## BINARY SEARCH

This chapter is all about binary search. If you don't know what binary search is— excellent! I'm excited for the opportunity to teach you a systematic, performant technique for isolating an optimal solution from among zillions of possible solutions. And if you do know what binary search is and think that it's just for searching a sorted array—excellent! You'll learn that binary search is for so much more than that. To keep things fresh, we will not search a sorted array in this entire chapter, not even once.

What do minimizing the amount of liquid needed to feed ants, maximizing the minimum jump distance between rocks, finding the best living area in a city, and flipping switches to open cave doors have in common? Let's find out.

## Problem 1: Feeding Ants

This is DMOJ problem coci14c4p4.

## The Problem

Bobi has a terrarium in the shape of a tree. Each edge of the tree is a pipe in which liquid flows down. Some pipes are superpipes that increase the amount of liquid that flows through them. Bobi keeps one of his pet ants in each of the tree's leaves. (Yes, this context is a reach. I won't pretend otherwise, but this problem is otherwise ace.)

Each pipe has a percentage value that indicates the percentage of the available liquid that flows through it. For example, suppose that a node $n$ has three downward pipes, where those pipes have percentage values of 20 percent, 50 percent, and 30 percent, respectively. If 20 liters of liquid arrive at Node $n$, then the 20 percent pipe gets $20 \times 0.2 = 4$ liters, the 50 percent pipe gets $20 \times 0.5 = 10$ liters, and the 30 percent pipe gets $20 \times 0.3 = 6$ liters.

Now consider the superpipes. For each superpipe, Bobi decides whether its special behavior is off or on. If it is off, then it behaves like a regular pipe. If it is on, then it squares the amount of liquid that it receives.

Bobi pours liquid into the root of the tree. His goal is to give each ant at least the amount of liquid that it requires and to do so by pouring as little liquid as possible.

Let's make this description concrete by studying a sample terrarium; see Figure 7-1.

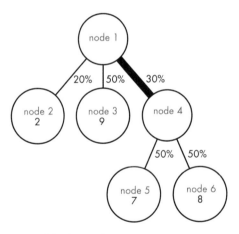

Figure 7-1: A sample terrarium

I've numbered the nodes from 1 to 6; the leaf nodes (2, 3, 5, and 6) have an additional annotation giving the amount of liquid required by each ant. I've also annotated each edge with its percentage value. Notice that the percentage values of the downward pipes leaving a given node always add up to 100 percent.

There's one superpipe in the tree, from Node 1 to Node 4; I've drawn that with a thicker edge. Suppose that 20 liters of liquid are poured into the root. The superpipe gets 30 percent of the 20 liters, which is 6 liters. If the superpipe's special behavior is off, then 6 liters flow through it. However, if the superpipe's special behavior is on, then, instead of 6 liters of liquid flowing through it, $6^2 = 36$ liters of liquid flow through it.

## Input

The input contains one test case, consisting of the following lines:

- A line containing $n$, the number of nodes in the tree. $n$ is between 1 and 1,000. The tree nodes are numbered from 1 to $n$, and the root of the tree is node 1.

- $n - 1$ lines used to build the tree. Each of these lines represents one pipe and consists of four integers: the two nodes connected by the pipe, the pipe's percentage value (between 1 and 100), and whether the pipe is a superpipe (with 0 meaning no and 1 meaning yes).

- A line containing $n$ integers, one for each node, giving the number of liters of liquid needed by the ant in that node. Each ant requires between 1 and 10 liters of liquid. For any nonleaf node (where there is no ant), a value of $-1$ is given.

Here's an input that could generate the sample terrarium in Figure 7-1:

```
6
1 2 20 0
1 3 50 0
1 4 30 1
4 5 50 0
4 6 50 0
-1 2 9 -1 7 8
```

Note how the first line (integer 6 here) indicates the number of nodes in the tree, not the number of lines that build the tree. The number of lines that build the tree (in this case five lines) is always one less than the number of nodes. (Why is it always one less? Each line that builds the tree effectively tells us the parent of one of the $n$ nodes. Each node except for the root has a parent, so we need $n - 1$ lines to tell us about all of the $n - 1$ parents.)

## Output

Output the minimum number of liters of liquid that Bobi must pour into the tree's root to feed all the ants. Include four digits of accuracy after the decimal point. The correct output is guaranteed to be at most 2,000,000,000 (two billion).

The time limit for solving the test case is 0.6 seconds.

## A New Flavor of Tree Problem

As in Chapter 2, we're in the domain of trees here. If we want to explore a terrarium tree, then we can use recursion. (A full graph-search algorithm such as BFS is overkill because there are no cycles.)

For the two problems in Chapter 2, our solutions were based on the structure of the tree and the values stored in nodes:

- In Halloween Haul, we calculated the total candy by adding up the values in the leaves, and we calculated the total street-walks using the height and shape of the tree.

- In Descendant Distance, we calculated the number of descendants at the desired distance by using the number of children of each node.

That is, what we needed—candy values, height, tree shape—were right there, encoded for us in the tree itself. In the present problem, we're asked to find the minimum number of liters that Bobi must pour—but the tree doesn't contain any values like that! The tree has information on pipe percentage, superpipe status, and ant appetite, but it has nothing directly informing us of the amount of liquid that should be poured into the root. In particular, the superpipes, with their liquid-squaring behavior, make unclear the relationship between the amount of liquid needed by the ants and the amount of liquid that should be poured.

Because the tree won't readily give us what we need, I'll just pick a value out of thin air—say, 10. There you go, Bobi. Pour 10 liters in there.

I hope you're very suspicious of what I just did, recklessly choosing a number like that. You should be surprised if 10 were the answer. I pulled 10 out of thin air, after all. You may also be surprised that we can in fact learn a lot by trying out the value 10 and seeing what happens.

Let's use Figure 7-1 again. Suppose that we pour 10 liters of liquid into the root. Twenty percent of 10 is 2, so 2 liters of liquid will make it to the ant in Node 2. Perfect: that ant needs 2 liters of liquid, so we're sending just enough liquid. Let's continue.

Since 50 percent of 10 is 5, the ant in Node 3 gets 5 liters of liquid. Now we're in trouble: that ant needs 9 liters of liquid, and 5 liters is not enough. More bad news: the pipe between Nodes 1 and 3 is not a superpipe, so there's nothing we can do except declare that 10 is not in fact the solution.

We could proceed by picking another number of liters out of thin air and similarly simulating the flow of liquid on that new number. However, because 10 liters was insufficient, now we should restrict our thin-air range to only values *greater than 10*. Since 10 liters was insufficient, any smaller value will be insufficient, too. There's no point trying 2 liters or 7 liters or 9.5 liters or anything less than 10. They're all too small.

Let's next try 20 liters. This time, the ant at Node 2 gets 4 liters, which is just fine because that ant only needs 2 liters. The ant at Node 3 gets 10 liters, which again is fine because that ant only needs 9 liters.

The pipe between Nodes 1 and 4 takes 30 percent of the liquid, so that's 6 liters of the total 20 liters. However, this pipe is a superpipe! If we use its special behavior, the pipe cranks up the 6 liters to $6^2 = 36$ liters, so 36 liters arrives at Node 4. Now the ants at Nodes 5 and 6 are fine: each ant gets 18 liters, and they only need 7 liters (Node 5) and 8 liters (Node 6).

Unlike 10 liters, then, 20 liters is a feasible solution, but is it the optimal (that is, minimal) solution? Maybe, maybe not. What we know for sure is that there's no point testing any number of liters greater than 20. We already have 20 as a feasible solution; why try values, such as 25 or 30, that are worse?

We've now reduced the problem to finding an optimal solution between 10 and 20 liters. We could keep choosing numbers, reducing the range at each step, until our range is so small that one of its endpoints serves as an accurate solution.

In the general case, what number of liters should we choose first? The optimal solution could be up to 2 billion, so starting with 10 may be way, way off. And, once we test a number of liters, where should we go next? The optimal solution might be considerably larger or smaller than our current guess, so adding or subtracting 10 at a time may not help us make much progress.

These are good questions, good questions that we will answer ... but not yet. Let's first tackle how to read the input (so that we can explore a tree) and how to determine whether a number of liters is a feasible solution. Then, we'll see a super-fast algorithm for searching massive ranges. A range of two billion? We'll eat that for breakfast.

## Reading the Input

In Chapter 2, we used a node struct at the core of how trees were represented. Then, in Chapter 5, Book Translation, we used the adjacency list representation of a graph with an edge struct. There we learned that whether we use a node or edge struct comes down to whether it's the nodes or the edges that carry additional attributes. In the present problem, the edges carry information (a percentage and a superpipe status), but so do the leaf nodes (the amount of liquid required by each ant). It's therefore tempting and reasonable to use *both* an edge struct and a node struct. Instead, to closely parallel the use of adjacency lists, I've chosen to stick with only an edge struct. As in the problem description, we number nodes starting at 1, but, with no node struct, we have nowhere to store the amount of liquid required by each ant. For that reason, we augment the adjacency list with a liquid_needed array, where liquid_needed[i] gives the amount of liquid required by the ant in Node i.

Here's the constant and typedef that we'll use throughout the code:

```
#define MAX_NODES 1000

typedef struct edge {
  int to_node, percentage, superpipe;
  struct edge *next;
} edge;
```

As in Book Translation (Chapter 5) and the two problems in Chapter 6, we can chain these edge structs together through next pointers to form a linked list of edges. If an edge is in the linked list for nNde i, then we know that the parent node of the edge is i. The to_node member tells us the child node at which this edge connects with the parent node; percentage is an integer between 1 and 100 that gives the percentage value for the pipe (edge); and superpipe is a flag whose value is 1 if the pipe is a superpipe and 0 if it's a regular pipe.

Now we can read the tree from the input, as shown in Listing 7-1.

```
int main(void) {
  static edge *adj_list[MAX_NODES + 1] = {NULL};
  static int liquid_needed[MAX_NODES + 1];
  int num_nodes, i;
  int from_node, to_node, percentage, superpipe;
  edge *e;
  scanf("%d", &num_nodes);

  for (i = 0; i < num_nodes - 1; i++) {
    scanf("%d%d%d%d", &from_node, &to_node, &percentage, &superpipe);
    e = malloc(sizeof(edge));
    if (e == NULL) {
      fprintf(stderr, "malloc error\n");
      exit(1);
    }
    e->to_node = to_node;
    e->percentage = percentage;
    e->superpipe = superpipe;
    e->next = adj_list[from_node];
❶   adj_list[from_node] = e;
  }

  for (i = 1; i <= num_nodes; i++)
❷   scanf("%d", &liquid_needed[i]);
  solve(adj_list, liquid_needed);
  return 0;
}
```

Listing 7-1: The main function for building the tree

The code is similar to, but simpler than, Listing 5-16 (Book Translation). In particular, each edge is read from the input, its members are set, and then it's added to the list of edges for from_node ❶. You may expect a corresponding edge to be added for to_node, since the graph is undirected, but I've left out such edges: liquid moves down the tree, not up, so adding backward edges would needlessly complicate the code that explores a tree.

Once the edge information is read in, all that's left is to read the values for the amount of liquid required by each ant. We'll use the liquid_needed array for that ❷. The combination of adj_list and liquid_needed captures everything we need to know about the test case.

## Testing Feasibility

Our next milestone is this: determine whether a given amount of liquid is a feasible solution. This is a crucial step, because once we have a function that can test a value for feasibility, we'll be able to use it to progressively narrow the search space until we find the optimal solution. Here's the signature for the function that we'll write:

```
int can_feed(int node, double liquid,
             edge *adj_list[], int liquid_needed[])
```

Here, node is the root node of the tree, liquid is the amount of liquid that we pour into the root of the tree, adj_list is the adjacency list for the tree, and liquid_needed is the amount of liquid required by each ant. We'll return 1 if liquid is enough to feed the ants (that is, if liquid is a feasible solution) and 0 if it is not.

We spent a whole chapter (Chapter 2) writing recursive functions on trees. Let's think about whether we can use recursion again.

Remember that, to use recursion, we need a base case—a case that can be solved with no recursion. Luckily, we have one! If the tree is a single leaf node, then we can determine right away whether liquid is sufficient. If liquid is greater than or equal to the amount of liquid needed by the ant in this leaf, then we have a feasible solution; otherwise, we don't.

We can tell whether a node is a leaf by checking the corresponding value in liquid_needed: if it's -1, then it isn't a leaf; otherwise, it is. (We could have also used the adjacency list to check whether or not the linked list for the node was empty.) Here's what we've got:

```
if (liquid_needed[node] != -1)
  return liquid >= liquid_needed[node];
```

Now, consider the recursive case. Imagine that the root node of some tree has $p$ downward pipes (that is, $p$ children). We're given the amount of liquid that's poured into the root. Using the pipe percentage values, we can determine the amount of liquid that goes into each pipe; using the super-pipe statuses, we can determine the amount of liquid that reaches the bottom end of each pipe. If enough liquid reaches the bottom end of each pipe, then the liquid poured into the root was sufficient and we should return 1. Otherwise, the amount of liquid that reaches the bottom end of some pipe isn't sufficient, and we should return 0. This suggests that we should make $p$ recursive calls, one for each pipe that leaves the root. We'll do that in a loop that uses the adjacency list to go through each such pipe.

The full code for the function is given in Listing 7-2.

```
int can_feed(int node, double liquid,
             edge *adj_list[], int liquid_needed[]) {
  edge *e;
  int ok;
  double down_pipe;
  if (liquid_needed[node] != -1)
```

```
        return liquid >= liquid_needed[node];
    e = adj_list[node];
❶ ok = 1;
    while (e && ok) {
        down_pipe = liquid * e->percentage / 100;
        if (e->superpipe)
        ❷ down_pipe = down_pipe * down_pipe;
        if (!can_feed(e->to_node, down_pipe, adj_list, liquid_needed))
        ❸ ok = 0;
        e = e->next;
    }
    return ok;
}
```

*Listing 7-2: Testing the feasibility of the amount of liquid*

The ok variable tracks whether liquid is a feasible solution for the tree. If ok is 1, then the solution is still feasible; if ok is 0, then it's definitely not. We initialize ok to 1 ❶, and we set it to 0 if the amount of liquid through one of the pipes isn't sufficient ❸. If ok is still 1 at the bottom of the function, then we've satisfied all pipes and we conclude that liquid is feasible.

We determine the amount of liquid that enters each pipe by using that pipe's percentage value. Then, if the pipe is a superpipe, we square that value ❷ . . . but hey, wait! The problem description says that Bobi gets to decide whether or not to use the special behavior of each superpipe. However, here we're just indiscriminately squaring the amount of liquid, thereby always using the special behavior.

The reason we can get away with this is that squaring makes values bigger: compare 2 to $2^2 = 4$, 3 to $3^2 = 9$, and so on. Since we want to know whether the given amount of liquid is feasible and there's no penalty for using the special behavior of a superpipe, we may as well generate as much liquid as possible. Maybe we could have gotten away without using some superpipe special behavior, but no one's asking us to be economical.

Don't worry that squaring makes positive values less than one, such as 0.5, smaller. $0.5^2 = 0.25$, so indeed we wouldn't want to activate superpipe behavior in such cases. Each ant requires at least 1 liter of liquid, though. So, if we're down to 0.5 liters of liquid at some node, then nothing we do is going to feed the ants in the node's subtree anyway. We'd eventually return 0 whether or not we squared the value.

Let's show how useful this can_feed function is by continuing the work we did in "A New Flavor of Tree Problem" on page 233. We showed there that 10 liters was not sufficient for the sample instance from the problem description. Comment out the solve call at the bottom of Listing 7-1 (don't worry: we'll write that solve function soon), and add a call to can_feed to test 10 liters of liquid:

```
printf("%d\n", can_feed(1, 10, adj_list, liquid_needed));
```

You should see a result of 0, which means that 10 liters isn't sufficient. We also showed that 20 liters was sufficient. Change the can_feed call to test 20 liters instead of 10:

```
printf("%d\n", can_feed(1, 20, adj_list, liquid_needed));
```

You should see a result of 1, which means that 20 liters is sufficient.

Now, we know that 10 is not enough but 20 is. Let's squeeze this range down further. Try 15, and you should see an output of 0. So, it seems 15 is not enough. Our optimal answer is now greater than 15 and at most 20.

Try 18 next: you should see that 18 is enough. How about 17? No, 17 is not enough, nor is 17.5 or 17.9. It turns out that the optimal solution is indeed 18.

That's enough of the ad hoc searching. Let's systematize this.

## Searching for a Solution

From the problem description, we know that the optimal solution is at most two billion. There's therefore a massive search space in which the optimal solution lies. Our goal is to cut down this space as quickly as possible by never wasting a guess.

It's easy to waste a guess. For example, if we start with a guess of 10, and the optimal solution is in fact two billion, then we've essentially wasted that guess: all we've done is eliminate the numbers between 0 and 10. It's true that a guess of 10 would be fantastic if the optimal solution were, say, 8, because that one step would cut the range down to 0 to 10 and we'd find 8 soon after. Nonetheless, taking shots like this isn't worth it, because getting lucky once in a while won't offset the very likely case that our guess tells us almost nothing. It's for this reason that you don't guess 10 as your first guess when someone asks you to guess their number between 1 and 1,000. Sure, if they say "lower," you look like a full-on rock star, but if they say "higher," as they most likely will, you've all but wasted that first guess.

To guarantee that we learn as much as possible with each guess, we'll always guess the middle of the range. To do so, we maintain two variables, low and high, holding the low end and high end, respectively, of our current range. We then calculate the middle of the range, mid, test the feasibility of mid, and update low or high based on what we learn. We'll implement this strategy in Listing 7-3.

```
#define HIGHEST 2000000000

void solve(edge *adj_list[], int liquid_needed[]) {
  double low, high, mid;
  low = 0;
  high = HIGHEST;
❶ while (high - low > 0.00001) {
❷   mid = (low + high) / 2;
❸   if (can_feed(1, mid, adj_list, liquid_needed))
```

```
        high = mid;
      else
        low = mid;
  }
❹ printf("%.4lf\n", high);
}
```

*Listing 7-3: Searching for the optimal solution*

It's important to initialize low and high so that their range is guaranteed to contain the optimal solution. At all times, we'll maintain that low is less than or equal to the optimal solution and that high is greater than or equal to the optimal solution. We start low off with a value of 0; as each ant requires at least 1 liter, 0 liters is definitely less than or equal to the optimal solution. We start high off with a value of 2 billion, because it's guaranteed by the problem description that 2 billion is the maximum value of the optimal solution.

The while loop condition forces the range between low and high to be very small by the time the loop ends ❶. We need four digits of accuracy, hence the four 0s after the decimal point in 0.00001.

The first thing to do in the loop body is to calculate the middle of the range. We'll do that by taking the average of low and high, storing that result in mid ❷.

Now it's time to test mid liters for feasibility, using can_feed ❸. If mid is feasible, we have learned that guessing anything larger than mid would be a waste. We therefore set high = mid to cut the range off at a maximum of mid.

If mid is not feasible, then guessing anything smaller than mid would be a waste. We therefore set low = mid to cut the range off at a minimum of mid.

Once the loop terminates, low and high are very close together. We're printing high ❹, but printing low would work just as well.

This technique, where we keep dividing the range in half until it's very small, is called *binary search*. It's a surprisingly subtle and powerful algorithm, further evidence of which will come from the remaining problems in this chapter. It's also very fast, able to handle ranges of billions or trillions with ease.

Submit the solution to the judge, and then let's keep going. There's a lot more to know about binary search.

## Binary Search

Feeding Ants is an exemplar of the types of problems where binary search thrives. There are two ingredients to such problems; if you see these ingredients in a new problem you're facing, it's worth your time to try binary search.

**Ingredient 1: Hard optimality and easy feasibility**   For some problems, it's hard to come up with a way to find an optimal solution. Fortunately, in many such cases, it's considerably easier to determine whether or not some proposed solution is feasible. This was the situation in the

Feeding Ants problem: we didn't know how to find an optimal solution directly, but we did see how to determine whether some number of liters was feasible.

**Ingredient 2: Infeasible–feasible split**   We need the problem to exhibit the property that there is a border between infeasible and feasible solutions. All solutions on one side of the border must be infeasible, and all solutions on the other side must be feasible. In Feeding Ants, small values were infeasible and large values were feasible. Imagine considering values from small to large and asking whether each is infeasible or feasible. In doing so, we'll see a bunch of infeasible values and then a feasible value; after our first feasible value, we won't see infeasible values again. Suppose we try a value of 20 liters and find that it's infeasible. This means that we're still in the infeasible part of the search space, and we must search larger values. If 20 liters is feasible, then we're in the feasible part of the search space, and we should search smaller values. (Not meeting Ingredient 2 renders binary search useless. For example, suppose we have a problem where small values are infeasible, larger values are feasible, and even-larger values are infeasible again. We try a value of 20 and find that it is infeasible. Don't even think about focusing on values greater than 20: for all we know, values less than 10 could be infeasible and 10 to 15 could be feasible, giving 10 as the optimal solution here.) It's also okay if the search space transitions from feasible to infeasible, rather than from infeasible to feasible. Our next problem will offer such an example.

## Runtime of Binary Search

The reason why binary search is so powerful is that it makes a huge amount of progress with just a single iteration. For example, suppose that we're searching for an optimal solution in a range of two billion. A single iteration of binary search throws out half of this range, leaving a range of only one billion. Let that sink in: with just a single if statement and one variable update to mid, we make one billion units of progress! If binary search takes $q$ iterations to search a range of one billion, then it takes only one more iteration, $q + 1$, to search a range of two billion. The number of iterations grows very slowly compared to the width of the range.

The number of iterations taken by binary search to cut a range $n$ to range 1 is roughly the number of times that $n$ must be divided by 2 to get down to 1. For example, say that we start with a range of 8. After one iteration, we'll have reduced the range to at most 4. After two iterations, we'll have reduced the range to at most 2. After three iterations, we'll have reduced the range to 1. Moreover, if we don't care about decimal digits of accuracy, then that's it: three iterations.

There's a mathematical function called the *base-2 logarithm*, which, given value $n$, tells you how many times you have to divide $n$ by 2 to get 1 or less. It's written $\log_2 n$ or, when the discussion makes it clear that two is the base, as just $\log n$. For example, $\log_2 8$ is 3 and $\log_2 16$ is 4. $\log_2 2{,}000{,}000{,}000$

(that's two billion) is 30.9, so it takes about 31 iterations to knock this range down to 1.

Binary search is an example of a *logarithmic-time* algorithm. We therefore say that it's $O(\log m)$. (You'd ordinarily use $n$ here instead of $m$, but we're going to use $n$ for something else later in this section.) To reduce a range to 1, $m$ is the initial width of the range. However, in Feeding Ants, we needed to go further, obtaining four decimal digits of accuracy. What is $m$ there?

It's time to come clean on how we used binary search in Feeding Ants: we do more than $\log_2 2{,}000{,}000{,}000$ iterations of binary search, because we don't stop when the width of the range is 1. Instead, we stop once we've achieved four digits of accuracy after the decimal point. Adding five zeros gives us the number of iterations that we do: $\log_2 200{,}000{,}000{,}000{,}000$ rounds up to 48. Only 48 iterations are needed to pull a solution with four decimal digits of accuracy from a bewildering range of trillions. That's what binary search is made of.

On a tree of $n$ nodes, the can_feed function in Listing 7-2 (Feeding Ants) takes linear time; that is, time proportional to $n$. We call that function $\log_2 m \times 10^4$ times, where $m$ is the width of the range (two billion in the test cases). This is proportional to $\log m$ work. In total, then, we do $n$ work a total of $\log m$ times. This is an $O(n \log m)$ algorithm. It is not quite linear, because of that extra $\log m$ factor, but still very fast.

## Determining Feasibility

What I like most about binary search algorithms is that determining whether a value is feasible often requires the use of some other type of algorithm. That is, on the outside we have binary search, but on the inside—to test if each value is feasible—we have something else. That something else could be anything. In Feeding Ants, it was a tree search. In our next problem, it will be a greedy algorithm. In our third problem, it will be a dynamic-programming algorithm. We won't see one in this book, but there are problems where checking feasibility requires running a graph algorithm. That stuff you've learned in the previous chapters will all be in play again.

Determining feasibility often requires considerable creativity (just hopefully not as much creativity as needed for finding optimality!).

## Searching a Sorted Array

If you were familiar with binary search prior to reading this chapter, odds are that it was in the context of searching a sorted array. A typical scenario is that we are given an array a and a value v, and we want to find the smallest index of a whose value is greater than or equal to v. For example, if we were given the array {-5, -1, 15, 31, 78} and v were 26, we'd return index 3, because the value at index 3 (31) is the first one that's greater than or equal to 26.

Why does binary search work here? Take a look at the two ingredients:

**Ingredient 1**    Without a binary search, finding the optimal value would involve a costly scan through the array. Therefore, optimality is hard to obtain, but feasibility is easy: if I give you an index i, you can tell me right away whether a[i] is greater than or equal to v just by comparing a[i] to v.

**Ingredient 2**  Any values smaller than v come before any values that are greater than or equal to v—remember that a is sorted! That is, the infeasible values come before the feasible values.

It's true that binary search can be used to find a suitable index in an array in logarithmic time; later, in Chapter 10, we'll use it for that very purpose. But we solved Feeding Ants with binary search, with no such array in sight. Don't restrict yourself to thinking about binary search only when you have an array to search. Binary search is far more flexible than that.

# Problem 2: River Jump

We'll now see a problem in which we need a greedy algorithm to determine feasibility.

This is POJ problem 3258.

## The Problem

There's a river of length $L$ along which rocks have been placed. There's a rock at Location 0 (the beginning of the river), a rock at Location $L$ (the end of the river), and then $n$ other rocks between these. For example, on a river of length 12, we might have rocks at the following locations: 0, 5, 8, and 12.

A cow begins on the first rock (Location 0), jumps from there to the second rock, jumps from the second rock to the third rock, and so on, until it gets to the rock at the end of the river (Location $L$). Its minimum jump distance is the minimum distance between any consecutive pair of rocks. In the above example, the minimum jump distance is 3, witnessed by the distance between the rocks at Locations 5 and 8.

Farmer John is bored by the short jumps made by the cow, so he wants to increase the minimum jump distance as much as possible. He can't remove the rock at Location 0 or Location $L$, but he is able to remove $m$ of the other rocks.

In the above example, suppose that Farmer John is able to remove one rock. His choice is then to remove the rock at Location 5 or Location 8. If he removes the rock at Location 5, the minimum jump distance is 4 (from Location 8 to Location 12). However, he shouldn't do that, because if he removes the rock at Location 8, then he achieves a greater minimum jump distance of 5 (from Location 0 to Location 5).

Our task is to maximize the minimum jump distance that Farmer John can achieve by removing $m$ rocks.

### Input

The input contains one test case, consisting of the following lines:

- A line containing the three integers $L$ (the length of the river), $n$ (the number of rocks, not including the rocks at the beginning and end), and $m$ (the number of rocks that Farmer John can remove). $L$ is between 1 and 1,000,000,000 (one billion), $n$ is between 0 and 50,000, and $m$ is between 0 and $n$.

- $n$ lines, each giving the integer location of a rock. No two rocks will be at the same location.

### Output

Output the maximum achievable minimum jump distance. For the above example, we would output 5.

The time limit for solving the test case is two seconds.

## A Greedy Idea

In Chapter 3, when solving the Moneygrubbers problem, we introduced the idea of a greedy algorithm. A greedy algorithm does what looks promising right now, with no regard to the long-term consequences of its choices. Such an algorithm is often easy to propose: just state the greedy rule that it uses to make its next choice. When solving the Moneygrubbers problem, for example, I proposed the greedy algorithm that chooses the option of cheapest cost per apple. That greedy algorithm was incorrect. That lesson is worth remembering: while it's easy to propose a greedy algorithm, it's not easy to find one that's correct.

For two reasons, I didn't dedicate a chapter of the book to greedy algorithms. First, they're not as broadly applicable as other algorithm design approaches (such as dynamic programming). Second, when they do happen to work, it's often for subtle, problem-specific reasons. I've been duped many times over the years by seemingly correct but ultimately flawed greedy algorithms. A careful proof of correctness is often required to distinguish between the ones that are right and the ones that only feel right.

Nevertheless, greedy algorithms did make a concealed—and this time correct—appearance in Chapter 6 in the form of Dijkstra's algorithm. Algorithmists generally classify Dijkstra's algorithm as greedy. Once the algorithm declares that a node's shortest path has been found, it never goes back on that decision. It commits, once and for all, and does not let future discoveries influence what it has done in the past.

Greedy algorithms are now going to reappear. When I was introduced to River Jump several years ago, my instinct was that I could use a greedy algorithm to solve it. I wonder if you'll find the proposed algorithm as natural as I did. Here's the greedy rule: find the two rocks that are closest together, remove the one that's closest to its other neighbor rock, and repeat.

Let's return to the example from the problem description. Here it is as a test case:

```
12 2 1
5
8
```

For convenience, here are the rock locations: 0, 5, 8, and 12. We're allowed to remove one rock. The two rocks that are closest together are those at Locations 5 and 8, so the greedy rule will result in one of these being removed. The rock at Location 8 is a distance of 4 from its neighbor to the right; the rock at Location 5 is a distance of 5 from its neighbor to the left. Therefore, the greedy algorithm removes the rock at Location 8. It works correctly in this example.

Let's throw a bigger example in here and see what the greedy algorithm does. Suppose that the river has a length of 12 and we're allowed to remove two rocks. Here's the test case:

```
12 4 2
1
3
8
9
```

The rock locations are 0, 1, 3, 8, 9, and 12. What will the greedy algorithm do? The rocks that are closest together are the ones at Locations 0 and 1 and those at Locations 8 and 9. We'll have to choose one pair—let's choose 0 and 1. Since removing the rock at Location 0 is not allowed, we remove the rock at Location 1. The remaining rock locations are 0, 3, 8, 9, and 12.

Now the closest rocks are at Locations 8 and 9. The distance between 9 and 12 is less than the distance between 8 and 3, so the greedy algorithm removes the rock at Location 9. We're left with 0, 3, 8, and 12. The minimum jump distance here, and the correct answer, is 3. The greedy algorithm wins again.

Isn't that right? Keep knocking off the smallest distance between two rocks. How could we possibly do better than that? The greedy algorithm charms.

Sadly, the greedy algorithm is not correct. I encourage you to try to come up with a counterexample before I spoil it in the next paragraph.

Here's a counterexample:

```
12 4 2
2
4
5
8
```

We're allowed to remove two rocks. The rock locations are 0, 2, 4, 5, 8, and 12. The greedy rule identifies the rocks at Locations 4 and 5 as the closest rocks. It will remove the rock at Location 4, since the distance between

4 and 2 is less than the distance between 5 and 8. Here's what's left: 0, 2, 5, 8, and 12.

Now the greedy rule identifies the rocks at Locations 0 and 2 as the closest pair. It isn't allowed to remove the rock at 0, so it removes the rock at 2. We're left with 0, 5, 8, and 12. That's a minimum jump distance of 3. Here we have a mistake made by the greedy algorithm, because the maximum achievable minimum jump distance is 4. To see this, rather than remove the rocks at Locations 2 and 4, remove the ones at Locations 2 and 5. That leaves us with 0, 4, 8, and 12.

What went wrong? By removing the rock at Location 4 as its first move, the greedy algorithm creates a situation involving a jump distance of 2 and a jump distance of 3. It can only fix one of those two with its second move, so it has no chance of producing a minimum jump distance of anything greater than 3.

I don't know a greedy algorithm that directly solves this problem. Like Feeding Ants, this is a tough one to solve head-on. Fortunately, we don't have to.

### Testing Feasibility

In "Binary Search" on page 240, I offered two signals that point to a binary search solution: that it's easier to test feasibility than produce optimality and that the search space transitions from infeasible to feasible (or feasible to infeasible). We'll see that the River Jump problem passes on both counts.

Instead of solving for the optimal solution outright, let's solve for a different question: Is it possible to achieve a minimum jump distance of at least $d$? If we can nail this, then we can use binary search to find the largest feasible value of $d$.

Here's the test case that ended the previous subsection:

```
12 4 2
2
4
5
8
```

We're allowed to remove two rocks. The rock locations are 0, 2, 4, 5, 8, and 12.

Here's a question: What is the minimum number of rock removals that are needed to achieve a minimum jump distance of at least 6? Let's work from left to right and check. The rock at Location 0 has to stay—that's spelled out in the problem description. It's then evident that we have no choice of what to do with the rock at Location 2: we must remove it. If we didn't, then the distance between the rocks at Locations 0 and 2 would be less than 6. So, one rock is removed. The remaining rocks are at 0, 4, 5, 8, and 12.

Now, consider the rock at Location 4—do we keep it or remove it? Again, we're forced to remove it. If we keep it, then the rocks at Locations 0 and 4 would be closer together than 6. That's our second removal, and we're left with rocks at 0, 5, 8, and 12.

The rock at Location 5 has to be removed, too, because it's only a distance of 5 from the 0 rock. That's our third removal, leaving us with rocks at 0, 8, and 12.

We have to remove the rock at Location 8, too! It's far enough from Location 0 but too close to Location 12. That's our fourth removal, ultimately leaving us with just two rocks at 0 and 12.

So it takes four removals to achieve a minimum jump distance of at least 6, but we're only allowed to remove two rocks. As such, 6 is not a feasible solution. It's too big.

Is 3 a feasible solution? That is, can we achieve a minimum jump distance of at least 3 by removing two rocks? Let's see.

The rock at Location 0 stays. The rock at Location 2 has to go. That's our first removal, and it leaves us with this: 0, 4, 5, 8, and 12.

The rock at Location 4 can stay: it's more than a distance of 3 from Location 0. The rock at Location 5, though, has to go, because it's too close to the rock at Location 4. That's our second removal, giving us this: 0, 4, 8, and 12.

The rock at Location 8 is fine: it's far enough away from the rocks at Locations 4 and 12. We're done: it took us only two removals to achieve a minimum jump distance of at least 3. So, 3 is feasible.

We seem to be homing in on a greedy algorithm for checking feasibility. The rule is this: consider each rock in order, and remove it if it's too close to the previously kept rock. Also check the rightmost rock that we kept, and remove it if it's too close to the end of the river. Then, count the number of rocks that we removed; that count tells us whether the proposed minimum jump distance is feasible given the number of rocks we're allowed to remove. (To be clear, this is a proposed greedy algorithm for checking feasibility of a specified jump distance, not for finding the optimal solution in one shot.)

The code for this algorithm is in Listing 7-4.

```
int can_make_min_distance(int distance, int rocks[], int num_rocks,
                          int num_remove, int length) {
  int i;
  int removed = 0, prev_rock_location = 0, cur_rock_location;
  if (length < distance)
    return 0;
  for (i = 0; i < num_rocks; i++) {
    cur_rock_location = rocks[i];
❶ if (cur_rock_location - prev_rock_location < distance)
      removed++;
    else
      prev_rock_location = cur_rock_location;
  }
❷ if (length - prev_rock_location < distance)
    removed++;
```

```
    return removed <= num_remove;
}
```

*Listing 7-4: Testing the feasibility of the jump distance*

The function has five parameters:

**distance**   The minimum jump distance whose feasibility we're testing

**rocks**   An array giving the location of each rock, not including the rocks at the beginning and end of the river

**num_rocks**   The number of rocks in the rocks array

**num_remove**   The number of rocks that we're allowed to remove

**length**   The length of the river

The function returns 1 (true) if distance is a feasible solution and returns 0 otherwise.

The variable prev_rock_location tracks the location of the most recent rock that we've kept. Inside the for loop, cur_rock_location holds the location of the rock that we're currently considering. We then have our crucial test to determine whether to keep or remove the current rock ❶. If the current rock is too close to the previous rock, then we remove the current rock and increase the number of removals by one. Otherwise, we keep the current rock and update prev_rock_location accordingly.

When the loop terminates, we've counted the number of rocks that we must remove. Well... almost. We still need to check whether the rightmost rock that we've kept is too close to the end of the river ❷. If it is, then we remove that rock. (Don't worry about the possibility of removing the rock at Location 0. If we really have removed all the rocks, then prev_rock_location will be 0. However, length - 0 < distance cannot be true; if it were, then we would have returned in the if statement at the start of the function.)

Now we have no rocks within the minimum jump distance of each other, and we have not removed rocks unnecessarily. How could we possibly do better than that? The greedy algorithm charms... but here we go again. The last time this occurred, in "A Greedy Idea" on page 244, the greedy algorithm turned out to be incorrect. Don't be convinced by a couple of examples where things happen to work out. Don't let me sweet-talk you into believing that everything is okay.

Before moving on, I'd like to give a fairly precise argument for why this greedy algorithm is correct. Specifically, I'll show that it removes the minimum number of rocks required to achieve a minimum jump distance of at least $d$. I'll assume that $d$ is at most the length of the river; otherwise, the greedy algorithm immediately and correctly determines that a minimum jump distance of $d$ is infeasible.

For each rock from left to right, our greedy algorithm decides whether to keep the rock or remove it. Our goal will be to show that it matches, step for step, what an optimal solution does. When the greedy algorithm decides to keep a rock, we'll show that an optimal solution keeps that rock, too. When the greedy algorithm decides to remove a rock, we'll show that an optimal solution removes that rock, too. If the greedy algorithm does exactly what an optimal solution does, then what we get from it must be correct. In this example, "optimal" will be used to refer to an optimal solution. For each rock, we have four possibilities: greedy and optimal both remove the rock, greedy and optimal both keep the rock, greedy removes it but optimal keeps it, and greedy keeps it but optimal removes it. We have to show that the third and fourth cases cannot actually occur.

Before we proceed to the four cases, consider again removing two rocks from these rock locations: 0, 2, 4, 5, 8, and 12. When asked whether it's possible to achieve a minimum jump distance of at least 3, we have seen that greedy will remove the rocks at Locations 2 and 5, leaving us with 0, 4, 8, and 12. So we might expect that the optimal solution is also to remove the same two rocks. Although that is optimal, another optimal solution is to remove the rocks at Locations 2 and 4, resulting in these rocks: 0, 5, 8, and 12. That's another way to get a minimum distance of at least 3 by removing two rocks, and it's as good as what the greedy algorithm produces. Rather than match *the* optimal solution, we'll be just as happy matching *an* optimal solution. We don't care which one greedy matches: all optimal solutions are equally optimal.

We have some optimal solution $S$ that we want greedy to match. Greedy starts running, and for some time there are no discrepancies: it does whatever $S$ does. Greedy at least does the right thing for the rock at Location 0: that one has to stay, no matter what.

Greedy is thus looking at the rocks from left to right, doing the right stuff, keeping rocks and removing rocks just like optimal solution $S$ ... and then, boom, greedy and $S$ disagree on what to do with some rock. We think about the *first* rock on which greedy and $S$ disagree.

### Greedy removes it, but optimal keeps it.

The greedy algorithm only removes a rock when it's too close to another rock. If greedy removes a rock because it's less than $d$ from the rock to the left, then $S$ must have removed the rock, too. Because this is the first disagreement, $S$ includes exactly the same rocks to the left as greedy. So if $S$ did not remove the rock, then it would have two rocks within a distance of less than $d$. However, that can't happen: $S$ is an optimal (and necessarily feasible) solution where all distances between rocks are at least $d$. We can conclude that $S$ really does remove the rock, agreeing with greedy. Similar reasoning shows that, if greedy removes a rock because it's too close to the end of the river, then $S$ must remove it, too.

### Greedy keeps it, but optimal removes it.

We're not going to be able to make greedy and $S$ match here, but that's okay, because we'll be able to form a new optimal solution $U$ that keeps this rock. Let $r$ be the current rock; the one that greedy keeps and $S$ removes. Think about a new set of rocks $T$ that has exactly the same rocks as $S$ plus rock $r$. Therefore, $T$ removes one fewer rock than $S$. Because of this, $T$ can't be a feasible solution. If it were, then it would be better (by one rock) than $S$, contradicting the fact that $S$ is an optimal solution.

Since the only difference between $S$ and $T$ is that $T$ has rock $r$, it must be $r$ that causes $T$ to be infeasible. Therefore, in $T$, $r$ must be closer than $d$ to rock $r_2$ to its right. We know that $r_2$ can't be the rock at the end of the river, because then greedy wouldn't have kept $r$ (as $r$ would be too close to the end of the river). So $r_2$ is some rock that is allowed to be removed.

Now, think about another new set of rocks $U$ that has exactly the same rocks as $T$ except that it doesn't have $r_2$. We can say that $U$ has the same number of rocks as $S$: we added one rock $r$ to $S$ to get $T$, and we removed one rock $r_2$ from $T$ to get $U$. Also, $U$ has no rocks that are less than a distance of $d$ apart, because it doesn't include the offending rock $r_2$. That is, $U$ is an optimal solution, just like $S$. Crucially, $U$ contains rock $r$! So greedy agrees with optimal solution $U$ to include $r$.

Let's give our feasibility tester a whirl before we continue. Here's how to call it on the example that we used throughout this section:

```
int main(void) {
  int rocks[4] = {2, 4, 5, 8};
  printf("%d\n", can_make_min_distance(6, rocks, 4, 2, 12));
  return 0;
}
```

The code above asks whether it's possible to achieve a minimum jump distance of at least 6 by removing two rocks. The answer is "no," so you should see 0 (false) as the output. Change the first argument from 6 to 3, and now you're asking whether a minimum jump distance of at least 3 is feasible. Run the program again, and you should see 1 (true).

Excellent: now we have a way to check feasibility. It's time to bring out binary search to give us optimality.

### Searching for a Solution

To use binary search, let's adapt the code from Listing 7-3. In Feeding Ants, we had to achieve four digits of accuracy after the decimal point. Here, however, we're looking to optimize the minimum jump distance, and that's guaranteed to be an integer value because all rocks are at integer locations. So we'll stop when high and low are within one, rather than within the four decimal digits. Listing 7-5 gives the new code.

```
// bugged!
void solve(int rocks[], int num_rocks,
           int num_remove, int length) {
  int low, high, mid;
  low = 0;
  high = length;
  while (high - low > 1) {
    mid = (low + high) / 2;
❶ if (can_make_min_distance(mid, rocks, num_rocks, num_remove, length))
❷   low = mid;
```

```
  else
❸   high = mid;
  }
  printf("%d\n", high);
}
```

*Listing 7-5: Searching for the optimal solution (bugged!)*

On each iteration, we calculate the midpoint mid of the range, and we use our helper function to test its feasibility ❶.

If mid is feasible, then everything less than mid is also feasible, so we update low to cut off the low half of the range ❷. Notice the contrast to Listing 7-3: there, a feasible mid means that everything greater than mid is feasible, so we cut off the high half of the range instead.

If mid is infeasible, then everything greater than mid is also infeasible, so we update high to cut off the high half of the range ❸.

Unfortunately, this binary search is not correct. To see why, run it on this test case:

```
12 4 2
2
4
5
8
```

You should get an output of 5, but the optimal solution is in fact 4.

Ahh, I know what to do. Let's change the printf call at the bottom to output low instead of high. When the loop terminates, low will be one less than high, so this change will result in an output of 4 instead of 5. The new code is given in Listing 7-6.

```
// bugged!
void solve(int rocks[], int num_rocks,
            int num_remove, int length) {
  int low, high, mid;
  low = 0;
  high = length;
  while (high - low > 1) {
    mid = (low + high) / 2;
    if (can_make_min_distance(mid, rocks, num_rocks, num_remove, length))
      low = mid;
    else
      high = mid;
  }
  printf("%d\n", low);
}
```

*Listing 7-6: Searching for the optimal solution (still bugged!)*

That fixes the problematic test case, but now we get this test case wrong:

```
12 0 0
```

This is a perfectly valid test case, if a little strange: the length of the river is 12, and there are no rocks. The maximum achievable minimum jump distance is 12, but our binary search returns 11 on this example. Again, we are off by one.

Binary search is legendarily difficult to implement correctly. Should that > be a >=? Should that be a mid or a mid + 1? Do we want low + high or low + high + 1? If you keep on with binary search problems, you'll grapple with all of this eventually. I don't know any other algorithm with the bug-density potential of binary search.

Let's be a little more careful for our next attempt. Suppose we knew at all times that low and everything smaller than low are feasible and that high and everything larger than high are infeasible. Such a claim is called an *invariant*, which simply means that it's always true as the code runs.

When the loop terminates, low will be one less than high. If we've managed to maintain our invariant, then we know that low is feasible. We also know that nothing greater than low can be feasible: high is next, and the invariant tells us that high is infeasible. So low will be the maximum feasible value, and we'll need to output low.

However, in all of this we assume that we can make this invariant true at the beginning of the code and keep it true at all times thereafter.

Let's start with the code above the loop. This code does *not* necessarily make the invariant true:

```
low = 0;
high = length;
```

Is low feasible? Certainly! A minimum jump distance of at least 0 is always achievable, because every jump has a nonzero distance. Is high infeasible? Well, it could be, but what if we can jump the whole river after we remove the allowed number of rocks? Then length is feasible, and our invariant is broken. Here's a better initialization:

```
low = 0;
high = length + 1;
```

Now high certainly isn't feasible: we can't achieve a minimum jump distance of length + 1 when the river is only of length length.

We next have to figure out what to do for the two possibilities in the loop. If mid is feasible, then we can set low = mid. The invariant is okay, because low and everything to its left are feasible, and, if mid is not feasible, then we can set high = mid. The invariant is again okay, because high and everything to its right are infeasible. Thus, in both cases, we maintain the invariant.

We now see that nothing in the code invalidates the invariant, and so we're safe to output low when the loop terminates. The correct code is given in Listing 7-7.

```c
void solve(int rocks[], int num_rocks,
           int num_remove, int length) {
  int low, high, mid;
  low = 0;
  high = length + 1;
  while (high - low > 1) {
    mid = (low + high) / 2;
    if (can_make_min_distance(mid, rocks, num_rocks, num_remove, length))
      low = mid;
    else
      high = mid;
  }
  printf("%d\n", low);
}
```

Listing 7-7: Searching for the optimal solution

For a river of length $L$, we're calling can_make_min_distance a total of $\log L$ times. If we have $n$ rocks, then can_make_min_distance (Listing 7-4) takes $O(n)$ time. Therefore, our solution to this problem is an $O(n \log L)$ algorithm.

## Reading the Input

We're nearly there. All that's left is to read the input and call solve. The code is provided in Listing 7-8.

```c
#define MAX_ROCKS 50000

int compare(const void *v1, const void *v2) {
  int num1 = *(const int *)v1;
  int num2 = *(const int *)v2;
  return num1 - num2;
}

int main(void) {
  static int rocks[MAX_ROCKS];
  int length, num_rocks, num_remove, i;
  scanf("%d%d%d", &length, &num_rocks, &num_remove);
  for (i = 0; i < num_rocks; i++)
    scanf("%d", &rocks[i]);
❶ qsort(rocks, num_rocks, sizeof(int), compare);
  solve(rocks, num_rocks, num_remove, length);
```

```
    return 0;
}
```

Listing 7-8: The main function for reading the input

We've been analyzing this problem by thinking about locations of rocks from left to right, that is, from smallest location to largest location. However, the rocks could come from the input in any order. Nothing in the problem description guarantees that they'll be sorted.

It's been a while, but we did use qsort to sort nodes in Chapter 2 when solving the Descendant Distance problem. Sorting rocks is a little easier than sorting those nodes. Our comparison function compare takes pointers to two integers, and it returns the result of subtracting the second from the first. This leads to a negative integer if the first integer is smaller than the second, 0 if the two integers are equal, and a positive integer if the first integer is larger than the second. We use qsort with this comparison function to sort the rocks ❶. We then call solve with the array of sorted rocks.

If you submit this solution to the judge, then you should see that all test cases pass.

## Problem 3: Living Quality

So far in this chapter, we've seen two approaches to check feasibility: a recursive traversal of a tree and a greedy algorithm. Now, we'll see an example where we'll use ideas from dynamic programming (Chapter 3) to efficiently check feasibility.

This is the first problem in the book where we don't read from standard input or write to standard output. We'll write a function with a name specified by the judge. In lieu of standard input, we'll use an array passed by the judge. In lieu of standard output, we'll return the correct value from our function. This is rather nice: we won't have to bother with scanf and printf at all!

Incidentally, this will also be our first problem from a world championship programming competition (IOI 2010). You've got this!

This is DMOJ problem ioi10p3.

### The Problem

A city consists of a rectangular grid of blocks. Each block is identified by its row and column coordinates. There are $r$ rows numbered 0 to $r - 1$ from top to bottom and $c$ columns numbered 0 to $c - 1$ from left to right.

Each block has been given a distinct *quality rank* between 1 and $rc$. For example, if we have seven rows and seven columns, then the ranks of each block will be some permutation of the numbers from 1 to 49. See Table 7-1 for an example city.

**Table 7-1:** A Sample City

|   | 0 | 1 | 2 | 3 | 4 | 5 | 6 |
|---|---|---|---|---|---|---|---|
| **0** | 48 | 16 | 15 | 45 | 40 | 28 | 8 |
| **1** | 20 | 11 | 36 | 19 | 24 | 6 | 33 |
| **2** | 22 | 39 | 30 | 7 | 9 | 1 | 18 |
| **3** | 14 | 35 | 2 | 13 | 31 | 12 | 46 |
| **4** | 32 | 37 | 21 | 3 | 41 | 23 | 29 |
| **5** | 42 | 49 | 38 | 10 | 17 | 47 | 5 |
| **6** | 43 | 4 | 34 | 25 | 26 | 27 | 44 |

The *median quality rank* of a rectangle is the quality rank such that half of the quality ranks in the rectangle are smaller and half are larger. For example, consider the five-row-by-three-column (5×3) rectangle in the top left of Table 7-1. It consists of 15 quality ranks: 48, 16, 15, 20, 11, 36, 22, 39, 30, 14, 35, 2, 32, 37, and 21. The median quality rank is 22, because seven numbers are less than 22 and the other seven are greater.

We'll be provided integers $h$ and $w$ that specify the height (number of rows) and width (number of columns) of candidate rectangles. Our task is to identify the minimum median quality rank of any rectangle with $h$ rows and $w$ columns. (In this problem, low-quality ranks correspond to high qualities; finding the minimum median quality rank therefore corresponds to finding a high-quality living area of the city.)

Let's use $(x, y)$ to refer to row $x$, column $y$. Suppose $h$ is 5 and $w$ is 3. Then, for the city in Table 7-1, we would identify 13 as the minimum median quality rank. The rectangle whose median quality rank is 13 is the one whose top-left coordinate is $(1, 3)$ and whose bottom-right coordinate is $(5, 5)$.

## Input

There's nothing to read from standard input. Everything we need will come from the judge through function parameters. Here's the signature for the function that we'll write:

```
int rectangle(int r, int c, int h, int w, int q[3001][3001])
```

Here, $r$ and $c$ are the numbers of rows and columns in the city, respectively. Similarly, $h$ and $w$ are the numbers of rows and columns in the candidate rectangles, respectively; $h$ will be at most $r$ and $w$ will be at most $c$. It's also guaranteed that $h$ and $w$ will be odd numbers. (Why is that? Since multiplying two odd numbers results in an odd number, *hw*, the number of blocks in a candidate rectangle, will be an odd number. The median is precisely defined in this case: the quality rank such that half of the remaining quality ranks are smaller and the other half are larger. What if we had an even number of quality ranks, such as the four ranks 2, 6, 4, and 5? What would the median be? We'd have to choose between 4 and 5. The problem author has spared us this choice.)

The final parameter q gives the quality rank of the blocks. For example, q[2][3] gives the quality of the block at row 2, column 3. Notice how the dimensions on q tell us the maximum number of rows and columns in the city: 3,001, in each case.

### Output

We won't produce anything on standard output. Instead, from the rectangle function just described, we'll return the minimum median quality rank.

The time limit for solving the test case is 4.5 seconds.

## *Sorting Every Rectangle*

It's hard to make much progress toward an efficient solution that doesn't use binary search, but we'll try here, anyway. It'll give us practice looping through all of the candidate rectangles. We'll get to binary search in the next subsection.

To start, we need a couple of constants and a type definition:

```
#define MAX_ROWS 3001
#define MAX_COLS 3001

typedef int board[MAX_ROWS][MAX_COLS];
```

Much as we did in Chapter 5, we'll use board whenever we need a two-dimensional array of the correct size.

Suppose you are given the top-left and bottom-right coordinates of a rectangle and asked to determine the median quality rank of its blocks. How can you do it?

Sorting can help. Sort the quality ranks from smallest to largest, and then pick out the element at the middle index. For example, say we have these 15 quality ranks again: 48, 16, 15, 20, 11, 36, 22, 39, 30, 14, 35, 2, 32, 37, and 21. If we sort them, we get 2, 11, 14, 15, 16, 20, 21, 22, 30, 32, 35, 36, 37, 39, and 48. There are 15 quality ranks, so all we do is take the eighth one, 22, and that's our median.

There are slightly faster algorithms for finding the median directly, without taking the scenic route through sorting. Sorting gives us an algorithm that takes $O(n \log n)$ time to find the median; there's a sophisticated $O(n)$ algorithm for finding the median that I encourage you to look up if you are interested.

We won't go there, though. What we do in this subsection is going to be so slow that no improved algorithm for finding the median is going to be of benefit.

Listing 7-9 gives the code for finding the median of a given rectangle.

```
int compare(const void *v1, const void *v2) {
  int num1 = *(const int *)v1;
  int num2 = *(const int *)v2;
  return num1 - num2;
}


int median(int top_row, int left_col, int bottom_row, int right_col,
           board q) {
  static int cur_rectangle[MAX_ROWS * MAX_COLS];
  int i, j, num_cur_rectangle;
  num_cur_rectangle = 0;
  for (i = top_row; i <= bottom_row; i++)
    for (j = left_col; j <= right_col; j++) {
      cur_rectangle[num_cur_rectangle] = q[i][j];
      num_cur_rectangle++;
    }
❶ qsort(cur_rectangle, num_cur_rectangle, sizeof(int), compare);
  return cur_rectangle[num_cur_rectangle / 2];
}
```

*Listing 7-9: Finding the median of a given rectangle*

The first four parameters of median delimit the rectangle by specifying the top-left row and column and the bottom-right row and column. The final parameter, q, holds the quality ranks. We use the one-dimensional array cur_rectangle to accumulate the quality ranks for the rectangle. The nested for loops go through each block in the rectangle and add the block's quality rank to cur_rectangle. After corralling the quality ranks, we're all set to feed them to qsort ❶. Then we know exactly where the median is—it's in the middle of the array—so we just return it.

With that function in hand, we can now proceed to loop through each candidate rectangle, keeping track of the one whose median quality rank is the smallest. Check out Listing 7-10 for the code.

```
int rectangle(int r, int c, int h, int w, board q) {
  int top_row, left_col, bottom_row, right_col;
❶ int best = r * c + 1;
  int result;
  for (top_row = 0; top_row < r - h + 1; top_row++)
    for (left_col = 0; left_col < c - w + 1; left_col++) {
❷ bottom_row = top_row + h - 1;
❸ right_col = left_col + w - 1;
❹ result = median(top_row, left_col, bottom_row, right_col, q);
  if (result < best)
```

```
        best = result;
    }
    return best;
}
```

*Listing 7-10: Finding the smallest median of all candidate rectangles*

The variable best tracks the best (smallest) median that we've found so far. We start it off with a big value, bigger than the median of any candidate rectangle ❶. There's no way for a rectangle to have a median of r * c + 1: that would mean that half of its quality ranks were larger than r * c, but by the problem description, *no* quality ranks can be larger than r * c. The nested for loops consider each possible top-left coordinate for a rectangle. That gives us the top row and left column, but we also need the bottom row and right column in order to call median. To calculate the bottom row, we take the top row, add h (the number of rows in the candidate rectangles), and then subtract 1 ❷. It's really easy to make an off-by-one error here, but that - 1 is required. If the top row is 4 and h is 2, then we want the bottom row to be 4 + 2 - 1 = 5; if we made the bottom row be 4 + 2 = 6, then we'd have a rectangle with three rows instead of the desired two. We use a similar calculation to find the right column ❸. With the four coordinates available, we call median to calculate the median of the rectangle ❹. The remainder of the code updates best if we've found a better median.

We're done with this solution. There's no main function, because the judge calls rectangle directly, but the absence of main means that we can't test our code on our own computer. For testing purposes, you can introduce a main function, but don't keep that in there when you submit to the judge. Here's an example main function on the city in Table 7-1:

```
int main(void) {
static board q = {{48, 16, 15, 45, 40, 28, 8},
                  {20, 11, 36, 19, 24, 6, 33},
                  {22, 39, 30, 7, 9, 1, 18},
                  {14, 35, 2, 13, 31, 12, 46},
                  {32, 37, 21, 3, 41, 23, 29},
                  {42, 49, 38, 10, 17, 47, 5},
                  {43, 4, 34, 25, 26, 27, 44}};
    int result = rectangle(7, 7, 5, 3, q);
    printf("%d\n", result);
    return 0;
}
```

You should see an output of 13 when you run the program.

Feel free to submit our solution, minus the main function, to the judge. It'll pass a few test cases but time-out on the rest.

To get a feel for why our code is so slow, let's focus on the case where *r* and *c* are both the same number *m*. To exhibit the worst case, take *h* and *w* to both be *m*/2. (We don't want the rectangles to be too big, because then there won't be many rectangles; and we don't want them to be too small, because then each is easy to process.) The slowest part of our median function is the call to qsort. It's given an array with $m/2 \times m/2 = m^2/4$ values. On an array of $n$ values, qsort takes $n \log n$ steps. Replacing $n$ by $m^2/4$ gives $(m^2/4) \log(m^2/4) = O(m^2 \log m)$. So we're already slower than quadratic—and all we've done is calculate the median for one rectangle! The rectangle function calls median a total of $m^2/4$ times, so our total runtime is $O(m^4 \log m)$. That power of 4 relegates this solution to only very small problem instances.

There are two bottlenecks here. The first is sorting each rectangle. The second is doing a lot of work from scratch for each rectangle. Using a binary search disposes the former, and a neat dynamic-programming trick disposes the latter.

## Using Binary Search

Why should we be optimistic that binary search will lead to a speedup here? First, in the previous subsection, we saw that finding optimality head-on is a costly endeavor; our approach that piggybacked on sorting was slightly slower than an $m^4$ algorithm. Second, we have another example of a problem where all infeasible solutions come first and are followed by all feasible solutions. Suppose I tell you that there is no rectangle with median quality rank of at most five. Then there'd be no point looking for rectangles with median quality five, or four, or three, or anything else less than five. Conversely, suppose I tell you that there is a rectangle with median quality rank of at most five. Now, there'd be no point looking for rectangles with median quality of six, or seven, or anything greater than five. This is tailor-made binary search territory.

In the Feeding Ants problem, small values were infeasible and large values were feasible. In the River Jump problem, small values were feasible and large values were infeasible. Here, we're back in the Feeding Ants case: small values are infeasible and large values are feasible. We'll therefore need a change to the River Jump invariant, flipping the locations of the feasible and infeasible portions of the solution space.

Here's the invariant that we'll use: low and everything smaller than low are infeasible; high and everything larger than high are feasible. This tells us that we should return high when we're done, as it will be the smallest feasible value. The code, in Listing 7-11, is otherwise very similar to Listing 7-7.

```
int rectangle(int r, int c, int h, int w, board q) {
  int low, high, mid;
  low = 0;
  high = r * c + 1;
  while (high - low > 1) {
    mid = (low + high) / 2;
    if (can_make_quality(mid, r, c, h, w, q))
      high = mid;
    else
      low = mid;
  }
```

```
    return high;
}
```

*Listing 7-11: Searching for the optimal solution*

To finish the job, we need an implementation of can_make_quality to test feasibility.

## Testing Feasibility

Here's the signature for the feasibility-checking function that we'll write:

```
int can_make_quality(int quality, int r, int c, int h, int w, board q)
```

In "Sorting Every Rectangle" on page 256, we were saddled by having to calculate the median quality rank of each rectangle. Now this is no longer the case: we're content to determine whether the median value of some rectangle is at most some cutoff quality rank value.

This is an easier problem for which a sorting step is unnecessary. Here's the key observation: the specific values themselves no longer matter; all that matters is the relationship between each value and quality. To exploit this observation, we'll replace all values that are less than or equal to quality by −1 and all values greater than quality by 1. We then add up these −1 and 1 values for a given rectangle. If we have at least as many −1 values as 1 values (that is, there are at least as many small values as large values, relative to quality), then the sum will be zero or negative, and we can conclude that this rectangle has a median quality rank of quality or less.

Let's work an example. Here are the 15 quality ranks again for the 5×3 rectangle in the top left of Table 7-1: 48, 16, 15, 20, 11, 36, 22, 39, 30, 14, 35, 2, 32, 37, and 21. Does this rectangle have a median quality rank of 16 or less? Take each value and replace it by −1 if it's less than or equal to 16 and 1 if it's greater than 16. Here are the new values: 1, −1, −1, 1, −1, 1, 1, 1, 1, −1, 1, −1, 1, 1, and 1. If we add these up, we get a value of 5. This means that there are five more large values than small values, and we must conclude that a median of 16 or smaller is not possible for this rectangle. If we wanted to know whether a median of 30 was feasible, we'd get this after replacing the numbers by −1s and 1s: 1, −1, −1, −1, −1, 1, −1, 1, −1, −1, 1, −1, 1, 1, and −1. Adding these up, we get a total of −3.

Aha! So 30 is a feasible median. Crucially, we're making this feasible–infeasible decision with no sorting at all.

We need to loop through each rectangle, testing whether it has a median quality rank of quality or less. Listing 7-12 does exactly this.

```
int can_make_quality(int quality, int r, int c, int h, int w, board q) {
❶ static int zero_one[MAX_ROWS][MAX_COLS];
  int i, j;
  int top_row, left_col, bottom_row, right_col;
  int total;
```

```
for (i = 0; i < r; i++)
  for (j = 0; j < c; j++)
❷ if (q[i][j] <= quality)
    zero_one[i][j] = -1;
  else
    zero_one[i][j] = 1;

for (top_row = 0; top_row < r - h + 1; top_row++)
  for (left_col = 0; left_col < c - w + 1; left_col++) {
    bottom_row = top_row + h - 1;
    right_col = left_col + w - 1;
    total = 0;
    for (i = top_row; i <= bottom_row; i++)
      for (j = left_col; j <= right_col; j++)
      ❸ total = total + zero_one[i][j];
    if (total <= 0)
      return 1;
  }
  return 0;
}
```

*Listing 7-12: Testing the feasibility of quality*

We can't just obliterate the q array with −1s and 1s, because then we couldn't use the original quality ranks to later test other values of quality. Therefore, we use a new array to hold the −1s and 1s ❶. Notice how this array is filled in based on whether each value is less than or equal to (−1) or greater than (1) the cutoff quality parameter that we're checking ❷.

We then go through each rectangle, just as we did in Listing 7-10. We add up all of its −1 and 1 values ❸ and return 1 (true) if it has a median quality rank that's small enough.

All right! We have sidestepped the sorting—crafty, eh? What we did in this subsection is crucial to a fast solution to solving our problem, but we're not there yet, because if you count the number of nested loops, you'll see that there are four of them.

At the end of "Sorting Every Rectangle" we observed that our first solution—with no binary search anywhere!—was a very slow $O(m^4 \log m)$, where $m$ is the number of rows or columns in the city. Here, our feasibility check is already $m^4$; multiply by the log factor for the binary search, and it's not clear that we've made any progress.

Oh, but we have! It's just locked up behind too many nested loops, involving too much recomputation. Dynamic programming is now going to take us the rest of the way.

## A Quicker Way to Test Feasibility

Suppose we start with Table 7-1 and are interested in whether any $5 \times 3$ rectangle has a median quality rank of 16 or less. Changing all values less than or equal to 16 to −1 and all values greater than 16 to 1 results in Table 7-2.

**Table 7-2:** A City with Quality Ranks Replaced

|   | 0 | 1 | 2 | 3 | 4 | 5 | 6 |
|---|---|---|---|---|---|---|---|
| 0 | 1 | −1 | −1 | 1 | 1 | 1 | −1 |
| 1 | 1 | −1 | 1 | 1 | 1 | −1 | 1 |
| 2 | 1 | 1 | 1 | −1 | −1 | −1 | 1 |
| 3 | −1 | 1 | −1 | −1 | 1 | −1 | 1 |
| 4 | 1 | 1 | 1 | −1 | 1 | 1 | 1 |
| 5 | 1 | 1 | 1 | −1 | 1 | 1 | −1 |
| 6 | 1 | −1 | 1 | 1 | 1 | 1 | 1 |

We might begin by summing the elements of the 5×3 rectangle whose top-left coordinate is $(0, 0)$. As we saw in the previous section, the sum of that rectangle is 5. Next, maybe we want to sum the elements of the 5×3 rectangle whose top-left coordinate is $(0, 1)$. Adding up all 15 numbers here is what we would have done in the previous subsection. However, doing so fails to lean on the work we did to compute the sum of the first rectangle. Indeed, this second rectangle has 10 values in common with the first rectangle. We should be able to prevent this kind of duplication of effort for this and all other rectangles.

Dodging the repeated work here amounts to efficiently solving what's known as a two-dimensional *range sum query*. The one-dimensional case uses similar ideas, but in a simpler context, so we'll briefly study that before returning to finish the Living Quality problem. (About half of Chapter 8 will be devoted to range queries, so stay tuned!)

### One-Dimensional Range Sum Queries

Here's a one-dimensional array:

| Index | 0 | 1 | 2 | 3 | 4 | 5 | 6 |
|-------|---|---|----|---|----|---|----|
| Value | 6 | 2 | 15 | 9 | 12 | 4 | 11 |

If asked to find the sum of the array from index 2 to index 5, we could directly sum the values in that range: $15 + 9 + 12 + 4 = 40$. That's not very fast, and it would be particularly unfortunate if we were asked for the sum of the entire array. However, if we had to answer just a few such queries, we could get away with answering each by summing the appropriate values.

Now imagine that we're getting peppered by hundreds or thousands of these queries. It makes sense to have done a little up-front work, once, if it means that we can then answer the queries more quickly.

Consider the "index 2 to 5" query. What if we could look up the sum from index 0 to 5? That sum is 48. That's not 40, the answer that we want. Far from useless, though, is that 48 is quite close to what we need. It's only wrong because it includes the values at index 0 and index 1, stuff that we now need to exclude. We could do that if we could look up the sum from index 0 to 1. That sum is 8. If we subtract this 8 from 48, we get 40.

What's needed, then, is a new array, one where index $i$ holds the sum of all values from index 0 to index $i$. This new array is included in the Prefix Sum row in the following table:

| Index | 0 | 1 | 2 | 3 | 4 | 5 | 6 |
|---|---|---|---|---|---|---|---|
| Value | 6 | 2 | 15 | 9 | 12 | 4 | 11 |
| Prefix Sum | 6 | 8 | 23 | 32 | 44 | 48 | 59 |

No matter the query, we can now quickly answer it using the prefix sum array: to calculate the sum of the range from index $a$ to $b$, take the value at index $b$ and subtract the value at index $a - 1$. For 2 to 5, we get $48 - 8 = 40$, and for 1 to 6, we get $59 - 6 = 53$. These are constant-time answers, for eternity, and all we had to do was one preprocessing pass over the array.

### Two-Dimensional Range Sum: Queries

Let's return to the two-dimensional world of our quality ranks. Summing the elements of each rectangle is too slow, so we'll extend what we did in one dimension to two dimensions. Specifically, we'll produce a new array, where index $(i, j)$ is the sum of the elements of the rectangle whose top-left coordinate is $(0, 0)$ and whose bottom-right coordinate is $(i, j)$.

Let's look again at Table 7-2.

|  | 0 | 1 | 2 | 3 | 4 | 5 | 6 |
|---|---|---|---|---|---|---|---|
| **0** | 1 | −1 | −1 | 1 | 1 | 1 | −1 |
| **1** | 1 | −1 | 1 | 1 | 1 | −1 | 1 |
| **2** | 1 | 1 | 1 | −1 | −1 | −1 | 1 |
| **3** | −1 | 1 | −1 | −1 | 1 | −1 | 1 |
| **4** | 1 | 1 | 1 | −1 | 1 | 1 | 1 |
| **5** | 1 | 1 | 1 | −1 | 1 | 1 | −1 |
| **6** | 1 | −1 | 1 | 1 | 1 | 1 | 1 |

The corresponding prefix array is in Table 7-3. (It may seem a little strange to call it a "prefix array" here, but let's stick with it to match the terminology from the one-dimensional case.)

**Table 7-3:** An Array for Two-Dimensional Range Sum Queries

|   | 0 | 1 | 2 | 3 | 4 | 5 | 6 |
|---|---|---|---|---|---|---|---|
| **0** | 1 | 0 | −1 | 0 | 1 | 2 | 1 |
| **1** | 2 | 0 | 0 | 2 | 4 | 4 | 4 |
| **2** | 3 | 2 | 3 | 4 | 5 | 4 | 5 |
| **3** | 2 | 2 | 2 | 2 | 4 | 2 | 4 |
| **4** | 3 | 4 | 5 | 4 | 7 | 6 | 9 |
| **5** | 4 | 6 | 8 | 6 | 10 | 10 | 12 |
| **6** | 5 | 6 | 9 | 8 | 13 | 14 | 17 |

Let's make sure we know what this array tells us before worrying about how to quickly build it. The value in row 4, column 2 gives the sum of the values of the rectangle whose top-left coordinate is $(0, 0)$ and whose bottom-right coordinate is $(4, 2)$. We have seen in "Testing Feasibility" that this sum is 5 and, indeed, that's what this array has there.

How could we compute that $(4, 2)$ value of 5 using other values that we've already computed? We need to start with its value in Table 7-2, add what's in range above it, and add everything in its row to the left. We can do this with judicious use of the array in Table 7-3, as shown in Table 7-4.

**Table 7-4:** Quickly Calculating a Given Sum

|   | 0 | 1 | 2 | 3 | 4 | 5 | 6 |
|---|---|---|---|---|---|---|---|
| **0** | ● ■ | ● ■ | ● |   |   |   |   |
| **1** | ● ■ | ● ■ | ● |   |   |   |   |
| **2** | ● ■ | ● ■ | ● |   |   |   |   |
| **3** | ● ■ | ● ■ | ● |   |   |   |   |
| **4** | ■ | ■ | 1 |   |   |   |   |
| **5** |   |   |   |   |   |   |   |
| **6** |   |   |   |   |   |   |   |

We need to start with the 1, capture the cells that include a circle (those above), capture the cells that include a square (those to the left), and add them all up. We can capture the cells that include a circle by looking up the element at row 3, column 2. We can also capture the cells that include a square by looking up the element at row 4, column 1. However, adding those together double-counts the cells that include both a circle and a square (those both above and to the left), but this is not an issue because the element at row 3, column 1 captures exactly those circle-and-square cells, whose subtraction undoes the double-counting. In all, we have $1 + 2 + 4 - 2 = 5$, as desired. As long as we work from top to bottom and left to right, we can build this array with only two additions and one subtraction per cell.

We now know how to build an array like that in Table 7-3. So what?

The "so what" is that it enables us to quickly calculate the sum of any rectangle. Suppose we wanted the sum of the rectangle whose top-left coordinate is $(1, 3)$ and whose bottom-right coordinate is $(5, 5)$. We can't just use the value 10 in row 5, column 5 of Table 7-3. That captures everything in the desired rectangle but also includes more than we want: it includes elements that are outside (above or to the left) of our desired rectangle. However, just as in the one-dimensional case, we'll be able to adjust that value to include only the elements in the rectangle. See Table 7-5 for how to do this. In this table, the cells of the desired rectangle are marked by stars.

**Table 7-5:** Quickly Calculating the Sum of a Rectangle

|   | 0 | 1 | 2 | 3 | 4 | 5 | 6 |
|---|---|---|---|---|---|---|---|
| 0 | ● ■ | ● ■ | ● ■ | ● | ● | ● |   |
| 1 | ■ | ■ | ■ | ★ | ★ | ★ |   |
| 2 | ■ | ■ | ■ | ★ | ★ | ★ |   |
| 3 | ■ | ■ | ■ | ★ | ★ | ★ |   |
| 4 | ■ | ■ | ■ | ★ | ★ | ★ |   |
| 5 | ■ | ■ | ■ | ★ | ★ | ★ |   |
| 6 |   |   |   |   |   |   |   |

This time, we need to subtract the cells that include a circle and the cells that include a square. We can get the cells with a circle from row 0, column 5 and the cells with a square from row 5, column 2. But subtracting both will double-subtract the cells that have both a circle and a square, so we need to add back the cell in row 0, column 2. That is, we have $10 - 2 - 8 + (-1) = -1$, which is the sum of the rectangle.

Here's a general expression for this calculation:

```
sum[bottom_row][right_col] - sum[top_row - 1][right_col] -
  sum[bottom_row][left_col - 1] + sum[top_row - 1][left_col - 1]
```

This will be used in the code presented next.

### Two-Dimensional Range Sum: Code

We're ready to put it all together—the −1 and 1 idea, building the prefix array, and using the prefix array for fast rectangle sums—in Listing 7-13.

```
int can_make_quality(int quality, int r, int c, int h, int w, board q) {
  static int zero_one[MAX_ROWS][MAX_COLS];
  static int sum[MAX_ROWS + 1][MAX_COLS + 1];
  int i, j;
  int top_row, left_col, bottom_row, right_col;
  int total;

❶ for (i = 0; i < r; i++)
    for (j = 0; j < c; j++)
      if (q[i][j] <= quality)
        zero_one[i][j] = -1;
      else
        zero_one[i][j] = 1;

  for (i = 0; i <= c; i++)
    sum[0][i] = 0;
  for (i = 0; i <= r; i++)
    sum[i][0] = 0;
❷ for (i = 1; i <= r; i++)
    for (j = 1; j <= c; j++)
      sum[i][j] = zero_one[i - 1][j - 1] + sum[i - 1][j] +
                  sum[i][j - 1] - sum[i - 1][j - 1];

❸ for (top_row = 1; top_row <= r - h + 1; top_row++)
    for (left_col = 1; left_col <= c - w + 1; left_col++) {
      bottom_row = top_row + h - 1;
      right_col = left_col + w - 1;
      total = sum[bottom_row][right_col] - sum[top_row - 1][right_col] -
              sum[bottom_row][left_col - 1] + sum[top_row - 1][left_col - 1];
      if (total <= 0)
        return 1;
    }
  return 0;
}
```

*Listing 7-13: Testing the feasibility of quality quickly*

Step 1 is to build the zero_one array ❶, exactly as we did in Listing 7-12. Step 2 is to build the prefix sum array sum ❷. We'll use indices that start at 1, rather than 0, so that we don't have to worry about staying within bounds when we later process cells on the edges of the array. Finally, Step 3 is to use the prefix sum array to quickly calculate the sum of each rectangle ❸. Notice how each rectangle can be summed in constant time here! We paid for the preprocessing work of Step 2, but that work pays for itself every time we sum a rectangle without summing its elements.

Compared to Listing 7-12, we've removed two levels of nesting from the for loops. Therefore, this is an $O(m^2 \log m)$ algorithm, which is fast enough to pass all of the test cases. Go for it! Then take a well-deserved break, because we've got one more big problem to solve before we're through with this chapter.

# Problem 4: Cave Doors

Another IOI championship problem? Bring it on! This one is unique to the chapter because it uses binary search not to find an optimal solution, but to quickly zone-in on a desired element. As we did in the Living Quality problem, we won't read anything from standard input, and we won't write anything to standard output. Rather, we'll learn about the problem instance and submit our answer through calls to functions provided by the judge. As you read the problem description, try to anticipate why binary search is still appropriate here.

This is DMOJ problem ioi13p4.

## The Problem

You are at the entrance to a long, narrow cave, and you want to get through the cave to the other side. There are $n$ doors that you must pass through: the first door is Door 0, the second is Door 1, and so on.

Each door can be open or closed. You can walk through any open door, but you can't get past or see through a closed door. So if Door 0 and Door 1 are open but Door 2 is closed, then you progress to Door 2 but no further.

At the entrance to the cave is a panel of $n$ switches. Like the doors, the switches are numbered starting from 0. Each switch can be in the up (0) position or the down (1) position. Each switch is associated with a different door, and it determines whether that door is open or closed. If a switch is set to the correct position, then its associated door is open; otherwise, its associated door is closed. You don't know which switch is associated with which door, and you don't know whether the switch should be up or down for the door to be open. For example, maybe Switch 0 is associated with Door 5, and the switch has to be down for Door 5 to be open. And maybe Switch 1 is associated with Door 0, and the switch has to be up for Door 0 to be open.

You can set the switches to whatever positions you choose and then walk through the cave to determine the first door that is closed. You have the stamina to do this at most 70,000 times. Your goal is to determine both the correct position (0 or 1) and the associated door for each switch.

We have to write the function with this signature:

```
void exploreCave(int n)
```

where n is the number of doors and switches (between 1 and 5,000). To implement this function, you call two functions provided by the judge. These are described next.

### Input

We're not reading anything from standard input. The only way to learn about the problem instance is to call the function tryCombination provided by the judge. Its signature is

```
int tryCombination(int switch_positions[])
```

The parameter switch_positions is an array of length $n$ giving the position (0 or 1) of each switch. That is, switch_positions[0] gives the position of Switch 0, switch_positions[1] gives the position of Switch 1, and so on. The tryCombination function simulates what would happen if we set the switches as in switch_positions and walked through the cave. If some door is still closed, it returns the number of the first closed door; otherwise, it returns -1 to indicate that all doors are open.

### Output

We're not writing anything to standard output. Instead, when we're ready, we submit our answer by calling the function answer provided by the judge. Its signature is

```
void answer(int switch_positions[], int door_for_switch[])
```

We have one shot at this: when we call answer, we can't then do anything else, so we had better submit the correct answer the first time. The parameter switch_positions is our proposed switch positions, in the same format as for tryCombination. The parameter door_for_switch is our proposed association between switches and doors: door_for_switch[0] gives the door for Switch 0, door_for_switch[1] gives the door for Switch 1, and so on.

The number of calls to tryCombination, rather than execution time, is the scarce resource here. We're allowed to make at most 70,000 calls; if we make more, then our program is terminated and we do not solve the problem.

## Solving a Subtask

The author of this problem has split the points across five *subtasks*. The fifth subtask is the problem in its full generality as I've presented it here. The other subtasks impose additional constraints on the problem instances to make the problem easier.

I like when problem authors use subtasks, especially when I'm struggling to solve a problem. I can then target each subtask in turn, improving my solution as I go, until I solve the full problem. Moreover, if I can't solve the full problem, then I still get points for the subtasks that I was able to solve.

The first subtask in the Cave Doors problem is to solve the problem when each switch i is associated with door number i. That is, Switch 0 is associated with Door 0, Switch 1 is associated with Door 1, and so on. What we need to deduce is the correct position (0 or 1) for each switch.

Don't worry: we won't stop with this problem until we solve it fully. But let's start by solving Subtask 1 here, so we can focus on correctly calling the tryCombination and answer judge functions before we tackle the other aspects of the problem.

We don't have access to the code for the two judge functions, so we're not going to be able to locally compile and run our program. (If you'd like to get things set up locally, you can google "IOI 2013 tasks" and find the test data and templates for the Cave Doors problem, but you won't need to do any of that to follow the discussion here.) Whenever we want to test what we're doing, we can submit our code to the judge. In particular, once we successfully solve Subtask 1 and submit our code, the judge should give us some points. The code for Subtask 1 is given in Listing 7-14.

```
void exploreCave(int n) {
  int switch_positions[n], door_for_switch[n];
  int i, result;
  for (i = 0; i < n; i++) {
❶ switch_positions[i] = 0;
❷ door_for_switch[i] = i;
  }

  for (i = 0; i < n; i++) {
❸ result = tryCombination(switch_positions);
    if (result == i) // door i is closed
❹ switch_positions[i] = 1;
  }
❺ answer(switch_positions, door_for_switch);
}
```

*Listing 7-14: Solving Subtask 1*

To begin, we use a for loop to set each switch position to 0 ❶ and associate Door i with Switch i ❷. We'll update the switch positions when needed, but (as per the subtask constraints) we'll have no reason to touch the door associations again.

The second for loop loops through each switch. Its job is to determine if the current switch should stay in Position 0 or change to Position 1. Let's work through the first iteration, when i is 0. We call tryCombination ❸, which returns to us the number of the first door that is closed. If it returns 0, then Switch 0 is not set correctly; if Switch 0 were set correctly, Door 0 would be open, and tryCombination would return a number other than 0. So, if Door 0 is closed, then we change the position of Switch 0 from 0 to 1 ❹. That opens Door 0, and we can move on to Door 1.

When i is 1, we again call tryCombination. We won't get a result of 0, because our code has already done the work to guarantee that Door 0 is open. If we get a result of 1, it means that Door 1 is closed, and we have to change Switch 1 from Position 0 to Position 1.

Generalizing, we can say that, when we start a new iteration of the loop, all of the doors up to and including Door i - 1 are open. If Door i is closed, then we change the position of Switch i from 0 to 1; otherwise, Door i is already open, and Switch i is already correctly set.

Once we're finished with that second for loop, we've figured out the correct position of each switch. We communicate this to the judge through the call to the answer function ❺.

I suggest submitting this code to the judge to verify that you're correctly calling tryCombination and answer. Once you're ready, we'll move on to solve the real deal.

### Using Linear Search

It's a good thing we solved Subtask 1, beyond the fact of getting our feet wet. That's because there's a nice strategy in our solution that paves our way. That strategy is to figure out how to open each door and never let that door interfere again.

In our solution to Subtask 1, we focus first on Door 0 and get that door open. Once it's open, we never mess with its switch again. With Door 0 out of the way, we next focus on getting Door 1 open. Once Door 1 is open, we never mess with its switch again. As far as we are concerned, Doors 0 and 1 are gone; the Doors may as well start with Door 2. We continue in this way, knocking off one door after another, until all doors are open.

In Subtask 1, we knew exactly which door was associated with each of the switches. There was no searching required to figure out this correspondence. But, to solve the full problem, we do need a search, because we don't know which switch controls the current door. We start by getting Door 0 closed. Then we search through the switches. We change the position of the current switch and ask whether or not Door 0 opened. If not, then this was not the correct switch. If so, then we've found the switch for Door 0. We keep Door 0 open from this point onward, and we repeat the process for Door 1: getting it closed and then looping through the switches to find the one that opens it.

Let's start with the new exploreCave code given in Listing 7-15. It's brief, because it offloads the search to a helper function.

```
void exploreCave(int n) {
  int switch_positions[n], door_for_switch[n];
  int i;
  for (i = 0; i < n; i++)
❶  door_for_switch[i] = -1;
```

```
  for (i = 0; i < n; i++)
❷ set_a_switch(i, switch_positions, door_for_switch, n);
  answer(switch_positions, door_for_switch);
}
```

*Listing 7-15: The exploreCave function*

As with solving Subtask 1, each element of switch_positions will end up being a 0 or 1, indicating the position of each switch. door_for_switch indicates the door associated with each switch. We initialize each element of door_for_switch to -1 ❶ to indicate that the door for each switch is unknown. When the door for Switch i becomes known, we'll update switch_positions[i] and door_for_switch[i] accordingly.

Pop quiz: If door_for_switch[5] is 8, what does that mean? Does it mean that Switch 5 is associated with Door 8 or that Door 5 is associated with Switch 8?

It's the former! Make sure you're clear on this before continuing.

For each Door i, we call the set_a_switch helper function ❷. Its task is to search through the switches to determine the one that is associated with Door i. It also determines whether that switch should be in Position 0 or 1.

The code for set_a_switch is given in Listing 7-16.

```
void set_a_switch(int door, int switch_positions[],
                  int door_for_switch[], int n) {
  int i, result;
  int found = 0;

  for (i = 0; i < n; i++)
    if (door_for_switch[i] == -1)
❶   switch_positions[i] = 0;

  result = tryCombination(switch_positions);
  if (result != door) { // door is open
    for (i = 0; i < n; i++)
      if (door_for_switch[i] == -1)
❷     switch_positions[i] = 1;
  }

  i = 0;
  while (!found) {
    if (door_for_switch[i] == -1) {
❸     switch_positions[i] = 1 - switch_positions[i];
      result = tryCombination(switch_positions);
❹     if (result != door)
        found = 1;
      else
        i++;
  }
```

```
        else
            i++;
    }
    door_for_switch[i] = door;
}
```

*Listing 7-16: Finding and setting the switch for the current door using a linear search*

The `door` parameter dictates which door we want to solve next.

We begin with a loop through the switches. We set the position of the switches to 0 ❶, but only for those switches that are not associated with a door yet. (Remember that, if a switch is already associated with a door, we don't want to change that switch's position ever again.)

With all relevant switches set to Position 0, we determine whether the current door is open or closed. If it's open, then we want to close it so that we can later change switch positions, one at a time, to see which switch opens it. To close the door, we just set all switch positions to 1 ❷. This works because the door was open when the switch positions were all 0; one of those switches controls this door, so the door will close when that switch position changes.

With the door closed, it's time to search for the switch that opens it. For each switch not already associated with a door, we *toggle* its position from 0 to 1 or 1 to 0 ❸. Notice how subtracting the position from 1 changes the position: if it was 1 before, then it's 0 now; if it was 0 before, then it's 1 now. Then, we check the new status of the door. If it's open ❹, then we've found the associated switch! If it's still closed, then this wasn't the right switch and the loop continues.

What we're doing in `set_a_switch` is a linear search through all of the remaining switches. We could have up to 5,000 switches, so finding the switch for a single door could take up to 5,000 calls of `tryCombination`.

We can call `tryCombination` up to 70,000 times. If we get unlucky and the search for the first door takes 5,000 calls, the second takes 4,999 calls, the third takes 4,998 calls, and so on, then we can only handle about 14 doors before we go over the limit. Only 14 doors is not much. We could have 5,000 doors—we're not even close! This is the end of the line for a linear search.

## Using Binary Search

The numbers 5,000 (maximum number of doors) and 70,000 (maximum number of `tryCombination` calls) subtly encode the fact that binary search is a plausible solution strategy. Notice that $\log_2 5,000$ rounds up to 13. If we can find a way to use binary search, then it'll pick out the switch for the current door in only 13 calls of `tryCombination`, not 5,000. If we take 13 calls per door, and we have 5,000 doors, that's $13 \times 5,000 = 65,000$ calls in all. We'll need one extra call per door to tell us whether the door is closed but, still, we should be able to get in under the 70,000 limit.

How can binary search be used here? It must have something to do with eliminating half of the switch range on each step. Take some time to think through this before continuing!

I'll explain the idea through an example. Suppose we have eight doors and eight switches and that Door 0 is currently closed. If we flip Switch 0, and Door 0 doesn't open, then we've learned very little: all we've learned is that Switch 0 isn't the switch associated with Door 0. (It's like starting with "1" when guessing someone's number between 1 and 1,000.) A better idea is to flip half of the switches. So let's flip Switches 0, 1, 2, and 3. No matter what that does to Door 0, we learn a lot. If Door 0 is still closed, then Switches 0 to 3 have nothing to do with Door 0, and we can focus only on Switches 4 to 7. If Door 0 is now open, we know that one of the Switches 0 to 3 is the switch that's associated with Door 0, and we can focus only on Switches 0 to 3. One step: half the range gone. We continue in this way until we find the switch (and its position) associated with Door 0.

Suppose that we go all the way, cutting the range of switches in half again and again until we have only one switch remaining. Let's say we find that Switch 6 is associated with Door 0. We'll then set Switch 6 so that Door 0 is open. That's how it stays. When we next solve Door 1, or indeed any other door later, we'll be careful not to change the position of Switch 6.

I can now present the binary search solution to this problem. The new set_a_switch code is given in Listing 7-17. The exploreCave function is the same as before (Listing 7-15).

```
void set_a_switch(int door, int switch_positions[],
                  int door_for_switch[], int n) {
  int i, result;
  int low = 0, high = n-1, mid;

  for (i = 0; i < n; i++)
    if (door_for_switch[i] == -1)
      switch_positions[i] = 0;

  result = tryCombination(switch_positions);
  if (result != door) {
    for (i = 0; i < n; i++)
      if (door_for_switch[i] == -1)
        switch_positions[i] = 1;
  }

❶ while (low != high) {
    mid = (low + high) / 2;
    for (i = low; i <= mid; i++)
      if (door_for_switch[i] == -1)
        switch_positions[i] = 1 - switch_positions[i];
❷   result = tryCombination(switch_positions);
    if (result != door) {
      high = mid;
      for (i = low; i <= mid; i++)
        if (door_for_switch[i] == -1)
          switch_positions[i] = 1 - switch_positions[i];
```

```
      }
      else
        low = mid + 1;
    }
    door_for_switch[low] = door;
  ❸ switch_positions[low] = 1 - switch_positions[low];
}
```

*Listing 7-17: Finding and setting the switch for the current door using a binary search*

Compared to Listing 7-16, the only real change is the replacement of the linear search with a binary search. Prior to each evaluation of the binary search condition ❶, we'll arrange so that the current door is closed. In particular, once low and high are equal and the loop terminates, the door will still be closed. Then all we have to do is change the position of switch low to open the door.

Let's now study the binary search itself. On each iteration, we calculate the midpoint mid, then change the position of the first half of the switches (but only those that are not already associated with doors). What effect did that have on the current door ❷? There are two possibilities:

**The door is now open.**   We now know that the switch we seek is between low and mid, so we throw away all switches greater than mid. We also flip each switch between low and mid back to what they were prior to this iteration. This closes the door again so that we're ready for the next iteration.

**The door is still closed.**   The switch we want is therefore between mid + 1 and high, so we throw away all switches that are mid or less. That's all we do! No switches get flipped here, because the door is still closed, just as we want it.

When we finish the binary search, low and high will be equal, and they tell us the switch associated with the current door. The current door is still closed at this point, so we flip the switch to open it ❸.

There are no more caveats: we have a clean, fast, binary-search-based solution. Send this off to the judge and you should pass all of the test cases.

## Summary

Sometimes it's much tougher to find an optimal solution than it is to check whether some proposed solution is feasible. How much liquid should be poured in a tree? I don't know. Is 10 liters enough liquid? Now that question I can handle.

When the conditions are right, binary search can convert a hard optimization problem into an easier feasibility-check problem. Sometimes it feels like cheating! We pay just an extra logarithmic factor for adding the binary search. A logarithmic factor is practically free. In return, we get to deal with an easier problem.

I'm not claiming that binary search is the only way to solve the problems in this chapter. For example, it's possible to solve Feeding Ants without binary search along the lines of what we did in Chapter 2, but I find that solution trickier than the one I presented in this chapter. Some problems that can be solved by binary search can also be solved by dynamic programming, but, again, doing so may be very challenging and there'd likely be little practical payoff anyway.

What I am claiming is that binary search can offer solutions that are both nearly as fast as and easier to design than anything else we might try. If you're not convinced, you might revisit each problem in this chapter, this time considering how you might solve it without binary search. But, really: if you're working on a problem and see that you can use binary search, just do it and don't look back.

## Notes

Feeding Ants is originally from the 2014 Croatian Open Competition in Informatics, Round 4. River Jump is originally from the December 2006 USA Computing Olympiad, Silver Division. Living Quality is originally from the 2010 International Olympiad in Informatics. Cave Doors is originally from the 2013 International Olympiad in Informatics.

Binary search is one manifestation of a general algorithm design technique called *divide and conquer (D&C)*. D&C algorithms solve one or more independent subproblems, then combine those solutions to solve the original problem. Binary search solves just one subproblem—the one corresponding to the part of the input that we know contains the solution. Other D&C algorithms typically solve two or more subproblems; in Chapter 10, we'll see such an example. To learn about other problems that are solved efficiently by D&C algorithms, see *Algorithms Illuminated (Part 1): The Basics* by Tim Roughgarden (2017).

# 8

## HEAPS AND SEGMENT TREES

Data structures organize our data to make
it possible to accelerate certain operations.
For example, in Chapter 1, we learned about
hash tables, which speed up the search for a
specified element in a collection.

In this chapter, we'll learn two new data structures: heaps and segment
trees. A heap is what you want whenever you need the maximum (or minimum) element; a segment tree is what you want when you need to perform
queries on pieces of an array. In our first problem, we'll see how heaps turn
slow maximum computations into fast heap operations; in our second and
third problems, we'll see how segment trees do similarly for more general
array queries.

## Problem 1: Supermarket Promotion

This is SPOJ problem PRO.

### *The Problem*

In a supermarket, each shopper picks up the items that they want to buy,
then goes through the checkout to pay for their items. Once a shopper pays,
the shopper is given a receipt that has the total cost of what they purchased.

For example, if someone picks up some items and the total is $18, then the cost written on their receipt is $18. We don't care about the cost of individual items.

The supermarket is having a promotion that will last $n$ days. During the promotion, each receipt is placed in a ballot box. At the end of each day, two receipts are removed from the ballot box: one of maximum cost $x$ and one of minimum cost $y$. The shopper who produced the maximum-cost receipt gets a prize worth $x - y$ dollars. (Don't worry about how the supermarket identifies that shopper based on their receipt.) The $x$ and $y$ receipts are then gone, never to reappear, but all other receipts from that day stay in the ballot box (and may be removed on some future day).

It's guaranteed that there will be at least two receipts in the ballot box at the end of each day.

Our task is to compute the total prize money that will be given out by the supermarket as part of the promotion.

### Input

The input contains one test case, consisting of the following lines:

- A line containing $n$, the duration in days of the promotion. $n$ is between 1 and 5,000.

- $n$ lines, one for each day of the promotion. Each such line begins with integer $k$, indicating that there are $k$ receipts on this day. The line then contains $k$ integers, representing the cost of each receipt for this day. $k$ is between 0 and 100,000; each receipt cost is a positive number that's at most 1,000,000.

The total number of receipts produced throughout the entire promotion is at most 1,000,000.

### Output

Output the total prize money given out by the supermarket.

The time limit for solving the test case is 0.6 seconds.

## Solution 1: Maximum and Minimum in an Array

For many of the problems in this book, it's a challenge to devise a correct algorithm, let alone an efficient one. At least for the current problem, correctness doesn't seem so hard. Determining the prize on each day simply involves searching the ballot box for the maximum cost and then searching again for the minimum cost. Maybe that will be efficient enough, too?

Let's look at a test case:

```
2
16 6 63 16 82 25 2 43 5 17 10 56 85 38 15 32 91
1 57
```

Remember that the first number on each line of receipts tells us the number of receipts and is not itself a receipt cost. After the first day and before removing any receipts, we have these 16 receipt costs:

```
6 63 16 82 25 2 43 5 17 10 56 85 38 15 32 91
```

The maximum receipt is 91 and the minimum is 2. Those two receipts are removed, and they contribute 91 − 2 = 89 in prize money. Here's what's left after removing 91 and 2:

```
6 63 16 82 25 43 5 17 10 56 85 38 15 32
```

Now we move on to the second day. We add the 57 to get:

```
6 63 16 82 25 43 5 17 10 56 85 38 15 32 57
```

The maximum now is 85 and the minimum is 5, so that's 85 − 5 = 80 added to the prize money. The total prize money for this promotion is therefore 89 + 80 = 169.

One implementation idea involves storing the receipts in an array. To remove a receipt, we could literally remove it, as we just did. That would involve shifting later receipts to the left, to fill the vacated array entry. But it's simpler to keep the receipts where they are and associate a used flag with each receipt. If used is 0, then the receipt hasn't been used yet; if it's 1, then it has been used and is logically removed (so we had better ignore it from here on out).

Here are a couple of constants and the receipt struct:

```
#define MAX_RECEIPTS 1000000
#define MAX_COST 1000000

typedef struct receipt {
  int cost;
  int used;
} receipt;
```

We're going to need helper functions to identify and remove the maximum receipt cost and minimum receipt cost, so let's knock those out now. Listing 8-1 gives the code.

```
int extract_max(receipt receipts[], int num_receipts) {
  int max, max_index, i;
❶ max = -1;
  for (i = 0; i < num_receipts; i++)
❷  if (!receipts[i].used && receipts[i].cost > max) {
      max_index = i;
      max = receipts[i].cost;
    }
```

```
❸ receipts[max_index].used = 1;
  return max;
}

int extract_min(receipt receipts[], int num_receipts) {
  int min, min_index, i;
❹ min = MAX_COST + 1;
  for (i = 0; i < num_receipts; i++)
  ❺ if (!receipts[i].used && receipts[i].cost < min) {
      min_index = i;
      min = receipts[i].cost;
    }
❻ receipts[min_index].used = 1;
  return min;
}
```

*Listing 8-1: Finding and removing maximum and minimum costs*

The standard term for the operation that removes and returns the maximum value is *extract-max*. Likewise, the operation that removes and returns the minimum value is called *extract-min*.

These functions operate very similarly. The extract_max function sets max to -1 ❶, which is smaller than any receipt cost. When it finds a "real" receipt cost, max will be set to that cost, and from then on it will track the largest cost found so far. Similar reasoning explains why extract_min initializes min with a cost higher than any valid cost ❹. Notice that, in each function, the only receipts that are considered are those whose used value is 0 ❷ ❺ and that each function sets the identified receipt's used value to 1 ❸ ❻.

With those two helper functions in hand, we can write a main function to read the input and solve the problem. One interesting aspect here is that reading input and solving the problem are interleaved: we read a little input (the receipts for the first day), calculate the prize for that day, read a little more input (the receipts for the second day), calculate the prize for that day, and so on. This is implemented in Listing 8-2.

```
int main(void) {
  static struct receipt receipts[MAX_RECEIPTS];
  int num_days, num_receipts_today;
  int num_receipts = 0;
❶ long long total_prizes = 0;
  int i, j, max, min;
  scanf("%d", &num_days);

  for (i = 0; i < num_days; i++) {
    scanf("%d", &num_receipts_today);
    for (j = 0; j < num_receipts_today; j++) {
      scanf("%d", &receipts[num_receipts].cost);
      receipts[num_receipts].used = 0;
      num_receipts++;
```

```
    }
    max = extract_max(receipts, num_receipts);
    min = extract_min(receipts, num_receipts);
    total_prizes += max - min;
  }
  printf("%lld\n", total_prizes);
  return 0;
}
```

*Listing 8-2: The main function for reading input and solving the problem*

The only gotcha here is the type of the total_prizes variable ❶. An integer or long integer may not be enough. A typical long integer can hold values up to about 4 billion; the total prize money could be up to 5,000 × 1,000,000, which is 5 billion. Long long integers can hold integers that are billions, trillions, and way beyond that, so we're certainly safe using a long long integer here.

The outer for loop runs once for each day, and the inner for loop reads each receipt for the day. Once each day's receipts have been read, we extract the maximum receipt, extract the minimum receipt, and update the total prize money.

This is a complete solution to the problem. It correctly outputs 169 for our sample test case, and you should spend some time convincing yourself that it's correct in general.

Unfortunately, it's too slow, and you would get a "Time-Limit Exceeded" error from the judge.

We can explore the inefficiency by thinking about a worst-case test case. Let's say that the promotion lasts 5,000 days and that on each of the first 10 days we get 100,000 receipts. After the tenth day, we'll have about a million receipts in the array. Finding the maximum and minimum involves a linear scan through the array. However, since we remove only two receipts per day, we'll have close to a million receipts in there all the way through the promotion. So, we're looking at 5,000 days, almost all of which require about a million steps to find the maximum and another million steps to find the minimum. That's about 5,000 × 2,000,000, or 10 billion, steps! There is no chance of solving this, given the stringent time limit. If only we could speed up those maximum and minimum computations.

Let's quickly disarm sorting as a possible improvement here. If we kept the receipts array sorted, then finding and removing the maximum would take constant time, as the maximum would be at the rightmost index. Finding the minimum would take constant time, too, but it would take linear time to remove the minimum since we'd have to shift all other elements to the left. Sorting also ruins the efficiency of adding a receipt: when we're not sorting, we can just plunk it at the end of the array, but when sorting we have to find its proper position. No, sorting isn't the answer. The answer is heaps.

## Max-Heaps

We'll begin by focusing on how to quickly find and extract the maximum element from an array. That's only solving half the problem—we need to be able to do this for the minimum, too—but we'll get to that.

### Finding the Maximum

Take a look at the tree in Figure 8-1. It has 13 nodes corresponding to the following 13 receipts (the first 13 receipts in our sample test case): 6, 63, 16, 82, 25, 2, 43, 5, 17, 10, 56, 85, and 38.

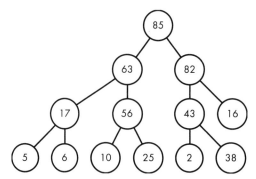

*Figure 8-1: A max-heap*

Quick—what's the maximum receipt cost in that tree?

It's 85, and it's right there at the root. If you were promised that the maximum element of some tree was at its root, then you could just return the element at the root and not search or traverse the tree at all.

Our plan is to maintain the tree such that the maximum receipt cost is always at the root. We'll have to be vigilant, because we're going to be bombarded by two kinds of events that can mess up our tree:

**A new receipt comes in.** We have to figure out how to reorganize the tree to incorporate this receipt. The new receipt could even be higher than everything else in the tree, in which case we need to get the receipt to the root.

**A receipt gets extracted from the tree.** We have to figure out how to reorganize the tree so that the maximum element remaining in the tree is at the root.

Of course, we have to do these inserts and extracts quickly. In particular, we need to be quicker than linear time, as a linear-time scan through an array is what brought us here in the first place!

### What Is a Max-Heap?

Figure 8-1 is an example of a *max-heap*. The "max" there means that this tree enables us to quickly find the maximum element.

A max-heap has two important properties. First, it's a *complete* binary tree. This means that each level in the tree is full (that is, it has no missing nodes), except possibly the bottom level, whose nodes are filled in from left to right. In Figure 8-1, notice how each level is completely full. Well, the bottom level isn't completely full, but that's okay because its nodes are filled in from the left. (Don't confuse complete binary trees here with full binary trees from Chapter 2.)

The fact that a max-heap is a complete binary tree doesn't directly help us find the maximum, insert an element, or extract the maximum, but it does lead to a lightning-fast implementation of heaps, as we'll see.

Second, the value of a node is greater than or equal to the values of its child nodes. (The values in Figure 8-1 are all distinct, so a parent's value is strictly greater than those of its children.) This is called the *max-heap-order* property.

Consider the node in Figure 8-1 with a value of 56. As promised, 56 is greater than the values of its child nodes (10 and 25). This property is true everywhere in the tree, and it's why the maximum value must be at the root. Every other node has a parent node with greater value!

## Inserting into a Max-Heap

When a new receipt arrives, we'll insert it into the max-heap, but we have to do it carefully so that the max-heap-order property is maintained.

Starting with Figure 8-1, let's insert 15. There's only one place we can put it without breaking the complete-tree property: on the bottom level, to the right of the 38 (see Figure 8-2).

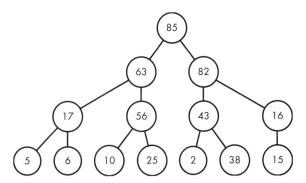

Figure 8-2: A max-heap with 15 inserted

It's a complete binary tree, for sure, but does the max-heap-order property hold? It does! 15's parent is 16, and 16 is greater than 15, just as we require. There's no additional work to do.

Now consider a tougher one. We'll insert 32 into Figure 8-2, resulting in Figure 8-3.

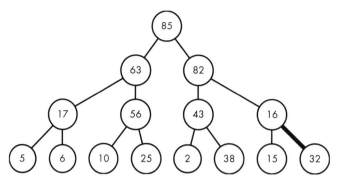

*Figure 8-3: A max-heap with 32 inserted*

There's some trouble here. Inserting 32 has broken the max-heap-order property, because its parent 16 is less than 32. (Here, and in subsequent figures, the thick edge shows a max-heap-order violation.) We can fix this problem by swapping the 16 and 32, as in Figure 8-4.

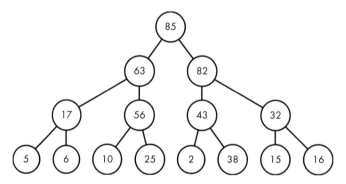

*Figure 8-4: A max-heap with the max-heap-order violation repaired*

Ahh, order has been restored: 32 must be greater than both of its children at this point. It's greater than its child 16 because that's why we performed the swap, and it's greater than its other child 15 because 15 used to be a child of 16. In general, performing such a swap is guaranteed to maintain the max-heap-order property between the new node and its children.

We're back to a max-heap, and it only took us one swap to do it. It could take more swaps, though, which I'll demonstrate now by inserting 91 into Figure 8-4. See Figure 8-5 for the result.

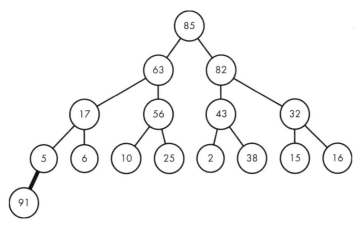

*Figure 8-5: A max-heap with 91 inserted*

We had to start a new level at the bottom of the tree, since the previous bottom level is full. We can't keep the 91 as a child of 5, though, because it violates the max-heap-order property. A swap will fix it . . . well, sort of. See Figure 8-6.

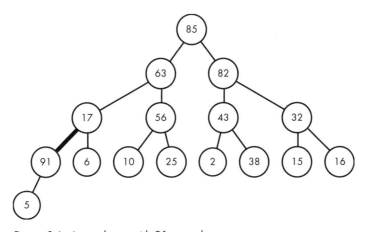

*Figure 8-6: A max-heap with 91 moved up*

We've fixed the problem between 5 and 91, but now we have a new problem between 17 and 91. We can fix this one by another swap; see Figure 8-7.

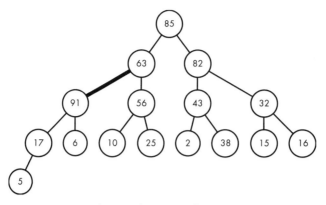

*Figure 8-7: A max-heap with 91 moved up again*

We have yet another max-heap-order violation, this time between 63 and 91. However, notice that the violation is moving up the tree, becoming closer and closer to the root. At worst, we'll end up shuttling 91 up to the root of the tree. That's exactly what will happen here, because 91 is the maximum element. It takes two more swaps to finish the job: the first is shown in Figure 8-8.

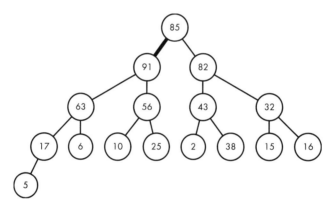

*Figure 8-8: A max-heap with 91 moved up yet again*

And the second swap is shown in Figure 8-9.

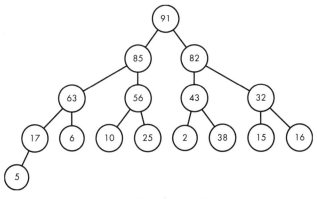

*Figure 8-9: A max-heap with the heap-order violation repaired*

We've got a max-heap again! We only had to perform four swaps to fix the heap of 16 elements, and that was for a value that bubbled up all the way to the root. As we've seen, inserting other values that don't make it all the way to the root will be even faster than that.

### Extracting from a Max-Heap

At the end of each day of the promotion, we'll need to extract the maximum receipt from the max-heap. As with insertion, we must be careful to fix the tree so that it's a max-heap again. We'll see that the process mirrors that of insertion, this time with a value bubbling down rather than up.

Let's start with Figure 8-1 and extract the maximum. Here is that figure again:

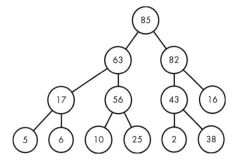

Extracting the maximum removes 85 as the root of the tree, but we need to put something else at the root; otherwise, we would no longer have a tree. The only node we can use, without breaking the complete-tree property, is the rightmost node on the bottom level. That is, we can swap 85 with 38, arriving at Figure 8-10.

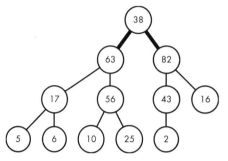

*Figure 8-10: A max-heap with 85 extracted*

We just took a small value from the bottom of the tree and blasted it up to the top. In general, that's going to break the max-heap-order property. It certainly does so here, because 38 is less than both 63 and 82.

We'll again fix the max-heap-order property by using swaps. Unlike insertion, extraction presents us with a choice. Should we swap 38 and 63, or should we swap 38 and 82? Swapping 38 and 63 doesn't solve the problem at the root, because 82 would end up as a child of 63. Swapping 38 and 82 is the right move. In general, we want to perform the swap with the larger child, so the max-heap-order property is fixed between the larger child and its new children. Figure 8-11 shows the result of swapping 38 and 82.

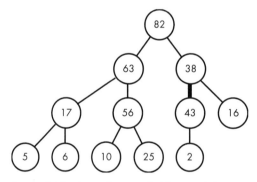

*Figure 8-11: A max-heap with 38 moved down*

We're not out of the woods yet—there's still a max-heap-order violation between 38 and 43. The good news is that the max-heap-order violation is moving down the tree. If we keep pushing the violations down, then in the worst case we'll have a max-heap again when 38 hits the bottom of the tree.

Let's swap 38 and 43; see Figure 8-12.

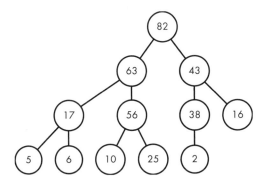

Figure 8-12: A max-heap with 38 moved farther down

The 38 is now fine right where it is, so we've restored the max-heap-order property.

### Height of a Max-Heap

Both insertion and extraction perform at most one swap per level: insertion swaps up the tree and extraction swaps down the tree. Are insertion and extraction fast? That depends on the height of the max-heap: if the height is small, then these operations are fast. Thus we need to understand the relationship between the number of elements in a max-heap and the height of the max-heap.

Take a look at Figure 8-13, where I've drawn the complete binary tree of 16 nodes.

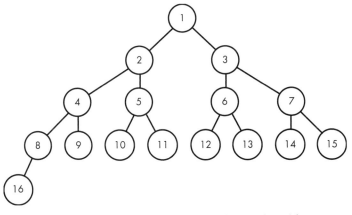

Figure 8-13: A complete binary tree of 16 nodes (numbered from top to bottom and left to right)

I've numbered the nodes from top to bottom, left to right. That's why the root is 1; its two children are 2 and 3; their children are 4, 5, 6, and 7;

and so on. We can observe that each new level starts with a number that is a power of 2: the root is 1, the level below that starts at 2, the level below that starts at 4, then 8, then 16. That is, we need to double the number of nodes to produce just one more level in the tree. This is like binary search, where doubling the number of elements leads to just one more iteration of the loop. As with binary search, then, the height of a complete binary tree, and therefore the height of a max-heap, is $O(\log n)$, where $n$ is the number of elements in the tree.

We are victorious! Inserting into a max-heap is $O(\log n)$. Extracting from a max-heap is $O(\log n)$. We no longer have to be slowed down by $O(n)$ linear-time work.

## Max-Heaps as Arrays

A max-heap is just a binary tree, and we know how to implement binary trees. While it is possible to implement a max-heap as such, it's quite challenging to do so.

Think back to when we solved Halloween Haul in Chapter 2. We used a node struct with pointers to the left and right children. That would be enough for us to be able to bubble a value down a max-heap. However, it would not be enough for us to be able to bubble a value up a max-heap, because doing so requires access to parent nodes. So we might add a parent pointer:

```
typedef struct node {
  fields for receipts
  struct node *left, *right, *parent;
} node;
```

Even if we added the parent like that, we still have direct access only to the root of our tree. When inserting a value, how are we supposed to quickly find where to insert it? When extracting, how are we supposed to quickly find the rightmost node on the bottom level? There is a better way.

Let's again use Figure 8-13, where I've numbered the nodes from top to bottom and left to right. The parent of node number 16 is 8. The parent of node number 12 is 6. The parent of node number 7 is 3. What is the relationship between the number of a node and the number of its parent?

The answer is: divide by 2! 16/2 = 8. 12/2 = 6. 7/2 = 3. Well, that last one is really 3.5, so just drop the fractional part.

We integer-divide by 2 to move up the tree. Let's see what happens if we reverse that process and multiply by two instead. $8 \times 2 = 16$, so multiplying by 2 takes us from 8 to its left child. However, most nodes have two children, and we may also want to move from a node to its right child. We can do that, too: we just add 1 to the number of the left child. For example, we can move from 6 to its left child by $6 \times 2 = 12$ and move from 6 to its right child by $6 \times 2 + 1 = 13$. (The relationship between 13/2 and 6 is an example of why it's safe to drop the 0.5 to move from a child to its parent.)

These relationships between nodes hold only because max-heaps are complete binary trees. In general, binary trees can have more chaotic structure, having a long chain of nodes here and a short chain there. We can't breeze around such a tree by multiplying and dividing by 2 unless we inserted placeholder nodes to maintain the illusion that the tree is complete. That would waste a huge amount of memory if the tree were very unbalanced.

If we store a max-heap in an array—first the root, then its children, then their children, and so on—then the index of a node in the array corresponds to its node number. We'll have to start indexing at 1, not 0, to match the numbering in Figure 8-13. (It's possible to start at index 0, but that would result in slightly messier relationships between nodes: the parent of the node at index $i$ would be at $(i - 1)/2$, and the children would be at indices $2i + 1$ and $2i + 2$.)

Here again is Figure 8-1, the heap of 13 receipt costs:

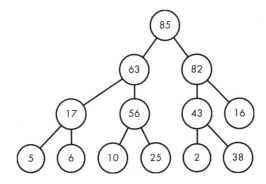

Here is the corresponding array:

| Index | 1 | 2 | 3 | 4 | 5 | 6 | 7 | 8 | 9 | 10 | 11 | 12 | 13 |
|---|---|---|---|---|---|---|---|---|---|---|---|---|---|
| Value | 85 | 63 | 82 | 17 | 56 | 43 | 16 | 5 | 6 | 10 | 25 | 2 | 38 |

Index 6 in the array has a value of 43. What is 43's left child? To answer that, just look up index $6 \times 2 = 12$ in the array: it's 2. What is 43's right child? Look up index $6 \times 2 + 1 = 13$: it's 38. What is 43's parent? Check index $6/2 = 3$: it's 82. No matter which node we're currently focused on in the tree, we can use the array to move to a child or the parent with just a tiny bit of math.

### Implementing a Max-Heap

Each element of our heaps will hold both a receipt index and a receipt cost. These are the two pieces of information that we'll want to know about a receipt when we extract it.

Here's the struct:

```
typedef struct heap_element {
  int receipt_index;
  int cost;
} heap_element;
```

Now we're ready to implement a max-heap. The two key operations are inserting into the heap and extracting the maximum from the heap. Let's start with inserting into the heap; see Listing 8-3.

```
void max_heap_insert(heap_element heap[], int *num_heap,
                     int receipt_index, int cost) {
  int i;
  heap_element temp;
❶ (*num_heap)++;
❷ heap[*num_heap] = (heap_element){receipt_index, cost};
❸ i = *num_heap;
❹ while (i > 1 && heap[i].cost > heap[i / 2].cost) {
    temp = heap[i];
    heap[i] = heap[i / 2];
    heap[i / 2] = temp;
❺ i = i / 2;
  }
}
```

Listing 8-3: Inserting into max-heap

The max_heap_insert function takes four parameters. The first two are for the heap: heap is the array that holds the max-heap, and num_heap is a pointer to the number of elements in the heap. The reason why num_heap is a pointer is because we'll need to increase the number of elements in the heap by one and make the caller aware of that increase. The latter two parameters are for the new receipt: receipt_index is the index of the receipt that we're inserting, and cost is its associated cost.

We begin by increasing the number of elements in the heap by one ❶ and then storing the new receipt in the new heap slot ❷. Variable i tracks the index in the heap of the newly inserted element ❸.

We have no guarantee that we still have a max-heap. What we just inserted may be larger than its parent, so we need to perform the required swaps. That's the point of the while loop ❹.

There are two conditions required for the while loop to continue. First, we need i > 1, because otherwise i is 1 and has no parent. (Remember that the heap starts at index 1, not 0.) Second, we need the node's receipt cost to be greater than that of its parent. The body of the while loop performs the swap, then it moves us from the current node to its parent ❺. Ahh, again, we have that divide-by-2 scheme to move up the tree. Such spare, pleasing, and correct code is the best kind.

Now let's turn to extracting from the max-heap. Listing 8-4 provides the code.

```
heap_element max_heap_extract(heap_element heap[], int *num_heap) {
  heap_element remove, temp;
  int i, child;
❶ remove = heap[1];
❷ heap[1] = heap[*num_heap];
```

```
❸ (*num_heap)--;
❹ i = 1;
❺ while (i * 2 <= *num_heap) {
  ❻ child = i * 2;
     if (child < *num_heap && heap[child + 1].cost > heap[child].cost)
     ❼ child++;
  ❽ if (heap[child].cost > heap[i].cost) {
       temp = heap[i];
       heap[i] = heap[child];
       heap[child] = temp;
     ❾ i = child;
     } else
       break;
  }
  return remove;
}
```

*Listing 8-4: Extracting the maximum from max-heap*

We begin by saving the receipt that we're about to extract, which is at the root of the heap ❶. We then replace the root with the bottom-most, right-most node ❷ and decrease the number of elements in the heap by one ❸. That new root element might not meet the max-heap-order property, so we use variable i to track its position in the heap ❹. Then, just as in Listing 8-3, we have a while loop that will perform the necessary swaps. This time, the while loop condition ❺ says that the left child of Node i is in the heap; if it's not, then Node i has no children and a max-heap-order violation cannot exist.

Inside the loop, child is set to the left child ❻. Then, if the right child exists, we check whether its cost is higher than that of the left child. If it is, then we set child to be that right child ❼. Now child is the biggest child, so we check whether it is involved in a max-heap-order violation ❽. If it is, then we perform the swap. Finally, we move down the tree ❾ so that we're ready to check for another max-heap-order violation.

Notice what happens if the node and its largest child are already correctly ordered: we break out of the loop, since there can't be any more violations in the tree.

The last thing the function does is return the maximum-cost receipt. We'll be able to use that to help determine the prize for the day and to make sure that we never consider this receipt again. First, however, let's learn about min-heaps, so we can extract minimums in addition to maximums.

## Min-Heaps

A *min-heap* allows us to quickly insert a new receipt and extract the minimum-cost receipt.

### Definition and Operations

Guess what? You know almost everything you need to know about min-heaps, because they are almost identical to max-heaps.

A min-heap is a complete binary tree. It will have height $O(\log n)$, where $n$ is the number of elements in the heap. We'll be able to store it in an array just as we did a max-heap. To find the parent of a node, divide by 2; to find the left child, multiply by 2; to find the right child, multiply by 2 and add 1. There is nothing new here.

The only new thing is the *min-heap-order* property: the value of a node is less than or equal to the values of its child nodes. This results in the smallest value, not the largest value, at the root. That's exactly where we want it to make minimum-extractions fast.

Let's again consider the following 13 receipt costs: 6, 63, 16, 82, 25, 2, 43, 5, 17, 10, 56, 85, and 38. Figure 8-14 shows a min-heap for these costs.

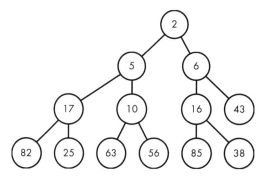

*Figure 8-14: A min-heap*

Inserting into a min-heap and extracting the minimum from a min-heap are analogous to the corresponding max-heap operations.

To insert, add the new node to the right of all nodes on the bottom level, or start a new level if the bottom level is full. Then swap the node up until it becomes the root or is greater than or equal to its parent.

To extract the minimum, replace the root by the bottom-most, right-most value, and then swap it down the tree until it becomes a leaf or is less than or equal to its children.

### Implementing a Min-Heap

Implementing a min-heap is a copy-and-paste job using our max-heap code. Just change the function names and change the comparisons from > to <. That's it. See Listing 8-5 for the insertion code.

```
void min_heap_insert(heap_element heap[], int *num_heap,
                     int receipt_index, int cost) {
  int i;
  heap_element temp;
  (*num_heap)++;
  heap[*num_heap] = (heap_element){receipt_index, cost};
```

```
  i = *num_heap;
  while (i > 1 && heap[i].cost < heap[i / 2].cost) {
    temp = heap[i];
    heap[i] = heap[i / 2];
    heap[i / 2] = temp;
    i = i / 2;
  }
}
```

*Listing 8-5: Inserting into min-heap*

Listing 8-6 gives the minimum-extraction code.

```
heap_element min_heap_extract(heap_element heap[], int *num_heap) {
  heap_element remove, temp;
  int i, child;
  remove = heap[1];
  heap[1] = heap[*num_heap];
  (*num_heap)--;
  i = 1;
  while (i * 2 <= *num_heap) {
    child = i * 2;
    if (child < *num_heap && heap[child + 1].cost < heap[child].cost)
      child++;
    if (heap[child].cost < heap[i].cost) {
      temp = heap[i];
      heap[i] = heap[child];
      heap[child] = temp;
      i = child;
    } else
      break;
  }
  return remove;
}
```

*Listing 8-6: Extracting a minimum from min-heap*

There is big-time code duplication here! In practice, what you'd do is write more general heap_insert and heap_extract functions that take a comparison function as a parameter (much like qsort does). It's simpler, though, to understand the code without that, so let's keep it as is.

## Solution 2: Heaps

Now that we've got max-heaps and min-heaps, we're ready for round 2 with this problem.

All we need is a main function that reads the input and uses heaps to quickly insert and extract receipts. See Listing 8-7 for the code. As you read through it, you'll come across two while loops. What on earth are those doing?

```
int main(void) {
❶ static int used[MAX_RECEIPTS] = {0};
❷ static heap_element max_heap[MAX_RECEIPTS + 1];
   static heap_element min_heap[MAX_RECEIPTS + 1];
   int num_days, receipt_index_today;
   int receipt_index = 0;
   long long total_prizes = 0;
   int i, j, cost;
   int max_num_heap = 0, min_num_heap = 0;
   heap_element max_element, min_element;
   scanf("%d", &num_days);

   for (i = 0; i < num_days; i++) {
     scanf("%d", &receipt_index_today);
     for (j = 0; j < receipt_index_today; j++) {
       scanf("%d", &cost);
❸     max_heap_insert(max_heap, &max_num_heap, receipt_index, cost);
❹     min_heap_insert(min_heap, &min_num_heap, receipt_index, cost);
       receipt_index++;
     }

❺   max_element = max_heap_extract(max_heap, &max_num_heap);
     while (used[max_element.receipt_index])
       max_element = max_heap_extract(max_heap, &max_num_heap);
     used[max_element.receipt_index] = 1;

❻   min_element = min_heap_extract(min_heap, &min_num_heap);
     while (used[min_element.receipt_index])
       min_element = min_heap_extract(min_heap, &min_num_heap);
     used[min_element.receipt_index] = 1;
     total_prizes += max_element.cost - min_element.cost;
   }
   printf("%lld\n", total_prizes);
   return 0;
}
```

*Listing 8-7: The main function for solving the problem using heaps*

We have a used array ❶ that will store for each receipt a 1 if it has been
used and a 0 if not. The max-heap ❷ and min-heap are one element larger
than the used array; this accounts for us not using index 0 in the heaps.

For a given day, we insert the index of each receipt into both the max-
heap ❸ and min-heap ❹. We then extract a receipt from the max-heap ❺
and extract a receipt from the min-heap ❻. This is where those two while
loops come in, looping until we get a receipt that hasn't yet been used. Let
me explain what's going on.

When we extract a receipt from the max-heap, it would be nice to also
extract it from the min-heap so that the two heaps always contain exactly the

same receipts. Notice, though, that we don't actually extract that same receipt from the min-heap. Why? Because we have no idea where that receipt *is* in the min-heap! At some later time, that receipt might be extracted from the min-heap—but it has already been used, so we want to throw it away and not process it again.

The opposite can happen, too, because we extract a receipt from the min-heap and leave it in the max-heap. At some later time, that used receipt might come out of the max-heap. We need to ignore it and extract from the max-heap again.

So that's what the while loops do: ignore receipts that have already been processed by one of the heaps.

A new test case may help. Here it is:

```
2
2 6 7
2 9 10
```

The prize money here is 7 − 6 = 1 from the first day and 10 − 9 = 1 from the second day, so the total prize money is 2.

After reading the two receipts on the first day, each heap holds the two receipts. For the max-heap, we have:

| receipt_index | cost |
|---|---|
| 1 | 7 |
| 0 | 6 |

For the min-heap, we have:

| receipt_index | cost |
|---|---|
| 0 | 6 |
| 1 | 7 |

We then do the heap extractions, removing one receipt from each heap. Here's what's left for the max-heap:

| receipt_index | cost |
|---|---|
| 0 | 6 |

Here's what's left for the min-heap:

| receipt_index | cost |
|---|---|
| 1 | 7 |

Receipt 0 is still in the max-heap, and Receipt 1 is still in the min-heap. However, they have been used, so we'd better not use them again.

Now consider the second day. Receipts 2 and 3 get added to each heap, so for the max-heap, we have:

| receipt_index | cost |
|---|---|
| 3 | 10 |
| 0 | 6 |
| 2 | 9 |

For the min-heap, we have:

| receipt_index | cost |
|---|---|
| 1 | 7 |
| 2 | 9 |
| 3 | 10 |

When we extract from the max-heap, we get Receipt 3. That's great. However, when we extract from the min-heap, we get Receipt 1. Without the while loop to throw it away, this would be big trouble, because Receipt 1 has already been used.

At the end of a given day, one or both of the while loops might iterate many times. If this kept happening, day after day, then we'd have to be concerned about the impact on our program's efficiency. Notice, though, that a receipt can be removed from a heap at most once. If there are $r$ receipts in a heap, then there can be at most $r$ extractions from the heap, whether they are clustered in a single day or across many days.

It is time to submit to the judge. Unlike Solution 1, which frittered away its time with slow searches, our heap-based solution should pass all of the test cases well within the time limit.

## Heaps

If you have a stream of values coming in and at any given time you may be asked to process the maximum or minimum value, then a heap is what you want. A max-heap is used to extract and process the maximum; a min-heap is used to extract and process the minimum.

A heap can be used to implement a *priority queue*. In a priority queue, each element has a priority that determines its importance. In some applications, the priorities of important elements are big numbers, in which case a max-heap should be used; in others, the priorities of important elements are small numbers, in which case a min-heap should be used. Of course, if we need both high- and low-priority elements, we can use two heaps as we did when solving the Supermarket Promotion problem.

### Two More Applications

I find that min-heaps are used more often than max-heaps. Let's explore two examples where min-heaps can be used.

## Heapsort

There's a famous sorting algorithm called *heapsort* that we can implement now that we understand min-heaps. All we do is insert all of the values into the min-heap and then extract the minimum one by one. The extractions pull out the smallest value, then the second-smallest value, then the third-smallest value, and so on, handing us the values sorted from smallest to largest. It's literally four lines. Check it out in Listing 8-8.

```
#define N 10

int main(void) {
  static int values[N] = {96, 61, 36, 74, 45, 60, 47, 6, 95, 93};
  static int min_heap[N + 1];
  int i, min_num_heap = 0;

  // Heapsort. 4 lines!
  for (i = 0; i < N; i++)
    min_heap_insert(min_heap, &min_num_heap, values[i]);
  for (i = 0; i < N; i++)
    values[i] = min_heap_extract(min_heap, &min_num_heap);

  for (i = 0; i < N; i++)
    printf("%d ", values[i]);
  printf("\n");
  return 0;
}
```

*Listing 8-8: Heapsort*

We're inserting integers into the heap here, so you should change `min_heap_insert` and `min_heap_extract` to use and compare integers rather than `heap_element` structs.

Heapsort performs $n$ inserts and $n$ extracts. A heap implements each of those in $\log n$ time, so heapsort is an $O(n \log n)$ algorithm. That's the same worst-case runtime as the fastest possible sorting algorithms. (The q in C's qsort function probably gets its name from *quicksort*, which is a sorting algorithm that is faster than heapsort in practice. We'll encounter quicksort in Chapter 10.)

## Dijkstra's Algorithm

Dijkstra's algorithm (Chapter 6) spends a lot of its time finding the next node to process. It does that by searching through node distances, looking for the smallest one. To speed up Dijkstra's algorithm, we can use a min-heap! This is demonstrated in "Dijkstra's Algorithm: Using a Heap" in Appendix B.

### Choosing a Data Structure

A data structure is typically good for only a few different operation types. There's no super data structure that makes everything fast, so it's up to you to choose the appropriate data structure for the problem you're solving.

Think back to Chapter 1, when we learned about the hash table data structure. Could we have used a hash table to solve Supermarket Promotion?

No! A hash table is good for speeding up the search for a specific item that we're searching for. What are the snowflakes that might be similar to snowflake $s$? Is word $c$ in this word list? Those are the kinds of questions you want to ask of a hash table. What is the minimum element in this array? No hashing is going to help there. You'd have to search through the hash table, which is no faster than searching a regular array. It's our job to choose a data structure specifically designed for the task at hand. For finding the minimum element in an array, that data structure is a min-heap.

As with any general-purpose data structure, heaps can be used to solve a surprisingly diverse set of problems—but the heap data structure itself remains as is, just as you've learned it here. So instead of solving another heap problem, let's proceed to a problem where we'll need a new data structure called a *segment tree*. As with heaps, segment trees speed up only a small number of types of operations. Even so, it's impressive how many problems are in the wheelhouse of segment trees, where those speedups are exactly what we need.

## Problem 2: Building Treaps

In this problem, we'll produce a representation of a *treap*. A treap is a flexible data structure that can solve a variety of search problems, and I encourage you to learn more about treaps if you're interested. Here we're concerned only with building a treap, not using it. Of course, I'll provide all you need to know about treaps for our purposes.

This is POJ problem 1785.

### The Problem

A treap is a binary tree where each node has both a label and a priority. Figure 8-15 shows an example treap, in which the uppercase letters are the labels and the positive integers are the priorities. I've separated the label and priority for each node by a slash. For example, the root node has label C and priority 58.

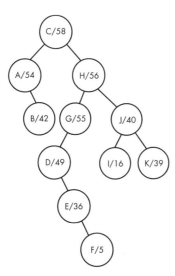

*Figure 8-15: A treap*

A treap has to satisfy two properties: one on its labels and one on its priorities.

First, let's talk about labels. For any node *x*, the labels in its left subtree are all less than the label of *x*, and the labels in its right subtree are all greater than the label of *x*. This is called the *binary search tree (BST)* property.

You can verify that the treap in Figure 8-15 meets this label property. For our alphabetic labels, one label is less than another if it comes earlier in the alphabet. Take the root node as an example. Its label is C. Both labels in its left subtree are less than C, and all labels in its right subtree are greater than C. As another example, consider the node with label G. All of the labels in its left subtree—D, E, and F—are less than G. What about all of the labels in its right subtree? Well, there are none, so there's nothing to check!

Second, let's talk about priorities. For any node *x*, the priorities of its children are less than the priority of *x*. Hey, this is like the max-heap-order property!

Take a look at the root again. Its priority is 58. Its children had better have lower priorities—and they do, with priorities 54 and 56. How about that G node, with priority 55? We need its child to have a lower priority—and it does, with priority 49.

So that's a treap: a binary tree whose labels satisfy the BST property and whose priorities satisfy the max-heap-order property. Notice that there's no shape requirement: a treap can have any structure whatsoever. There's certainly no complete tree requirement like there is for heaps.

In this problem, we are provided the label/priority of each node. Our task is to assemble and output a treap for these nodes.

## Input

The input contains zero or more test cases. Each line of input begins with an integer *n*. Each *n* is between 0 and 50,000. If *n* is 0, then there are no further test cases to process.

If $n$ is greater than zero, then it indicates the number of nodes in the test case. Following $n$ is $n$ space-separated tokens, one for each node. Each token is of the form L/P, where L is the label and P is the priority for this node. Labels are strings of letters; priorities are positive integers. All labels are unique, and all priorities are unique.

Here is possible input that leads to the treap in Figure 8-15:

```
11 A/54 I/16 K/39 E/36 B/42 G/55 D/49 H/56 C/58 J/40 F/5
0
```

### Output

For each test case, output the treap on its own line. Here is the required format for the treap:

```
(<left_subtreap><L>/<P><right_subtreap>)
```

Here `<left_subtreap>` is the left subtreap, `<L>` is the label of the root, `<P>` is the priority of the root, and `<right_subtreap>` is the right subtreap. The subtreaps are output in the same format.

Here is the output corresponding to the sample input:

```
((A/54(B/42))C/58(((D/49(E/36(F/5)))G/55)H/56((I/16)J/40(K/39))))
```

The time limit for solving the test cases is two seconds.

## Recursively Outputting Treaps

Let's again consider our sample nodes and reason through how we can produce a treap from them. Here are those nodes:

```
A/54 I/16 K/39 E/36 B/42 G/55 D/49 H/56 C/58 J/40 F/5
```

Remember that treap priorities must obey the max-heap-order property. In particular, this means that a node with maximum priority must be the root node. In addition, because the input guarantees that all priorities are distinct, there is only one node that has the maximum priority. So it's settled: the root node must be C/58.

We now must decide for each other node whether it should go in C's left subtreap or right subtreap. The priorities of these nodes are all less than 58, so priority won't help us make any kind of left–right split—but the BST property will! The BST property of treaps tells us that the labels in the left subtreap must be less than C and the labels in the right subtreap must be greater than C. We can therefore split the remaining nodes into two groups, one for the left subtreap and one for the right subtreap, as follows:

```
A/54 B/42
I/16 K/39 E/36 G/55 D/49 H/56 J/40 F/5
```

That is, the left subtreap will have Nodes A and B, and the right subtreap will have Nodes I, K, E, G, and so on.

Now, we're done! We've split the original problem into two smaller sub-problems of exactly the same form. We were asked to produce a treap for 11 nodes. We've reduced that problem to producing a treap for two nodes and a treap for eight nodes. We can do those recursively!

Let's nail down the specific rules that we'll use. For the base case, we can use a treap of zero nodes, which requires no output at all. For the recursive case, we'll identify the root as the node with highest priority and then split the remaining nodes into those with smaller labels and those with larger labels. We output an open parenthesis, recursively output the treap for the smaller labels, output the root node of the treap, output the treap for the larger labels, and finally output a closing parenthesis.

For our sample input, we'll output an opening parenthesis. Then we'll output the left subtreap:

```
(A/54(B/42))
```

This is followed by the root node:

```
C/58
```

then the right subtreap:

```
(((D/49(E/36(F/5)))G/55)H/56((I/16)J/40(K/39)))
```

and finally a closing parenthesis.

## Sorting by Label

I have one other implementation idea before we turn to the code. As I've described things so far, it seems that we'd need to literally create a new array with small-labeled nodes to pass to the first recursive call and a new array with large-labeled nodes to pass to the second recursive call. That would result in lots of copying between arrays. Fortunately, we can avoid all that by sorting the nodes by label, from smallest to largest, at the outset. Then we can just tell each recursive call the starting and ending indices of the array that it is responsible for.

For example, if we sort our sample input by label, we get this:

```
A/54 B/42 C/58 D/49 E/36 F/5 G/55 H/56 I/16 J/40 K/39
```

We can then tell the first recursive call to produce the subtreap for the first two nodes and the second recursive call to produce the subtreap for the latter eight.

## Solution 1: Recursion

Here are some constants and a struct:

```
#define MAX_NODES 50000
#define LABEL_LENGTH 16
```

```
typedef struct treap_node {
  char * label;
  int priority;
} treap_node;
```

We don't know how long the labels are, so we'll go with an initial size of 16. You'll see that we call a read_label function to read each label; if a length of 16 proves insufficient, that function will allocate more memory until the label fits. (This is probably overkill, since it looks like the test cases use short labels of up to only five letters, but it's better to be safe than sorry.)

### The main Function

Let's look at the main function, as given in Listing 8-9. It uses some helper functions—read_label that we just talked about and compare for comparing treap nodes—and calls solve for actually outputting the treap. We'll discuss those shortly.

```
int main(void) {
  static treap_node treap_nodes[MAX_NODES];
  int num_nodes, i;
  scanf("%d ", &num_nodes);
  while (num_nodes > 0) {
    for (i = 0; i < num_nodes; i++) {
      treap_nodes[i].label = read_label(LABEL_LENGTH);
      scanf("%d ", &treap_nodes[i].priority);
    }
    qsort(treap_nodes, num_nodes, sizeof(treap_node), compare);
    solve(treap_nodes, 0, num_nodes - 1);
    printf("\n");
    scanf("%d ", &num_nodes);
  }
  return 0;
}
```

Listing 8-9: The main function for reading input and solving the problem

Be careful with scanf in a program that reads a mix of numbers and strings. Here, each number from the input is followed by whitespace, and we don't want those space characters prefixing the labels that follow. To read and throw away those spaces, we use a space following each %d scanf format specifier.

### Helper Functions

We use scanf to read the priorities but not the labels. The labels are read by the read_label function in Listing 8-10.

```
/* based on https://stackoverflow.com/questions/16870485 */
char *read_label(int size) {
```

```
    char *str;
    int ch;
    int len = 0;
    str = malloc(size);
    if (str == NULL) {
      fprintf(stderr, "malloc error\n");
      exit(1);
    }
❶ while ((ch = getchar()) != EOF && (ch != '/')) {
      str[len++] = ch;
      if (len == size) {
        size = size * 2;
        str = realloc(str, size);
        if (str == NULL) {
          fprintf(stderr, "realloc error\n");
          exit(1);
        }
      }
    }
    str[len] = '\0';
    return str;
}
```

*Listing 8-10: Reading a label*

We've used essentially the same function once before in Listing 5-15. The only difference this time is that we stop reading at the / character that separates the label from the priority ❶. As usual, qsort needs a comparison function, and the one we want, given in Listing 8-11, compares nodes by label.

```
int compare(const void *v1, const void *v2) {
  const treap_node *n1 = v1;
  const treap_node *n2 = v2;
  return strcmp(n1->label, n2->label);
}
```

*Listing 8-11: A comparison function for sorting*

The strcmp function works perfectly as a comparison function, because it returns a negative integer if the first string is alphabetically less than the second string, 0 if the strings are equal, and a positive integer if the first string is alphabetically greater than the second string.

### Outputting the Treap

Before we get to the main event—the solve function—we need a helper function to return the index of the node with maximum priority. This is provided in Listing 8-12. It's a slow, linear search from index left to index right (and this should worry you!).

```
int max_priority_index(treap_node treap_nodes[], int left, int right) {
  int i;
  int max_index = left;
  for (i = left + 1; i <= right; i++)
    if (treap_nodes[i].priority > treap_nodes[max_index].priority)
      max_index = i;
  return max_index;
}
```

*Listing 8-12: Finding the maximum priority*

Now we're ready to output the treap! See Listing 8-13 for the solve function.

```
void solve(treap_node treap_nodes[], int left, int right) {
  int root_index;
  treap_node root;
❶ if (left > right)
    return;
❷ root_index = max_priority_index(treap_nodes, left, right);
  root = treap_nodes[root_index];
  printf("(");
❸ solve(treap_nodes, left, root_index - 1);
  printf("%s/%d", root.label, root.priority);
❹ solve(treap_nodes, root_index + 1, right);
  printf(")");
}
```

*Listing 8-13: Solving the problem*

This function takes three parameters: the array of treap nodes and left and right indices determining the range of nodes over which we'd like the treap to be built. In order for the treap to be built for all of the nodes, the initial call from main will pass 0 for left and num_nodes - 1 for right.

The base case for this recursive function occurs when there are no nodes in the treap ❶. In this case, we simply return without outputting anything. With no nodes, there is no output.

Otherwise, from nodes with indices between left and right, we find the index of the node with maximum priority ❷. That's the root of the treap, and it splits the problem in two: outputting a treap for those nodes with smaller labels and outputting a treap for those nodes with larger labels. We solve each of these subproblems with a recursive call ❸ ❹.

There we have it: our first solution. It's quite nice, I'd say. In fact, it does two important things right. First, it sorts the nodes, once and for all, so that each call of solve needs only its left and right indices. Second, it uses recursion to make short work of the otherwise-daunting process of outputting a treap.

However, submit this code to the judge and you'll see that everything grinds to a halt because of that linear search to find the node with maximum priority (Listing 8-12). What's so wrong with it? What kind of treap triggers its worst-case performance? We'll talk about that next.

### Range Maximum Queries

In the previous chapter, we talked about solving the range sum query problem. That one asked, "Given an array a, left index `left`, and right index `right`, what is the *sum* of all elements from a[`left`] to a[`right`]?"

Here, in Building Treaps, we're being asked to solve a related problem known as the *range maximum query (RMQ)* problem. This asks, "Given an array a, left index `left`, and right index `right`, what is the index of the *maximum* element of all elements from a[`left`] to a[`right`]?" (Rather than the index, for some problems it might suffice to get the maximum element itself, but for Building Treaps we need the index.)

In Solution 1, we offered an implementation of RMQ in Listing 8-12. It iterates from `left` to `right`, checking whether we've found an index whose node has higher priority than what we've discovered so far. We call that function for each subtreap, and each call involves a linear search through the active segment of the array. If most of those linear searches were on small array segments, then we might get away with this. However, there are some inputs that cause many of the searches to be on huge segments of the array. Here's such a list of nodes that we might read from the input:

---

A/1 B/2 C/3 D/4 E/5 F/6 G/7

---

We scan all seven nodes, finding G/7 as the node with maximum priority. We then recursively output the treap for the small-labeled nodes and recursively output the treap for the large-labeled nodes. Unfortunately, the first recursive call gets all but the G/7 node, as the second recursive call is on zero nodes. The first recursive call gets this:

---

A/1 B/2 C/3 D/4 E/5 F/6

---

Now we need another scan of these six elements to identify the node with highest priority. We'll identify F/6 as that node, make it the root of this subtreap, and then make two more recursive calls. Again, however, the first recursive call is saddled with all remaining nodes, leading to another expensive array scan. This pattern of expensive array scans can continue until there are no nodes remaining.

Generalizing, we can say that, for $n$ nodes, the first RMQ could take $n$ steps, the second could take $n - 1$ steps, and so on, all the way down to 1 step. That's $1 + 2 + 3 + \ldots + n$ steps in all. A closed form for this formula is $n(n + 1)/2$. In Chapter 1, we saw a very similar formula in "Diagnosing the Problem" on page 9. We can similarly conclude that we're doing $O(n^2)$ (quadratic) work here.

Here's another way to see that we're doing $O(n^2)$ work. Throw away the $n/2$ smallest terms and focus on only the remaining $n/2$ larger terms.

(Let's assume that $n$ is even so that $n/2$ is an integer.) This leaves us with $n + (n-1) + (n-2) + \ldots + (n/2 + 1)$. There are $n/2$ terms here, each of which is larger than $n/2$, so in total they add up to at least $(n/2)(n/2) = n^2/4$. This is quadratic!

Therefore, a linear search to solve the RMQ problem is not satisfactory.

In the previous chapter, we used a prefix array to speed up range sum queries. Give that a quick refresher now, because I'm about to ask you a question: Can we use that technique to solve the RMQ, too?

Unfortunately, no. (Or, fortunately no, because I can teach you one of my favorite data structures as a result.) To sum the elements from index 2 to 5, we can look up the prefix sum for index 5 and subtract the prefix sum for index 1. That's because subtraction undoes addition: the prefix sum for index 5 contains the prefix sum for index 1, so we can just subtract the latter out of there. Unfortunately, we cannot "undo" a maximum computation in the same way. If the maximum for the elements up to index 5 is 10, and the maximum for the elements up to index 1 is also 10, what is the maximum from index 2 to index 5? Who knows! With that 10 gone, it could be whatever is at index 2, or 3, or 4, or 5. A huge, early element prevents later elements from making any change at all to the prefix array. When that huge element is gone, we lose our bearings. Contrast that to a prefix sum array, where every element leaves its mark.

As a last-ditch effort, let's try a heap. Can we use a max-heap to solve the RMQ? No, again. A max-heap gives us the maximum element in the entire heap, with no provision for restricting that to a given range.

It's time for something new.

## Segment Trees

Shoo, treaps, shoo! We'll return to treaps later, just as soon as we have a better implementation of RMQ.

A *segment tree* is a full binary tree where each node is associated with a particular segment of an underlying array. (In Building Treaps, the underlying array is the array of priorities.) Each node stores the answer for the query on its segment. For the RMQ, each node stores the index of the maximum element in its segment, but segment trees can be used for other queries, too. The segments are arranged such that a small number of them can be assembled to answer any query.

### The Segments

The root node of a segment tree covers the entire array. So, if we're ever asked for the RMQ on the entire array, we can solve that in one step by just looking at the root. For other queries, we'll have to use other nodes. The root node has two children: the left child covers the first half of the array and the right child covers the second half. Each of these nodes has two children of its own, which subdivide the segments even further, and so on, until we get to segments of just one element.

Figure 8-16 shows a segment tree that supports queries on an eight-element array. Each node is labeled with its left and right endpoints. There's no information in the segment tree about the RMQ yet; for now, we'll just focus on the segments themselves.

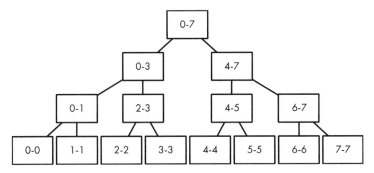

Figure 8-16: A segment tree for an eight-element array

Notice that the sizes of segments are cut in half for each level that we descend in the tree. For example, the root segment covers eight elements, each of its children covers four elements, each of their children covers two elements, and so on. Like a heap, the height of a segment tree is $\log n$, where $n$ is the number of elements in the array. We'll be able to answer any query by doing a constant amount of work per level, so we'll obtain $O(\log n)$ time per query.

Figure 8-16 is a complete binary tree. Through our study of heaps, we know what to do with these: store them in an array! We can then use the same math to find the children of a parent, which we'll need when processing segment trees.

Now, I'm going to hit you with another segment tree, one that exposes a bit of a surprise. See Figure 8-17.

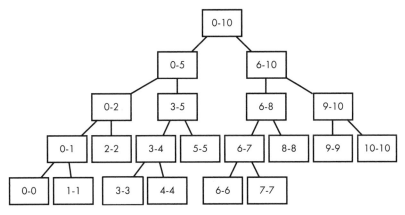

Figure 8-17: A segment tree for an 11-element array

That's not a complete binary tree at all, because the bottom level is not filled in from left to right! For example, Node 2-2 has no children, even though 3-4 does.

Everything's okay, though. We'll continue to store a segment tree in an array. We'll continue to multiply a node's index by 2 to get its left child and to multiply by 2 and add 1 to get its right child. All that will happen is a little bit of waste in the array. For example, the order of elements in the array for Figure 8-17 is as follows, where * is an unused element:

```
0-10
0-5 6-10
0-2 3-5 6-8 9-10
0-1 2-2 3-4 5-5 6-7 8-8 9-9 10-10
0-0 1-1 * * 3-3 4-4 * * 6-6 7-7 * * * * * *
```

This waste *does* make it a little more difficult to determine the number of array elements we need for the segment tree.

If the number of elements, $n$, in the underlying array is a power of 2, then we'll be safe with a segment tree that can hold $2n$ elements. For example, count the nodes in Figure 8-16: it takes 15 nodes, which is less than $8 \times 2 = 16$. ($2n$ is safe because all powers of 2 less than $n$ add up to exactly $n - 1$. For example, $4 + 2 + 1 = 7$, which is 1 less than 8.) If $n$ isn't a power of 2, then $2n$ isn't enough. For proof, look no further than Figure 8-17, which would require an array of 31 elements (more than $2 \times 11 = 22$) to hold it.

The more elements to cover in the segment tree, the bigger we need to make the segment tree array—but how big should it be? Suppose that we have an underlying array of $n$ elements for which we want to build a segment tree. I'll argue that the segment tree should be allocated an array of $4n$ elements to be safe.

Let $m$ be the smallest power of 2 greater than or equal to $n$. For example, if $n$ is 11, then $m$ is 16. We can store a segment tree for $m$ elements in an array with $2m$ elements. Since $m \geq n$, an array with $2m$ elements is enough to store a segment tree for $n$ elements, too.

Fortunately, $m$ can't be that high: it's at most twice the value of $n$. (The worst case occurs for values of $n$ that are just above powers of 2. For example, if $n$ is 9, then $m$ is 16, which is almost twice as large as 9.) Therefore, if we need an array of $2m$ elements and $m$ is at most $2n$, then $2m$ is at most $2 \times 2n = 4n$.

### Initializing the Segments

In each node of the segment tree, we'll store three things: the left index of its segment, the right index of its segment, and the index of the maximum element in the range. We'll initialize the first two of these before moving to the third.

Here's the struct that we'll use for a segment tree node:

```c
typedef struct segtree_node {
  int left, right;
  int max_index;
} segtree_node;
```

To initialize the `left` and `right` members for each node, we'll write the body for the following function signature:

```
void init_segtree(segtree_node segtree[], int node,
                  int left, int right)
```

We assume that `segtree` is an array with sufficient space for the segment tree. The `node` parameter is the root index of the segment tree; `left` and `right` are its segment's left and right indices, respectively. An initial call of `init_segtree` would look like this:

```
init_segtree(segtree, 1, 0, num_elements - 1);
```

Here `num_elements` is the number of elements in the underlying array (for example, the number of nodes in a treap).

We can use recursion to implement `init_segtree`. If `left` and `right` are equal, then we have a one-element segment and there is no subdividing to do. Otherwise, we're in the recursive case and have to split the segment in two. Listing 8-14 provides the code.

```
void init_segtree(segtree_node segtree[], int node,
                  int left, int right) {
  int mid;
  segtree[node].left = left;
  segtree[node].right = right;
❶ if (left == right)
    return;
❷ mid = (left + right) / 2;
❸ init_segtree(segtree, node * 2, left, mid);
❹ init_segtree(segtree, node * 2 + 1, mid + 1, right);
}
```

*Listing 8-14: Initializing segment tree segments*

We first store the values of `left` and `right` in the node. Then, we check the base case ❶, returning from the function if no children are required.

If children are required, then we calculate the midpoint of the current range ❷. We then need to build the left segment tree for the indices from `left` to `mid` and the right segment tree for the indices from `mid + 1` to `right`. This is accomplished by two recursive calls: one for the left ❸ and one for the right ❹. Notice how we use `node * 2` to move to the left child and `node * 2 + 1` to move to the right child.

### Filling the Segment Tree

With the segment tree initialized, it's time to add the index of the maximum element in its segment to each node. For an example, we'll need both a segment tree and the array on which the segment tree will be based. For the segment tree, let's use Figure 8-17, and, for the array, let's use the 11 priorities from "Sorting by Label" on page 303. Figure 8-18 shows the filled segment tree. The maximum index for each node is given below its segment endpoints.

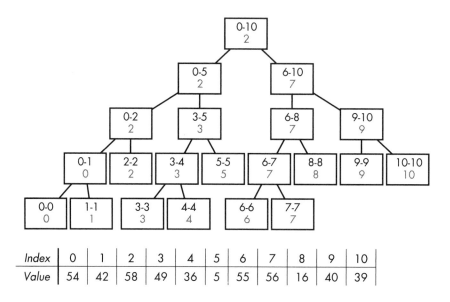

| Index | 0  | 1  | 2  | 3  | 4  | 5 | 6  | 7  | 8  | 9  | 10 |
|-------|----|----|----|----|----|---|----|----|----|----|----|
| Value | 54 | 42 | 58 | 49 | 36 | 5 | 55 | 56 | 16 | 40 | 39 |

*Figure 8-18: A segment tree and an array of priorities*

Let's perform a couple of quick checks. Consider the 0-0 node on the bottom of the tree. That's a segment of only index 0, so the only choice for the index of the maximum element is 0. This sounds like a base case to me!

Now consider Node 6-10. The node says that 7 is the index of the maximum element from index 6 to index 10. Index 7 holds 56, and you can verify that this is the largest element in the segment. To quickly calculate this, we can use the maximum indices stored in 6-10's child nodes: the left child says that 7 is the desired index for the 6-8 segment, and the right child says that 9 is the desired index for the 9-10 segment. For 6-10, then, we really have only two choices: index 7 or index 9, the elements that we get back from these subtrees. This sounds like a recursive case to me!

That's right: we're going to use recursion to fill the tree, much as we did to initialize the tree's segments. Listing 8-15 gives the code.

```
int fill_segtree(segtree_node segtree[], int node,
                 treap_node treap_nodes[]) {
  int left_max, right_max;

❶ if (segtree[node].left == segtree[node].right) {
    segtree[node].max_index = segtree[node].left;
  ❷ return segtree[node].max_index;
  }
```

❸ `left_max = fill_segtree(segtree, node * 2, treap_nodes);`
❹ `right_max = fill_segtree(segtree, node * 2 + 1, treap_nodes);`

❺ `if (treap_nodes[left_max].priority > treap_nodes[right_max].priority)`
   `    segtree[node].max_index = left_max;`
   `else`
   `    segtree[node].max_index = right_max;`
❻ `return segtree[node].max_index;`
`}`

*Listing 8-15: Adding the maximums*

The segtree parameter is the array where the segment tree is stored; we assume that it has already been initialized by Listing 8-14. The node parameter is the root index of the segment tree, and treap_nodes is an array of treap nodes. We need the treap nodes here so we can access their priorities, but otherwise this doesn't have anything to do with treaps. You could easily replace the treap nodes with whatever you need for solving a given problem.

This function returns the index of the maximum element for the root node of the segment tree.

The code begins with the base case check: that the node spans just a single index ❶. If it does, then the maximum index for the node is just its left index (or its right—they're the same, after all). We then return that maximum index ❷.

If we're not in the base case, then we're looking at a segment that spans more than one index. We make a recursive call to the left subtree ❸. That call figures out the max_index value for each node in that subtree and returns to us the max_index value of that subtree's root. We then do the same for the right subtree ❹. Then we compare the indices we got back from those recursive calls ❺, choosing the one whose priority is higher, and setting this node's max_index accordingly. The last thing to do is to return that maximum index ❻.

Filling the tree in this way takes linear time: for each node, we do a constant amount of work to find its maximum index.

### Querying the Segment Tree

Let's recap. We were stymied in our attempts to solve Building Treaps because we didn't have a fast way to respond to the range maximum queries. As a result, we've spent a lot of time developing segment trees, deciding how to choose the segments, how big to make the segment tree array, and how to store the index of the maximum element for each node.

Of course, all of this segment tree stuff would be for naught unless it gives us fast queries. Finally, then, it's time for the payoff: getting fast queries using a segment tree. It's go time! Don't worry—it doesn't involve much more than the kind of recursion we've been using on segment trees so far.

To get a feel for this, we'll make some sample queries on Figure 8-18. Here's that figure again:

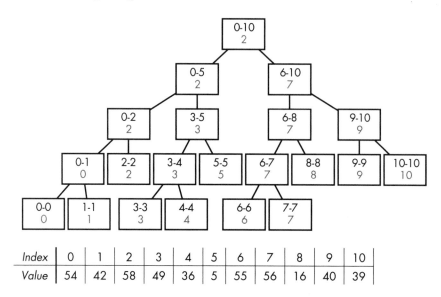

| Index | 0 | 1 | 2 | 3 | 4 | 5 | 6 | 7 | 8 | 9 | 10 |
|-------|---|---|---|---|---|---|---|---|---|---|----|
| Value | 54 | 42 | 58 | 49 | 36 | 5 | 55 | 56 | 16 | 40 | 39 |

For our first query, let's do 6-10. This range covers only some of what the root's 0-10 segment covers, so returning the root's maximum index wouldn't be justified. Instead, we'll ask each of the root's children for the maximum relevant index and use those answers to return the maximum index overall. The root's left child covers Segment 0-5, and that has no overlap at all with our 6-10 range. The left recursive call tells us nothing. The root's right child, however, covers exactly Segment 6-10. The recursive call on that right child will return 7, and that's what we should return overall: 7 is the index of the maximum element in the 6-10 range.

For our second query, let's do 3-8. Again, we'll ask each of the root's children for the maximum relevant index—except that, this time, both children will have something to say, because 3-8 overlaps both 0-5 and 6-10. The recursive call on the left child will return 3, and the recursive call on the right child will return 7. At the root, then, all we do is compare the element at index 3 with the element at index 7. The one at index 7 is higher, so that's our answer.

I don't normally unwind recursion, but I'll make an exception here because I think it might help. Let's further dive into the recursive call on the left subtree. We're still querying 3-8, and the range of the node is 0-5. The left child of 0-5 is 0-2. 0-2 doesn't have any indices in common with our 3-8 query range, so it's out. That leaves the 3-5 node to do the work. Importantly, 3-5 is completely contained within our desired 3-8 range, so we stop here and return 3 from the 3-5 recursive call.

Querying the node of a segment tree falls into one of three cases, and we have seen them all in our examples here. Case 1 is when the node has no indices in common with the query range, case 2 is when the node's segment is completely contained within the query range, and case 3 is when the node's segment contains part of the query range but also contains indices not in the query range.

I recommend pausing here, just before we look at the code, to work a few more query examples by hand. In particular, try the query 4-9. You'll notice that it requires tracing two long paths down the tree. This is the worst-case behavior: we split into two nodes near the top of the tree, and then we trace those two paths all the way down. Convince yourself through further examples, perhaps on larger segment trees, that those paths cannot further subdivide into two long paths of their own. So, although querying a segment tree does do a little more work than a heap operation—sometimes tracing two paths rather than one—it still accesses a small number of nodes per level, giving an $O(\log n)$ runtime.

The code for querying a segment tree is given in Listing 8-16.

```
int query_segtree(segtree_node segtree[], int node,
                  treap_node treap_nodes[], int left, int right) {
    int left_max, right_max;

❶ if (right < segtree[node].left || left > segtree[node].right)
      return -1;

❷ if (left <= segtree[node].left && segtree[node].right <= right)
      return segtree[node].max_index;

❸ left_max = query_segtree(segtree, node * 2,
                           treap_nodes, left, right);
❹ right_max = query_segtree(segtree, node * 2 + 1,
                            treap_nodes, left, right);

   if (left_max == -1)
     return right_max;
   if (right_max == -1)
     return left_max;
❺ if (treap_nodes[left_max].priority > treap_nodes[right_max].priority)
     return left_max;
   return right_max;
}
```

*Listing 8-16: Querying the segment tree*

The function parameters are similar to those of Listing 8-15, except that we've added the left and right indices of our query. The code handles each of the three cases in turn.

In case 1, the node has nothing in common with the query. This holds exactly when the query range ends before the node's segment starts or when the query range starts after the node's segment ends ❶. We return -1 to indicate that this node has no maximum index to return.

In case 2, the node's segment is completely within the query range ❷. We therefore return the maximum index of this node's segment.

That leaves case 3, where the node's segment partially overlaps the query range. We make two recursive calls: one to get the maximum index from the left child ❸ and one to get the maximum index from the right child ❹. If one of those returns -1, then we return the other. If they both return valid indices, then we choose the index whose element is larger ❺.

## Solution 2: Segment Trees

Our final order of business is to alter our first solution (specifically the main function in Listing 8-9 and the solve function in Listing 8-13) to use segment trees. It won't take much: we'll just make the appropriate calls to the segment tree functions that we've already written.

Listing 8-17 contains the new main function.

```
int main(void) {
  static treap_node treap_nodes[MAX_NODES];
❶ static segtree_node segtree[MAX_NODES * 4 + 1];
  int num_nodes, i;
  scanf("%d ", &num_nodes);
  while (num_nodes > 0) {
    for (i = 0; i < num_nodes; i++) {
      treap_nodes[i].label = read_label(LABEL_LENGTH);
      scanf("%d ", &treap_nodes[i].priority);
    }
    qsort(treap_nodes, num_nodes, sizeof(treap_node), compare);
❷   init_segtree(segtree, 1, 0, num_nodes - 1);
❸   fill_segtree(segtree, 1, treap_nodes);
❹   solve(treap_nodes, 0, num_nodes - 1, segtree);
    printf("\n");
    scanf("%d ", &num_nodes);
  }
  return 0;
}
```

Listing 8-17: The main function with segment trees added

The only additions are the declaration of the segment tree ❶, a call to initialize the segment tree's segments ❷, a call to compute the maximum index for each segment tree node ❸, and a new argument to pass the segment tree along to the solve function ❹.

The new solve function itself is given in Listing 8-18.

```
void solve(treap_node treap_nodes[], int left, int right,
           segtree_node segtree[]) {
  int root_index;
  treap_node root;
  if (left > right)
    return;
❶ root_index = query_segtree(segtree, 1, treap_nodes, left, right);
```

```
root = treap_nodes[root_index];
printf("(");
solve(treap_nodes, left, root_index - 1, segtree);
printf("%s/%d", root.label, root.priority);
solve(treap_nodes, root_index + 1, right, segtree);
printf(")");
}
```

*Listing 8-18: Solving the problem with segment trees added*

There's only one substantive change: the call to query_segtree to implement the RMQ ❶!

Phew! We had to work pretty hard there. This segment tree solution should pass all of the judge's test cases within the time limit. In the end, it was worth it, though, because segment trees insinuate themselves into fast solutions to all kinds of problems.

## Segment Trees

Segment trees go by several other names in the wild, including interval trees, tournament trees, order-statistic trees, and range query trees. It doesn't help that "segment tree" is also used to refer to an entirely different data structure than what we've studied here! Perhaps through my chosen terminology I have unknowingly aligned myself with some particular segment of the programmer population.

Whatever you call them, segment trees are must-know structures for those learning algorithms and those interested in competitive programming. On an underlying array of $n$ elements, you can build a segment tree in $O(n)$ time and query a range in $O(\log n)$ time.

In Building Treaps, we used segment trees to solve the RMQ, but segment trees can be used for other queries, too. If you can answer a query by quickly combining answers to two subqueries, then a segment tree is likely the tool of choice. What about a minimum range query? With a segment tree, you just take the minimum (not the maximum) of the children's answers. What about a range sum query? With a segment tree, you just take the sum of the children's answers.

Perhaps you're wondering whether segment trees apply only when the elements of the underlying array remain constant through the execution of the program. In Building Treaps, for example, the treap nodes never changed, so there was no way in which our segment tree could ever become out of sync with what was stored in the array. Indeed, many segment tree problems share this characteristic: an array to be queried, not modified. However, a neat bonus feature of segment trees is that they can be used even when the underlying array is allowed to change. Problem 3 shows you how this is done, and it also shows us a new type of query that we haven't seen before.

# Problem 3: Two Sum

There is no context this time—this is just a pure problem for segment trees. As you'll see, we'll need to support updates to the array, and the query we'll need is not the same as the RMQ.

This is SPOJ problem KGSS.

## *The Problem*

We are given a sequence of integers $a[1], a[2], \ldots, a[n]$, where each integer is at least 0. (Think of the sequence as an array that starts at index 1 rather than 0.)

We need to support two types of operations on the sequence:

**Update**   Given integers $x$ and $y$, change $a[x]$ to $y$.

**Query**   Given integers $x$ and $y$, return the maximum sum of two elements in the range $a[x]$ to $a[y]$.

### Input

The input contains one test case, consisting of the following lines:

- A line containing $n$, the number of elements in the sequence. $n$ is between 2 and 100,000.

- A line containing $n$ integers, each giving one element of the sequence in order from $a[1]$ to $a[n]$. Each integer is at least 0.

- A line containing $q$, the number of operations to be performed on the sequence. $q$ is between 0 and 100,000.

- $q$ lines, each giving one update or query operation to be performed on the sequence.

Here are the operations that can be performed in those $q$ lines.

**Update**   An update operation is specified as the letter U, a space, an integer $x$, a space, and an integer $y$. It indicates that $a[x]$ should be changed to $y$. For example, U 1 4 means that $a[1]$ is to be changed from its current value to 4. $x$ is between 1 and $n$; $y$ is at least 0. This operation does not result in any output.

**Query**   A query operation is specified as the letter Q, a space, an integer $x$, a space, and an integer $y$. It indicates that we should output the maximum sum of two elements in the range $a[x]$ to $a[y]$. For example, Q 1 4 asks us for the maximum sum of two elements in the range $a[1]$ to $a[4]$. $x$ and $y$ are between 1 and $n$, and $x$ is less than $y$.

### Output

Output the result of each query operation, one per line.

The time limit for solving the test case is one second.

### Filling the Segment Tree

In Building Treaps, we needed the segment tree to give us indices of the underlying array, which we used to characterize the recursion and split the treap nodes. This time, however, there's no reason to store indices in the segment tree. All we care about is the sum of elements, not the indices of those elements.

We'll initialize the segments of our segment tree just like we did in "Initializing the Segments" on page 310. We now need the segments to start covering the array at index 1, not index 0, but otherwise there's nothing new here.

Figure 8-19 shows a segment tree that supports a seven-element array. It covers indices 1 to 7, not 0 to 6, to correspond to the problem description.

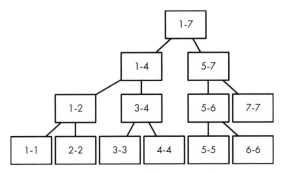

*Figure 8-19: A segment tree for a seven-element array*

Add the code from Listing 8-14 to your program.

Now let's think about how to fill each node with the maximum sum of two elements in its segment. Suppose that we've already found the maximum sum of two elements for Node 1-2 and already found the maximum sum of two elements for Node 3-4. We want to find the maximum sum of two elements for Node 1-4. How do we do this?

Life was good when we were solving the RMQ, because the maximum for a node is just the maximum of its children. For example, if the maximum value in the left subtree is 10 and the maximum in the right subtree is 6, then the maximum for their parent node is 10. No surprises there. In contrast, with this "maximum sum of two elements" segment tree, something weird happens.

Suppose we have these four sequence elements: 10, 8, 6, and 15. The maximum sum of two elements in Segment 1-2 is 18, and the maximum sum of two elements in Segment 3-4 is 21. Is 18 the answer for Segment 1-4, or is 21? Neither is correct! The answer is 10 + 15 = 25. We can't conjure up that 25 if all we know is the 18 from the left and 21 from the right. We need the left and right children to tell us more about their segment—more than just "Oh hey, here's my maximum sum of two elements."

To be clear, sometimes getting back just the maximum sum of two elements from each child *is* enough. Consider this sequence: 10, 8, 6, and 4. The maximum sum of two elements for Segment 1-2 is 18, and the maximum sum of two elements in Segment 3-4 is 10. The maximum sum of two elements in 1-4 is 18, which happens to be the answer from its child segment 1-2—but that was lucky!

There are at most three options for the maximum sum of two elements for a segment. (There are fewer than three options if a node's child doesn't have a valid maximum sum.) Those options are as follows:

**Option 1**   The maximum sum is in the left child. This is like the lucky case that we just did. We get the answer from what the left child tells us.

**Option 2**   The maximum sum is in the right child. This is another lucky case, where the answer is what the right child tells us.

**Option 3**   The maximum sum includes one element from the left child and one element from the right child. This one requires more work, because the answer is not one of the maximums of our children. This is where we need more information from the children.

If the maximum sum of two elements for some segment consists of one element from the left and one from the right, then it must use the maximum element from the left and the maximum element from the right. Let's return to the sequence 10, 8, 6, and 15. The maximum sum here is an example that involves one element from the left (10) and one element from the right (15). Notice that these are the largest elements in the left and right segments, respectively. There's no way to take an element from each side and do better than this.

Now we see what the segment tree nodes have to tell us. In addition to what the outside world cares about—the maximum sum of two elements—we also need the maximum element on its own. Combined, these two pieces of information about child segments enable us to fill in the information for the parent segment.

Figure 8-20 shows an example segment tree built for an array. Notice that each node contains both maxsum (the maximum sum of two elements) and maxelm (the maximum element).

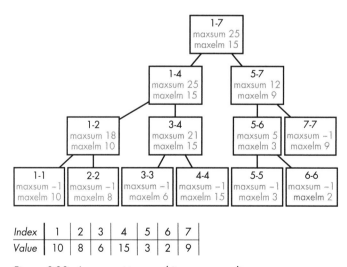

Figure 8-20: A segment tree and its corresponding array

Computing the maximum element for each node is something that we know how to do: it's just the RMQ problem that we solved in Building Treaps.

That leaves the maximum sum of two elements for each node. To begin, we set the maximum sum for the nodes with one-element segments, such as 1-1, 2-2, and so on, to the special value −1. The reason we do this is that there aren't even two elements in these segments to choose from! The −1 alerts us that the parent's maximum sum cannot be the maximum sum of this child.

The maximum sum for each other node is set based on the maximum sums of its children. Consider Node 1-7. There are three options for its maximum sum. We could take the maximum sum 25 from the left, or we could take the maximum sum 12 from the right, or we could take the maximum element 15 from the left and the maximum element 9 from the right to get $15 + 9 = 24$. Of these, 25 is the largest number, so that's what we choose.

We make a special case of the fake −1 maximum sum values to highlight that those cannot be taken as options for the maximum sum of the parent node. Look out for this in the upcoming code.

We'll use a struct for the segment tree nodes:

```
typedef struct segtree_node {
  int left, right;
  int max_sum, max_element;
} segtree_node;
```

We'll use another struct for what we will return from the fill_segtree and query_segtree functions:

```
typedef struct node_info {
  int max_sum, max_element;
} node_info;
```

We need node_info because it lets us return both the maximum sum and the maximum element; returning one integer, without the struct, would not be sufficient.

The code for computing the maximum sum and the maximum element for each segment is given in Listing 8-19.

```
int max(int v1, int v2) {
  if (v1 > v2)
    return v1;
  else
    return v2;
}

node_info fill_segtree(segtree_node segtree[], int node,
                       int seq[]) {
  node_info left_info, right_info;
```

```
❶ if (segtree[node].left == segtree[node].right) {
      segtree[node].max_sum = -1;
      segtree[node].max_element = seq[segtree[node].left];
  ❷ return (node_info){segtree[node].max_sum, segtree[node].max_element};
   }

❸ left_info = fill_segtree(segtree, node * 2, seq);
   right_info = fill_segtree(segtree, node * 2 + 1, seq);

❹ segtree[node].max_element = max(left_info.max_element,
                                  right_info.max_element);

❺ if (left_info.max_sum == -1 && right_info.max_sum == -1)
  ❻ segtree[node].max_sum = left_info.max_element +
                            right_info.max_element;

❼ else if (left_info.max_sum == -1)
      segtree[node].max_sum = max(left_info.max_element +
                                  right_info.max_element,
                                  right_info.max_sum);

❽ else if (right_info.max_sum == -1)
      segtree[node].max_sum = max(left_info.max_element +
                                  right_info.max_element,
                                  left_info.max_sum);

   else
  ❾ segtree[node].max_sum = max(left_info.max_element +
                                right_info.max_element,
                                max(left_info.max_sum, right_info.max_sum));
   return (node_info){segtree[node].max_sum, segtree[node].max_element};
}
```

*Listing 8-19: Adding the maximum sum and maximum element*

When the segment contains just one element, we're in the base case ❶.
We set the maximum sum to the special -1 value, which indicates that there
is no valid sum of two elements here, and we set the maximum element to
the only element in the segment. We then return the maximum sum and
maximum element ❷.

Otherwise, we're in the recursive case. We use left_info to hold the information for the left segment and right_info to hold the information for the
right segment. Each of those variables is initialized using a recursive call ❸.

As we discussed, the maximum element in a segment is just the maximum of the maximum element in the left and the maximum element in the
right ❹.

Now consider the maximum sum of two elements. If neither of the children has a maximum sum ❺, then we know that each child's segment contains just one element. This parent therefore has only two elements in its segment, and adding up those elements is the only choice for the maximum sum of two elements ❻.

Next, what do we do if the left child has only one element and the right child has more than one element ❼? Well, now we have two options for the maximum sum for the parent. The first option is to add the maximum elements from each half. The second is to take the maximum sum from the right segment. We use max to take the best of these two. The case when the right child has only one element and left child has more than one element is analogous ❽.

The final case is when both children have more than one element ❾. Now we have three options: add the maximum elements from each half, take the maximum sum from the left, or take the maximum sum from the right.

### Querying the Segment Tree

The work we just did to fill in the segment information is going to pay off again, right now, for the code to query the segment tree. See Listing 8-20.

```
node_info query_segtree(segtree_node segtree[], int node,
                        int seq[], int left, int right) {
  node_info left_info, right_info, ret_info;

❶ if (right < segtree[node].left || left > segtree[node].right)
     return (node_info){-1, -1};

❷ if (left <= segtree[node].left && segtree[node].right <= right)
     return (node_info) {segtree[node].max_sum, segtree[node].max_element};

  left_info = query_segtree(segtree, node * 2, seq, left, right);
  right_info = query_segtree(segtree, node * 2 + 1, seq, left, right);

  if (left_info.max_element == -1)
    return right_info;
  if (right_info.max_element == -1)
    return left_info;

  ret_info.max_element = max(left_info.max_element, right_info.max_element);

  if (left_info.max_sum == -1 && right_info.max_sum == -1) {
    ret_info.max_sum = left_info.max_element + right_info.max_element;
    return ret_info;
  }
```

```
    else if (left_info.max_sum == -1) {
      ret_info.max_sum = max(left_info.max_element + right_info.max_element,
                             right_info.max_sum);
      return ret_info;
    }

    else if (right_info.max_sum == -1) {
      ret_info.max_sum = max(left_info.max_element + right_info.max_element,
                             left_info.max_sum);
      return ret_info;
    }

    else {
      ret_info.max_sum = max(left_info.max_element + right_info.max_element,
                             max(left_info.max_sum, right_info.max_sum));
      return ret_info;
    }
}
```

*Listing 8-20: Querying the segment tree*

The structure of this code parallels the RMQ code in Listing 8-16. If the node's segment has nothing in common with the query range ❶, we return a struct where both the maximum sum and maximum element are -1. We can use this special value of -1 for the maximum element to tell us that there is no information available from a recursive call.

If the node's segment is completely within the query range ❷, then we return the maximum sum and maximum element for this node.

Finally, if the node's segment partially overlaps the query range, then we follow the same logic as when we filled in the segment information in Listing 8-19.

## Updating the Segment Tree

When an element of the sequence array is updated, we have to adjust the segment tree to keep pace. Otherwise, queries on the segment tree would use now-stale array elements and may therefore yield results at odds with what's currently in the array.

One option is to start from scratch and ignore whatever segment information is already in the tree. We can do that by rerunning Listing 8-19 each time an array element is updated. That would certainly bring the segment tree back up to date, so correctness is not a concern.

Efficiency is a concern, though! Rebuilding the segment tree takes $O(n)$ time. All it would take to tank our performance is a stream of $q$ update operations, with no query operations at all. That would force $n$ work to be done a total of $q$ times, for $O(nq)$ performance. That's especially grim if you think about the cost of updates with no segment tree at all: they're constant-time operations on an array! We can't afford to trade constant time for linear time. However, we *can* afford to trade constant time for logarithmic time, because the latter is very close to constant time.

The way we escape the linear-time work is to realize that only a small number of segment tree nodes need to be updated when an element of the array is updated. Dismantling the entire tree for a single update is a gross overreaction.

Let me explain what I mean by example. Here again is Figure 8-20:

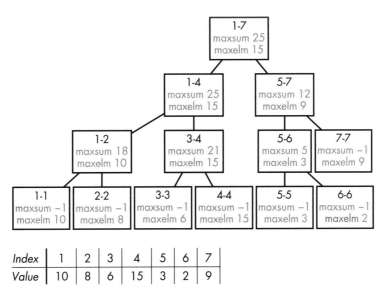

| Index | 1 | 2 | 3 | 4 | 5 | 6 | 7 |
|-------|---|---|---|---|---|---|---|
| Value | 10 | 8 | 6 | 15 | 3 | 2 | 9 |

Now imagine the next operation is U 4 1, which means that index 4 of the sequence should be changed to value 1 (as the 15 that was there is gone). The new segment tree and array are shown in Figure 8-21.

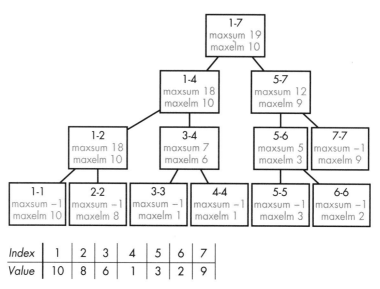

| Index | 1 | 2 | 3 | 4 | 5 | 6 | 7 |
|-------|----|----|----|----|----|----|----|
| Value | 10 | 8 | 6 | 1 | 3 | 2 | 9 |

*Figure 8-21: A segment tree and its corresponding array following an array update*

Notice that only three nodes have changed. Node 4-4 has to change, of course, because the only element in its segment changed. However, the impact of that change can't ripple too far: the only other nodes that can change are ancestors of 4-4, because those are the only other nodes that have an index of 4 in their segments! Indeed, in this example, you can confirm that the only other nodes that changed are the three ancestors 3-4, 1-4, and 1-7. At worst, then, we go from a leaf of the tree to the root, updating nodes along that path. Since the height of the tree is $O(\log n)$, this path has only $O(\log n)$ nodes.

As long as we don't waste time on recursion through inoperative parts of the segment tree, we will end up with an $O(\log n)$ update procedure. Listing 8-21 gives the code.

```
node_info update_segtree(segtree_node segtree[], int node,
                         int seq[], int index) {
  segtree_node left_node, right_node;
  node_info left_info, right_info;

❶ if (segtree[node].left == segtree[node].right) {
    segtree[node].max_element = seq[index];
    return (node_info) {segtree[node].max_sum, segtree[node].max_element};
  }

  left_node = segtree[node * 2];
  right_node = segtree[node * 2 + 1];

❷ if (index <= left_node.right ) {
  ❸ left_info = update_segtree(segtree, node * 2, seq, index);
```

```
❹ right_info = (node_info){right_node.max_sum, right_node.max_element};
  } else {
    right_info = update_segtree(segtree, node * 2 + 1, seq, index);
    left_info = (node_info){left_node.max_sum, left_node.max_element};
  }

  segtree[node].max_element = max(left_info.max_element,
                                  right_info.max_element);

  if (left_info.max_sum == -1 && right_info.max_sum == -1)
    segtree[node].max_sum = left_info.max_element +
                            right_info.max_element;

  else if (left_info.max_sum == -1)
    segtree[node].max_sum = max(left_info.max_element +
                                right_info.max_element,
                                right_info.max_sum);

  else if (right_info.max_sum == -1)
    segtree[node].max_sum = max(left_info.max_element +
                                right_info.max_element,
                                left_info.max_sum);

  else
    segtree[node].max_sum = max(left_info.max_element +
                                right_info.max_element,
                                max(left_info.max_sum, right_info.max_sum));
  return (node_info) {segtree[node].max_sum, segtree[node].max_element};
}
```

*Listing 8-21: Updating the segment tree*

This function is designed to be called *after* the array element at the given index has been updated. Every call of this function is required to ensure that node is the root of a segment tree whose segment contains index.

Our base case is when the segment contains just one element ❶. Since we never make a recursive call unless index is in the node's segment, we know this segment contains exactly our desired index. We thus update max_element of the node to whatever is now stored at seq[index]. We don't update max_sum: it's staying at -1, because this segment still has just one element in it.

Now suppose we're not in the base case. We have a node, and we know that exactly one of its elements, index, has been updated. There's absolutely no reason, then, to make *two* recursive calls, since only one of the node's children can house the updated element. If index is in the left child, then we want to make a recursive call on the left child to update the left subtree. If index is in the right child, then we want to make a recursive call on the right child to update the right subtree.

To determine which child index is in, we compare it to the rightmost index of the left child. If index comes before the left child's segment ends ❷, then we need a recursive call on the left; otherwise, we need a recursive call on the right.

Let's talk a little about the case where we make a recursive call on the left ❸; the else branch, where we make a recursive call on the right, is similar. We make the recursive call that updates the left subtree and returns to us the information for that updated segment. For the right subtree, we just inherit what was there before ❹—there's no update occurring there, so nothing can change.

The rest of the code parallels that of Listing 8-19.

### The main Function

We're now ready to use our souped-up segment tree to solve the problem. The code for the main function is given in Listing 8-22.

```
#define MAX_SEQ 100000

int main(void) {
    static int seq[MAX_SEQ + 1];
    static segtree_node segtree[MAX_SEQ * 4 + 1];
    int num_seq, num_ops, i, op, x, y;
    char c;
    scanf("%d", &num_seq);
    for (i = 1; i <= num_seq; i++)
        scanf("%d", &seq[i]);
    init_segtree(segtree, 1, 1, num_seq);
    fill_segtree(segtree, 1, seq);
    scanf("%d", &num_ops);
    for (op = 0; op < num_ops; op++) {
        scanf(" %c%d%d ", &c, &x, &y);

❶       if (c == 'U') {
            seq[x] = y;
            update_segtree(segtree, 1, seq, x);

❷       } else {
            printf("%d\n", query_segtree(segtree, 1, seq, x, y).max_sum);
        }
    }
    return 0;
}
```

Listing 8-22: The main function for reading input and solving the problem

The only thing to highlight here is the logic for processing the operations. If the next operation is an update operation ❶, we respond by updating the array element and then updating the segment tree. Otherwise, the operation is a query operation ❷, and we respond by querying the segment tree.

It is time to submit the code. The judge should enjoy this fast, segment-tree-based solution.

## Summary

In this chapter, we studied how to implement and use heaps and segment trees. Like any useful data structure, these data structures support a small number of highly efficient operations. It's not often that a data structure solves a problem on its own. More typically, you already have an algorithm whose speed is reasonable, and a data structure helps you make it even faster. For example, our implementation of Dijkstra's algorithm in Chapter 6 already does quite well, but add a min-heap and it does even better.

Whenever you're performing the same kind of operation over and over, you should seek out an opportunity to bolster your algorithm with a data structure. Are you searching for specified items in an array? Then hash tables are called for. Are you trying to find the maximum or minimum? Then heaps will do the trick. Are you querying segments of an array? Then employ segment trees. What about deciding whether two elements are in the same set? Well now, you'll have to read the next chapter for that one!

## Notes

Supermarket Promotion is originally from the 2000 Polish Olympiad in Informatics, Stage 3. Building Treaps is originally from the 2004 Ulm University Local Contest. Two Sum is originally from the 2009 Kurukshetra Online Programming Contest.

For more about segment trees and many other data structures, I recommend Matt Fontaine's *Algorithms Live!* series of videos (see *http://algorithms-live.blogspot.com*). Matt's segment tree video gave me the idea to explicitly store left and right segment indices in each node. (Most of the segment tree code you'll see out there doesn't do this, instead passing those indices around as additional function parameters that I always have trouble keeping straight.)

# 9

## UNION-FIND

We used the adjacency list data structure—and algorithms on it—to solve graph problems in Chapters 5 and 6. That's an efficient data structure that works no matter the graph problem. However, if we constrain the types of problems we want to solve, we can design an even more efficient data structure. Constrain the problems just a little, and we likely wouldn't be able to do any better than an adjacency list. Constrain them too much, and few people would use our data structure because it would be unlikely to solve problems that they cared about solving. Constrain the problems just right and you have the union-find data structure, the topic of this chapter. It solves graph problems—not all, only some. For the ones it does solve, though, it's much faster than a general-purpose graph data structure.

Keeping track of communities in a social network, maintaining groups of friends and enemies, and organizing items into specified drawers are all graph problems. Importantly, they're special graph problems, ones that can be solved with incredible speed by using union-find. Let's do this!

# Problem 1: Social Network

This is SPOJ problem SOCNETC.

## *The Problem*

You are asked to write a program that tracks the people and communities in a social network.

There are $n$ people, numbered $1, 2, \ldots, n$.

A *community* is a person plus that person's friends, their friends' friends, their friends' friends' friends, and so on. For example, if Person 1 and Person 4 are friends, and Person 4 and Person 5 are friends, then this community consists of the three people, 1, 4, and 5. People in the same community are all friends with each other.

Each person starts in a community alone; the person's community can get bigger as friendships between people are made.

Your program must support three operations:

**Add**   Make the two provided people be friends. If this operation takes place, and if these people were not in the same community before, then they will be in the same (larger) community now.

**Examine**   Report whether the two provided people are in the same community.

**Size**   Report the number of people who are in the provided person's community.

Your program will run on a computer with limited resources, so there is a parameter $m$ that gives the maximum number of people in a community. We're required to ignore any Add operation that would result in a community with more than $m$ people.

### Input

The input contains one test case, consisting of the following lines:

- A line containing $n$, the number of people in the social network, and $m$, the maximum number of people allowed in a community. $n$ and $m$ are between 1 and 100,000.

- A line containing integer $q$, the number of operations to follow. $q$ is between 1 and 200,000.

- $q$ lines, one for each operation.

Each of the $q$ lines can be one of the following operations:

- An Add operation is of the form A *x y*, where *x* and *y* are people.

- An Examine operation is of the form E *x y*, where *x* and *y* are people.
- A Size operation is of the form S *x*, where *x* is a person.

### Output

There is no output for an Add operation. The output for each Examine and Size operation is on its own line.

**Examine**   For an Examine operation, output Yes if the two people are in the same community, and output No otherwise.

**Size**   For a Size operation, output the number of people in the person's community.

The time limit for solving the test case is one second.

## Modeling as a Graph

In Chapters 5 and 6, we practiced at length framing problems as graph explorations. We figured out what to use as the nodes and what to use as the edges and then used BFS or Dijkstra's algorithm to explore the graph.

We can similarly model a social network as a graph. The nodes are the people in the social network. If the test case tells us that *x* and *y* are friends, then we can add an edge between node *x* and node *y*. The graph is undirected, because friendship between two people is mutual.

One key difference compared to the problems that we previously solved in Chapters 5 and 6 is that the social network graph is dynamic. Each time we process an Add operation between two people that are not yet friends, we add a new edge to the graph. Compare that to Chapter 5's Book Translation. There, we knew all of the languages and translators at the outset, so we could build the graph once and never have to update it.

Let's use a test case to animate how our graph grows and to observe how the graph helps us implement the three required operations (Add, Examine, and Size). Here it is:

```
7 6
11
A 1 4
A 4 5
A 3 6
E 1 5
E 2 5
A 1 5
A 2 5
A 4 3
S 4
A 7 6
S 4
```

We start with seven people and no friendship connections, like this:

The A 1 4 operation makes People 1 and 4 friends, so we add an edge between those two nodes:

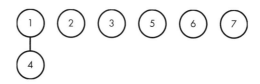

The A 4 5 operation does similarly for People 4 and 5:

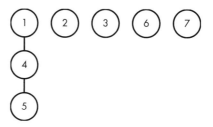

For A 3 6, we get:

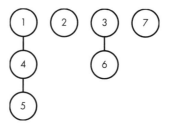

The next operation is E 1 5, which asks us whether People 1 and 5 are in the same community. The graph answers this for us: if there is a path from Node 1 to Node 5 (or, equivalently, from Node 5 to Node 1), then they are in the same community; otherwise, they are not. In this case, they are; the path from Node 1 to Node 4 to Node 5 is a path from Node 1 to Node 5.

The next operation is E 2 5. There's no path between Nodes 2 and 5, so these two people are not in the same community.

Next we have A 1 5, which will add an edge between Nodes 1 and 5. (Notice how we're interleaving operations that modify the graph with operations that query the graph.) Here's the result:

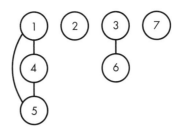

The addition of this edge caused a cycle, because it added a friendship link between two people who were already in the same community. Therefore, this new edge doesn't have any impact on the number of communities or their size. We could have left it out, but I've decided here to include all allowed friendship links.

Now consider A 2 5, which does unite two communities:

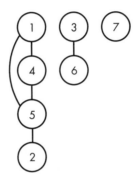

Next we have A 4 3, which again unites two communities:

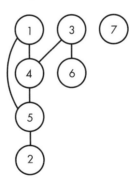

Now we have our first Size operation: S 4. How many people are in Person 4's community? This amounts to determining the number of nodes reachable from Node 4. There are six such nodes, with the only unreachable node being Node 7, so the answer is 6.

Now, consider A 7 6. We must add the edge between Nodes 7 and 6... whoa there! This edge would cause the formation of a new community with all seven people, but the test case forces an upper limit of six people in any given community. We must ignore this Add operation.

For that reason, the answer to the final operation, S 4, is the same as it was before: 6.

The correct output for our test case is:

---

Yes
No
6
6

---

This example shows what is needed to implement each operation. For Add, we add a new edge to the graph, unless that edge would produce a community with too many people. For Examine, we determine whether there is a path between two nodes or, equivalently, whether one node is reachable from the other. We can use BFS for that! For Size, we determine the number of nodes reachable from a given node. We can use BFS again!

## Solution 1: BFS

Let's take this graph-based solution in two steps. First, I'll show the main function that processes the operations, progressively building the graph as it goes. Then, I'll show the BFS code.

### The main Function

We need a constant and a struct to begin:

```
#define MAX_PEOPLE 100000

typedef struct edge {
  int to_person;
  struct edge *next;
} edge;
```

The main function is given in Listing 9-1. It reads the input, and it responds to the operations by incrementally building and querying the graph.

```
int main(void) {
  static edge *adj_list[MAX_PEOPLE + 1] = {NULL};
  static int min_moves[MAX_PEOPLE + 1];
  int num_people, num_community, num_ops, i;
  char op;
  int person1, person2;
  edge *e;
  int size1, size2, same_community;
  scanf("%d%d", &num_people, &num_community);
  scanf("%d", &num_ops);

  for (i = 0; i < num_ops; i++) {
    scanf(" %c", &op);
```

```
❶ if (op == 'A') {
      scanf("%d%d", &person1, &person2);
  ❷ find_distances(adj_list, person1, num_people, min_moves);
  ❸ size1 = size(num_people, min_moves);
      same_community = 0;
  ❹ if (min_moves[person2] != -1)
        same_community = 1;
  ❺ find_distances(adj_list, person2, num_people, min_moves);
  ❻ size2 = size(num_people, min_moves);
  ❼ if (same_community || size1 + size2 <= num_community) {
        e = malloc(sizeof(edge));
        if (e == NULL) {
          fprintf(stderr, "malloc error\n");
          exit(1);
        }
        e->to_person = person2;
        e->next = adj_list[person1];
        adj_list[person1] = e;
        e = malloc(sizeof(edge));
        if (e == NULL) {
          fprintf(stderr, "malloc error\n");
          exit(1);
        }
        e->to_person = person1;
        e->next = adj_list[person2];
        adj_list[person2] = e;
      }
    }

❽ else if (op == 'E') {
      scanf("%d%d", &person1, &person2);
      find_distances(adj_list, person1, num_people, min_moves);
      if (min_moves[person2] != -1)
        printf("Yes\n");
      else
        printf("No\n");
    }

❾ else {
      scanf("%d", &person1);
      find_distances(adj_list, person1, num_people, min_moves);
      printf("%d\n", size(num_people, min_moves));
    }
  }
  return 0;
}
```

*Listing 9-1: The main function for processing operations*

As we did in Book Translation in Chapter 5 and in the problems in Chapter 6, we use an adjacency list representation of the graph.

Let's see how the code handles each of the three types of operations, starting with Add ❶. We call the helper function find_distances ❷. That function, as we'll see shortly, implements the BFS: it fills min_moves with the shortest path in the graph from person1 to each person, using a value of -1 for any person that is not reachable. Then, we call helper function size ❸, which uses distance information in min_moves to determine the size of person1's community. We next determine whether person1 and person2 are in the same community: if person2 is reachable from person1, then they're in the same community ❹. We need this information to determine whether to add the edge: if the people are already in the same community, then the edge can be safely added without worrying about creating a community that violates the constraint on the maximum number of people in a community.

Having found the size of person1's community, we do the same for person2's community: first invoking BFS for person2 ❺ and then computing the community's size ❻.

Now, if there's no new community, or if the new community is small enough ❼, then we add the edge to the graph. Actually, we add two edges, because, remember, the graph is undirected.

The other operations take less code. For Examine ❽, we run the BFS and check whether person2 is reachable from person1. For Size ❾, we run the BFS and then count the number of nodes reachable from person1.

### The BFS Code

The BFS code we need here is very similar to the BFS code we wrote when solving Book Translation in Chapter 5, except without the book translation costs. See Listing 9-2.

```
void add_position(int from_person, int to_person,
                  int new_positions[], int *num_new_positions,
                  int min_moves[]) {
  if (min_moves[to_person] == -1) {
    min_moves[to_person] = 1 + min_moves[from_person];
    new_positions[*num_new_positions] = to_person;
    (*num_new_positions)++;
  }
}

void find_distances(edge *adj_list[], int person, int num_people,
                    int min_moves[]) {
  static int cur_positions[MAX_PEOPLE + 1], new_positions[MAX_PEOPLE + 1];
  int num_cur_positions, num_new_positions;
  int i, from_person;
  edge *e;
  for (i = 1; i <= num_people; i++)
    min_moves[i] = -1;
  min_moves[person] = 0;
```

```
    cur_positions[0] = person;
    num_cur_positions = 1;

    while (num_cur_positions > 0) {
      num_new_positions = 0;
      for (i = 0; i < num_cur_positions; i++) {
        from_person = cur_positions[i];
        e = adj_list[from_person];

        while (e) {
          add_position(from_person, e->to_person,
                       new_positions, &num_new_positions, min_moves);
          e = e->next;
        }
      }

      num_cur_positions = num_new_positions;
      for (i = 0; i < num_cur_positions; i++)
        cur_positions[i] = new_positions[i];
    }
}
```

*Listing 9-2: Minimum distance to people using BFS*

### Finding the Size of a Community

The last little helper function to write is size, which returns the number of
people in a given person's community. See Listing 9-3.

```
int size(int num_people, int min_moves[]) {
  int i, total = 0;
  for (i = 1; i <= num_people; i++)
    if (min_moves[i] != -1)
      total++;
  return total;
}
```

*Listing 9-3: The size of a person's community*

In this function, it is assumed that min_moves has already been filled in
by find_distances. Every person whose min_moves value is not -1 is therefore
reachable. We use total to add up those reachable people.

There we have it: a graph-based solution. For each of the $q$ operations,
we run one BFS. At worst, each operation adds one edge to the graph, so
each BFS call does work proportional to at most $q$. We therefore have an
$O(q^2)$, or quadratic, algorithm.

In Chapter 5, I advised you that it's important not to run BFS too many
times. It's best to make just one BFS call, if you can get away with that. Even
a few calls can be okay. After all, we got away with making a BFS call for each
pawn position when solving Knight Chase on page 151. The same sentiment

applies to Dijkstra's algorithm from Chapter 6: make as few calls as possible. Here again, making a few calls is okay. We solved Mice Maze on page 198 using about 100 calls of Dijkstra, and it was fast enough. Thriftless use of graph search hasn't bitten us yet.

It does bite us now, though. If you submit your solution to the judge, you'll get a "Time-Limit Exceeded" error—and it isn't even close. I'm playing around with an example here on my laptop with 100,000 people in the social network and 200,000 operations. The operations are divided equally among Add, Examine, and Size operations. Our graph-based solution takes over two minutes to run. You're about to learn a new data structure called union-find that, on the same example, runs 300 times faster. Union-find is an efficiency beast.

## Union-Find

For two reasons, BFS on a graph is not a satisfactory solution to the Social Network problem. First, it produces too much! It determines shortest paths between people. For example, it might tell us that the shortest path between People 1 and 5 is two, but who cares? All we want to know is whether or not two people are in the same community. How they ended up in the same community and the chain of friendships that connect them are not of interest.

Second, it remembers too little—or, rather, it remembers nothing: BFS starts afresh with each call. However, think about how wasteful this is. For example, an Add operation adds just one edge to the graph. The communities can't be much different than they were before. BFS doesn't use past information at all, instead reprocessing the complete graph on the next operation.

The goal, then, is to devise a data structure that doesn't remember anything about shortest paths and that does only a little work when a new friendship is made.

### Operations

The Add operation unites two communities into one. (Well, it does nothing when the resulting community would be too big or when two people are in the same community, but when it does something, it unites two communities.) This kind of operation is referred to in the algorithms world as a *Union*. In general, a Union replaces two sets by one larger set containing all of their elements.

The Examine operation tells us whether the two provided people are in the same community. One way to implement this is to designate one element of each community as its *representative* element. For example, a community with People 1, 4, and 5 might have 4 as its representative; a community with People 3 and 6 might have 3 as its representative. Are People 1 and 5 in the same community? Yes, because the representative of Person 1's community (4) is the same as the representative of Person 5's community (4). Are People 4 and 6 in the same community? No, because the representative of Person 4's community (4) is not the same as the representative of Person 6's community (3).

Determining the representative of a person's community is called a *Find*. We can implement Examine with two Finds: find the representative of the first person's community, find the representative of the second person's community, and compare them.

Since an Add is a Union and an Examine is a Find, data structures that implement these two operations are known as *union-find* data structures.

Once we have Union and Find working, we'll be in great shape to support Size operations as well. All we'll do is store the size of each community, being sure to keep sizes up to date whenever we do a Union. We'll then be able to respond to each Size operation by returning the size of the appropriate community.

### Array-Based Approach

One idea is to use an array community_of that indicates the representative for each person's community. For example, if People 1, 2, 4, and 5 are in the same community, People 3 and 6 are in the same community, and Person 7 is in their own community, then the array might look like this:

| Index | 1 | 2 | 3 | 4 | 5 | 6 | 7 |
|-------|---|---|---|---|---|---|---|
| Value | 5 | 5 | 6 | 5 | 5 | 6 | 7 |

For a community of a single person, there is no choice for who is the representative. That's why the representative for Person 7 is 7. In a community with multiple people, the representative is allowed to be any person in the community. For example, we're using 6 as a representative this time, but we could have used 3 instead.

Using this scheme, we can implement Find in constant time. All we do is look up the representative of the desired person, like this:

```
int find(int person, int community_of[]) {
  return community_of[person];
}
```

You can't do better than that!

Unfortunately, this scheme breaks down when we implement Union. Our only option is to change all representatives for one community to the representative of the other community. It would look like this:

```
void union_communities(int person1, int person2,
                       int community_of[], int num_people) {
  int community1, community2, i;
  community1 = find(person1, community_of);
  community2 = find(person2, community_of);
  for (i = 1; i <= num_people; i++)
    if (community_of[i] == community1)
      community_of[i] = community2;
}
```

I'm ignoring the maximum size restriction on social-network communities here so as not to distract from the essentials. The code uses find to set community1 and community2 to the representatives of person1's community and person2's community, respectively. It then loops through all people, changing anyone in community1 to community2. The effect is that community1 is gone, having been absorbed into community2.

If you build and submit a full solution based on the code I've given here, you should see that it still receives a "Time-Limit Exceeded" error. We need a better way to union two communities than looping through all of the people.

### Tree-Based Approach

The most efficient union-find data structures are based on trees. Each set is represented as its own tree, with the root of the tree serving as that set's representative. I'll describe how this works with the help of the example shown in Figure 9-1.

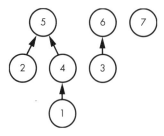

Figure 9-1: A tree-based union-find data structure

There are three trees here, so there are three distinct communities: one has People 1, 2, 4, and 5; one has People 3 and 6; and one has Person 7. Each tree's roots—People 5, 6, and 7—serve as community representatives.

I've drawn the tree edges with an arrow pointing from child to parent. You haven't seen that before in this book. The reason I'm doing it now is to emphasize the way that we'll be navigating these trees. As I describe how to support Find and Union in trees, we'll see that it's necessary to move up the tree (from child to parent) but never down.

Let's start with Find. Given a person, we have to return that person's representative. We can do that by moving up the appropriate tree until we reach its root element. For example, let's find the representative of Person 1 in Figure 9-1. Since 1 is not a root, we move to 1's parent. Person 4 is not a root, so we move to 4's parent. Person 5 is a root, so we're done: 5 is the representative of 1.

Compare this tree-hopping to what we were able to get away with in "Array-Based Approach" on page 341. Rather than simply looking up the representative in a single step, we have to move up the tree until we find the root. That sounds dicey—what if a tree gets really, really tall?—but we'll soon see that this concern is unfounded, as we'll be able to keep tree heights under control.

Now let's talk about Union. Given two people, we want to unite their two trees. In terms of correctness, it doesn't matter how we jam the two trees together. However, as was just mentioned in the context of Find, it helps to keep tree heights small. If we insert one tree at the bottom of the other, we might unnecessarily increase the height of the resulting tree. To avoid that, we'll insert one tree directly under the root of the other tree. To see how that looks, see Figure 9-2, where I've unioned the tree with root 5 and the tree with root 6.

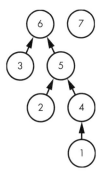

Figure 9-2: A tree-based union-find
data structure after a union

I've chosen to make 6 the root of the combined tree. We could have also chosen to make 5 the root of the combined tree. (Here's a teaser: Why will 5 turn out to be the better choice? We'll see why when we discuss union-find optimizations.)

We now have enough to design a union-find solution to the Social Network problem.

## Solution 2: Union-Find

Primed by our discussion of heaps and segment trees in Chapter 8, you may not be surprised that we're going to store the union-find data structure in an array!

Union-find trees are not necessarily binary trees, as their nodes can have any number of children. So we won't be able to move around these trees by multiplying and dividing by 2, as we did in Chapter 8. We're in luck, though, because the only travel we need to support is from a child to its parent. All we need is an array that maps from any given node to its parent. We can do that with the array parent, where parent[i] gives the parent of Node i.

Recall Figure 9-1, where we had three communities: one that has People 1, 2, 4, and 5; one with People 3 and 6; and one with Person 7. Here's the parent array corresponding to that figure:

| Index | 1 | 2 | 3 | 4 | 5 | 6 | 7 |
|---|---|---|---|---|---|---|---|
| Value | 4 | 5 | 6 | 5 | 5 | 6 | 7 |

What if we want to find the representative of Person 1's community? The value at index 1 is 4, which tells us that 4 is the parent of 1; the value at index 4 is 5, which tells us that the parent of 4 is 5; and the value at index 5 is 5, which means that 5 is the ... parent of 5? Certainly not! Whenever parent[i] is the same value as i, it means that we've reached the root of the tree. (The other common trick to distinguish roots is to use a value of -1, since that can't be confused with a valid array index. I won't use that in this book, but you may come across it in other code that you find.)

### The main Function

Now we're ready for some code. Let's start with the main function as given in Listing 9-4. (It's far briefer than Listing 9-1. In general, union-find code is compact.)

```
int main(void) {
❶ static int parent[MAX_PEOPLE + 1], size[MAX_PEOPLE + 1];
  int num_people, num_community, num_ops, i;
  char op;
  int person1, person2;
  scanf("%d%d", &num_people, &num_community);
❷ for (i = 1; i <= num_people; i++) {
    parent[i] = i;
    size[i] = 1;
  }
  scanf("%d", &num_ops);

  for (i = 0; i < num_ops; i++) {
    scanf(" %c", &op);

    if (op == 'A') {
      scanf("%d%d", &person1, &person2);
❸    union_communities(person1, person2, parent, size, num_community);
    }

    else if (op == 'E') {
      scanf("%d%d", &person1, &person2);
❹    if (find(person1, parent) == find(person2, parent))
        printf("Yes\n");
      else
        printf("No\n");
    }

    else {
      scanf("%d", &person1);
❺    printf("%d\n", size[find(person1, parent)]);
    }
  }
}
```

```
    return 0;
}
```

Listing 9-4: The main function for processing operations

In addition to the parent array that I've already described, there's a size array ❶. For each representative i, size[i] gives the number of people in its community. Never look up the size of a community using a nonrepresentative person. Once someone isn't a representative, we won't keep the size value updated anymore.

A for loop is used to initialize parent and size ❷. For parent, we let each person be their own representative, which corresponds to having each person in their own set. Because each set has just one person, we set each size value to 1.

To implement Add, we call the union_communities helper function ❸. It unites the communities of person1 and person2, subject to the num_community size constraint. We'll see its code soon.

To implement Examine, we make two calls to find ❹. If both calls return the same value, then the people are in the same community; otherwise, they are not.

Finally, to implement Size, we use the size array, looking up the representative of the person's set ❺.

I'll next supply implementations of find and union_communities, and that will finish off this implementation.

## The find Function

The find function takes a person as a parameter and returns that person's representative. See Listing 9-5.

```
int find(int person, int parent[]) {
  int community = person;
  while (parent[community] != community)
    community = parent[community];
  return community;
}
```

Listing 9-5: The find function

The while loop keeps moving up the tree, until it finds a root. That root person is the representative of the community, and so it is returned.

## The union Function

The union_communities function takes two people—in addition to the parent array, size array, and num_community constraint—and joins their two communities. (I would have called this function union, but that's not allowed because union is a C reserved word.) See Listing 9-6 for the code.

```
void union_communities(int person1, int person2, int parent[],
                       int size[], int num_community) {
  int community1, community2;
```

```
❶ community1 = find(person1, parent);
❷ community2 = find(person2, parent);
   if (community1 != community2 &&
       size[community1] + size[community2] <= num_community) {
❸  parent[community1] = community2;
❹  size[community2] = size[community2] + size[community1];
   }
}
```

Listing 9-6: The union_communities function

First, we find the representative for each person's community ❶ ❷. Two conditions must be met for a Union to take place: first, the communities must be different; second, the sum of the sizes of the two communities must not exceed the maximum-allowed community size. If both of these conditions pass, then we perform the Union itself.

I've chosen to fold community1 into community2. That is, community1 will be gone, and community2 will absorb community1. To make this happen, we must appropriately modify parent and size.

Before this Union, community1 was the root of a community, but now we want community1 to have community2 as its parent. So, that's precisely what we do ❸! Any person whose representative was previously community1 will now have community2 as their representative.

In terms of size, community2 has all of the people it had before plus all of the people that it inherited from community1. So the size is what it was before with the addition of the size of community1 ❹.

That's all! Feel free to submit this solution to the judge. It should finish within the time limit and pass all test cases.

Somehow, though, I maybe had hoped that it didn't pass within the time limit—because I'm sitting on two ace union-find optimizations here that I really want to teach you.

Hey, let's just do them! This may be overkill for this problem, but they offer such a speed boost that we'll apply them throughout this chapter and never worry about time limits again.

### Optimization 1: Union by Size

Our union-find solution generally runs fast, but test cases can be crafted to make it crawl. Here's what the worst kind of test case looks like:

```
7 7
7
A 1 2
A 2 3
A 3 4
A 4 5
A 5 6
A 6 7
E 1 2
```

Communities 1 and 2 are merged, that resulting community is merged with Community 3, that resulting community is merged with Community 4, and so on. After the six Unions, we have the tree as depicted in Figure 9-3.

Figure 9-3: A bad case of a tree-based union-find data structure

We have a long chain of nodes and, unfortunately, Finds and Unions may end up traversing the entire chain. For example, E 1 2 would invoke a Find on Person 1 and a Find on Person 2, each visiting almost every node. Of course, a seven-node chain is tiny, but we can replicate the unioning pattern to produce massive chains of whatever length we want. We can thereby force Find and Union operations to take linear time; with $q$ operations in all, we can force our tree-based union-find algorithm to take $O(q^2)$ time. This means that, in the worst case, the tree-based solution is not theoretically better than the BFS solution. It's better than BFS in practice, because most test cases will not produce long chains of nodes... but some test cases might!

Hold on! Why are we letting these officious test cases bully us into producing these awful trees? We don't care what the union-find data structure looks like. In particular, whenever a Union is requested, we have a choice of which old representative becomes the representative of the unioned community. Rather than always folding the first community into the second, we should make the choice that produces the best tree. Compare the nonsense in Figure 9-3 to the wonder that is Figure 9-4.

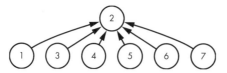

*Figure 9-4: An optimized tree-based union-find data structure*

Person 2 is the root, and everyone else is exactly one edge away. No matter what Union or Find comes next, we'll be able to perform it very efficiently.

How can our code make Figure 9-4 instead of Figure 9-3? The optimization is called *union by size*. Whenever you're about to union two communities together, union the community with fewer people into the community with more people.

In the test case that we've been discussing, we start with A 1 2. The two communities each have one person, so it doesn't matter which we choose to keep; let's keep Community 2. Now Community 2 has two people: the one that it had and the one from Community 1. To do A 2 3, we compare the size of Community 2 (two) to the size of Community 3 (one). We will keep Community 2 because it is larger than Community 3. Now Community 2 has three people. What about A 3 4? This gives us another person for Community 2. We then keep going, absorbing one person after another into Community 2.

Union by size certainly neutralizes the worst test cases, but there are still test cases whose trees need some work to go from nodes to roots. Here's one:

```
9 9
9
A 1 2
A 3 4
A 5 6
A 7 8
A 8 9
A 2 4
A 6 8
A 4 8
E 1 5
```

Union by size produces Figure 9-5.

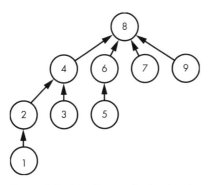

*Figure 9-5: A bad case of union by size*

Although it's true that some nodes are right below the root, there are now nodes that are further away (the worst offender being Node 1). Still, the tree is quite balanced, and it's certainly better than the long chain of nodes that we saw prior to the union-by-size optimization.

I'll next show that the maximum height of a tree when using union by size is $O(\log n)$, where $n$ is the total number of people. This means that a Find or Union takes $O(\log n)$ time, because a Find is just a traversal up the tree and a Union is just two Finds plus a change of parent.

Let's choose some arbitrary node $x$ and think about how many times the number of edges between $x$ and its root can increase. When $x$'s community absorbs another community, the number of edges between $x$ and its root doesn't change, because the root of its community is the same as it was. However, when $x$'s community is absorbed by another community, then the number of edges between $x$ and its new root is one more than it was before: the path from $x$ to its new root is what it was before (to get to its old root) plus one more edge to get to its new root.

Therefore, putting an upper bound on the number of edges between $x$ and its root amounts to determining the maximum number of times that $x$'s community can be absorbed into another community.

Say that $x$ is in a community of size four. Could it be absorbed into a community that was size two? No way! We're using union by size, remember. The only way $x$'s community can be absorbed into another community is if the other community is at least as large as $x$'s. In this example, the other community would have to be size four or greater. So we go from a community of size four to a community of at least size $4 + 4 = 4 \times 2 = 8$. That is, the size of $x$'s community at least doubles when it's absorbed into another community.

Starting off in a community of size one, $x$'s community gets absorbed and now it's in a community of at least size two. It gets absorbed again and now it's in a community of at least size four. Getting absorbed again puts it in a community of at least size eight. This doubling can't continue forever. It has to stop, at the latest, when $x$'s community contains all $n$ people. Starting from one, how many times can we double it before we get to $n$? That's $\log n$, and that's why the number of edges between any node and its root is capped at $\log n$.

Using union by size cuts linear runtime to logarithmic runtime. Better still, we don't need much new code to implement this optimization. In fact, for the Social Network problem, we're already maintaining sizes of communities—we can just use these sizes to decide which community gets absorbed into the other. Listing 9-7 gives the new code. Compare the code to Listing 9-6 to confirm that we're doing almost the same thing as before.

```
void union_communities(int person1, int person2, int parent[],
                       int size[], int num_community) {
  int community1, community2, temp;
  community1 = find(person1, parent);
  community2 = find(person2, parent);
  if (community1 != community2 &&
      size[community1] + size[community2] <= num_community) {
❶ if (size[community1] > size[community2]) {
      temp = community1;
      community1 = community2;
      community2 = temp;
    }
❷ parent[community1] = community2;
    size[community2] = size[community2] + size[community1];
  }
}
```

Listing 9-7: The union_communities function using union by size

By default, the code chooses community2 to absorb community1. This is the right thing to do if community2 is larger than or the same size as community1. If the size of community1 is larger than community2 ❶, then we swap community1 and community2 to reverse their roles. After that, community2 is guaranteed to be the bigger community, and we can proceed by absorbing community1 into community2 ❷.

## Optimization 2: Path Compression

Let's revisit the test case that produced Figure 9-5. Only this time, let's build the tree and then keep spamming the same Examine operation:

```
9 9
13
A 1 2
A 3 4
A 5 6
A 7 8
A 8 9
A 2 4
A 6 8
A 4 8
E 1 5
```

```
E 1 5
E 1 5
E 1 5
E 1 5
```

The E 1 5 operation is a little slow, each time requiring lengthy traversals to the root. To Find the representative of Person 1, for example, we go from Node 1 to Node 2 to Node 4 to Node 8. Now we know that Node 1's representative is Node 8. We would do a similar traversal for Person 5, but that knowledge is short-lived, because we don't remember that anywhere. Every single E 1 5 operation causes us to redo the work to Find Person 1 and Person 5, just to relearn what we learned last time.

Here we have another opportunity to benefit by controlling the structure of the tree. Remember that the particular shape of the tree doesn't matter: all that matters is that people in the same community are present in the same tree. Hence, as soon as we've determined the root of someone's community, we might as well move that person to be a child of the root. While we're at it, we might as well move that person's ancestors right below the root, too.

Consider again Figure 9-5, and suppose we next perform E 1 5. If we were using just the Union-by-size optimization, this Examine operation (like any Examine operation) would not change the structure of the tree. Watch what happens, though, if we use an optimization called *path compression*, as depicted in Figure 9-6.

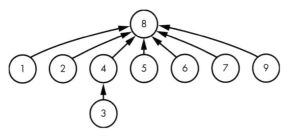

*Figure 9-6: An example of path compression*

This is nice, right? Finding Node 1 leads to Nodes 1 and 2 becoming children of a root; finding Node 5 leads to Node 5 becoming a child of a root. In general, path compression takes every node along a path and puts it as a child of the root node. Finding any of those nodes will therefore be extremely fast.

To implement path compression in the find function, we can make two traversals from the provided person to the root of the tree. The first traversal locates the root of the tree; that's the traversal that any find function does. The second traversal ensures that each node along the path has the root as its parent. Listing 9-8 implements the new code. Compare it to Listing 9-5 to see that what's new is the second traversal.

```
int find(int person, int parent[]) {
  int community = person, temp;
```

```
❶ while (parent[community] != community)
     community = parent[community];
❷ while (parent[person] != community) {
     temp = parent[person];
     parent[person] = community;
     person = temp;
  }
  return community;
}
```

*Listing 9-8: The find function with path compression implemented*

This code works in two phases. The first phase is the first `while` loop ❶, which results in `community` holding the representative (the root) of the community. With that representative in hand, the second phase, captured by the second `while` loop ❷, retraces the path from `person` to just below the root of the tree, updating each node's `parent` to be the tree's root. The `temp` variable is used to store the old parent of the current node. In that way, we can still move to the current node's old parent even after making it the root of the tree. (There's a shockingly concise though cryptic way to code path compression that you might see in the wild. Brace yourself, and then check out "Compressing Path Compression" in Appendix B.)

By using both union by size and path compression, it's still possible that a single Union or Find operation takes $O(\log n)$ time. However, taking all Unions and Finds together, the average time taken per operation—while not technically constant—is essentially constant. The runtime analysis is based on a function called the *inverse Ackermann function*, which grows very, very, *very* slowly. I won't define the inverse Ackermann function or show how it arises in the runtime analysis, but I'd like to give a sense of how strong this result is.

The logarithm function grows slowly, so let's start there. Taking the log of a huge number gives back a very small number. For example, log 1,000,000,000 is only about 30. However, the log isn't a constant: using a sufficiently large value of $n$, you can make log $n$ as big as you want.

The inverse Ackermann function is similarly not constant, but, unlike the log function, you'll never in practice get a value of 30 out of it. You can make $n$ as big as you want, as big as the biggest number representable in your computer, and the inverse Ackermann of $n$ will be at most 4. You can think of union-find with union by size and path compression as taking an average of just four steps per operation!

## Union-Find

The union-find data structure turbocharges solutions to graph problems whose primary operations are Union and Find. This doesn't help with problems such as those in Chapters 5 and 6, where we're required to calculate distances between nodes. But when union-find does apply, adjacency lists and graph search are overkill and just too slow.

### Relationships: Three Requirements

Union-find works on a collection of objects, where each object begins in its own set. At all times, objects in the same set are equivalent, whatever "equivalent" means for the problem that we're solving. For example, in the Social Network problem, people in the same set (community) are equivalent in the sense that they are all friends.

Union-find requires that the relationship between our objects satisfy three criteria. First, objects must be related to themselves. In terms of friendships from the Social Network, this just means that each person is one's own friend. A relationship that meets this criterion is called *reflexive*.

Second, the relationship has to be directionless: we can't have $x$ as a friend of $y$ and at the same time have $y$ as not a friend of $x$. A relationship that meets this criterion is called *symmetric*.

Third, the relationship must cascade: if $x$ is a friend of $y$, and $y$ is a friend of $z$, then $x$ is a friend of $z$. A relationship that meets this criterion is called *transitive*.

If any of these criteria is not met, then the Union operation we've been discussing is broken. For example, suppose that we have a friendship relationship where transitivity does not hold. If we learn that $x$ is a friend of $y$, we have no idea whether $x$'s friends are $y$'s friends. We're therefore not justified in uniting $x$'s community and $y$'s community; that might put people in the same set that are not in fact friends.

A relationship that is reflexive, symmetric, and transitive is called an *equivalence relation*.

### Choosing Union-Find

When deciding whether union-find might apply, ask yourself this: What is the relationship that I need to maintain between objects? Is it reflexive, symmetric, and transitive? If it is, and the primary operations can be mapped to Finds and Unions, then you should consider union-find as a viable solution strategy.

Beneath every union-find problem lies a graph problem that could be modeled (less efficiently!) using adjacency lists and graph search. Unlike what we did for the Social Network problem, for the remaining problems in this chapter, we won't take the scenic route through graphs.

### Optimizations

I introduced two union-find optimizations: union by size and path compression. They offer protection against bad test cases and generally increase performance no matter what the test case. They each take only a few lines of code, so I recommend using them whenever you can.

"Whenever you can" is not to be confused with "always." Unfortunately, there are some union-find problems where these optimizations are not appropriate. I haven't yet encountered a problem where path compression is problematic, but sometimes we need to remember the order in which sets are being united, and in those cases we can't swap roots of trees using union by size. You'll see in Problem 3 an example where we can't use union by size.

# Problem 2: Friends and Enemies

You might worry that the only kind of "Add" operation we can support is like that used in the Social Network problem: $x$ and $y$ are friends; $x$ and $y$ go to the same school; $x$ and $y$ live in the same city—that kind of thing. It turns out that we can support other types of Add information, too. $x$ and $y$ are *not* friends. Hmm ... that one's interesting, telling us not that $x$ and $y$ are in the same set but that they are *not* in the same set. How does union-find work now? Read on!

This is UVa problem 10158.

## The Problem

Two countries are at war. You have been granted permission to attend their peace meetings, during which you can listen to pairs of people talking to each other. There are $n$ people at these meetings, numbered $0, 1, \ldots, n - 1$. At first, you don't know anything about who are friends (citizens of the same country) or enemies (citizens of opposing countries). Your job is to record information about who are friends or enemies and to respond to queries based on what you know so far.

You must support four operations:

**SetFriends**   Record that the two provided people are friends.

**SetEnemies**   Record that the two provided people are enemies.

**AreFriends**   Report whether you know for sure that the two provided people are friends.

**AreEnemies**   Report whether you know for sure that the two provided people are enemies.

Friendship is an equivalence relation: it's reflexive ($x$ is a friend of $x$), symmetric (if $x$ is a friend of $y$, then $y$ is a friend of $x$), and transitive (if $x$ is a friend of $y$ and $y$ is a friend of $z$, then $x$ is a friend of $z$).

Enemyship is not an equivalence relation. It's symmetric: if $x$ is an enemy of $y$, then $y$ is likewise an enemy of $x$. It's neither, however, reflexive nor transitive.

There's a little more we need to know about friendship and enemyship. Suppose that $x$ has some friends and enemies, $y$ has some friends and enemies, and then we are told that $x$ and $y$ are enemies. What have we learned? Well, we learn directly that $x$ and $y$ are enemies—but that's not all. We can also conclude that $x$'s enemies are friends with everyone in $y$'s set. (Suppose that Alice and Bob are enemies and that David and Eve are friends—and then we are told that Alice and David are enemies. We should conclude that Bob is friends with David and Eve.) Similarly, we can conclude that $y$'s enemies are friends with everyone in $x$'s set. Here's this paragraph in one aphorism: the enemy of an enemy is a friend.

Now suppose that $x$ has some friends and enemies and that $y$ has some friends and enemies—but that this time, we are told that $x$ and $y$ are friends. Here, we should additionally conclude that $x$'s enemies and $y$'s enemies are friends. (Hang in there. We'll make all of this concrete as we work through some examples.)

### Input

The input contains one test case, consisting of the following lines:

- A line containing $n$, the total number of people attending the meetings. $n$ is less than 10,000.

- Zero or more lines, one for each operation.

- A line containing three integers, the first of which is 0. This signifies the end of the test case.

Each operation line has the same format: an operation code followed by two people ($x$ and $y$).

- A SetFriends operation is of the form 1 $x$ $y$.

- A SetEnemies operation is of the form 2 $x$ $y$.

- An AreFriends operation is of the form 3 $x$ $y$.

- An AreEnemies operation is of the form 4 $x$ $y$.

### Output

The output for each operation is on its own line.

- If a SetFriends operation succeeds, then it produces no output. If it conflicts with information that is already known, then output -1 and ignore the operation.

- If a SetEnemies operation succeeds, then it produces no output. If it conflicts with information that is already known, then output -1 and ignore the operation.

- For an AreFriends operation, output 1 if the two people are known to be friends and output 0 otherwise.

- For an AreEnemies operation, output 1 if the two people are known to be enemies and output 0 otherwise.

The time limit for solving the test case is three seconds.

## *Augmenting Union-Find*

If all we had to deal with were the SetFriends and AreFriends operations, then we could directly apply union-find as we did when solving the Social Network problem. We'd keep one set for each group of friends. Like Add in Social Network, SetFriends would be implemented as a Union and bring together two sets of friends into a larger set. Like Examine in Social Network, AreFriends would be implemented as a Find on each of the two people to determine whether they're in the same set.

We could start by solving the problem for just these two operations... actually, you know what? I'm confident you could solve that restricted problem, right now, without anything else from me. Where I may be helpful is in explaining the technique for incorporating SetEnemies and AreEnemies.

### Augmentation: Enemies

*Augmenting* a data structure refers to storing additional information in that data structure to support new or faster operations. Maintaining the size of each set in a union-find data structure is an example of augmentation: you could implement the data structure without it, but with it you can quickly report set sizes and perform union by size.

You should consider augmentation when an existing data structure *almost* does what you want. The key is to identify a suitable augmentation that adds the desired functionality without appreciably slowing down other operations.

We already have a union-find data structure that supports SetFriends and AreFriends. It maintains the parent of each node as well as the size of each set. We're going to augment that data structure to support SetEnemies and AreEnemies. Moreover, we're going to do it without slowing down SetFriends and AreFriends much at all.

Suppose we're told that *x* and *y* are enemies. From the problem description, we know that we're going to have to union *x*'s enemies with *y*'s set and union *y*'s enemies with *x*'s set. Who are *x*'s enemies? Who are *y*'s enemies? With the standard union-find data structure, we don't know. This is why we need to augment the union-find data structure.

In addition to the parent of each node and the size of each set, we're going to keep track of an enemy for each set. We'll store those enemies in an array called enemy_of. Suppose that s is the representative of some set. If that set has no enemies, then we'll arrange for enemy_of[s] to hold a special value that can't be confused with a person. If that set has one or more enemies, then enemy_of[s] will give us one of them.

That's right: *one* of them, not *all* of them. Knowing one enemy of each set is enough, because we can use that one enemy to find the representative of everyone in that enemy's set.

Let's now work through two test cases. They'll prepare us for the implementation that follows. The diagrams I will show are conceptual and do not correspond exactly to what an implementation might do. In particular, I won't use union by size or path compression in the diagrams, but we'll throw those optimizations into our implementation in the interest of performance.

### Test Case 1

Recall that the operation code for SetFriends is 1 and the code for SetEnemies is 2.

Here's our first test case:

```
    9
    1 0 1
    1 1 2
    1 3 4
    1 5 6
❶  2 1 7
❷  2 5 8
❸  1 2 5
    0 0 0
```

The first four operations are SetFriends operations. No one has any enemies yet, so these operations play out just as did Add operations in the Social Network problem. Figure 9-7 shows the state of the data structure after these operations.

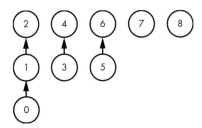

*Figure 9-7: The data structure after four SetFriends operations*

Next we have our first SetEnemies operation ❶, and it indicates that People 1 and 7 are enemies. This means that everyone in 1's set is enemies with everyone in 7's set. To incorporate this into the data structure, we add links between roots of these two sets: a link from 2 (the root of 1's set) to 7, and a link from 7 (the root of 7's set) to 1. (You could have decided that the latter should instead be a link from 7 to 2; that would be fine as well.) The result of this operation is shown in Figure 9-8. In this and subsequent figures, enemy links are realized as dashed lines; in our implementation, enemy links will be realized as the aforementioned enemy_of array.

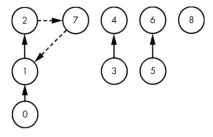

*Figure 9-8: The data structure after a SetEnemies operation*

Next is a SetEnemies operation between People 5 and 8 ❷; performing this operation might result in Figure 9-9.

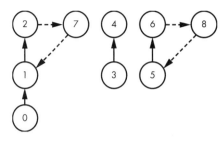

Figure 9-9: The data structure after another
SetEnemies operation

Now it's time for the final operation ❸, which says that People 2 and 5 are friends. This unites 2's set and 5's set into one larger set of friends, as expected. The surprise, perhaps, is that we also unite two enemy sets. Specifically, we unite the enemies of Person 2's set with the enemies of Person 5's set. After all, if we know that two people are in the same country, then each of their enemy sets must be together in the other country. The result of performing these *two* Union operations is shown in Figure 9-10.

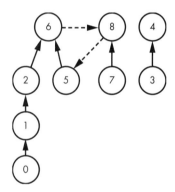

Figure 9-10: The data structure after
a final SetFriends operation

The reason I haven't drawn enemy links from Person 2 to Person 7 and from Person 7 to Person 1 is because we maintain enemy links only from root nodes. Once a node is no longer a root, we'll never use it again to find enemies.

Two key things can be learned from this test case: that one enemy of a set is stored at that set's root and that a SetFriends operation requires two Unions, not one. Now, what do we do when a set already has an enemy and then that set is involved in a SetEnemies operation? That's where our next test case comes in.

## Test Case 2

Our second test case differs from the first only in its final operation:

```
9
1 0 1
1 1 2
```

```
    1 3 4
    1 5 6
    2 1 7
    2 5 8
❶  2 2 5
    0 0 0
```

Prior to the final operation, the data structure appears as depicted in Figure 9-9. The final operation ❶ is now a SetEnemies operation rather than a SetFriends operation. Person 2's set already has an enemy, and now it has new enemies from Person 5's set. Hence we need to unite Person 2's enemies with Person 5's set. Similarly, Person 5's set already has an enemy and now has new enemies from Person 2's set, so we need to unite Person 5's enemies with Person 2's set.

The result of these two Unions is shown in Figure 9-11.

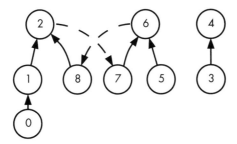

Figure 9-11: The data structure after a final SetEnemies operation

Having laid this background, we're ready for an implementation!

## The main Function

Let's start with the main function, which is given in Listing 9-9. It reads the input, and it calls one helper function for each of the four operations that we're supporting.

```
#define MAX_PEOPLE 9999

int main(void) {
  static int parent[MAX_PEOPLE], size[MAX_PEOPLE];
  static int enemy_of[MAX_PEOPLE];
  int num_people, i;
  int op, person1, person2;
  scanf("%d", &num_people);
  for (i = 0; i < num_people; i++) {
    parent[i] = i;
    size[i] = 1;
❶   enemy_of[i] = -1;
  }
```

```
    scanf("%d%d%d", &op, &person1, &person2);

    while (op != 0) {
❷  if (op == 1)
        if (are_enemies(person1, person2, parent, enemy_of))
          printf("-1\n");
        else
          set_friends(person1, person2, parent, size, enemy_of);

❸  else if (op == 2)
        if (are_friends(person1, person2, parent))
          printf("-1\n");
        else
          set_enemies(person1, person2, parent, size, enemy_of);

❹  else if (op == 3)
        if (are_friends(person1, person2, parent))
          printf("1\n");
        else
          printf("0\n");

❺  else if (op == 4)
        if (are_enemies(person1, person2, parent, enemy_of))
          printf("1\n");
        else
          printf("0\n");

      scanf("%d%d%d", &op, &person1, &person2);
    }
    return 0;
}
```

*Listing 9-9: The main function for processing operations*

Notice that, as part of the initialization, we set each enemy_of value to -1 ❶. That's our special value to indicate "no enemy."

To implement SetFriends ❷, we first check whether the two people are already known to be enemies. If they are, we output -1; if they aren't, we call the set_friends helper function. The implementation of SetEnemies ❸ follows the same pattern. For AreFriends ❹ and AreEnemies ❺, we call a helper function to determine whether the condition is true or false, and we output 1 or 0 accordingly.

## Find and Union

I'll present the Find and Union functions here; they'll be called by our helper functions, set_friends, set_enemies, are_friends, and are_enemies. The Find function is given in Listing 9-10. We've got path compression in there!

```
int find(int person, int parent[]) {
  int set = person, temp;
  while (parent[set] !=  set)
    set = parent[set];
  while (parent[person] != set) {
    temp = parent[person];
    parent[person] = set;
    person = temp;
  }
  return set;
}
```

*Listing 9-10: The find function*

The Union function is given in Listing 9-11. Union by size: you better believe it!

```
int union_sets(int person1, int person2, int parent[],
               int size[]) {
  int set1, set2, temp;
  set1 = find(person1, parent);
  set2 = find(person2, parent);
  if (set1 != set2) {
    if (size[set1] > size[set2]) {
      temp = set1;
      set1 = set2;
      set2 = temp;
    }
    parent[set1] = set2;
    size[set2] = size[set2] + size[set1];
  }
❶ return set2;
}
```

*Listing 9-11: The union_sets function*

The Union function does have one feature not present in our prior Union code: it returns the representative of the resulting set ❶. We'll turn to the SetFriends operation next, and you'll see there that we use this return value.

### SetFriends and SetEnemies

The SetFriends operation is implemented in Listing 9-12.

```
void set_friends(int person1, int person2, int parent[],
                 int size[], int enemy_of[]) {
  int set1, set2, bigger_set, other_set;
❶ set1 = find(person1, parent);
```

```
❷ set2 = find(person2, parent);
❸ bigger_set = union_sets(person1, person2, parent, size);
❹ if (enemy_of[set1] != -1 && enemy_of[set2] != -1)
  ❺ union_sets(enemy_of[set1], enemy_of[set2], parent, size);
❻ if (bigger_set == set1)
      other_set = set2;
   else
      other_set = set1;
❼ if (enemy_of[bigger_set] == -1)
      enemy_of[bigger_set] = enemy_of[other_set];
}
```

*Listing 9-12: Recording that two people are friends*

We begin by determining the representative of each of the two people: set1 is the representative of person1 ❶ and set2 is the representative of
person2 ❷. Since these two sets of people are now supposed to be all friends
with each other, we unite them into a bigger set ❸. We store the return value
of union_sets in bigger_set; we'll use that soon.

We've now unioned person1's set and person2's set, but we're not done,
because—remember this from our first test case—we might have to union
some enemies together as well. Specifically, if set1 has enemies and set2
has enemies, then we need to union those enemies into a single, bigger set.
That's just what the code does: if both sets have enemies ❹, we union those
enemy sets ❺.

It's tempting to think that we're done at this point. We've performed
the required union of friends and union of enemies—what else is there to
do? Well, imagine that set1 has some enemies and that set2 does not. The
representative of set2 therefore has an enemy_of value of -1. Now, maybe set1
ends up being folded into set2 so that set2 is the bigger set. If we just call it a
day here and do nothing else, then set2 will not be able to find its enemies!
The enemy_of value for set2's representative is still -1—and that's wrong, because set2 *does* have enemies now.

Here's how we handle this in the code. We already have bigger_set, indicating which set—set1 or set2—resulted from unioning set1 and set2. We
use an if–else to set other_set to the other set ❻: if bigger_set is set1, then
other_set will be set2, and vice versa. Then, if bigger_set has no enemies ❼,
we copy over the enemy link from other_set. The result is that bigger_set is
guaranteed to be able to find its enemies if set1 or set2 or both had enemies.

Now it's time for SetEnemies. Check it out in Listing 9-13.

```
void set_enemies(int person1, int person2, int parent[],
                 int size[], int enemy_of[]) {
  int set1, set2, enemy;
  set1 = find(person1, parent);
  set2 = find(person2, parent);
❶ enemy = enemy_of[set1];
  if (enemy == -1)
  ❷ enemy_of[set1] = person2;
```

```
    else
❸   union_sets(enemy, person2, parent, size);
❹ enemy = enemy_of[set2];
  if (enemy == -1)
    enemy_of[set2] = person1;
  else
    union_sets(enemy, person1, parent, size);
}
```

*Listing 9-13: Recording that two people are enemies*

We again begin by finding the representatives of each set, storing them in set1 and set2, respectively. We then look up an enemy of set1 ❶. If set1 has no enemy, then we set person2 to be its enemy ❷. If set1 does have an enemy, then we're in the territory of our second test case. We union set1's enemies with person2's set ❸, which ensures that person2 and all of person2's friends are all enemies of person1.

That takes care of set1. Now we do likewise for set2 ❹, setting its enemy to be person1 if it doesn't have an enemy yet or otherwise unioning its enemies with person1's set.

Importantly, this function maintains the symmetry of the enemy relationship: if from person1 we can find enemy person2, then from person2 we can find enemy person1. Consider a given call of set_enemies on person1 and person2. If person1 has no enemies, then its enemy becomes person2, but if person1 has enemies, its enemy set grows to include person2. Symmetrically, if person2 has no enemies, then its enemy becomes person1, and if person2 has enemies, then its enemy set grows to include person1.

## AreFriends and AreEnemies

The AreFriends operation amounts to checking whether the two people are in the same set or, equivalently, whether they have the same representative. This can be accomplished with two calls to Find, as shown in Listing 9-14.

```
int are_friends(int person1, int person2, int parent[]) {
  return find(person1, parent) == find(person2, parent);
}
```

*Listing 9-14: Determining whether two people are friends*

We have just one more operation to go! We can implement AreEnemies by checking whether one person is in the other person's set of enemies. The code is given in Listing 9-15.

```
int are_enemies(int person1, int person2, int parent[],
                int enemy_of[]) {
  int set1, enemy;
  set1 = find(person1, parent);
  enemy = enemy_of[set1];
```

```
❶   return (enemy != -1) &&
            (find(enemy, parent) == find(person2, parent));
    }
```

*Listing 9-15: Determining whether two people are enemies*

Two things must be true for person2 to be an enemy of person1 ❶. First, person1 must have an enemy. Second, person2 must be in its set of enemies.

Hey! Shouldn't we also check whether person1 is an enemy of person2? No, that's not needed, because the enemy relationship is symmetric. If person2 is not an enemy of person1, then there's no point checking whether person1 is an enemy of person2.

That's it! We have successfully augmented the vanilla union-find data structure to incorporate both friend and enemy information. If you submit your code to the judge, you should pass all test cases. What about exceeding the time limit? With union by size and path compression in there, the time limit can't stop us.

## Problem 3: Drawer Chore

In the Social Network and Friends and Enemies problems, we were able to use both union by size and path compression to speed up our implementations. In this next problem, we'll attach more meaning to the root of each set. We won't be able to use union by size, because the choice of root matters. Think about why this is as you read the problem description!

This is DMOJ problem coci13c5p6.

### The Problem

Mirko has $n$ items strewn around his room and $d$ empty drawers. The items are numbered $1, 2, \ldots, n$; the drawers are numbered $1, 2, \ldots, d$. Each drawer can hold at most one item. Mirko's goal is to consider each item in turn, placing it in a drawer if possible and throwing it away if not.

Each item has exactly two drawers in which it is allowed to be placed: Drawer A and Drawer B. (It's for organizational purposes. We wouldn't want to put the Halloween candy with the ants, after all.) For example, we might be allowed to place item 3 in Drawer 7 (A) or Drawer 5 (B).

To determine what happens with each item, we use the following five rules in order:

1. If Drawer A is empty, put the item in Drawer A and stop.

2. If Drawer B is empty, put the item in Drawer B and stop.

3. If Drawer A is full, move the existing item in Drawer A to its other drawer; if that drawer is full, too, move its existing item to its other drawer; and so on. If this process would terminate, place the item in Drawer A and stop.

4. If Drawer B is full, move the existing item in Drawer B to its other drawer; if that drawer is full, too, move its existing item to its other

drawer; and so on. If this process would terminate, place the item in Drawer B and stop.

5. If we have failed to place the item using the first four rules, we throw the item away.

Because of Rules 3 and 4, placing an item may result in other items moving to their other drawers.

We need to output whether each item is kept or thrown away.

### Input

The input contains one test case, consisting of the following lines:

- A line containing $n$, the number of items, and $d$, the number of drawers. $n$ and $d$ are between 1 and 300,000.

- $n$ lines, one for each item. Each line contains two integers $a$ and $b$, indicating that this item's Drawer A is $a$ and Drawer B is $b$. $a$ will not be the same integer as $b$.

### Output

The output for each item is on its own line. For each item, output LADICA if it is placed in a drawer and SMECE if it is thrown away. (These words come from the original COCI problem description: *ladica* is the Croatian word for drawer and *smece* is the Croatian word for trash.)

The time limit for solving the test case is one second.

## Equivalent Drawers

Here's an interesting scenario: We place a new item in Drawer 1—but, uh-oh, Drawer 1 happens to be full. Its existing item's other drawer is Drawer 2. So we move that existing item to Drawer 2 and, uh-oh again, Drawer 2 is full. Its existing item's other drawer is Drawer 6. Ugh—Drawer 6 is full, too! We move its existing item to its other drawer, Drawer 4. Phew! Drawer 4 is empty, so we stop.

In the process of ultimately filling Drawer 4, we moved three existing items: from Drawer 1 to 2, from Drawer 2 to 6, and finally from Drawer 6 to 4. However, those particular moves won't matter to us. All we'll need to know is that Drawer 4 ends up filled.

Prior to adding the new item, what Drawers 1, 2, 6, and 4 had in common is that if you try to place an item in any one of them, Drawer 4 ends up getting filled. This is the sense in which these four drawers are equivalent. For example, if you place an item in Drawer 4 directly, then Drawer 4 is filled right away. If you place an item in Drawer 6, Drawer 6's existing item moves to Drawer 4 and again Drawer 4 is filled. This pattern also holds if you place an item in Drawer 2 and, as we saw at the start of this example, if you place an item in Drawer 1. Drawer 4 is an empty drawer where the chain of drawers terminates and, thinking ahead to our union-find data structure, we see that this will be the representative of its set. Our set representatives will always be empty drawers; every other drawer in a set will be full.

To make all of this concrete, let's work through two test cases. In the first one, we'll have LADICA everywhere: we'll be able to place each item in a drawer. In the second, we'll see some SMECE: there are some items that we will not be able to place.

### Test Case 1

Here's our first test case:

```
6 7
1 2
2 6
6 4
5 3
5 7
2 5
```

We have seven drawers, each of which starts empty and in its own set. I'll place each set on its own line and highlight each set's representative in italics:

*1*

*2*

*3*

*4*

*5*

*6*

*7*

It's a good time to refresh your memory of the rules from the problem description before continuing.

The first item is 1 2; that's a Drawer A of 1 and a Drawer B of 2. Since Drawer 1 is empty, this item is placed in Drawer 1 (using Rule 1). In addition, Drawers 1 and 2 end up in the same set: placing a new item into Drawer 1 or Drawer 2 would result in the same drawer, Drawer 2, being filled. Here's our next snapshot of the sets:

1 *2*

*3*

*4*

*5*

*6*

*7*

Notice the new set has Drawer 2 as its representative. Using Drawer 1 as its representative would be incorrect: it would erroneously indicate that Drawer 1 is empty! This is why we won't use union by size: it might choose the wrong root to be the representative of the resulting set.

Now consider the second item: 2 6. Drawer 2 is empty, so we place this item there (using Rule 1 again). Now placing an item in Drawer 1, 2, or 6 would result in Drawer 6 being filled, so we union Drawers 1 and 2 with Drawer 6:

$$1\,2\,6$$
$$3$$
$$4$$
$$5$$
$$7$$

Drawer 6 is empty, so placing an item in Drawer 6 fills it immediately. Placing an item in Drawer 2 causes that drawer's existing item to move to Drawer 6, again filling Drawer 6. Placing an item in Drawer 1 causes its existing item to move to Drawer 2, and Drawer 2's existing item to move to Drawer 6..., so Drawer 6 is filled again. That's why we're justified in putting all three of these drawers in the same set, with Drawer 6 as its representative.

The next item is 6 4. We know what to do (using Rule 1 again):

$$1\,2\,6\,4$$
$$3$$
$$5$$
$$7$$

The next item is 5 3. Again, this poses no problem (using Rule 1):

$$1\,2\,6\,4$$
$$5\,3$$
$$7$$

Every item we've processed so far has succeeded by using Rule 1. Of course, that need not be the case, as is evinced by the next item: 5 7. Rule 1 does not apply, because Drawer 5 is already full. Rule 2 does apply, though, because Drawer 7 is empty. This item is therefore placed in Drawer 7. The empty drawer of the unioned set is Drawer 3, so that's our representative, as shown in the next snapshot:

$$1\,2\,6\,4$$
$$5\,7\,3$$

We have one more item to go, and it's a fun one: 2 5. Does Rule 1 apply? No, because Drawer 2 is full. Does Rule 2 apply? No, because Drawer 5 is full. Does Rule 3 apply? Yes! It applies because Drawer 2's set has an empty drawer (Drawer 4). How do we proceed?

The argument in this case is that Drawer 2's set and Drawer 5's set should be unioned, like this:

1 2 6 4 5 7 3

I'll explain why this works. The 2 5 item ends up placed in Drawer 2: existing items move from Drawer 2 to Drawer 6 and move from Drawer 6 to Drawer 4. Drawer 4 is now filled, so it can't be the representative of its set anymore. In fact, the only relevant, empty drawer is Drawer 3, so we're really hoping that Drawer 3 can serve as the set representative. Drawers 5, 7, and 3 should certainly be in the same set: placing an item in any of them ultimately fills Drawer 3, because they were in the same set prior to us introducing the 2 5 item.

It remains to explain why Drawers 1, 2, 6, and 4 should be in Drawer 3's set, as well. Drawer 2 is fine: placing an item in Drawer 2 moves its existing item to Drawer 5. Drawer 5 is in Drawer 3's set, so we know what happens from here: Drawer 3 will end up filled.

Drawer 1 is fine, too: placing an item in Drawer 1 moves its existing item to Drawer 2, and from here we can use the previous paragraph to argue that Drawer 3 will be filled. Similar logic applies to Drawers 6 and 4. For example, if we place an item in Drawer 4 and then we "undo" the moves that occurred when we filled Drawer 2, Drawer 4's existing item moves back to Drawer 6, Drawer 6's existing item moves back to Drawer 2, and now we're back in the case in the previous paragraph.

Each item in this test case is placed in a drawer, so the correct output is as follows:

---

LADICA
LADICA
LADICA
LADICA
LADICA
LADICA

---

Let's extract a general principle from this test case. Say we're processing item x y and that the item ends up in x's set. Then we union x's set and y's set, keeping y's representative as the representative of the union.

Why is this correct? Think about what happens when we try to place an item in the unioned set, whose components are x's old set and y's old set. Placing it in some drawer of y's set still fills y's representative, because we haven't messed with y's set at all. Placing it in drawer x fills y's representative, too, because we move x's existing item to y, and then we're back in the case of placing an item in a drawer of y's set. The only remaining option is that the new item is placed in drawer z (which is different from x) in x's set. There is a chain of drawers from drawer z to drawer x; moving items along that chain will fill drawer x, and from there y's representative will be filled.

What if we're processing item x y, and the item ends up in y's set? In this case, the roles of the two sets are reversed. In particular, we'll keep the representative of x's set as the representative of the union set.

## Test Case 2

Now let's see how some SMECE can arise. Here's our second test case:

---

```
7 7
1 2
2 6
6 4
❶ 1 4
2 4
1 7
7 6
```

---

The first three items are LADICAs and result in a familiar state:

1 2 6 *4*

*3*

*5*

*7*

Now, here's something different: item 1 4 ❶. For the first time, we see an item whose Drawer A and Drawer B are in the *same* set. It therefore provides no new empty drawer for this set. That is, using Rule 2 fills Drawer 4 (so it's a LADICA), but it gives us no set to union. Drawers 1, 2, 6, and 4 enter a new kind of state, whereby it becomes impossible to successfully place an item in any of them! If you try, you will cycle items around forever. For example, try to place an item in Drawer 1. We can push Drawer 1's existing item to Drawer 2, then push Drawer 2's existing item to Drawer 6, then push Drawer 6's existing item to Drawer 4, Drawer 4's existing item gets pushed to Drawer 1, Drawer 1's existing item to Drawer 2, Drawer 2's existing item to Drawer 6, and so on and so on, until I hit my book's page limit.

In our implementation, we're going to flag this state by giving this set a representative of 0:

1 2 6 4 *0*

*3*

*5*

*7*

Now we're dangerously close to a SMECE. If any item comes along, both of whose drawers are in this set, then there's no way to place it. Look at our next item: 2 4. Can we place it in Drawer 2? No; it's full. What about Drawer 4? No; it's also full. Can we follow a chain of drawers from Drawer 2 to find an empty drawer? No. Is there a chain of drawers from Drawer 4 to an empty drawer? No. Four strikes. SMECE.

Moving on, we have item 1 7. This will be processed by using Rule 2. We therefore perform a Union (because it's a LADICA)—but watch out: because it's another Union that gives us a set without an empty drawer! Here's the result:

1 2 6 4 7 *0*

*3*

*5*

The final item is 7 6, and that's another SMECE because none of the four LADICA rules apply: Drawers 7 and 6 are in the same set, and that set has no empty drawer.

The correct output for this test case is:

```
LADICA
LADICA
LADICA
LADICA
SMECE
LADICA
SMECE
```

The only rule we haven't explored in our test cases is Rule 4. I encourage you to play around with Rule 4 a bit before continuing. In particular, you can verify that whenever you apply Rule 4, the representative of the unioned set will be 0.

Now it's implementation time!

### The main Function

Let's start with the main function, which reads each item from the input and processes it. The code is given in Listing 9-16.

```
#define MAX_DRAWERS 300000

int main(void) {
  static int parent[MAX_DRAWERS + 1];
  int num_items, num_drawers, i;
  int drawer_a, drawer_b;
  scanf("%d%d", &num_items, &num_drawers);
❶ parent[0] = 0;
  for (i = 1; i <= num_drawers; i++)
    parent[i] = i;

  for (i = 1; i <= num_items; i++) {
    scanf("%d%d", &drawer_a, &drawer_b);

❷   if (find(drawer_a, parent) == drawer_a)
❸     union_sets(drawer_a, drawer_b, parent);
```

```
❹ else if (find(drawer_b, parent) == drawer_b)
  ❺ union_sets(drawer_b, drawer_a, parent);

❻ else if (find(drawer_a, parent) > 0)
  ❼ union_sets(drawer_a, drawer_b, parent);

❽ else if (find(drawer_b, parent) > 0)
  ❾ union_sets(drawer_b, drawer_a, parent);

    else
      printf("SMECE\n");
  }
  return 0;
}
```

*Listing 9-16: The main function for processing items*

As usual, the `parent` array records the parent of each node in the union-find data structure. Items are numbered starting from 1, so it's safe for us to use a representative of 0 for the drawers that can never have a new item placed in them. We give 0 a representative of 0 ❶ to indicate that this set, like all other sets, starts out empty.

Now, let's look at those five rules. We implement each of the four LADICA rules with one call to `find` and one call to `union`. If none of these rules applies, then we're in the SMECE case. Let's go through each LADICA rule in turn.

For Rule 1, we need to know whether `drawer_a` is empty. Remember that each set of drawers (not including the "0" set) has exactly one empty drawer and that this empty drawer is the representative of the set. The `find` function returns the representative of the given set. Putting these two facts together, we see that `find` returns `drawer_a` exactly when `drawer_a` is empty ❷.

If we are in the Rule 1 case, then we need to union `drawer_a`'s set with `drawer_b`'s set. We therefore call `union_sets` ❸. Careful, though: remember that we must make `drawer_b`'s representative be the representative of the new set, because `drawer_a`'s set has no empty drawers now that `drawer_a` is full. To make that happen, we'll use an implementation of `union_sets` that does not perform union by size. It guarantees that the representative of the second parameter that we pass—`drawer_b` here—will be the representative of the unioned set. It's also responsible for outputting the LADICA message. We'll see that code in the next subsection.

For Rule 2, we need to know if `drawer_b` is empty. We again use `find` to check this ❹, and we perform the Union operation if this rule applies ❺. This time, we call `union_sets` with the drawers in the opposite order so that `drawer_a`'s representative becomes the representative of the unioned set.

For Rule 3, we need to know whether `drawer_a`'s set has an empty drawer. A set has an empty drawer unless the set's representative is 0. We use `find` to check this condition ❻: if `find` returns a representative other than 0, then this set has an empty drawer. If this rule applies, then we perform the expected Union ❼. We'll see in the next subsection how union_sets is responsible for appropriately moving sets to the "0" set.

Finally, for Rule 4, we need to know whether drawer_b's set has an empty drawer. The logic is the same as that for Rule 3: use find to check whether this set has an empty drawer ❽; if it does, perform the Union ❾.

### Find and Union

The Find function is given in Listing 9-17. It uses path compression. That's a good thing, because I just submitted a solution without path compression and I received a "Time-Limit Exceeded" error. #PathCompressionWins.

```
int find(int drawer, int parent[]) {
  int set = drawer, temp;
  while (parent[set] != set)
    set = parent[set];
  while (parent[drawer] != set) {
    temp = parent[drawer];
    parent[drawer] = set;
    drawer = temp;
  }
  return set;
}
```

*Listing 9-17: The find function*

The Union function is given in Listing 9-18.

```
void union_sets(int drawer1, int drawer2, int parent[]) {
  int set1, set2;
  set1 = find(drawer1, parent);
  set2 = find(drawer2, parent);
❶ parent[set1] = set2;
❷ if (set1 == set2)
  ❸ parent[set2] = 0;
  printf("LADICA\n");
}
```

*Listing 9-18: The union_sets function*

As promised, there's no union by size here: we always use set2, the set of drawer2, as the new set ❶.

In addition, whenever an item is placed whose drawers are in the same set ❷, we set the representative of the resulting set to 0 ❸. Whenever find is later called on any element of this resulting set, 0 will be returned, correctly indicating that no item can ever be placed in this set again.

There we have it: a 50-line union-find solution to one of the most challenging problems in this book. Please submit your code to the judge!

# Summary

In this chapter, we've learned how to efficiently implement the union-find data structure. Of all the data structures in this book, the union-find data structure is the one that surprises me most with the breadth of its applications. "Really? This is a union-find problem?" I frequently have that thought. Perhaps you similarly had that thought when we solved Friends and Enemies or Drawer Chore. In any case, you're likely to encounter other problems, seemingly quite different from those that I presented here, where union-find nevertheless applies.

Happily, given its wide applicability and speedy performance, we don't need huge amounts of code to implement union-find: just a few lines for Union and a few lines for Find. In addition, you may find that the code isn't too tricky, once we've learned about the array representation for the trees. Even the optimizations, union by size and path compression, require little code.

# Notes

Drawer Chore is originally from the 2013 Croatian Open Competition in Informatics, Round 5. I found the "0 representative" idea from the COCI website (see *http://hsin.hr/coci/archive/2013_2014*).

# 10

## RANDOMIZATION

Think back to when we learned about binary search in Chapter 7. Rather than answering the question, "What is the optimal solution?" we instead asked, "Is this specific value the optimal solution?" While we were solving the Feeding Ants problem, you may have thought that my picking values out of thin air was outlandish, wondering how that was going to work at all. But it works great, as we now know.

You want something that's even more outlandish than binary search? How about just straight-up guessing a completely random solution. How could that possibly work? What is it about specific problems that makes this random guessing a viable strategy? And could random guessing still help us solve a problem even if we already have a solution? The surprising conclusions await.

# Problem 1: Yōkan

Yōkan is a Japanese candy. It's sweet. It has kind of a jelly or gummy texture. Buy a nice big block and cut it into little pieces and pair it with some fruit and chill it for a nice refreshing... oh, sorry. Back to algorithms.

This is DMOJ problem `dmpg15g6`.

## The Problem

Two friends have found a Yōkan consisting of $n$ pieces. The pieces are numbered $1, 2, \ldots, n$. Each piece of the Yōkan has a specific flavor, and each friend will eat only those pieces that are the same flavor.

A slab of Yōkan consists of all of the pieces from Piece $l$ to Piece $r$. A friend is *happy* with a slab if they can find at least one-third of that slab's pieces that have the same flavor. For example, if a slab has 9 pieces, then a friend would need to find $9/3 = 3$ pieces of the same flavor. For both friends to be happy with the slab, they would each need to find their own one-third of pieces that have the same flavor.

The friends will query about various slabs; for each, we need to determine whether both of them would be happy with that slab.

### Input

The input consists of the following lines:

- A line containing $n$, the number of pieces in the Yōkan, and $m$, the number of possible piece flavors. $n$ and $m$ are between 1 and 200,000.

- A line containing $n$ integers giving the flavors of the Yōkan pieces from Piece 1 to Piece $n$. Each integer is a flavor between 1 and $m$.

- A line containing $q$, the number of queries that the friends have. $q$ is between 1 and 200,000.

- $q$ lines, one for each query. Each such line contains the integers $l$ and $r$, indicating the slab from Piece $l$ to Piece $r$.

### Output

The output for each query is on its own line. For each query:

- If both friends are happy with this slab, output YES.

- Otherwise, output NO.

The time limit for solving the test case is 1.4 seconds.

## Randomly Choosing a Piece

Let's start with a test case:

---

```
14 4
1 3 4 2 1 1 2 4 1 2 2 4 1 1
```

```
3
3 11
8 11
5 6
```

The Yōkan here has 14 pieces. It looks like this:

| Piece | 1 | 2 | 3 | 4 | 5 | 6 | 7 | 8 | 9 | 10 | 11 | 12 | 13 | 14 |
|---|---|---|---|---|---|---|---|---|---|---|---|---|---|---|
| Flavor | 1 | 3 | 4 | 2 | 1 | 1 | 2 | 4 | 1 | 2 | 2 | 4 | 1 | 1 |

There are three queries to process. The first query starts at Piece 3 and ends at Piece 11. We're therefore interested in this slab of the Yōkan:

| Piece | 3 | 4 | 5 | 6 | 7 | 8 | 9 | 10 | 11 |
|---|---|---|---|---|---|---|---|---|---|
| Flavor | 4 | 2 | 1 | 1 | 2 | 4 | 1 | 2 | 2 |

This slab has 9 pieces, so we want to determine whether each friend can find $9/3 = 3$ pieces of the same flavor. And they can! The first friend could eat 3 pieces of Flavor 1. The second friend could eat 3 pieces of Flavor 2. (There are 4 pieces of Flavor 2 there, but that fourth one is overkill for what we need.) For this query, we would therefore output YES.

Think about how we might write code to determine whether the friends are happy with this slab. In general, it would be too slow to do this by checking each piece in the slab one by one; after all, a slab can have up to 200,000 pieces in it. This is a familiar roadblock for us by this point in the book; the usual thing to do would be to use some fancy data structure to make the queries fast.

But we're going to do something far less usual here. I'd like you to look at that Yōkan slab again and randomly pick one of its pieces. Pieces of Flavor 1 and pieces of Flavor 2 are prevalent here, so you may have ended up picking a piece of one of those two flavors. If you did, then you just found a way to satisfy the first friend. If not, please randomly pick another piece of that Yōkan slab. You may have gotten Flavor 1 or Flavor 2 that time. Still no? Then try a third time. If you're choosing randomly, you're bound to pick Flavor 1 or Flavor 2 within a small number of tries.

Let's say that you've found Flavor 1 for the first friend. Now, do it again, this time for the second friend. It'll be a little more difficult this time: the three Flavor 1 pieces are gone, so you'll have to land on Flavor 2. Still, try picking a random piece a few times, and I'm sure you'll eventually pick one of Flavor 2.

The program that we'll write to solve this problem is going to do exactly what you just did: picking pieces randomly, trying to find one whose flavor makes each friend happy.

Suppose that the two friends are happy with a given Yōkan slab. This means that there's a single flavor that shows up for 2/3 of the pieces, or two different flavors that each show up for 1/3 of the pieces. Regardless, we have a 2/3 chance of making the first friend happy by just choosing a piece at random. If we succeed, then we're done with the first friend and we move to the second friend. If we fail, well, we'll just try again, and we'll have a new 2/3 chance of success. If we fail that second time, we'll try a third time, and a fourth time, until we succeed.

We'll figure out how many attempts we need later. For now, though, I can promise that it won't be very many. The intuition for this can come from a coin-tossing experiment.

Imagine that you were playing a game with a fair coin. If you toss the coin and it comes up heads, you win. If you toss the coin and it comes up tails, you have to try again. Think of the coin coming up heads as making the friend happy, and the coin coming up tails as not making the friend happy and having to try again. How many times do you expect to have to toss the coin before it comes up heads? Not many, right? If there's a flavor in the slab that makes a friend happy, we'll toss only so many tails in a row before we find a heads.

We were in the middle of working through a test case before all of that randomizing and coin-tossing talk, so let's finish that before continuing.

The second query starts at Piece 8 and ends at Piece 11. The corresponding slab is:

| Piece | 8 | 9 | 10 | 11 |
|-------|---|---|----|----|
| Flavor | 4 | 1 | 2 | 2 |

Unfortunately, the two friends are not happy with this one. Each friend needs to find at least $4/3 = 1.\overline{3}$ pieces of the same flavor; as the available number of pieces of each flavor is an integer, what we really need is at least 2 pieces of the same flavor. We can do this for the first friend with Flavor 2, but we're stuck for the second friend. We need to output NO here.

The third query starts at Piece 5 and ends at Piece 6. That's this part of the Yōkan:

| Piece | 5 | 6 |
|-------|---|---|
| Flavor | 1 | 1 |

Each friend needs just one piece of a given flavor. We can therefore use Flavor 1 to make both friends happy: we can give one piece to the first friend and the other to the second friend! The correct output is therefore YES.

### Generating Random Numbers

We'll need a way to generate random numbers in order to randomly pick Yōkan pieces. We'll use C's rand function to do this.

If we call rand with an integer x, we're asking for rand to give us one of x possibilities. Specifically, we'll get back a random integer in the range 0 to x - 1. For example, if we call rand(4), we'll get back a 0, 1, 2, or 3.

Now, how can we use rand to pick a random piece of a slab? Let's use the term *width* to refer to the number of pieces in a slab. For example, the slab from Piece 8 to Piece 11 has a width of 4. In this case, we'd need rand to give us back 8, 9, 10, or 11. We can start by calling rand(4), because we need rand to give us one of four possibilities. That would give us a 0, 1, 2, or 3. This is a good start, but those numbers are not in the right range. To fix that, we can just add 8 to move that value into the 8–11 range that we need.

In code, generating a random number for a given width `width` and starting point `left` can be done as in Listing 10-1.

```
int random_piece(int left, int width) {
❶ return (rand() % width) + left;
}
```

Listing 10-1: Randomly choosing a piece

The code carries out the plan that we just outlined: it generates a random number from 0 to `width` - 1, then adds the starting point `left` to it ❶.

## Determining Number of Pieces

Suppose that we're working on a particular query. We're going to choose a random piece in that query's slab. Does the flavor of that piece make one or both of the friends happy? To answer that, we'll need to be able to quickly determine how many times that flavor shows up in the slab.

It will therefore be convenient for us to have a sorted array for each flavor that gives us the pieces of that flavor. I'll call such an array a *flavor array*.

Let's go back to the Yōkan from our test case:

| Piece | 1 | 2 | 3 | 4 | 5 | 6 | 7 | 8 | 9 | 10 | 11 | 12 | 13 | 14 |
|-------|---|---|---|---|---|---|---|---|---|----|----|----|----|----|
| Flavor | 1 | 3 | 4 | 2 | 1 | 1 | 2 | 4 | 1 | 2 | 2 | 4 | 1 | 1 |

The array for Flavor 1 would be [1, 5, 6, 9, 13, 14]; the array for Flavor 2 would be [4, 7, 10, 11]; and so on. As promised, each of these arrays is sorted: the piece numbers are in order from smallest to largest. We'll see how to generate these flavor arrays later; for now let's just assume they exist.

We can use such an array to determine the number of pieces of a given flavor that lie within a slab. For example, we could use the array [1, 5, 6, 9, 13, 14] to conclude that there are three pieces of Flavor 1 in the 3-11 slab: the pieces 5, 6, and 9.

Let's take stock. We have the query that we want to solve. We have a random flavor that we care about checking. We have the flavor array: a sorted array of piece numbers of that flavor. And we need to determine how many of those pieces are in the range of the query.

We could do this using a linear search through the flavor array. But that would be too slow—a linear amount of work per query.

If you think back to Chapter 7, you might wonder whether we can call on a binary search here. We can indeed, because the array is sorted! Well, actually, we'll need to call binary search twice rather than once, but that won't change the fact that we'll be able to find what we need in logarithmic time.

We're going to write a binary search function that takes a flavor array pieces and an integer at_least and returns the index of the leftmost value in the array that's greater than or equal to at_least.

Before we do, we should make sure that the specification of that function actually does what we need. To that end, let's use it to figure out how many pieces of Flavor 1 are in the 3-11 slab.

To figure out where the pieces of Flavor 1 begin in that slab, we can call our function with the array [1, 5, 6, 9, 13, 14] and an at_least value of 3. We'll get a result of 1. This tells us that the piece at index 1 is the first piece of this flavor whose number is at least 3. That piece is Piece 5, which is indeed the first piece that we're looking for.

Where do the pieces of Flavor 1 end in that slab? We can figure that out, too! Just call our function with the same array, but this time an at_least value of 12. Why 12? Because that's the first piece *not* in the slab. If we make this call, we'll get a result of 4. This refers to the piece at index 4, which is Piece 13. That's the first piece of this flavor that's not in the 3-11 slab. In general, to figure out where a flavor ends, we'll call our binary search function with an at_least value that's 1 larger than the right end of the slab.

Now we know where the relevant pieces start (index 1) and where the relevant pieces end (just to the left of index 4). If we subtract 1 from 4, we get an answer of 3, which is exactly the number of pieces of Flavor 1 in the 3-11 slab.

Let's write the code for our binary search function. (Soon, we'll see the function that calls this function twice.) As you learned in "Searching for a Solution" on page 250, the right way to write a binary search function is to first figure out the invariant. Our invariant will have two parts: that all values at indices less than low are < at_least, and that all values at indices high or greater are >= at_least. See Listing 10-2 for the code. In addition to the aforementioned pieces and at_least parameters, we have a parameter num_pieces that gives the number of pieces in the pieces array.

```
int lowest_index(int pieces[], int num_pieces, int at_least) {
  int low, high, mid;
❶ low = 0;
❷ high = num_pieces;
❸ while (high - low >= 1) {
    mid = (low + high) / 2;
    if (pieces[mid] < at_least)
      low = mid + 1;
    else
      high = mid;
  }
❹ return low;
}
```

Listing 10-2: Searching for the first satisfying value

We need to make both parts of the invariant true above the loop. For the first part, notice that the invariant isn't making any claim about the value at index low; it makes a claim only about the values to the left of index low. For that reason, we can set low to 0 above the loop ❶; there's nothing to the left of low now, so this part of the invariant is satisfied.

For the second part, the invariant claims something about all of the values at indices high or greater. Since we don't know anything about any value in the array, we need to make this part of the invariant claim nothing. We can do this by setting high to just beyond the right end of the array ❷: now there are no valid indices between high and the end of the array.

The code inside the while loop maintains the invariant. I encourage you to check this for yourself if you like, but you've had a lot of binary search practice already so I don't blame you if you'd rather not!

The while loop condition ❸ ensures that low and high are equal when the loop terminates. The invariant tells us that all values to the left of low are too small and that low is the first index of the value that's >= at_least. This is why we return low when the function terminates ❹.

Next, as promised, we're going to make two calls of that function to figure out how many pieces of a given flavor are within the range of a given slab. See Listing 10-3 for the code.

```
int num_in_range(int pieces[], int num_pieces, int left, int right) {
❶  int left_index = lowest_index(pieces, num_pieces, left);
❷  int right_index = lowest_index(pieces, num_pieces, right + 1);
❸  return right_index - left_index;
}
```

Listing 10-3: Determining number of pieces of a given flavor that are in range

Here, the pieces parameter is the flavor array, and the left and right parameters indicate the leftmost and rightmost pieces of the slab. The code first finds the index in the slab where the flavor starts ❶. Then it finds the index immediately to the right of where the flavor ends in the slab ❷. Finally, it subtracts the first of these indices from the second to determine the number of pieces of the flavor in the slab ❸.

### Guessing Flavors

At this point, we know what to do once we've guessed a flavor: use binary search to check whether the guessed flavor makes one or both friends happy. Now we need to work on the code that makes the guesses.

Our overall strategy can be broken down into three steps:

**Step 1**  Figure out the number of pieces that we need to make one friend happy.

**Step 2**  Try to make the first friend happy. Start by guessing a piece. If the flavor of that piece makes the friend happy, then we are done; otherwise, guess again. Keep guessing until we succeed or until we run out of guesses. It's possible for us to find a flavor that's so prevalent that it makes not just the first friend happy, but *both* friends happy. If that happens, we pump out a YES and stop right there, without doing Step 3.

**Step 3**   Try to make the second friend happy using the same strategy that we used for the first friend. If we happen to guess the flavor that made the first friend happy, then we need to ignore it and move on to our next attempt because that flavor isn't prevalent enough to make both friends happy.

We'll write the function for the following signature:

```
void solve(int yokan[], int *pieces_for_flavor[],
           int num_of_flavor[], int left, int right)
```

Here's what each parameter is for:

**yokan**   The array of Yōkan flavors; yokan[1] is the flavor of the first piece, yokan[2] is the flavor of the second piece, and so on. (We start at index 1 rather than 0 because the pieces are numbered from 1 in this problem.) We need this array so that we can choose a random piece.

**pieces_for_flavor**   The array of flavor arrays. Each flavor array is sorted from smallest piece number to largest piece number. For example, pieces_for_flavor[1] might be the array [1, 5, 6, 9, 13, 14], telling us all of the pieces that are of Flavor 1. We need these arrays so that we can binary search them.

**num_of_flavor**   An array giving the number of pieces of each flavor; num_of_flavor[1] is the number of pieces of Flavor 1, num_of_flavor[2] is the number of pieces of Flavor 2, and so on. That is, this array tells us how many elements are in each of the flavor arrays.

**left**   The beginning index of the current query.

**right**   The ending index of the current query.

The code for this function is in Listing 10-4. Look out for the three steps—figure out the happy threshold, make the first friend happy, make the second friend happy—as you read through the code.

```
void solve(int yokan[], int *pieces_for_flavor[],
           int num_of_flavor[], int left, int right) {
  int attempt, rand_piece, flavor, result;
  int width = right - left + 1;
❶ double threshold = width / 3.0;
  int first_flavor = 0;

❷ for (attempt = 0; attempt < NUM_ATTEMPTS; attempt++) {
  ❸ rand_piece = random_piece(left, width);
    flavor = yokan[rand_piece];
  ❹ result = num_in_range(pieces_for_flavor[flavor],
                          num_of_flavor[flavor], left, right);
  ❺ if (result >= 2 * threshold) {
      printf("YES\n");
      return;
    }
```

```
  ❻ if (result >= threshold)
      ❼ first_flavor = flavor;
    }

    if (first_flavor == 0) {
      printf("NO\n");
      return;
    }

❽ for (attempt = 0; attempt < NUM_ATTEMPTS; attempt++) {
      rand_piece = random_piece(left, width);
      flavor = yokan[rand_piece];
  ❾ if (flavor == first_flavor)
        continue;
      result = num_in_range(pieces_for_flavor[flavor],
                            num_of_flavor[flavor], left, right);
      if (result >= threshold) {
        printf("YES\n");
        return;
      }
    }

    printf("NO\n");
}
```

*Listing 10-4: Solving the problem*

For Step 1, we determine the number of pieces that will make a friend happy ❶.

For Step 2, we start guessing flavors for the first friend ❷. The for loop uses a NUM_ATTEMPTS constant that we haven't defined yet. We'll decide on this number after we finish walking through this function. In the for loop, we choose a random piece from the current slab ❸, then call our num_in_range helper function to get the number of pieces in the slab that have the same flavor as that random piece ❹.

Did our random flavor make one or both of the friends happy? We first check whether the flavor was so prevalent that it makes both friends happy. Specifically, if the flavor shows up 2/3 of the time (that is, twice the threshold value), it can be used to make both friends happy ❺. In this case, we're done: we just output YES and return. If the flavor doesn't make both friends happy, it might still be good enough to make the first friend happy, so we check for that next ❻. We also record the flavor that we found for the first friend ❼.

If in all our guessing we weren't able to find a flavor for the first friend, then we output NO and stop.

If we were able to find a flavor for the first friend, then we proceed to Step 3 ❽, where we try to find a flavor for the second friend. The logic is quite similar to what we did for the first friend. The only addition is to ensure that we don't inadvertently use the flavor that we already used for the first friend ❾.

If we get to the bottom of the function, it means that we weren't able to find a flavor for the second friend. We output NO in this case.

## How Many Attempts Do We Need?

Let's finally answer the question of how many attempts we need to ensure a ridiculously high probability of success.

We'll assume that each query asks about a slab of the Yōkan where exactly one third of the pieces are of some flavor $x$, exactly one third are of some other flavor $y$, and the rest of the pieces are distributed among a bunch of other flavors. That will be the hardest type of query of all for us. We may get lucky and run into a query where one flavor shows up 50 percent or 70 percent or 85 percent of the time, and for those we'll have an easier time with our guessing. But we're focusing on the hardest type of query because if we can nail that one, then we know that we can nail any others.

Don't worry if you haven't worked with probability before. A *probability* is just a value in the range 0 to 1. If something has a probability of 0 then it never occurs; if something has a probability of 1 then it occurs every time. You can multiply a probability value by 100 to turn it into a percentage. For example, when tossing a coin there is a 0.5 probability that it comes up heads; multiplied by 100, we see it equivalently has a $0.5 \times 100 = 50$ percent chance of coming up heads. We need a couple of other rules of probability as well, but I'll explain those as we go along.

Let's just pick a number of guesses out of nowhere and see how well we do. How about 10? We'll first figure out the probability that we make the first friend happy. On our first guess, we have a $2/3$ probability of success. That's because $2/3$ of the pieces in the slab are of one of the two flavors that each show up $1/3$ of the time. What's our probability of failure? There are only two outcomes here: success and failure. They have to add up to 1, because there's a 100 percent chance that one of these two outcomes happens. So we can find the probability of failure by subtracting the probability of success from 1. That gives us a $1 - 2/3 = 1/3$ probability of failure.

What's the probability of failure on all 10 guesses? For that to happen, we need to have failed on each guess independently. There's a $1/3$ probability that we fail on the first guess, a $1/3$ probability that we fail on the second guess, a $1/3$ probability that we fail on the third guess, and so on. There's a rule that we can use here to figure out the probability that we fail on all of these 10 independent guesses: just multiply all of the probabilities together. We see that the probability of failing on all 10 guesses is $(1/3)^{10}$, which is about 0.000017.

Now we are able to calculate our probability of success for this friend: $1 - 0.000017 = 0.999983$.

This is a better-than-99.99 percent probability of success. We're doing great!

What's the probability that we make the second friend happy given that we made the first friend happy? For this one, the probability of success on each attempt is 1/3, not 2/3, because the pieces of the first friend's flavor are gone. If you run through the calculation starting with 1/3 rather than 2/3, you should find a probability of success for the second friend of about 0.982658. That's over 98.2 percent! We're still looking good.

It's nice that we now have both the probability of success for the first friend and the probability of success for the second friend given success on the first friend. But what we care about more is the probability of success for both friends. To find that, we can multiply our two success probabilities together. Doing so, we find that the overall probability of making both friends happy is 0.999983 × 0.982658 = 0.982641.

This probability is more than 98.2 percent. Pretty good, right? Unfortunately, no. If we had to process one query, then this probability would be just fine. But we may need to process a massive 200,000 queries. And we need to get every single one of them right. If we get even one wrong, then we fail the test case.

Suppose you're throwing a ball into a basket and you have a 98.2 percent probability of success on each throw. You throw one ball. That one's probably going in. Now imagine that you throw 100 balls. You're probably going to botch at least a couple of those throws. And if you threw 200,000 balls? Your probability of getting every single one into the basket is near 0.

While 10 attempts was a good try, it isn't enough. We need more. Through some trial and error, I've settled on using 60 attempts for each friend. If you run through the calculations using 60 guesses instead of 10, you should find a success probability for each query of about 0.99999999997.

That's a lot of 9s! But we need them all because otherwise we'd take a massive probability hit when going from 1 query to 200,000. To find our probability of success for 200,000 queries, we can raise our per-query probability of success to the power of 200,000: $0.99999999997^{200,000} = 0.999994$.

It looks like we've lost a few 9s. Still, this is a staggeringly high probability, and this time it is for the probability that we get every single query right, not just one.

We're finally ready to set our NUM_ATTEMPTS constant. Let's use 60:

```
#define NUM_ATTEMPTS 60
```

### Filling the Flavor Arrays

We're almost ready for the main function; we just need one more little helper function first.

That helper function will take yokan (the Yōkan array) and num_pieces (the number of pieces in the Yōkan) and produce the pieces_for_flavor flavor arrays that we used in the solve function. See Listing 10-5 for the code.

```
#define MAX_FLAVORS 200000

void init_flavor_arrays(int yokan[], int num_pieces,
                        int *pieces_for_flavor[]) {
```

```
❶ static int cur_of_flavor[MAX_FLAVORS + 1];
   int i, flavor, j;
   for (i = 1; i <= num_pieces; i++) {
     flavor = yokan[i];
❷  j = cur_of_flavor[flavor];
     pieces_for_flavor[flavor][j] = i;
     cur_of_flavor[flavor]++;
   }
 }
```

*Listing 10-5: Filling in the flavor arrays*

The function assumes that each array in `pieces_for_flavor` already has memory assigned to it; that's a responsibility of the `main` function that's coming up next.

We use a local `cur_of_flavor` array ❶ to track the number of pieces we've found so far of each flavor. Inside the `for` loop, we use this array to determine the index in which to store the current piece number ❷.

### The main Function

We've made it to the `main` function! Check it out in Listing 10-6.

```
#define MAX_PIECES 200000

int main(void) {
   static int yokan[MAX_PIECES + 1];
   static int num_of_flavor[MAX_FLAVORS + 1];
   static int *pieces_for_flavor[MAX_FLAVORS + 1];
   int num_pieces, num_flavors, i, num_queries, l, r;
❶ srand((unsigned) time(NULL));
   scanf("%d%d", &num_pieces, &num_flavors);

❷ for (i = 1; i <= num_pieces; i++) {
     scanf("%d", &yokan[i]);
     num_of_flavor[yokan[i]]++;
   }

❸ for (i = 1; i <= num_flavors; i++) {
❹   pieces_for_flavor[i] = malloc(num_of_flavor[i] * sizeof(int));
     if (pieces_for_flavor[i] == NULL) {
       fprintf(stderr, "malloc error\n");
       exit(1);
     }
   }

❺ init_flavor_arrays(yokan, num_pieces, pieces_for_flavor);

   scanf("%d", &num_queries);
```

```
    for (i = 0; i < num_queries; i++) {
      scanf("%d%d", &l, &r);
❻   solve(yokan, pieces_for_flavor, num_of_flavor, l, r);
    }

    return 0;
}
```

*Listing 10-6: The main function*

Before we can use C's rand function, we need to use the srand function to initialize the random number generator with a seed. The seed determines the sequence of random numbers that are generated. We don't want to use the same seed every time, otherwise we'll generate the same sequence of numbers each time. What works well is to use the current time as the seed so that the random numbers change each time we run the program. We do that using C's time function ❶. To use that function, you'll need to add #include <time.h> at the top of your program.

There are two important for loops here. The first one ❷ fills in the yokan array and also uses the num_of_flavor array to keep track of the number of pieces of each flavor. Why do we need to know the number of pieces of each flavor? It's because, without knowing that, we wouldn't know how big to make each flavor array. The second for loop ❸ is responsible for allocating memory for the flavor arrays. It uses num_of_flavor to determine exactly how big each flavor array should be ❹.

Following these for loops, we call our helper function to fill in the flavor arrays whose memory we just allocated ❺.

And then we're off to the queries! For each one, we call our solve function ❻ to print YES or NO as needed.

If you submit our code to the judge, you should find that it passes all test cases within the time limit. If your code is correct and you somehow fail a test case, take a screenshot: you'll probably never see that again.

# Randomization

There are two main types of randomized algorithms. We just learned about one of them. Let's expand on that one here and preview the other.

## Monte Carlo Algorithms

The type of algorithm that we used to solve Yōkan, where there's a chance that we get the answer wrong, is called a *Monte Carlo Algorithm*. The key question when using such an algorithm is: How many attempts should we use? There's a tradeoff between the number of attempts and the probability of success: as we crank up the number of attempts, we increase the probability of success but slow down the algorithm. We generally want to find a sweet spot where the probability of success is high enough but our algorithm is still fast. Of course, what counts as a "high enough" probability of success depends on what we're using the algorithm for. Solving a programming competition problem? Ninety-nine percent probability of success is fine. (If the algorithm fails, who cares: just run it again.) For algorithms that impact the health and safety of people, though, 99 percent is not okay.

In our solution to Yōkan, if we answer YES, then we're guaranteed to be correct. We only answer YES when we're staring at the very flavors that show why the friends are happy with the slab. By contrast, if we answer NO, then we might be wrong. It might be the case that the friends aren't happy with the slab—but it could also be that we just got unlucky and kept picking bad flavors. Because only one of the two types of answers can be wrong, we say that our algorithm has *one-sided errors*. There are Monte Carlo algorithms that can be wrong in both the "yes" and "no" cases; those are said to have *two-sided errors*.

A Monte Carlo algorithm helped us solve Yōkan because the probability of randomly finding a useful flavor is so high. It might not seem that a $1/3$ or $2/3$ probability of success is that great, and indeed an algorithm that worked only one-third or two-thirds of the time wouldn't cut it. But remember that these probabilities are only our starting point. By the time we're done with our repeated attempts, we'll have converted that wonderful per-attempt probability to a wonderful per-answer probability.

Monte Carlo algorithms are useful for other problems as well. Consider a graph with $n$ nodes and imagine dividing the nodes into two groups. There are about $2^n$ ways to make this division, because for each of the $n$ nodes we have two options for where to put it. Such a division of nodes into two groups is called a *cut*. The *minimum cut problem* asks which of these $2^n$ divisions has the fewest edges that cross from one group to the other. Now, if we just randomly chose a cut, we'd have a per-attempt probability of success of $1/2^n$, which is terrible and not a promising start to a Monte Carlo algorithm. There *is* a Monte Carlo algorithm for this problem, though, and it hinges on the surprising fact that the per-attempt probability of success can be driven up to $1/n^2$. Relative to $1/2^n$, a probability of success of $1/n^2$ is high indeed.

If you can find a way to come up with a "surprisingly high" per-attempt probability of success, then you're well on your way to developing a useful Monte Carlo algorithm. Just crank up the number of attempts until you get the overall probability of success that you want.

## Las Vegas Algorithms

A Monte Carlo algorithm is always fast and almost always correct. A *Las Vegas Algorithm*, by contrast, is always correct and almost always fast. (These algorithms were given casino-related names to evoke the idea of gambling: with a Monte Carlo algorithm we're gambling with correctness, and with a Las Vegas algorithm we're gambling with speed.)

Suppose we had an algorithm that was quite fast for the vast majority of test cases but quite slow for the few remaining test cases. We might be okay to deploy this algorithm; we just have to hope that the Achilles' heel test cases don't happen very often.

But we can do better than that, and one way is through the use of a Las Vegas algorithm. In such an algorithm, we randomize the decisions that the algorithm makes as it runs. Because the algorithm has no fixed sequence of steps, no one can craft a test case that'll reliably slow it down because no one knows what decisions the algorithm will make on that test case!

Why can Las Vegas algorithms be effective? I like Ethan Epperly's article "Why Randomized Algorithms?" (see *https://www.ethanepperly.com/index.php/2021/08/11/why-randomized-algorithms/*). Suppose you were playing many rounds of Rock Paper Scissors against your friend. One approach would be to use a fixed pattern, like rock, paper, scissors, rock, paper, scissors, rock, paper . . . This might work for a little while—but eventually your friend will figure out what you're doing, and then you'll never win a round again. They'll just keep picking the option that beats you. A better approach is to randomly decide what to do on each round. If you do that, you're using a Las Vegas algorithm. Your friend will have no clue what's coming next! In our code for such an algorithm, we'll randomize the choices that we make so that no fixed test case can force us into poor performance.

Way back in Chapter 1, we solved two problems using hash tables. In each one, we chose one specific hash function and just went for it. A malicious actor could bring those solutions to a crawl by intentionally causing a huge number of hash collisions. It's possible to address that through a Las Vegas algorithm: rather than committing to a single hash function for all of time, sitting there waiting for someone to figure out what we're doing, we let our program randomly choose which hash function to use each time it runs. Doing so is called *random hashing*.

Random hashing is a frequently used Las Vegas algorithm. But there's one Las Vegas algorithm used even more frequently than that. We're going to see that one in Problem 2. First, let's talk about whether we really do need randomization in the first place.

### Deterministic vs. Randomized Algorithms

A *deterministic algorithm* is an algorithm that doesn't use randomness. Every algorithm we looked at in the first nine chapters of this book is a deterministic algorithm, and wow did we get a lot of mileage from those. Why not just forget about randomized algorithms and stick with deterministic ones, then? Why play around with guessing stuff and getting a 99.9999 percent probability of success when we can just have 100 percent success with a deterministic algorithm?

The reason is that a fast randomized algorithm can be easier to develop than a fast deterministic algorithm. If you're interested, you might try solving Yōkan without using randomization. It's certainly possible but requires additional ideas not needed in the randomized algorithm.

There are problems where the efficiency gulf between the currently best randomized algorithm and the currently best deterministic algorithm is huge. For example, to determine whether a number is prime, there's a randomized algorithm that runs in $O(n^2)$ time, but the best we've been able to do in terms of deterministic algorithms is $O(n^6)$.

Likewise, it's difficult to find a way to quickly solve our next problem with a deterministic algorithm. Good thing we don't have to. Let's do some more randomization!

# Problem 2: Caps and Bottles

This is DMOJ problem cco09p4.

## The Problem

We have $n$ caps and $n$ bottles. Each cap and bottle has a unique size, and there is exactly one cap that perfectly fits each bottle.

Our goal is to match the caps to their corresponding bottles. (I've seen this problem alternately phrased as matching nuts and bolts, keys and locks, hats and people's heads, you name it. Feel free to use one of these if it works as a better visual for you.)

The caps and bottles have very similar sizes, so we cannot make comparisons between two caps or between two bottles. The only thing we can do is try to put a cap on a bottle to learn whether the cap is too small, the right size, or too big for the bottle.

To solve the problem, we interact with the judge by making queries and progressively reporting our answer until we are done. (It's kind of like how we interacted with the judge when solving Cave Doors in Chapter 7, but here we communicate with the judge by using input and output rather than by calling functions.)

### Input and Output

Because input and output are interleaved in this problem, we'll look at them together.

To start, we read the integer $n$, which tells us the number of caps and bottles that we must match. $n$ is between 1 and 10,000. The caps are numbered from 1 to $n$, as are the bottles.

After reading $n$, we can interact with the judge in two ways.

**Query** We can make a query by outputting 0 cap_num bottle_num. This asks the judge to tell us about the relationship between the cap numbered cap_num and the bottle numbered bottle_num. We need to read from the input to get the answer to our query. We'll get a −1 if the cap is too small for the bottle, a 0 if it matches the bottle, or a 1 if it's too big for the bottle.

**Report** We can tell the judge part of our answer by outputting 1 cap_num bottle_num, which means that we are matching the cap numbered cap_num with the bottle numbered bottle_num. The judge doesn't produce anything for us to read in response.

We need to eventually make $n$ reports to the judge in order to match each of the $n$ caps with some distinct bottle. We can mix and match queries and reports as we prefer; that is, there's no requirement to make all queries before all reports or anything like that.

We are allowed to make at most 500,000 queries.

## Solving a Subtask

For most problems in this book, we read from standard input, do what the problem asks, and output the answer on standard output. Oftentimes, such as for each problem in the previous chapter, what we read from standard input are operations that tell us what to do next. The interaction for this Caps and Bottles problem is a little different. Rather than being asked to respond to queries, we are the ones making the queries to the judge.

The last time we had a nonstandard interaction with the judge was when we solved Cave Doors in Chapter 7. There, we first solved a small subtask, rather than the whole problem, to give us confidence that we were interacting correctly. Let's start that way here.

The first subtask for this problem guarantees that $n$ will be at most 700. The first algorithm that we come up with might make a lot of queries; the hope is that with only 700 caps and bottles we'll be able to pass at least those test cases.

We need to figure out which bottle goes with each cap. Well, why not go through the caps one by one, and just ask about each bottle for each cap? If we do that, we get the code in Listing 10-7.

```
int main(void) {
  int n, cap_num, bottle_num, result;
❶ scanf("%d", &n);
  for (cap_num = 1; cap_num <= n; cap_num++)
    for (bottle_num = 1; bottle_num <= n; bottle_num++) {
❷     printf("o %d %d\n", cap_num, bottle_num);
❸     scanf("%d", &result);
      if (result == 0) {
❹       printf("1 %d %d\n", cap_num, bottle_num);
        break;
      }
    }
  return 0;
}
```

*Listing 10-7: Solving subtask 1*

Let's make sure we've got the interaction right. We start by reading the value of n ❶, which tells us how many caps and bottles we're dealing with. Then we have a double for loop that considers matching each cap with each bottle. For each such cap-bottle pair, we query the judge ❷. We know that the judge will then produce a response, so we read that next ❸. If we've found a match, we tell the judge about it ❹.

It's a bit of a mind-bend to test this program locally, but let's do it anyway. We need to play the role of the judge, responding consistently to the queries that the program makes.

We'll work through a test case with three caps and bottles. To "play judge," we need to settle on some sizes for the caps and bottles so that we can respond consistently to the queries. The program will never know what these sizes are, but as the judge we need them so that we know whether a cap is too small or too large. Let's agree that the cap sizes are as follows:

| Cap number | 1 | 2 | 3 |
| --- | --- | --- | --- |
| Size | 23 | 85 | 8 |

and that the bottle sizes are as follows:

| Bottle number | 1 | 2 | 3 |
| --- | --- | --- | --- |
| Size | 85 | 23 | 8 |

If the program handles this test case correctly, it will match Cap 1 with Bottle 2, Cap 2 with Bottle 1, and Cap 3 with Bottle 3.

Run our program. Type 3 from the keyboard to indicate that n is 3.

Now the program starts making queries. You'll see those show up as part of the program's output. The first one is 0 1 1, which is asking us for the relationship between Cap 1 and Bottle 1. Cap 1 (size 23) is smaller than Bottle 1 (size 85), so we need to type -1 here. Go ahead—and once you do, we'll be asked another query.

The next query we get is 0 1 2, which asks us about Cap 1 and Bottle 2. This cap and bottle match, so type 0. The program correctly reports that Cap 1 and Bottle 2 are matched.

Now that our program has figured out how to match Cap 1, it should move on to Cap 2. That's exactly what it does, as we can see from the next query: 0 2 1. Cap 2 and Bottle 1 match, so we need to type 0 in response. The program now correctly reports a match between Cap 2 and Bottle 1.

All the program has to figure out now is what to do with Cap 3. It asks the query 0 3 1, to which we must type -1 because Cap 3 is smaller than Bottle 1. Then it asks 0 3 2, and again we type -1. Finally, we get the query 0 3 3; as Cap 3 and Bottle 3 match, we type 0. When we do so, the program should correctly report that Cap 3 is matched with Bottle 3 . . . and we're done! The program has successfully matched the caps and bottles.

If you submit our code to the judge, you should pass a few test cases.

The reason we don't pass more is because of the requirement that we make at most 500,000 queries. We can tell from our nested for loops that we have an $O(n^2)$ algorithm here. With 10,000 caps and bottles, we might make up to $10,000^2 = 100,000,000$ queries. That's way too many! We'll need new ideas to complete the remaining subtasks.

## Solution 1: Recursion

If we stay with our idea of choosing a cap and then figuring out which bottle matches it, we need to make better use of the information that the judge gives us.

### Piles of Caps and Bottles

In the algorithm that we used to solve the subtask, we ask the judge about the relationship between Cap 1 and Bottle 1, Cap 1 and Bottle 2, Cap 1 and Bottle 3, and so on, until we find the bottle that matches Cap 1. Maybe we finally find the match with bottle 5,000. That was a lot of work! For the cost of 5,000 queries, we match one cap and one bottle, and that's all we get. We're back to square one for the next cap.

We're throwing away a lot of information on our way to matching that first cap, though, and that's information we can use to make it easier for us to match other caps later. In particular, so far we're not doing anything with the "too small" and "too big" information that the judge gives us.

If you were doing this by hand, how could you use this information from the judge? One thing you might do is form two piles of bottles: one of small bottles and one of big bottles. suppose we find that Cap 1 is too small for Bottle 1. Throw that bottle into the big pile. Then maybe we find that Cap 1 is too big for Bottle 2. That bottle goes into the small pile. Cap 1 is too big for Bottle 3? That bottle goes into the small pile, as well. Do this for every bottle.

Now what we have are two piles of bottles. Maybe these are subproblems? The hope is that we could solve each subproblem and thereby solve the original problem.

This may feel like the setup to a dynamic-programming solution. But it's not, because the two subproblems are not overlapping. Solving one of them doesn't help us at all with the other one. Recursion, then? Can we use that?

For recursion to work, we need each subproblem to be a smaller version of the original problem. Our original problem had a bunch of caps and bottles. But, so far, our subproblems have only bottles. Where are the caps to go with those bottles? We need to find a way to split the caps into small caps and large caps, too. Once we do that, we'll truly have our two subproblems: one for the small caps and bottles and one for the big caps and bottles.

Here are the overall steps that we'll use.

**Step 1**   Choose a cap for our subproblem.

**Step 2**   Go through the bottles. If the cap is smaller than the bottle, put the bottle in the pile of big bottles; if the cap is bigger than the bottle, put the bottle in the pile of small bottles. At some point during this step, we're going to find the bottle that matches the cap. Call this the *matching bottle*. Report the match between the cap and the matching bottle.

At the end of Step 2, we'll have the two piles of bottles that we need. Now for the caps . . .

**Step 3**    Go through the caps. If the current cap is smaller than the matching bottle, put the cap in the pile of small caps; if the current cap is bigger than the matching bottle, put the cap in the pile of big caps. At the end of this step, we'll have the two piles of caps that we need.

**Step 4**    Recursively solve the subproblem on the small caps and small bottles.

**Step 5**    Recursively solve the subproblem on the big caps and big bottles.

Like binary search, this is an example of a divide and conquer algorithm. We're dividing the caps and bottles into smaller, independent subproblems and then conquering each of those subproblems recursively.

### The main Function

There's a bit of setup we need to do before we can implement our algorithm; let's get that out of the way first. See Listing 10-8 for our main function.

```
#define MAX_N 10000

int main(void) {
  int n, i;
❶ int cap_nums[MAX_N], bottle_nums[MAX_N];
  scanf("%d", &n);
  for (i = 0; i < n; i++) {
❷ cap_nums[i] = i + 1;
❸ bottle_nums[i] = i + 1;
  }
  solve(cap_nums, bottle_nums, n);
  return 0;
}
```

*Listing 10-8: The main function*

There are two important arrays here: cap_nums and bottle_nums ❶. We will initialize these arrays so that they contain all cap numbers ❷ and all bottle numbers ❸, respectively. This is our starting point for the caps and bottles that we're working with. In the code that we'll see next, we'll be making recursive calls on smaller subsets of those caps and bottles.

### Implementing Our Algorithm

Now let's turn our five-step algorithm into code. See Listing 10-9.

```
void *malloc_safe(int size) {
  char *mem = malloc(size);
  if (mem == NULL) {
    fprintf(stderr, "malloc error\n");
    exit(1);
```

```
  }
  return mem;
}

void solve(int cap_nums[], int bottle_nums[], int n) {
  int small_count, big_count, cap_num, i, result, matching_bottle;
  int *small_caps = malloc_safe(n * sizeof(int));
  int *small_bottles = malloc_safe(n * sizeof(int));
  int *big_caps = malloc_safe(n * sizeof(int));
  int *big_bottles = malloc_safe(n * sizeof(int));
  if (n == 0)
    return;

  small_count = 0;
  big_count = 0;

❶ cap_num = cap_nums[0];

❷ for (i = 0; i < n; i++) {
    printf("0 %d %d\n", cap_num, bottle_nums[i]);
    scanf("%d", &result);
  ❸ if (result == 0) {
      printf("1 %d %d\n", cap_num, bottle_nums[i]);
      matching_bottle = bottle_nums[i];
    } else if (result == -1) {
      big_bottles[big_count] = bottle_nums[i];
      big_count++;
    } else {
      small_bottles[small_count] = bottle_nums[i];
      small_count++;
    }
  }

  small_count = 0;
  big_count = 0;
❹ for (i = 0; i < n; i++) {
    printf("0 %d %d\n", cap_nums[i], matching_bottle);
    scanf("%d", &result);
    if (result == -1) {
      small_caps[small_count] = cap_nums[i];
      small_count++;
    } else if (result == 1) {
      big_caps[big_count] = cap_nums[i];
      big_count++;
    }
  }
```

⑤ `solve(small_caps, small_bottles, small_count);`
⑥ `solve(big_caps, big_bottles, big_count);`
`}`

*Listing 10-9: Solution 1*

Prior to our code that implements our five steps, we have some `malloc` calls. We need those so that we have memory for the piles of caps and bottles that we'll form.

For Step 1, we must choose a cap. We can make that easy if we just choose the first cap. Yeah, let's just do that ❶ and move on. Nothing to see here.

For Step 2, we use a `for` loop to go through all of the bottles ❷. For each cap, there are three possibilities for the if statement inside this loop. In the first, we find a match ❸, so we tell the judge about the match and remember the matching bottle for later. In the second, the cap is too small for the bottle, so we throw the bottle into the pile of big bottles. In the third, the cap is too big for the bottle, so we throw the bottle into the pile of small bottles.

Step 3 is similar to Step 2, but this time we go through all of the caps ❹ rather than all of the bottles. If the cap is too small for the bottle, we throw the cap into the pile of small caps. If the cap is too big for the bottle, we throw the cap into the pile of big caps. Be careful not to mix these up! It's easy to mess up a -1 or a 1 and throw caps or bottles in the wrong piles.

For Step 4, we solve the "small caps and small bottles" subproblem with a recursive call ❺.

And finally, for Step 5, we solve the "big caps and big bottles" subproblem through another recursive call ❻.

And that's it! Get the small stuff in one subproblem, get the big stuff in another subproblem, and solve both subproblems recursively. Pretty slick, right? . . . Right?

Unfortunately it isn't quite slick enough. If you submit our code to the judge, you will find that it times out before passing all test cases.

We are very close to nailing this problem, though. All we need to add is randomization. Why is our current solution not quite there? And how will randomization fix it? Those answers are next.

## Solution 2: Adding Randomization

Before we see how to add randomization, let's understand exactly the kind of test case that defeats Solution 1.

### Why Solution 1 Is Slow

Each call of our `solve` function operates on some caps and some bottles. Our choice of cap splits the caps and bottles into two groups: the group with the small caps and bottles and the group with the big caps and bottles. No matter which cap we choose, we get this correct behavior.

That said, the cap we choose does have a major impact on the number of queries that we'll need to solve the problem. The algorithm that we used to solve the subtask (Listing 10-7) was an $O(n^2)$ algorithm, and it was too slow. So to offer an explanation for why Solution 1 is too slow, what we can do is demonstrate that it, too, has test cases on which it takes $O(n^2)$ time.

The test case we'll use may intuitively feel like it should be an easy one. But that intuition is wrong.

As always for this problem, we'll have $n$ caps and $n$ bottles. The sizes of the caps will increase from Cap 1 to Cap $n$. For example, we can say that Cap 1 has size 1, Cap 2 has size 2, Cap 3 has size 3, and so on. Let's do similarly for the bottles: Bottle 1 has size 1, Bottle 2 has size 2, Bottle 3 has size 3, and so on.

Now, what will our Solution 1 algorithm do? On the first call of solve, it will choose Cap 1 on which to split the caps and bottles. It'll loop through the caps, which costs $n$ queries, and then it'll loop through the bottles, which costs another $n$ queries. So that's $2n$ queries so far. And what of our subproblems? Do they have similar sizes or are they very lopsided?

They are lopsided! There are no caps or bottles that are smaller than the chosen cap. So the "smaller caps and bottles" subproblem is empty. The "bigger caps and bottles" subproblem, then, has everything—all remaining $n - 1$ caps and bottles.

What happens on that subproblem with $n - 1$ caps and bottles? Again, we're going to pick the first cap, which is Cap 2 this time. We'll make $n - 1$ queries as we make our way through the first for loop and then another $n - 1$ queries as we make our way through the second loop. That's $2(n - 1)$ queries for this subproblem. And, again, the two subproblems stemming from this one are as lopsided as can be: an empty subproblem and a subproblem with $n - 2$ caps and bottles.

The situation here is very similar to the one on page 307 that clobbered us when we were solving Building Treaps. In each case, we were hoping for a nice, even split of our problem into two subproblems. When we don't get that, we end up doing a quadratic amount of work. Here, we'll make $2n$ queries, then $2(n - 1)$ queries, then $2(n - 2)$ queries, and so on. The total number of queries we'll make is $2(1 + 2 + 3 + \ldots + n)$, which is $O(n^2)$.

Darn! All of that fancy splitting and recursing, and yet we're still stuck at $O(n^2)$.

### What We Will Randomize

In Solution 1, we chose the first cap and split our problem around it. That first cap determines what counts as "small" and "big." As we just saw, if that cap does a poor job of splitting, then our algorithm can be quadratic.

You might wonder whether we can avoid that poor behavior by making a "smarter" choice of cap. Maybe we should have chosen the rightmost cap? Unfortunately not: the test case from the prior subsection would wreck that, too. Maybe we should have chosen the cap in the middle? Sure, but then someone could craft a test case where the middle caps are always the smallest caps. Then we'd be back to quadratic land again.

The best thing to do here is to choose our caps randomly! Each time we need a cap, we'll call rand to get it. If we do that, no test case can reliably cause poor performance because on each run we'll make different choices for how the algorithm executes. This converts our deterministic algorithm into a Las Vegas algorithm.

Contrast this use of randomization with the kind of randomization that we used when solving Yōkan. In Yōkan, the randomization determined whether we got the right answer. In Caps and Bottles, we always get the right answer; the randomization determines how fast we get it.

### Adding the Randomization

We need just two changes to Solution 1. First, we need to add the call of srand to the main function in Listing 10-8, just as we did when solving Yōkan.

Second, we need to choose a random cap in Listing 10-9. Rather than choosing the first cap:

```
cap_num = cap_nums[0];
```

we choose a random one:

```
cap_num = cap_nums[rand() % n];
```

If you make those two changes and submit the updated code to the judge, you should find that it passes all test cases. Randomization has done it again!

Believe it or not, in solving this problem we've also managed to secretly learn one of the most famous algorithms in computer science. Let's go there next.

# Quicksort

The key idea in our solution to Caps and Bottles is to choose a cap and then use that cap to split the problem into two subproblems: one subproblem with the small stuff and the other with the big stuff. This idea most famously powers a sorting algorithm called *Quicksort*.

## *Implementing Quicksort*

Quicksort is one of many algorithms that can be used to sort an array; in practice, it's one of the . . . quickest. In Caps and Bottles, the item that's used to split the problem is a cap; in Quicksort, the value that's used to split the array is called the *pivot*.

The code for Quicksort is similar to the code we used to solve Caps and Bottles. Check it out in Listing 10-10.

```
#define N 10

void *malloc_safe(int size) {
  char *mem = malloc(size);
  if (mem == NULL) {
    fprintf(stderr, "malloc error\n");
    exit(1);
```

```
    }
    return mem;
}

void swap(int *x, int *y) {
    int temp = *x;
    *x = *y;
    *y = temp;
}

void quicksort(int values[], int n) {
    int i, small_count, big_count, pivot_index, pivot;
    int *small_values = malloc_safe(n * sizeof(int));
    int *big_values = malloc_safe(n * sizeof(int));
    if (n == 0)
        return;

    small_count = 0;
    big_count = 0;

❶  pivot_index = rand() % n;
❷  swap(&values[0], &values[pivot_index]);
    pivot = values[0];

❸  for (i = 1; i < n; i++) {
        if (values[i] > pivot) {
            big_values[big_count] = values[i];
            big_count++;
        } else {
            small_values[small_count] = values[i];
            small_count++;
        }
    }

    quicksort(small_values, small_count);
    quicksort(big_values, big_count);

❹  for (i = 0; i < small_count; i++)
        values[i] = small_values[i];
❺  values[small_count] = pivot;
❻  for (i = 0; i < big_count; i++)
        values[small_count + 1 + i] = big_values[i];
}

int main(void) {
    static int values[N] = {96, 61, 36, 74, 45, 60, 47, 6, 95, 93};
    int i;
```

```
  srand((unsigned) time(NULL));

  quicksort(values, N);

  for (i = 0; i < N; i++)
    printf("%d ", values[i]);
  printf("\n");
  return 0;
}
```

*Listing 10-10: Quicksort*

We choose a random pivot index ❶ and move the pivot to the left end of the array ❷. We want the pivot out of the way like that so that we don't lose track of it—we'll need to put it in the correct place later.

Next, we go through all of the other values in the array ❸, adding each to big_values or small_values as appropriate. Once that's done, we make our two recursive calls to sort the small values and sort the big values.

What we want to do next is paste everything together: first the small values, then the pivot, then the big values. We copy the small values to the beginning of the values array ❹, then copy the pivot ❺, then copy the big values ❻.

Next, we'll see why our solution to Caps and Bottles is so fast. While we'll couch our discussion in terms of Caps and Bottles, what we learn about its runtime directly applies to the runtime of Quicksort as well.

### Worst-Case and Expected Runtime

Our solution to Caps and Bottles is a Las Vegas algorithm. The runtime depends on how well each of our randomly chosen caps splits the problem into the two subproblems. If we choose terrible cap after terrible cap, we get $O(n^2)$ runtime. But that's the worst-case behavior; the whole reason we introduced randomization was to make it extremely unlikely that this would actually happen. Rather than focusing on the worst-case runtime of such an algorithm, then, algorithm designers tend to focus on the *expected runtime*, which tells us what we can expect to happen in practice.

What can we expect in practice for our randomized solution to Caps and Bottles? We already know what happens if we're shockingly unlucky: we get $O(n^2)$ performance. What happens if we're shockingly lucky, picking caps that perfectly split each problem in half?

To begin, we'll choose our cap and make our $2n$ queries, as we always do. If that cap perfectly splits the problem in half, then we'll need to work on two subproblems each with $n/2$ caps and bottles. Each of those two subproblems will generate $2n/2 = n$ queries of their own before they in turn recurse. So those two subproblems with $n/2$ caps and bottles will generate $2n$ queries, just like our original problem did.

Now, if each subproblem with $n/2$ caps and bottles is split perfectly, then we get four problems of size $n/4$. Each of those four will generate $2n/4 = n/2$ queries before they recurse, for a total of $2n$ queries.

To summarize, we make $2n$ queries for our original problem of size $n$, $2n$ queries in total for our subproblems of size $n/2$, $2n$ queries in total for our subproblems of size $n/4$, and so on. We can only do this about $\log n$ times before we reach base case subproblems. So, we do $2n$ queries a total of $\log n$ times, for a total of $O(n \log n)$ queries.

Another way to see this $O(n \log n)$ bound is through a *recursion tree*. Such a tree characterizes how much work is done in each call of a recursive function. When we have perfect splits all the way down, our recursion tree looks like the one in Figure 10-1.

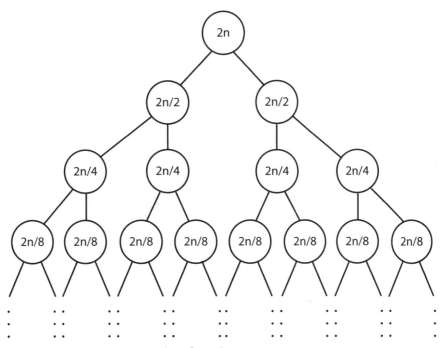

Figure 10-1: A recursion tree with perfect splits

Notice that each node splits into two nodes below, representing the fact that each problem splits into two. The quantity in each node indicates the number of queries that are directly made to solve that subproblem. The $2n$ at the top, for example, means that the initial call makes $2n$ queries. It's not saying that the total number of queries made in the entire algorithm is $2n$, only that the initial call makes $2n$ queries of its own prior to recursing. Notice that each level in this tree—the node at the top, the two nodes below that, and the four nodes below those—make a total of $2n$ queries. If we drew the entire tree, it would have about $\log n$ levels in it. In all, then, we have $O(n \log n)$ queries.

Now, $O(n \log n)$ is a wonderful thing, but all I've argued so far is that this is what happens when the algorithm gets super lucky with perfect splits. The algorithm is generally not going to get this lucky, though, just as it's generally not going to get super unlucky with horrible cap choices.

It turns out that the expected runtime is very close to what is predicted by the super lucky case rather than the super unlucky case. For example, let's imagine that each time we choose a cap, one subproblem will end up with 90 percent of the caps and bottles and the other subproblem will end up with the remaining 10 percent of the caps and bottles. You might consider that pretty unlucky. But even in this case, our algorithm is $O(n \log n)$! Our biggest subproblem would go from size $n$, to size $n/(10/9)$, to size $n/(10/9)^2$, and so on. That is, rather than dividing by 2 each time, we're dividing by $10/9$. How many times do we need to do this to get down to a base case? It's still logarithmic! The base of the log changes—it goes from $\log_2$ to $\log_{10/9}$—but it's still log. Yes: even if we get *this* unlucky, we're still not going to hit $O(n^2)$.

## Summary

When I teach randomization in my algorithms classes, I often have at least a few flummoxed students. "Really, Dan? Picking random numbers? This feels like the kind of thing I would have tried *before* learning about real algorithms." But as I hoped I've demonstrated in this chapter, randomization is no rookie move. Compared to deterministic algorithms, randomized algorithms can be faster and easier to design.

In Chapter 7, I gave this advice: if you see an opportunity to use binary search to solve a problem, just do it. Who cares if there's a slightly more efficient solution that doesn't use binary search. I offer similar advice here: if you see an opportunity to use randomization, and you can tolerate the randomness in correctness or runtime, just do it. Who cares if there's a deterministic algorithm: even if you can come up with one (which may not be easy!), it'll probably be slower in practice anyway.

## Notes

Yōkan is originally from the 2015 Don Mills Programming Gala programming competition, Gold Division. Caps and Bottles is originally from the 2009 Canadian Computing Olympiad.

There's a way to cut down the amount of memory needed by our solution to Caps and Bottles. It's a neat trick that applies to implementations of Quicksort as well. Check it out in "Caps and Bottles: In-Place Sorting" in Appendix B.

For a deep dive into sorting algorithms, I recommend *Compared to What?: An Introduction to the Analysis of Algorithms* by Gregory J.E. Rawlins (1991). It's an oldie but a goodie. There are many sorting algorithms: some of them are slow, some of them are fast; some of them merge sorted pieces, some of them split and sort the pieces. The book compares and contrasts many sorting algorithms. This is also the book that originally introduced me to the Caps and Bottles problem.

# AFTERWORD

I wrote this book to teach you how to think about and design data structures and algorithms. On our way, we studied many durable ideas from computer science. Hash tables free us from expensive linear searches. Trees organize hierarchical data. Recursion solves problems whose solutions involve solving subproblems. Memoization and dynamic programming keep recursion fast even when subproblems overlap. Graphs generalize what is representable by trees. Breadth-first search and Dijkstra's algorithm find shortest paths in graphs; since graphs are so general, "paths" can mean many things. Binary search turns a "solve this" problem into a "check this" problem. Heaps make it fast to find minimum or maximum elements; segment trees do similarly for other kinds of queries. Union-find speeds up graph problems that maintain equivalent sets of nodes. Randomization makes it easier to design fast algorithms and protects us from worst-case test cases. That's quite the list, and I hope you're pleased with what you've learned. I also hope that I've helped you dig into why these data structures and algorithms are useful, why they work so well, and what we can learn from their design.

I wrote this book to motivate you to think about and design data structures and algorithms. I used programming problems that I hope you found intriguing (so that you'd want to solve them) and challenging (so that you'd have to learn how to solve them). Perhaps you're motivated by the problems themselves. Perhaps you're motivated by the ways that computer scientists pose and solve problems. Perhaps you're itching to solve problems that are personally meaningful to you. Whatever the case, I hope that I've helped you develop your skills and motivation to pursue what matters.

One nice thing about programming problems like those in this book is that they wait patiently for us to solve them. They don't change. They don't adapt—but we do. When we're stuck on a problem, we can go away, learn new things, and come back to try again. Real-world problems certainly aren't going to present to us their precise inputs and outputs. Some of their features may change over time. It's up to us to find out in what ways these problems wait patiently, too.

I wrote this book to teach. Thank you for trusting me and making time to read through what I had to say.

# A

## ALGORITHM RUNTIME

 Each competitive programming problem that we solve in this book specifies a time limit on how long our program will be allowed to run. If our program exceeds the time limit, then the judge terminates our program with a "Time-Limit Exceeded" error. A time limit is designed to prevent algorithmically naive solutions from passing the test cases. The problem author has some model solutions in mind and sets the time limit as an arbiter of whether we have demonstrated those solution ideas. As such, in addition to being correct, we need our programs to be fast.

### The Case for Timing...and Something Else

Most books on algorithms do not use time limits when discussing runtime. Time limits and execution times do, however, appear frequently in this book. The primary reason is that such times can give us intuitive understanding of the efficiency of our programs. We can run a program and measure how long it takes. If our program is too slow, according to the time limit for the problem, then we know that we need to optimize the current code or find a wholly new approach. We don't know what kind of computer the judge is using, but running the program on our own computer is still informative. Say that we run our program on our laptop and it takes 30 seconds on some small test case. If the problem time limit is three seconds, we can be confident that our program is simply not fast enough.

An exclusive focus on execution times, however, is limiting. Here are five reasons why:

**Execution time depends on the computer.**   As just suggested, timing our program tells us only how long our program takes on one computer. That's very specific information, and it gives us little in the way of understanding what to expect when it is run on other computers. When working through the book, you may also notice that the time taken by a program varies from run to run, even on the same computer. For example, you might run a program on a test case and find that it takes 3 seconds; you might then run it again, on the same test case, and find that it takes 2.5 seconds or 3.5 seconds. The reason for this difference is that your operating system is managing your computing resources, shunting them around to different tasks as needed. The decisions that your operating system makes influence the runtime of your program.

**Execution time depends on the test case.**   Timing our program on a test case tells us only how long our program takes on that test case. Suppose that our program takes one second to run on a small test case. That may seem fast, but here's the truth about small test cases: every reasonable solution for a problem will be able to solve those. If I ask you to sort a few numbers, or optimally schedule a few events, or whatever, you can quickly do it with the first correct idea that you have. What's interesting, then, are large test cases. They are the ones where algorithmic ingenuity pays off. How long will our program take on a large test case or on a huge test case? We don't know. We'd have to run our program on those test cases, too. Even if we did that, there could be specific kinds of test cases that trigger poorer performance. We may be led to believe that our program is faster than it is.

**The program requires implementation.**   We can't time something that we don't implement. Suppose that we're thinking about a problem and come up with an idea for how to solve it. Is it fast? Although we could implement it to find out, it would be nice to know, in advance, whether or not the idea is likely to lead to a fast program. You would not implement a program that you knew, at the outset, would be incorrect. It would similarly be nice to know, at the outset, that a program would be too slow.

**Timing doesn't explain slowness.**   If we find that our program is too slow, then our next task is to design a faster one. However, simply timing a program gives us no insight into why our program is slow. It just is. Further, if we manage to think up a possible improvement to our program, we'd need to implement it to see whether or not it helps.

**Execution time is not easily communicated.** For many of the reasons above, it's difficult to use execution time to talk to other people about the efficiency of algorithms. "My program takes two seconds to run on this computer that I bought last year, on a test case with eight chickens and four eggs, using a program that I wrote in C. How about yours?"

Not to worry: computer scientists have devised a notation that addresses these shortcomings of timing. It's independent of the computer, independent of test case, and independent of a particular implementation. It signals why a slow program is slow. It's easily communicated. It's called *big O*, and it's coming right up.

# Big O Notation

Big O is a notation that computer scientists use to concisely describe the efficiency of algorithms. It assigns each algorithm to one of a small number of efficiency classes. An efficiency class tells you how fast an algorithm is or, equivalently, how much work it does. The faster an algorithm, the less work it does; the slower an algorithm, the more work it does. Each algorithm belongs to an efficiency class; the efficiency class tells you how much work that algorithm does relative to the amount of input that it must process. To understand big O, we need to understand these efficiency classes. I'll introduce three of them here: linear time, constant time, and quadratic time.

## Linear Time

Suppose that we are provided an array of integers in increasing order, and we want to return its maximum integer. For example, given the array

```
[1, 3, 8, 10, 21]
```

we want to return 21.

One way to do this is to keep track of the maximum value that we have found so far. Whenever we find a larger value than the maximum, we update the maximum. Listing A-1 implements this idea.

```
int find_max(int nums[], int n) {
  int i, max;
  max = nums[0];
  for (i = 0; i < n; i++)
    if (nums[i] > max)
      max = nums[i];
  return max;
}
```

*Listing A-1: Finding the maximum in an array of increasing integers*

The code sets max to the value at index 0 of nums, and then loops through the array, looking for larger values. Don't worry that the first iteration of the loop compares max to itself: that's just one iteration of unnecessary work.

Rather than timing specific test cases, let's think about the amount of work that this algorithm does as a function of the size of the array. Suppose that the array has five elements. What does our program do? It performs one variable assignment above the loop, then iterates five times in the loop, and then returns the result. If the array has 10 elements, then our program does similarly, except now it iterates 10 times in the loop rather than 5. What about a million elements? Our program iterates a million times. Now we see that the assignment above the loop and return below the loop pale in comparison to the amount of work done by the loop. What matters, especially as the test case gets large, is the number of iterations of the loop.

If our array has $n$ elements, then the loop iterates $n$ times. In big O notation, we say that this algorithm is $O(n)$. Interpret this as follows: for an array of $n$ elements, the algorithm does work proportional to $n$. An $O(n)$ algorithm is called a *linear-time algorithm* because there is a linear relationship between the problem size and the amount of work done. If we double the problem size, then we double the work done and thereby double the runtime. For example, if it takes one second to run on an array with two million elements, we can expect it to take about two seconds to run on an array of four million elements.

Notice that we didn't have to run the code to arrive at this insight. We didn't even have to write the code out. (Well . . . yeah, I did write the code, but that was just to make the algorithm clear.) Saying that an algorithm is $O(n)$ offers us the fundamental relationship between the problem size and the growth in runtime. It's true no matter what computer we use or which test case we look at.

### Constant Time

We know something about our arrays that we didn't exploit yet: that the integers are in increasing order. The biggest integer will therefore be found at the end of the array. Let's just return that directly, rather than eventually finding it through an exhaustive search of the array. Listing A-2 presents this new idea.

```
int find_max(int nums[], int n) {
  return nums[n - 1];
}
```

Listing A-2: Finding the maximum in an array of increasing integers

How much work does this algorithm do as a function of the size of the array? Interestingly, array size no longer matters! The algorithm accesses and returns nums[n - 1], the final element of the array, no matter if it has 5 elements or 10 or a million. The algorithm doesn't care. In big O notation, we say that this algorithm is $O(1)$. It's called a *constant-time algorithm* because the amount of work it does is constant, not increasing as the problem size increases.

This is the best kind of algorithm. No matter how large our array, we can expect about the same runtime. It's surely better than a linear-time algorithm, which gets slower as the problem size increases. Not many interesting problems can be solved by constant-time algorithms, though. For example, if we were given the array in arbitrary order, rather than increasing order, then constant-time algorithms are out. There's no way we could look at a fixed number of array elements and hope to be guaranteed to find the maximum.

## Another Example

Consider the algorithm in Listing A-3: is it $O(n)$ or $O(1)$ or something else? (Notice that I've left out the function and variable definitions so that we're not tempted to compile and run this.)

```
total = 0;
for (i = 0; i < n; i++)
  total = total + nums[i];
for (i = 0; i < n; i++)
  total = total + nums[i];
```

Listing A-3: What kind of algorithm is this?

Suppose that array nums has $n$ elements. The first loop iterates $n$ times, and the second loop iterates $n$ times. That's $2n$ iterations in total. As a first attempt, it's natural to say that this algorithm is $O(2n)$. While saying that is technically true, computer scientists would ignore the 2, simply writing $O(n)$.

This may seem weird, since this algorithm is twice as slow as the one in Listing A-1, yet we declare both to be $O(n)$. The reason comes down to a balancing act between simplicity and expressiveness of our notation. If we kept the 2, then we'd perhaps be more accurate, but we'd obscure the fact that this is a linear-time algorithm. Whether it's $2n$ or $3n$ or anything times $n$, it's fundamental linear runtime growth does not change.

## Quadratic Time

We have now seen linear-time algorithms (which are very fast in practice) and constant-time algorithms (which are even faster than linear-time algorithms). Now let's look at something slower than linear time. The code is in Listing A-4.

```
total = 0;
for (i = 0; i < n; i++)
  for (j = 0; j < n; j++)
    total = total + nums[j];
```

Listing A-4: A quadratic-time algorithm

Compared to Listing A-3, notice that the loops are now nested rather than sequential. Each iteration of the outer loop causes $n$ iterations of the inner loop. The outer loop iterates $n$ times. Therefore, the total number of iterations for the inner loop, and the number of times that we update total, is $n^2$. (The first iteration of the outer loop costs $n$ work, the second costs $n$ work, the third costs $n$ work, and so on. The total is $n + n + n + \ldots + n$, where the number of times we add $n$ is $n$.)

In big O notation, we say that this algorithm is $O(n^2)$. It's called a *quadratic-time algorithm* because quadratic is the mathematical term referring to a power of 2.

Let's now probe why quadratic-time algorithms are slower than linear-time algorithms. Suppose that we have a quadratic-time algorithm that takes $n^2$ steps. On a problem size of 5, it would take $5^2 = 25$ steps; on a problem size of 10, it would take $10^2 = 100$ steps; and on a problem size of 20, it would take $20^2 = 400$ steps. Notice what's happening when we double the problem size: the work done *quadruples*. That's far worse than linear-time algorithms, where doubling the problem size leads to only a doubling of work done.

Don't be surprised that an algorithm that takes $2n^2$ steps, $3n^2$ steps, and so on is also classified as a quadratic-time algorithm. The big O notation hides what's in front of the $n^2$ term, just as it hides what's in front of the $n$ term in a linear-time algorithm.

What if we have an algorithm that we find takes $2n^2 + 6n$ steps? This, too, is a quadratic-time algorithm. We're taking a quadratic runtime of $2n^2$ and adding a linear runtime of $6n$ to it. The result is still a quadratic-time algorithm: the quadrupling behavior of the quadratic part quickly comes to dominate the doubling behavior of the linear part.

## Big O in This Book

There's much more that can be said about big O. It has a formal mathematical basis used by computer scientists to rigorously analyze the runtime of their algorithms. There are other efficiency classes besides the three that I've introduced here (and I'll introduce the few others that appear in this book as needed). There is certainly more to learn if you are interested in going further, but what I've presented here is enough for our purposes.

Big O generally arises in this book on an as-needed basis. We may pursue an initial solution for a problem, only to find that we get a "Time-Limit Exceeded" error from the judge. In those cases, we need to understand where we went wrong, and the first step in such an analysis is to appreciate the way that our runtime grows as a function of problem size. A big O analysis not only confirms that slow code is slow, but it often uncovers the particular bottlenecks in our code. We can then use that enhanced understanding to design a more efficient solution.

# B

## BECAUSE I CAN'T RESIST

In this appendix, I include additional material related to some of the problems studied in this book. I consider this appendix as optional: it doesn't concern material that I think is core to the goal of learning about data structures and algorithms. However, if you're keen to learn more about a problem, this appendix is for you.

### Unique Snowflakes: Implicit Linked Lists

It's often the case that at compile time we don't know how much memory our program will need. If you've ever asked, "How big should I make this array?" or "Will this array be big enough?" then you've experienced first-hand the inflexibility of C arrays: we have to choose an array size, but we might not know the size we need until the array starts filling up. In many such cases, linked lists neatly solve the problem. Whenever we require new memory to store some data, we just call malloc at runtime to add a node to a linked list.

In the first problem in Chapter 1, Unique Snowflakes, we used linked lists to chain together the snowflakes that reside in the same bucket. For every snowflake that we read in, we used malloc to allocate memory for exactly one snowflake. If we read 5,000 snowflakes, we'll have made 5,000 `malloc` calls. The time taken by these `malloc` calls can add up.

Wait! We just said that linked lists are useful when we don't know how much memory we might need. In Unique Snowflakes, we *do* know! Or, at least, we know the *maximum* that we'll need: it's whatever is required to store at most 100,000 snowflakes.

That raises questions. Why are we using `malloc`, anyway? Is there a way to avoid using `malloc` and linked lists? Indeed, we can solve Unique Snowflakes in a way that doesn't use `malloc` and leads to a doubling of speed. How?

The key idea is to preallocate an array of the maximum number of nodes (100,000) that we might use. The array is called `nodes`, and it stores the nodes from all of the (now-implicit) linked lists. Each element of `nodes` is an integer giving the index of the next node in its list of nodes. Let's get a handle on this by deciphering a sample `nodes` array:

```
[-1, 0, -1, 1, 2, 4, 5]
```

Suppose we know that one of the lists starts at index 6. The value of index 6, 5, tells us that index 5 is the next node in the list. Similarly, index 5 tells us that index 4 is the next node in the list. Index 4 tells us that index 2 is the next node in the list. What about index 2, with the value of -1? We'll use -1 as our `NULL` value: it indicates that there's no "next" element. We have discovered the list of indices 6, 5, 4, and 2.

There's one more nonempty list in that array. Suppose we know this list starts at index 3. Index 3 tells us that index 1 is the next node in the list. Index 1 tells us that index 0 is the next node in the list. That's all then— index 0 is a -1, so the list is over. We have discovered the list of indices 3, 1, and 0.

That's the `nodes` array. If some index has a value of -1, then it's the end of a list. Otherwise, it gives the index of the next element in the list.

Notice that `nodes` doesn't tell us anything about where the lists start. We had to assume that we somehow knew that the list heads were at indices 6 and 3. How could we have known that? By using another array, `heads`, that gives the index of the first node in a list. `heads` uses -1 for the value of any element that does not start a list.

Our `malloc`-less solution uses a total of three arrays in the `main` function: `snowflakes`, `nodes`, and `heads`. The `snowflakes` array stores the actual snowflakes so that we can look up a snowflake according to the indices in `nodes` and `heads`. Here are the three arrays:

```
static int snowflakes[SIZE][6];
static int heads[SIZE];
static int nodes[SIZE];
```

Only two of our functions must be adjusted to move from linked lists to the implicit lists that we use here: `identify_identical` and `main`. These adjustments are about syntax, not substance: `identify_identical` still performs pairwise comparisons of all snowflakes in a list, and `main` still reads in the snowflakes and builds the lists.

The new `identify_identical` is in Listing B-1—compare this to what we had before in Listing 1-12!

```
void identify_identical(int snowflakes[][6], int heads[],
                        int nodes[]) {
  int i, node1, node2;
  for (i = 0; i < SIZE; i++) {
    node1 = heads[i];
    while (node1 != -1) {
  ❶ node2 = nodes[node1];
      while (node2 != -1) {
        if (are_identical(snowflakes[node1], snowflakes[node2])) {
          printf("Twin snowflakes found.\n");
          return;
        }
      ❷ node2 = nodes[node2];
      }
    ❸ node1 = nodes[node1];
    }
  }
  printf("No two snowflakes are alike.\n");
}
```

*Listing B-1: Identifying identical snowflakes in implicit linked lists*

Inside the for loop, node1 is set to the head of the current list. If this list is empty, then the outer while loop won't run at all for this node. If it isn't empty, then, by using the nodes array, node2 is set to the node after node1 ❶. Rather than linked-list code like node2 = node2->next, we again use the nodes array to find the next node ❷ ❸.

The new main function is given in Listing B-2.

```
int main(void) {
  static int snowflakes[SIZE][6];
  static int heads[SIZE];
  static int nodes[SIZE];
  int n;
  int i, j, snowflake_code;
  for (i = 0; i < SIZE; i++) {
    heads[i] = -1;
    nodes[i] = -1;
  }
  scanf("%d", &n);
  for (i = 0; i < n; i++) {
    for (j = 0; j < 6; j++)
      scanf("%d", &snowflakes[i][j]);
    snowflake_code = code(snowflakes[i]);
  ❶ nodes[i] = heads[snowflake_code];
  ❷ heads[snowflake_code] = i;
```

```
    }
    identify_identical(snowflakes, heads, nodes);
    return 0;
}
```

*Listing B-2: The main function for implicit linked lists*

Suppose we have just read a snowflake and we have stored it in row i of snowflakes. We want this snowflake to become the head of its list. To accomplish this, we store the old list head at nodes[i] ❶, and then we set the head of the list to be snowflake i ❷.

Take some time to compare this solution to our linked-list solution. Which do you prefer? Is the malloc-less solution harder or easier for you to understand? Submit both to the judge; is the speedup worth it?

## Burger Fervor: Reconstructing a Solution

In Chapter 3, we solved three problems—Burger Fervor, Moneygrubbers, and Hockey Rivalry—that involved minimizing or maximizing the value of a solution. In Burger Fervor, we maximized Homer's time spent eating burgers; we gave an answer such as 2 2, meaning two burgers and two minutes drinking beer. In Moneygrubbers, we minimized the amount of money required to purchase apples; we gave an answer such as Buy 3 for $3.00. In Hockey Rivalry, we maximized the number of goals in rivalry games; we gave an answer such as 20.

Notice, though, that what we are doing here is giving the *value* of an optimal solution. We are not giving the optimal solution itself. We are not indicating which burgers to eat, or how to purchase the apples, or which games are the rivalry games.

The vast majority of optimization problems in competitive programming ask for the value of an optimal solution, which was the focus in Chapters 3 and 4. However, we can, if we like, use memoization and dynamic programming to return an optimal solution itself.

Let's see how this is done using Burger Fervor as an example. Given the following test case:

```
4 9 15
```

let's output not only the value of an optimal solution, but an optimal solution itself, like this:

```
2 2
Eat a 4-minute burger
Eat a 9-minute burger
```

The first line is what we had before; the other lines constitute an optimal solution itself, proof that the 2 2 is indeed achievable.

Outputting an optimal solution like this is known as *reconstructing* or *recovering* a solution. Both of these words suggest that we already have the pieces that can be put together to produce the optimal solution. And that's true: what we need is sitting right there in the memo or dp array. Here, let's use the dp array; the memo array could be used in precisely the same way.

We're going to write the body for this function signature:

```
void reconstruct(int m, int n, int dp[], int minutes)
```

Recall that we have $m$-minute and $n$-minute burgers. The m and n parameters are these values and come from the current test case. The dp parameter is the array that is produced by the dynamic-programming algorithm in Listing 3-8. Finally, the minutes parameter is the number of minutes spent eating burgers. The function will print, one per line, the number of burgers that should be eaten in an optimal solution.

What is the last burger that Homer should eat in an optimal solution? If we were solving this problem from scratch, then we wouldn't know this answer. We'd have to see what happens if we choose an $m$-minute burger to be last and also see what happens if we choose an $n$-minute burger to be last. Indeed, that's what we did when solving this problem in Chapter 3. Remember, though, that we now have the dp array at our disposal. That array is going to tell us which of the two options is the best.

Here's the key idea: take a look at dp[minutes - m] and dp[minutes - n]. Both of those values are available to us, because the dp array has already been constructed. Whichever of these values is larger tells us what we should use as the last burger. That is, if dp[minutes - m] is larger, then an $m$-minute burger is last; if dp[minutes - n] is larger, then an $n$-minute burger is last. (If dp[minutes - m] and dp[minutes - n] are equal, then you can choose arbitrarily whether to make the last burger an $m$-minute or $n$-minute burger.)

This reasoning parallels that used in Listing 3-8 to build the dp array. There, we chose the maximum of first and second; here, we reverse engineer which of those choices the dynamic-programming algorithm made.

Once we have deduced the final burger, we remove the time taken to eat that burger and then repeat the process. We keep going until we get down to zero minutes, at which point our reconstruction is complete. Listing B-3 gives the code for the function.

```
void reconstruct(int m, int n, int dp[], int minutes) {
  int first, second;
  while (minutes > 0) {
    first = -1;
    second = -1;
    if (minutes >= m)
      first = dp[minutes - m];
    if (minutes >= n)
      second = dp[minutes - n];
    if (first >= second) {
      printf("Eat a %d-minute burger\n", m);
      minutes = minutes - m;
    } else {
      printf("Eat a %d-minute burger\n", n);
```

```
        minutes = minutes - n;
      }
    }
}
```

*Listing B-3: Reconstructing the solution*

This function should be called in two places in Listing 3-8, once after each `printf` call. The first is:

```
reconstruct(m, n, dp, t);
```

The second is:

```
reconstruct(m, n, dp, i);
```

I encourage you to reconstruct optimal solutions for the Moneygrubbers and Hockey Rivalry problems, following this same style.

## Knight Chase: Encoding Moves

In the Knight Chase problem of Chapter 5, we designed a BFS algorithm to find the number of moves needed for a knight to reach each square from its starting point. The knight has eight possible moves, and we wrote each of them out in our code (see Listing 5-1). For example, here's what we did to have the knight explore moving up one and right two:

```
add_position(from_row, from_col, from_row + 1, from_col + 2,
             num_rows, num_cols, new_positions,
             &num_new_positions, min_moves);
```

Here's what we did for up one and left two:

```
add_position(from_row, from_col, from_row + 1, from_col - 2,
             num_rows, num_cols, new_positions,
             &num_new_positions, min_moves);
```

There is gross code duplication there: the only change is a plus sign to a minus sign! In fact, all eight moves are encoded in a very similar way, just messing around with some pluses and minuses and 1s and 2s. That kind of thing is quite error-prone.

Fortunately, there is a neat technique to dodge this kind of code duplication. It applies to many problems where you're asked to explore an implicit graph of multiple dimensions (such as rows and columns).

Here are the knight's eight possible moves, as presented in the problem description in Chapter 5:

- Up 1, right 2
- Up 1, left 2
- Down 1, right 2

- Down 1, left 2
- Up 2, right 1
- Up 2, left 1
- Down 2, right 1
- Down 2, left 1

Let's first focus on the rows and write down how each move changes the row number. The first move increases the row number by one, as does the second move. The third and fourth moves, by contrast, reduce the row number by one. The fifth and sixth moves increase the row number by two, and the seventh and eighth moves reduce the row number by two. Here's an array of those numbers:

```
int row_dif[8] = {1, 1, -1, -1, 2, 2, -2, -2};
```

It's called row_dif because it gives the difference in row numbers between the current row and the row after making a move.

Now let's do the same thing for the columns. The first move increases the column number by two, the second move decreases the column number by two, and so on. As an array, the column differences are:

```
int col_dif[8] = {2, -2, 2, -2, 1, -1, 1, -1};
```

What's useful about these two parallel arrays is that they characterize the effect that each move has on the current row and column. The numbers in row_dif[0] and col_dif[0] tell you that the first move increases the row by one and increases the column by two, those in row_dif[1] and col_dif[1] tell you that the second move increases the row by one and decreases the column by two, and so on.

Now, instead of typing out eight near-identical calls to add_position, we can use a loop of eight iterations, typing out just one call to add_position in there. Here's how it's done, using a new integer variable m to loop through the moves:

```
for (m = 0; m < 8; m++)
  add_position(from_row, from_col,
            from_row + row_dif[m], from_col + col_dif[m],
            num_rows, num_cols, new_positions,
            &num_new_positions, min_moves);
```

That's better! Update your Knight Chase code from Chapter 5 and give it a go with the judge. You should still pass all of the test cases and your code shouldn't be noticeably faster or slower, but you've shaved off quite a bit of repetitive code, and that's a win.

We had only eight moves here, so we managed to survive Knight Chase in Chapter 5 without using this encoding trick. However, if we had many more moves than this, then pasting the call to add_position over and over simply wouldn't be feasible. What we've seen here scales much more nicely.

# Dijkstra's Algorithm: Using a Heap

In Chapter 6, we learned Dijkstra's algorithm for finding shortest paths in weighted graphs. The runtime of our Dijkstra implementation was $O(n^2)$, where $n$ is the number of nodes in the graph. Dijkstra's algorithm spends a lot of its time searching for minimums: on each iteration, it has to find the node whose distance is minimum of all nodes that are not done.

Then, in Chapter 8, we learned about max-heaps and min-heaps. A max-heap won't help here—but a min-heap will, because its job is to quickly find the minimum. We can therefore use a min-heap to speed up Dijkstra's algorithm. This is a match made in computer-science heaven.

The min-heap will hold all of the nodes that have been discovered and that are not done. It might also hold some discovered nodes that *are* done. That's okay, though: as we did when solving the Supermarket Promotion problem with heaps in Chapter 8, we'll just ignore any done node that happens to come off the min-heap.

## Mice Maze: Tracing with Heaps

Let's enhance our solution to the Mice Maze problem from Chapter 6 to use a min-heap. Here's the graph that we used there (Figure 6-1):

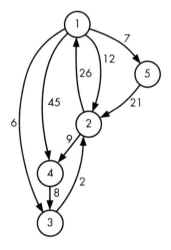

In Chapter 6, we traced Dijkstra's algorithm starting from Node 1. Let's do that again, this time using a min-heap. Each heap element will consist of a node and a time necessary to reach that node. We'll see that there can be multiple occurrences of the same node on the heap. However, because it's a min-heap, we'll be able to process each node using only its minimum time.

In each min-heap snapshot that follows, I've arranged the rows in the same order as they'd be stored in the heap array.

We start with only Node 1 in the heap, with a time of 0. We have no time information for other nodes. We therefore have this snapshot:

Min-heap

| node | time |
|------|------|
| 1 | 0 |

Rest of State

| node | done | min_time |
|------|------|----------|
| 1 | false | 0 |
| 2 | false | |
| 3 | false | |
| 4 | false | |
| 5 | false | |

Extracting from the min-heap gives us its sole element, Node 1. We then process Node 1 to update the shortest paths to Nodes 2, 3, 4, and 5 and place these nodes on the min-heap. Here's our state now:

Min-heap

| node | time |
|------|------|
| 3 | 6 |
| 2 | 12 |
| 5 | 7 |
| 4 | 45 |

Rest of State

| node | done | min_time |
|------|------|----------|
| 1 | true | 0 |
| 2 | false | 12 |
| 3 | false | 6 |
| 4 | false | 45 |
| 5 | false | 7 |

Node 3 is next out of the min-heap and gives us a shorter path to Node 2. We therefore add another occurrence of Node 2 to the heap, this one with a shorter path than before. Here's what we've got now:

Min-heap

| node | time |
|------|------|
| 5 | 7 |
| 2 | 8 |
| 4 | 45 |
| 2 | 12 |

Rest of State

| node | done | min_time |
|------|------|----------|
| 1 | true | 0 |
| 2 | false | 8 |
| 3 | true | 6 |
| 4 | false | 45 |
| 5 | false | 7 |

Next out is Node 5. It doesn't lead to any shortest-path updates, so nothing new gets added to the heap. Here's where we are:

Min-heap

| node | time |
|------|------|
| 2 | 8 |
| 2 | 12 |
| 4 | 45 |

Rest of State

| node | done | min_time |
|------|------|----------|
| 1 | true | 0 |
| 2 | false | 8 |
| 3 | true | 6 |
| 4 | false | 45 |
| 5 | true | 7 |

Node 2 is next out of the min-heap—specifically the one with 8 time, not the one with 12 time! It leads to an update of Node 4's shortest path, and consequently a new occurrence of Node 4 on the min-heap. Here's the result:

Min-heap

| node | time |
|------|------|
| 2 | 12 |
| 4 | 45 |
| 4 | 17 |

Rest of State

| node | done | min_time |
|------|------|----------|
| 1 | true | 0 |
| 2 | true | 8 |
| 3 | true | 6 |
| 4 | false | 17 |
| 5 | true | 7 |

The next node to come out of the min-heap is Node 2. Again! Node 2 is already done, so we simply extract it from the heap and do nothing else. We certainly don't process this node again. Here's what's left:

Min-heap

| cell | time |
|------|------|
| 4 | 17 |
| 4 | 45 |

Rest of State

| node | done | min_time |
|------|------|----------|
| 1 | true | 0 |
| 2 | true | 8 |
| 3 | true | 6 |
| 4 | false | 17 |
| 5 | true | 7 |

The two occurrences of Node 4 will be extracted from the min-heap in turn. The first Node 4 won't lead to any shortest-path updates—all other nodes are done—but will set Node 4 to done. The second Node 4 will therefore be skipped.

In most textbook heap-based implementations of Dijkstra's algorithm, it is assumed that there's a way to decrease the shortest-path distance of a node in a heap. That way, a node can be updated in the heap, and there's no need to have multiple occurrences of a node hanging around. The heaps that we developed in Chapter 8, though, don't support such a "decrease" operation. Rest assured that what we're doing here, with the insertions instead of updates, has the same worst-case time complexity. Which is what, exactly?

Let's use $n$ to represent the number of nodes in the graph and $m$ the number of edges. We process each edge $u \to v$ at most once, when $u$ is extracted from the heap. Each edge can lead to at most one insertion into the heap, so we insert at most $m$ elements. The biggest the heap could ever get, then, is size $m$. We can only extract what's been inserted, so there are at most $m$ extractions. That's $2m$ heap operations in all, each of which takes at most $\log m$ time. Therefore, we have an $O(m \log m)$ algorithm.

Compare this to the $O(n^2)$ implementation from Chapter 6. The heap-based implementation is a clear win when the number of edges is small in relation to $n^2$. For example, if there are $n$ edges, then the heap-based implementation is $O(n \log n)$, which blows away the $O(n^2)$ runtime in Chapter 6. If the number of edges is large, then it matters less which implementation we use. For example, if there are $n^2$ edges, then the heap-based implementation is $O(n^2 \log n)$, which is competitive with, but a little slower than, $O(n^2)$. If you don't know in advance whether your graph will have few or many edges, using a heap is a safe bet: the only cost is the extra $\log n$ factor on graphs with many edges, but that's a small price to pay in exchange for much better performance on graphs with few edges.

## Mice Maze: Implementation with Heaps

Now let's solve Mice Maze using heaps. We use this struct for the heap elements:

```
typedef struct heap_element {
  int cell;
  int time;
} heap_element;
```

I won't replicate the min-heap insertion code (Listing 8-5) or extraction code (Listing 8-6) here. The only change is to compare time rather than cost; I'll leave that to you.

The main function is the same as it was in Chapter 6 (Listing 6-1). All we need is a replacement of find_time (Listing 6-2) to use a min-heap instead of linear searches. That code is given in Listing B-4.

```
int find_time(edge *adj_list[], int num_cells,
              int from_cell, int exit_cell) {
  static int done[MAX_CELLS + 1];
  static int min_times[MAX_CELLS + 1];
❶ static heap_element min_heap[MAX_CELLS * MAX_CELLS + 1];
  int i;
  int min_time, min_time_index, old_time;
  edge *e;
  int num_min_heap = 0;
  for (i = 1; i <= num_cells; i++) {
    done[i] = 0;
    min_times[i] = -1;
  }
  min_times[from_cell] = 0;
  min_heap_insert(min_heap, &num_min_heap, from_cell, 0);

❷ while (num_min_heap > 0) {
    min_time_index = min_heap_extract(min_heap, &num_min_heap).cell;
    if (done[min_time_index])
❸    continue;
    min_time = min_times[min_time_index];
```

```
        done[min_time_index] = 1;

    e = adj_list[min_time_index];
❹ while (e) {
        old_time = min_times[e->to_cell];
        if (old_time == -1 || old_time> min_time + e->length) {
            min_times[e->to_cell] = min_time + e->length;
❺ min_heap_insert(min_heap, &num_min_heap,
                e->to_cell, min_time + e->length);
        }
        e = e->next;
    }
  }
  return min_times[exit_cell];
}
```

*Listing B-4: Shortest path to exit using Dijkstra's algorithm and heaps*

Each cell can result in at most MAX_CELLS elements added to the min-heap, and there are at most MAX_CELLS. We're safe from overflowing the min-heap, then, if we allocate space for MAX_CELLS * MAX_CELLS elements plus one, since we index starting at 1 rather than 0 ❶.

The main while loop continues as long as there's something in the min-heap ❷. If the node that we extract from the min-heap is already done, then we don't do anything on its iteration ❸. Otherwise, we process the outgoing edges as usual ❹, adding nodes to the min-heap when shorter paths are found ❺.

## Compressing Path Compression

In Chapter 9, you learned about path compression, an optimization to the tree-based union-find data structure. We saw its code in the context of the Social Network problem in Listing 9-8. Written like that, with the two while loops, is not how you'll see the code in practice.

I generally don't like to dwell on opaque code—and I hope I haven't presented you with any such code in the book—but I'll make an exception here, because you may at some point run into a particularly dense, one-line implementation of path compression. It's presented in Listing B-5.

```
int find(int p, int parent[]) {
  return p == parent[p] ? p : (parent[p] = find(parent[p], parent));
}
```

*Listing B-5: Path compression in practice*

I changed person to p to get the code on one line (since readability is already shot, why not?).

There's a lot going on here: the ? : ternary if operator, using the result of the = assignment operator, and even recursion. We're going to unravel this in three steps.

## Step 1: No More Ternary If

The ? : operator is a form of if–else that returns a value. Programmers use it when they want to save space and jam an entire if statement on one line. A quick example looks like this:

```
return x >= 10 ? "big" : "small";
```

If x is greater than or equal to 10, "big" is returned; otherwise, "small" is returned.

The ? : operator is called a *ternary* operator because it takes three operands: the first expression is the boolean expression whose truth we are testing, the second expression is the result when the first expression is true, and the third is the result when the first expression is false.

Let's rewrite Listing B-5 to use a standard if...else statement rather than the ternary if:

```
int find(int p, int parent[]) {
  if (p == parent[p])
    return p;
  else
    return parent[p] = find(parent[p], parent);
}
```

That's a little better. Now we explicitly see that the code has two paths: one if p is already the root and the other if p is not the root.

## Step 2: Cleaner Assignment Operator

What do you think this code snippet does?

```
int x;
printf("%d\n", x = 5);
```

The answer is that it prints 5! You know that x = 5 assigns 5 to x, but it's also an expression whose value is 5. That's right: = assigns a value, but it also returns the value that it stored in the variable. It's also why we can do

```
a = b = c = 5;
```

to assign the same value to multiple variables.

In the path-compression code, we have a return statement and an assignment statement on the same line. That line both assigns a value to parent[p] and returns that value. Let's split those two actions out:

```
int find(int p, int parent[]) {
  int community;
  if (p == parent[p])
    return p;
  else {
    community = find(parent[p], parent);
```

```
      parent[p] = community;
      return community;
  }
}
```

We're explicitly finding the representative for p, assigning parent[p] to that representative, and then returning the representative.

### Step 3: Understand the Recursion

Now we have the recursion isolated on its own line:

```
community = find(parent[p], parent);
```

The find function performs path compression from its argument to the root of the tree, and it returns the root of the tree. Therefore, this recursive call performs path compression from p's parent to the root of the tree, and it returns the root of the tree. That handles all of the path compression except for p itself. We need to set p's parent to the root of the tree as well, which we do with this:

```
parent[p] = community;
```

There we have it: proof that the one-line path-compression code really does work!

## Caps and Bottles: In-Place Sorting

In Chapter 10, we solved the Caps and Bottles problem using a famous "splitting" idea from Quicksort. If you look back at Listing 10-9, you'll notice that we're allocating a lot of additional memory as our algorithm runs. Specifically, on each invocation of solve, we use malloc to allocate memory for four arrays: the small caps, the small bottles, the big caps, and the big bottles.

It's possible to avoid this use of additional memory and perform the splitting directly in the cap_nums and bottle_nums arrays. This won't decrease the number of queries that we need to make, but it does decrease the memory that our program uses. It's also a common optimization that people perform when implementing Quicksort.

To make this work, we need to keep track of the border between small values and large values. We'll maintain a variable called border to make this happen. Once we finish going through all of the caps and bottles, that border variable will tell us exactly where our problem is split in two; we need that in order to make our recursive calls. See Listing B-6 for our new solution that uses this idea.

```
#define MAX_N 10000

void swap(int *x, int *y) {
  int temp = *x;
```

```
    *x = *y;
    *y = temp;
  }

  int random_value(int left, int width) {
    return (rand() % width) + left;
  }

❶ void solve(int cap_nums[], int bottle_nums[], int left, int right) {
    int border, cap_index, cap_num, i, result, matching_bottle;
    if (right < left)
      return;

    border = left;
❷ cap_index = random_value(left, right - left + 1);
    cap_num = cap_nums[cap_index];

    i = left;
    while (i < right) {
      printf("0 %d %d\n", cap_num, bottle_nums[i]);
      scanf("%d", &result);
❸   if (result == 0) {
        swap(&bottle_nums[i], &bottle_nums[right]);
❹   } else if (result == 1) {
❺     swap(&bottle_nums[border], &bottle_nums[i]);
        border++;
        i++;
      } else {
        i++;
      }
    }

    matching_bottle = bottle_nums[right];
❻ printf("1 %d %d\n", cap_num, matching_bottle);

    border = left;

    i = left;
    while (i < right) {
      printf("0 %d %d\n", cap_nums[i], matching_bottle);
      scanf("%d", &result);
      if (result == 0) {
        swap(&cap_nums[i], &cap_nums[right]);
      } else if (result == -1) {
        swap(&cap_nums[border], &cap_nums[i]);
        border++;
        i++;
```

```
      } else {
        i++;
      }
    }

❼ solve(cap_nums, bottle_nums, left, border - 1);
❽ solve(cap_nums, bottle_nums, border, right - 1);
  }

int main(void) {
  int n, i;
  int cap_nums[MAX_N], bottle_nums[MAX_N];
  srand((unsigned) time(NULL));
  scanf("%d", &n);
  for (i = 0; i < n; i++) {
    cap_nums[i] = i + 1;
    bottle_nums[i] = i + 1;
  }
  solve(cap_nums, bottle_nums, 0, n - 1);
  return 0;
}
```

*Listing B-6: Solution with no extra memory allocation*

Rather than an n parameter giving the number of caps and bottles, now we need left and right parameters delimiting the operative part of the arrays ❶.

Prior to the first while loop, we choose our random cap ❷. The key invariant for the first while loop is that all bottles from left to border - 1 are small bottles and all bottles from border to i - 1 are big bottles. The loop will also eventually find the matching bottle; when it does, it puts that at the right ❸. We'll then be able to ignore that bottle in future recursive calls.

If we find that the cap is too big for the current bottle ❹, it means that the current bottle is on the wrong side of border. After all, it's a small bottle, and small bottles have to go to the left of border. To fix it, we swap that small bottle with the big bottle at bottle_nums[border] ❺, and then we increment border to take into account that we now have one more small bottle to the left of border.

When that while loop is done, we'll have rearranged the bottles so the small bottles are first and the big bottles follow. We'll also have placed the matching bottle at the right, so we tell the judge about that match now ❻.

The second while loop is nearly identical to the first, though this time it's splitting the caps rather than the bottles.

The final thing we need to do is make our two recursive calls. The first one goes from left to border - 1 ❼—that's all of the small caps and bottles. The second one goes from border to right - 1 ❽—that's all of the big caps and bottles. Be careful: we need right - 1 here, not right. The bottle and cap at index right have already been matched and should therefore never again be passed to a recursive call.

# C

## PROBLEM CREDITS

 I'm grateful for the time and expertise offered by anyone who helps people learn through competitive programming. For each problem in this book, I have sought to identify its author and where it was used. If you have additional information or credits for any of the following problems, please let me know. Updates will be posted on the book's website.

Here are the abbreviations that are used in the following table:

**CCC**   Canadian Computing Competition

**CCO**   Canadian Computing Olympiad

**COCI**   Croatian Open Competition in Informatics

**DMPG**   Don Mills Programming Gala

**ECNA**   East Central North America Regional Programming Contest

**IOI**   International Olympiad in Informatics

**NOIP**   National Olympiad in Informatics in Provinces

**POI**   Polish Olympiad in Informatics

**SAPO**   South African Programming Olympiad

| 8 | Building Treaps | Binary Search; Heap Construction | 2004 Ulm; Walter Guttmann |
|---|---|---|---|
| 8 | Two Sum | Maximum Sum | 2009 Kurukshetra Online Programming Contest; Swarnaprakash Udayakumar |
| 9 | Social Network | Social Network Community | Prateek Agarwal |
| 9 | Friends and Enemies | War | Petko Minkov |
| 9 | Drawer Chore | Ladice | 2013 COCI; Luka Kalinovcic, Gustav Matula |
| 10 | Yōkan | Yōkan | 2015 DMPG; FatalEagle |
| 10 | Caps and Bottles | Bottle Caps | 2009 CCO |

CCC and CCO problems are owned by the Centre for Education in Mathematics and Computing (CEMC) at the University of Waterloo.

# INDEX

## N

National Olympiad in Informatics in Province (NOIP), xxix
negative-weight edge in graph, 211
node
  in graph, 169
  in tree, 40
node struct
  in binary tree, 42
  in linked list, 14

## O

$O(1)$ (constant time), 408–409
oaat (one-at-a-time) hash function, 36
  in hash table, 18–19, 24
$O(\log n)$ (logarithmic time), 242
$O(n^2)$ (quadratic time), 10, 23, 410
$O(n)$ (linear time), 20, 408
$O(n \log n)$, 299, 400–401
open addressing in hash table, 19–20
optimal solution, 80
optimization problem, 80
output of problem description, xxxi

## P

parent in tree, 40
parity of an integer, 167
path compression in union-find, 351, 422
pointer, void, 74
POJ judge, xxix
pop in stack, 47
priority queue, 298
probability, 384
  multiplication rule, 384
  subtracting, 384
problem description
  components, xxx–xxxi
  input, xxx
  output, xxxi
  problem of, xxx
  subtask, 268
programming judge, xxviii
push in stack, 47

## Q

qsort function for sorting, 10–11, 74
quadratic-time algorithm ($O(n^2)$), 10, 23, 410
querying the segment tree, 313–316
queue, 50
  first-in, first-out, 50
Quicksort, 398–400
  pivot, 398

## R

rand function, 378–379
random hashing, 389
randomized algorithm, 389
  Las Vegas algorithm, 388–389
  Monte Carlo algorithm, 387–388
  randomization, 377, 397–398
  random numbers, 378
range maximum query, 307–308
range sum query, 262
  one dimension, 262–263
  two dimensions, 263–266
Rawlins, Gregory J.E., 402
reading integers
  from line, 106
  from string, 62–63
reading lines, 188–189
recursion, 52, 54, 65
  base case, 55
  recursive call, 54
  recursive case, 55
reflexive in union-find, 353
representative in union-find, 340–341
reversed in graph, 208
right child in binary tree, 40
River Jump problem, 243–254.
      *See also* binary search
  comparison function for sorting, 254
  feasible solution, 246
  greedy algorithm, 244, 247
  invariant, 252
Roberts, Eric, 76
root in tree, 40

The fonts used in *Algorithmic Thinking, 2nd Edition*, are New Baskerville, Futura, The Sans Mono Condensed and Dogma. The book was typeset with LaTeX $2_\varepsilon$ package nostarch by Boris Veytsman *(2008/06/06 v1.3 Typesetting books for No Starch Press)*.

# RESOURCES

Visit *https://nostarch.com/algorithmic-thinking-2nd-edition* for errata and more information.

*More no-nonsense books from*  **NO STARCH PRESS**

### LEARN TO CODE BY SOLVING PROBLEMS

**A Python Programming Primer**
*BY* DANIEL ZINGARO
336 PP., $34.99
ISBN 978-1-7185-0132-4

### EFFECTIVE C

**An Introduction to Professional C Programming**
*BY* ROBERT C. SEACORD
272 PP., $49.99
ISBN 978-1-7185-0104-1

### C++ CRASH COURSE

**A Fast-Paced Introduction**
*BY* JOSH LOSPINOSO
792 PP., $59.95
ISBN 978-1-59327-888-5

### DATA STRUCTURES THE FUN WAY

**An Amusing Adventure with Coffee-Filled Examples**
*BY* JEREMY KUBICA
304 PP., $39.99
ISBN 978-1-7185-0260-4

### THE RECURSIVE BOOK OF RECURSION

**Ace the Coding Interview with Python and JavaScript**
*BY* AL SWEIGART
328 PP., $39.99
ISBN 978-1-7185-0202-4

### THE RUST PROGRAMMING LANGUAGE, 2ND EDITION

*BY* STEVE KLABNIK *AND* CAROL NICHOLS
560 PP., $49.99
ISBN 978-1-7185-0310-6

**PHONE:**
800.420.7240 OR
415.863.9900

**EMAIL:**
SALES@NOSTARCH.COM
**WEB:**
WWW.NOSTARCH.COM

Never before has the world relied so heavily on the Internet to stay connected and informed. That makes the Electronic Frontier Foundation's mission—to ensure that technology supports freedom, justice, and innovation for all people—more urgent than ever.

For over 30 years, EFF has fought for tech users through activism, in the courts, and by developing software to overcome obstacles to your privacy, security, and free expression. This dedication empowers all of us through darkness. With your help we can navigate toward a brighter digital future.